# Masterin Flutter

*Learn to develop Flutter apps for iOS, Android, desktop and web*

**Kevin Moore**

www.bpbonline.com

First Edition 2025

Copyright © BPB Publications, India

ISBN: 978-93-65899-177

To View Complete
BPB Publications Catalogue
Scan the QR Code:

www.bpbonline.com

# Dedicated to

*My wife, two sons and two cats*

# About the Author

**Kevin Moore** is currently working as a Flutter developer for two companies and has been an Android developer for over 14 years and a Flutter developer for over 4 years. He has written several books on mobile development, including Android, Flutter, and Kotlin Multi-platform. He is a Google Developer Expert in Flutter and speaks at conferences around the country.

# About the Reviewers

❖ **Randal Schwartz** is a self-taught programmer, writer, trainer, and new media host with a passion for technology and creative pursuits.

Throughout his career, Randal has honed his skills in various programming languages, including Perl, Dart, and Flutter, and has become a recognized expert in the field. Notably, he has authored several influential books on Perl programming, including "Programming Perl," "Learning Perl," and "Effective Perl Programming."

He is currently recognized as a Google Developer Expert in the areas of Dart and Flutter (one of 10 in the United States and 150 in the world).

Randal's professional journey has taken him through diverse roles, from software developer and system administrator to consultant and technical writer. He has contributed his expertise to numerous organizations, including Stonehenge Consulting Services, Inc., O'Reilly & Associates, and TWiT.tv, where he hosted the popular show "FLOSS Weekly."

Beyond his technical prowess, Randal is also a gifted communicator and educator. He has lectured at conferences, provided technical training, and shared his insights through magazine articles and online platforms. Randal's unique blend of technical expertise, writing talent, and engaging personality has made him a sought-after speaker, author, and consultant in the tech industry.

❖ **Roman Jaquez** is a Google Developer Expert in Flutter as well as a Google Certified Cloud Architect who loves sharing his passion for Flutter with the wider developer community. He is also the lead organizer at GDG Lawrence and has 10+ years of experience as a software engineer. He enjoys spreading the word about best practices in the industry, ranging from mobile, web, and cloud.

# Acknowledgement

I would like to express my gratitude to all those who contributed to the completion of this book.

First and foremost, I extend my heartfelt appreciation to my family and friends for their unwavering support and encouragement throughout this journey. Their love and encouragement have been a constant source of motivation.

I would like to extend a special thanks to the following individuals for their valuable input and contributions to this project: Simon Lightfoot, Randal Schwartz, Roman Jaquez, and Scott Stoll. Thank you for your invaluable support and all the things you have taught me.

I would also like to thank Yiru Gan for the incredible design on the Movie App.

I am immensely grateful to BPB Publications for their guidance and expertise in bringing this book to fruition. Their support and assistance were invaluable in navigating the complexities of the publishing process.

Last but not least, I want to express our gratitude to the readers who have shown interest in the book. Your support and encouragement have been deeply appreciated.

Thank you to everyone who has played a part in making this book a reality.

# Preface

Flutter has become one of the most popular multi-platform frameworks available. While others have died out, Flutter continues to grow stronger and have a larger community. It has done so because it is easy to use and easy to create apps for every major platform. Instead of learning each platform and language, you can just learn one.

Comprising nineteen chapters, this book covers a wide range of topics essential for learning Flutter. From the Dart programming language needed to write Flutter apps, to the widget system provided by Flutter you will learn everything you need to start creating apps for every platform.

**Chapter 1: Introduction to Flutter** - Learn all about Flutter and why you should use it. Learn how to install Flutter and get started. You will also choose which IDE you will use to develop apps. You will learn about the Flutter architecture and the basics of how it is put together.

**Chapter 2: Dart Essentials** - Learn about the Dart programming language that is used to write Flutter apps. Dart is a modern programming language with a lot of great features. You will need to know this language if you are to write Flutter apps. You will learn about basic programming fundamentals like variables, control flow, functions, and classes, as well as some more advanced topics like null safety.

**Chapter 3: Building the Movie App** - Learn about the app you will build with this book. This is a beautiful app that showcases popular movies and allows users to learn all about the movie and the cast. You will start the app from scratch, learning how to create your own apps. You will also learn about the different types of widgets Flutter uses. Finally, you will learn about the amazing hot reload feature of Flutter that allows you to keep changing your app while it is running and not have to rebuild each time.

**Chapter 4: Basic Widgets** - Get started with learning some of the most important widgets that Flutter offers. Mastering these building block widgets will help you build screens.

**Chapter 5: Themes, Colors and Fonts** - An app is boring and ugly unless you have a good set of consistent colors and fonts. Learn how to create a theme that has the colors and fonts you need to build the movie app.

**Chapter 6: State Management Fundamentals** - How you manage the state of your data will either make your programming life difficult or easy. Learn some of the state management packages available to Flutter developers.

**Chapter 7: Advanced Widgets** - Now that you know the basic widgets, learn more advanced widgets like ListViews, Grids, Cards, and Slivers.

**Chapter 8: Navigation and Routing** - Learn an easy way to transition from one page to another. Learn how to push and pop pages with ease.

**Chapter 9: Animations and Transitions** - Let your app look professional with engaging animations.

**Chapter 10: Futures and Async/Await** - Prevent your UI from slowing down by performing background tasks asynchronously. Learn all about Dart's Futures.

**Chapter 11: Networking** - Learn how to retrieve data from the cloud. This is really important as there is a lot of great information out there to show your users.

**Chapter 12: Local Storage and Databases** - Learn how to save data for both simple and complex data needs. Learn about shared preferences for simple data and databases for more complex needs.

**Chapter 13: Web and Desktop** - Now that you have created mobile apps, learn how to develop for the desktop (both the Mac and Windows) and the web.

**Chapter 14: Handling User Input and Gestures** - Learn how to handle input from the user, from text fields, and gestures to focus management.

**Chapter 15: Firebase** - Learn how to use one of the most popular cloud databases to store your data remotely.

**Chapter 16: Packages** - Learn how to create your own Dart package. This is really useful to create shared code, either for yourself, your team, or others in the community.

**Chapter 17: Platform Channels and Plugins** - Learn about how you can write code that runs natively on each platform. This is useful if you cannot find a plugin that does what you need. You will build a plugin to save and retrieve native preferences.

**Chapter 18: Testing and Performance** - Learn about the different types of testing, from unit to widget and then to integration. This will allow you to feel confident in your code and will show you any problems that may crop up when you are changing your code. You will also learn about the tools available to measure your app's performance and find and fix those problems.

**Chapter 19: Building and Publishing** - In this final chapter you will learn how to build release versions of your app and publish them to both the Google Play Store and the Apple App Store. This will allow you to reach your users on both platforms.

# Code Bundle and Coloured Images

Please follow the link to download the
*Code Bundle* and the *Coloured Images* of the book:

# https://rebrand.ly/d0ff3b

The code bundle for the book is also hosted on GitHub at
**https://github.com/bpbpublications/Mastering-Flutter**.
In case there's an update to the code, it will be updated on the existing GitHub repository.

We have code bundles from our rich catalogue of books and videos available at
**https://github.com/bpbpublications**. Check them out!

# Errata

We take immense pride in our work at BPB Publications and follow best practices to ensure the accuracy of our content to provide with an indulging reading experience to our subscribers. Our readers are our mirrors, and we use their inputs to reflect and improve upon human errors, if any, that may have occurred during the publishing processes involved. To let us maintain the quality and help us reach out to any readers who might be having difficulties due to any unforeseen errors, please write to us at :

**errata@bpbonline.com**

Your support, suggestions and feedbacks are highly appreciated by the BPB Publications' Family.

# Join our book's Discord space

Join the book's Discord Workspace for Latest updates, Offers, Tech happenings around the world, New Release and Sessions with the Authors:

**https://discord.bpbonline.com**

# Table of Contents

# CHAPTER 1
# Introduction to Flutter

## Introduction

In this chapter, you will take your first steps towards mastering Flutter, *Google's UI toolkit* for crafting beautiful, natively compiled applications for mobile, web, and desktop from a single codebase. You will learn about and install Flutter. You will also learn about the Movie application that you will be creating in this book.

## Structure

The chapter covers the following topics:

- Overview of Flutter
- Flutter architecture
- Benefits of Flutter
- Flutter's language: Dart
- Installing Flutter SDK
- Development application

# Objectives

By the end of this chapter, you will have an understanding of what Flutter is and the incredible possibilities it unlocks. You will be eager to dive into the next chapters and embark on your journey to become a Flutter master!

# Overview of Flutter

Flutter is a UI toolkit developed by *Google*. It has the ability to run on mobile (both Android and iOS), desktop (macOS, Windows, and Linux), and the web. The Flutter toolkit uses a declarative UI built of Widgets. In fact, *Google* likes to say that everything is a widget. There are widgets for almost every task you need, and if not, you just need to create your own, by building a widget with other widgets inside or going all the way and creating a custom widget with its own rendering code. You will learn more in later chapters.

As mentioned above, Flutter works on almost every platform using almost the same code (some separate code needs to be written for platform-specific areas like menus). In fact, *Google* used Flutter on their Nest displays.

# History

Flutter has an interesting history; the first version was introduced in 2015 and was known as **Sky**. It ran on Android. It used Dart as the development language. Then in 2018 Flutter 1.0 was released. In 2021, Flutter 2 was released at the *Flutter Engage event*. This version had a canvas-based engine for the web and early desktop support. This was a very important version as it introduced Dart 2.0 with null safety. This made development safer (but broke existing code). In 2021, Flutter 2.5 was released with Material Design support. In 2022 Flutter 3 was introduced with full desktop support and iOS Objective-C and Swift interop.

There have been many attempts at cross-platform frameworks, many of which have failed. Java was supposed to be the one language to rule them all but never quite achieved it. Since then, there have been other attempts such as React Native (by *Facebook*) and Xamarin (by *Microsoft*). React Native is still in use but Microsoft has ended support for Xamarin and now uses .Net MAUI. React Native uses HTML web pages and Xamarin uses C#.

# Flutter architecture

The Flutter framework is made up of several layers. Each layer can be replaced if needed but does not have any special access to the layer below it. The top-level layer is the Framework. This is written in Dart. The entire Flutter framework looks like the following figure:

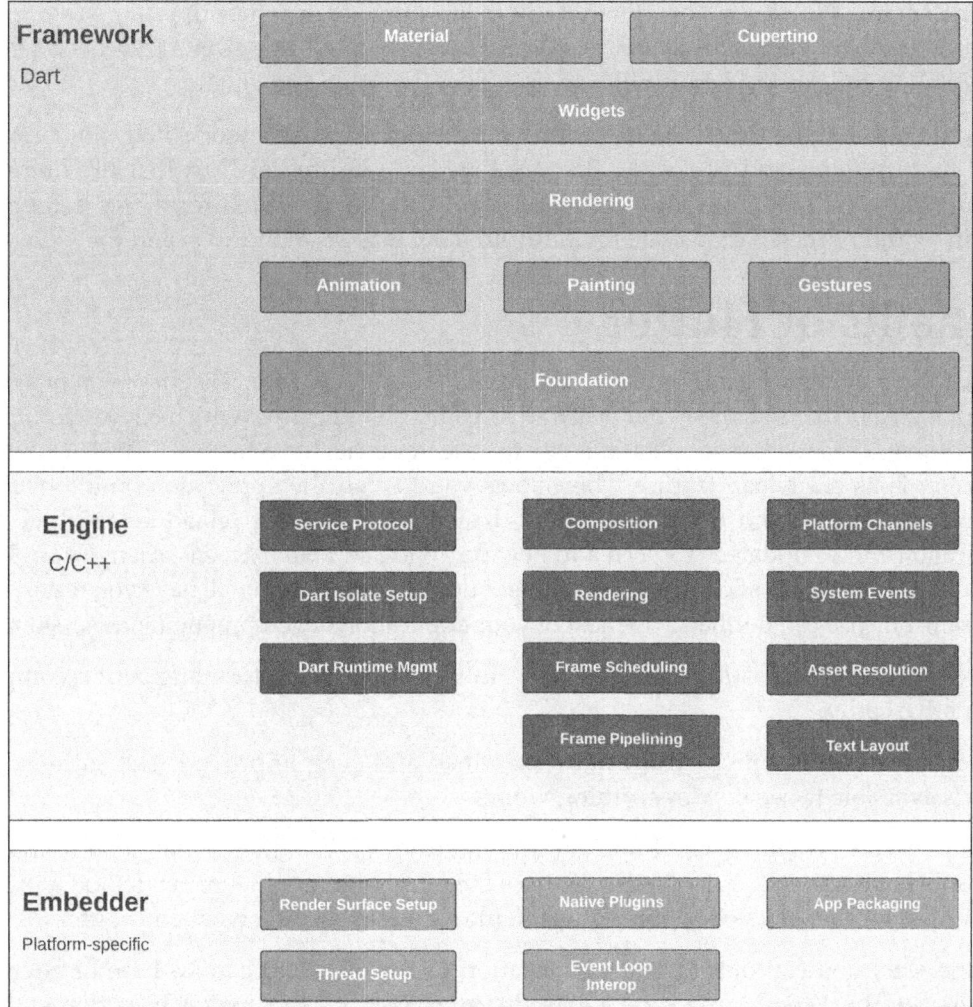

**Figure 1.1**: *Flutter architecture*

This layer contains the widgets you will be using/creating. The Framework layer contains many different common widgets that you will use as well as the rendering code needed to display those widgets. The **Material** and **Cupertino** libraries are for *Google* and *Apple's UI* look and feel. The Rendering, Animation, Painting, and Foundation are lower-level Dart codes that form the essential drawing framework.

The next layer is the Engine and is written in C/C++. This is not a layer you need to use. The final layer is the Embedder and is different for each platform. One of the nice features of Flutter is that each application is compiled into native code just like any other application on that platform. This means that applications run as fast as native applications (or faster).

**Note: That there is a small overhead for the built-in Flutter code.**

For the engine, Flutter was originally built using the Skia graphics drawing system. The Flutter team is moving this system to a newer version called **Impeller**. It has been written for both iOS and Android and will be coming to other platforms later.

If you do not find the functionality you need in the Flutter framework, you can use many third-party plugins and packages. Packages are code written in Dart that provide extra functionality. Plugins are built with lower-level code for each platform. For example, a plugin would need separate code for Android, iOS, macOS, Windows, and the web.

# Benefits of Flutter

One of the main benefits of Flutter is its rapid development time. This happens in several different areas. The first one is the declarative UI that Flutter uses, which allows you to use widgets that contain other widgets and only update those that have changed. The killer feature of Flutter is its hot reload feature. This allows you to start the application on the platform you are working on and make almost any change. Click the **Hot reload** button, and your application will be updated. You can add new packages, add new screens, change your logic, and just have the application instantly update. Adding a new plugin will have you restart your program, but you can normally do most of your application development in one session.

Unlike many other cross-platform systems, Flutter has native performance as it is compiled into native code.

Flutter is also open source, so it can be examined and even improved. The entire source code is available to see how everything works.

More importantly, Flutter can build for any platform. This makes development faster as you only have one code base. It also reduces the number of engineers needed on a project. Flutter can also be developed for the web (although that is still a work in progress).

For the web, you can output your application using HTML, a canvas-based system, or **WebAssembly** (**Wasm**). The canvas-based system is faster but makes it so that systems like *Google search* cannot index your web pages. This is bad for **search engine optimization** (**SEO**). This means *Google* will not be able to find and index individual pages. This problem is currently being worked on.

# Flutter's language: Dart

Flutter uses the Dart language which was developed by *Google*. Since it was originally developed for the web, it is similar to JavaScript. The syntax is very similar with variables being defined with the var keyword and both having async/await keywords. *Google* has made a lot of improvements to the language, especially the 2.0 version with null safety. Null safety solves many inadvertent crashes. The language is object-oriented, uses classes, and is garbage-collected (which just means that it handles all allocation/disposal of classes in memory). The language was released in 2013 and Flutter 2.0 was released in 2018. They then introduced the dart2native tool to create native code. This means that you do not have to have the Dart SDK installed on a machine to run applications (unlike Java, which needs a JDK or JRE to run). Dart 3.0 was released in May 2023 with null safety, records, patterns, and class modifiers. There is also work being done for Wasm, but it is not finished yet. Wasm is a binary instruction format designed to run code at near-native speed in web browsers, complementing JavaScript. It enables developers to compile high-performance applications written in various languages (like C++, Rust, or Go) and run them efficiently on the web, expanding the possibilities for web applications beyond what JavaScript alone could traditionally handle.

Flutter is a single-threaded toolkit with a main thread. Dart provides a way to create asynchronous methods using the async and await keywords. This is for running methods in a semi-asynchronous way (they are put in a queue to be run on the main thread). To get true multi-threading, you need to use Dart's isolates. This is the way to truly run things on another thread. They are called **isolates** because they are totally isolated from any other thread. You cannot share variables or anything in memory. You can pass data back and forth with send and receive ports, which are part of the Dart language. Isolates are pretty advanced. There are a few methods that will allow you to write simple isolates but to pass data back and forth is difficult.

# Installing Flutter SDK

To get started with Flutter you will want to download the Flutter SDK.

1.  Go to **https://docs.flutter.dev/get-started/install** and follow the instructions for the desktop platform you are on.

2.  Find the Install the Flutter SDK section of the instructions and download the zip.

3.  Unzip the files and put them in an easy-to-find location on your computer. Make sure the path is simple and does not contain any spaces or special characters. A good example is *flutter*. Next, you will need to add the flutter installation to your path.

# Windows

For Windows, go to **Advanced System Settings | Advanced | Environment Variables**. In the **User variables** section edit the **Path** entry. Double-click on an empty row and type the path to Flutter. For example: **C:\flutter**. Click on the **OK** buttons until you are out of all dialogs.

# macOS

For macOS, you will need to update your path by opening or creating a file called **~/.zshenv**. Add the following line:

```
export PATH=$HOME/flutter/bin:$PATH
```

When you have installed Flutter in a folder called **flutter** you can save the file.

# CocoaPods

iOS and MacOS applications usually use CocoaPods for library management (although that is changing). This tool is used for managing iOS and MacOS libraries. For Flutter you will need this tool as it generates a library needed to run Flutter on these platforms. CocoaPods is located at: **https://cocoapods.org/**. There are two ways to install it. Since the Mac has several tools already installed (ruby and gems), you can simply install it from the command line with this line **(you will need your password for this)**:

```
sudo gem install cocopods
```

Another alternative is the Homebrew package manager. This is a very popular package manager that allows you to easily install other command line programs. This makes it very simple to install command line software on a Mac. You can find this at: **https://brew. sh/**. After installing it, use this:

```
brew install cocopods
```

# Flutter Doctor

A really good tool to use is Flutter itself. There are several flutter tools available. The most important one is Flutter doctor. This tool does a diagnostic on Flutter and will let you know if you need to install any additional tools or fix a problem. From a command line type:

```
flutter doctor
```

You should see something like this (refer to the following figure):

```
01.   flutter doctor
02.   Doctor summary (to see all details, run flutter doctor -v):
03.   [✓] Flutter (Channel stable, 3.19.6, on macOS 14.2.1 23C71 darwin-arm64, locale en-US)
04.   [✓] Android toolchain - develop for Android devices (Android SDK version 34.0.0)
05.   [✓] Xcode - develop for iOS and macOS (Xcode 15.1)
06.   [✓] Chrome - develop for the web
07.   [✓] Android Studio (version 2022.3)
08.   [✓] VS Code (version 1.88.1)
09.   [✓] Connected device (4 available)
10.   [✓] Network resources
11.
12.
```

*Figure 1.2: Flutter doctor*

If there are any errors, follow the directions for fixing them.

# Development application

When developing a Flutter application, you can use any text editor you want, but if you want to be more productive, you can use an **integrated development environment (IDE)**. It will help you organize your code and make it easy to run and test. There are several IDEs that can run Flutter applications.

The first one is called **Visual Studio Code** from *Microsoft*. This is a free IDE that is very lightweight. It has extensions for Flutter development. It has become very popular. The next two are from *Google* and *JetBrains*. *JetBrains* is the maker of many different IDEs. *Google* has written one called **Android Studio** based on *JetBrain's* framework. The other is called **Intellij** from *JetBrains*. This is not specific to Android and can be used for Java/Kotlin development as well as Flutter. In this book, we will be using Android Studio (all these IDEs are free, and there is a free and paid version of Intellij).

1.  To install Android Studio, go to **https://developer.android.com/studio**.

2.  Download the latest stable version. As of this writing that was *Android Studio Ladybug* (animal names are given for each version). Follow the instructions on the website for installing Android Studio.

3.  Once installed, start the application. The first time you run the application you will be prompted to download the Android SDK. Follow those instructions.

For mobile devices you will need to install an emulator for Android and on macOS you will need a simulator for iOS.

For iOS, you will need to install Xcode. Follow the given steps:

1.  Open tahe **App Store** and search for **Xcode**. Download and install it, as shown in the following figure:

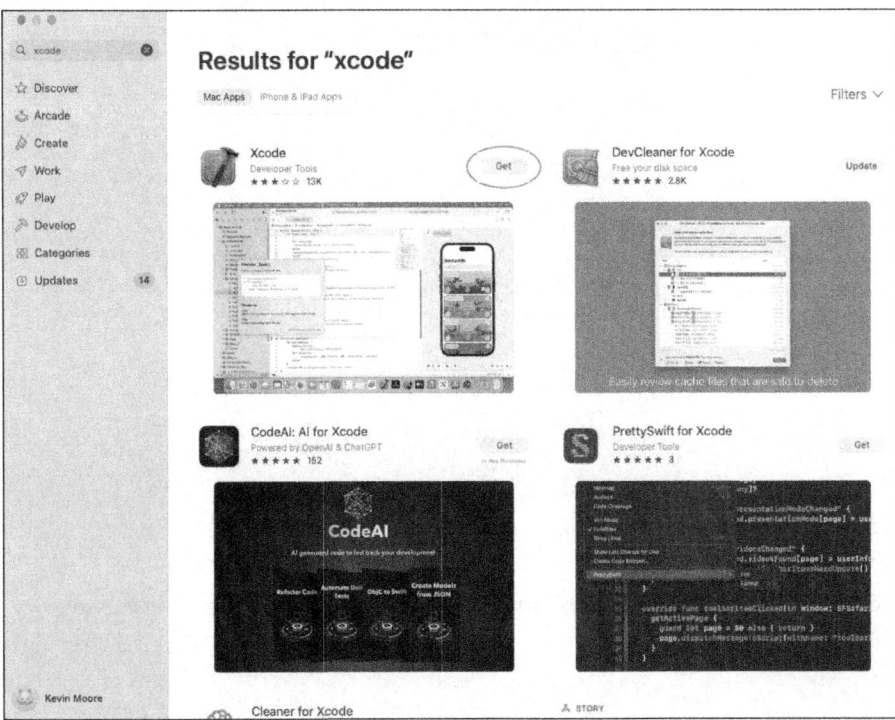

*Figure 1.3*: App Store

2. Next, you will run the **xcode-select** command to set the directory for other tools to find Xcode tools. This tool will set the directory for where to find Xcode tools. The **runFirstLaunch** command will allow you to accept *Apple terms and conditions* and install any missing components. From a command line (open the Terminal application) type:

```
sudo sh -c 'xcode-select -s /Applications/Xcode.app/Contents/
Developer && xcodebuild -runFirstLaunch'
```

3. Next, open XCode and from the **Window** menu choose **Devices and Simulators**, as shown in the following figure:

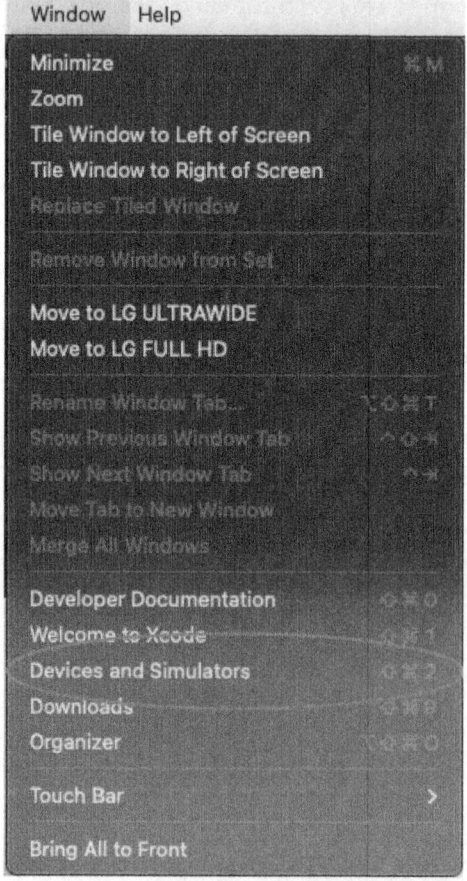

*Figure 1.4*: *Xcode devices menu*

4. Next, choose the **Simulators** button, as shown in the following figure:

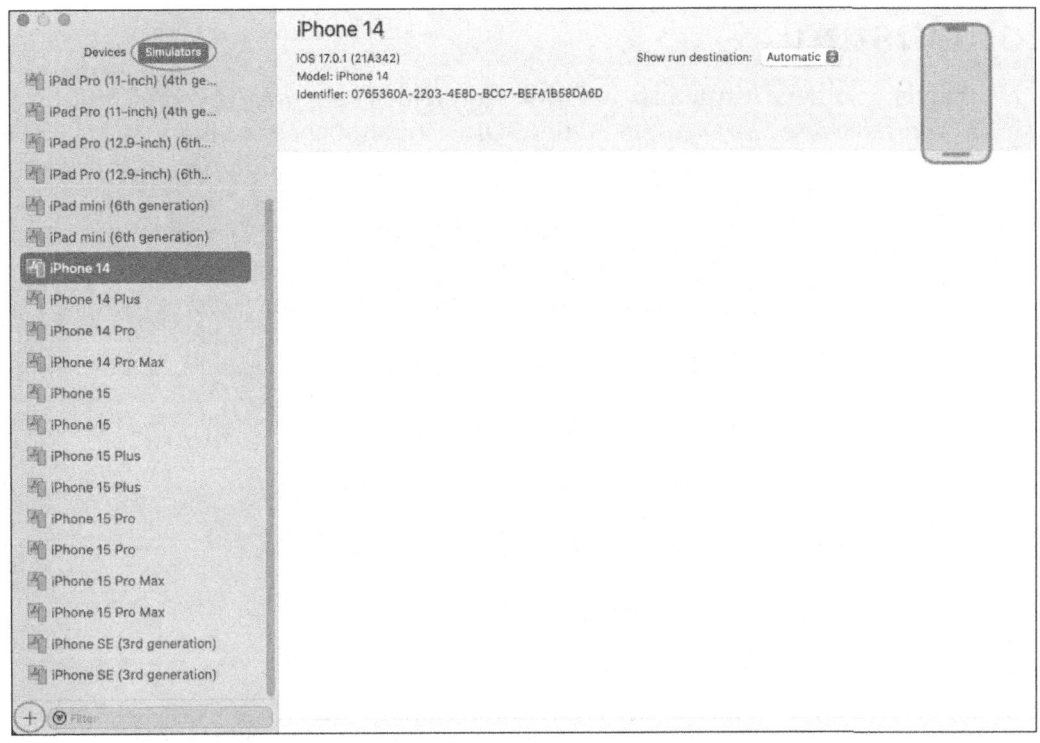

*Figure 1.5: Xcode devices*

5. Then click the plus button at the bottom left; type in a name for your simulator and choose the **Device Type** and **OS Version** you want. Then click **Create**, as shown in the following figure:

*Figure 1.6: Create new simulator*

You should see your new simulator in the list, on the left. You will be able to use this simulator when you test your application on iOS. You can make as many different types of simulators as you need.

# Conclusion

In this chapter, you have learned about Flutter, its architecture, and why you would want to use it. You have also installed the Flutter SDK with all its needed tools, as well as an IDE. You now have an overview of the application you will be reading about, in this book.

In the next chapter, you will learn more about the Dart language.

## Join our book's Discord space

Join the book's Discord Workspace for Latest updates, Offers, Tech happenings around the world, New Release and Sessions with the Authors:

**https://discord.bpbonline.com**

# CHAPTER 2
# Dart
# Essentials

## Introduction

Before you begin writing Flutter applications, it is important that you understand the language that is used to build them. This language is Dart. Dart was created by *Google* and was originally intended just for the web. It has evolved over the years. The language is constantly improving and new innovative features are coming soon. It is now at version 3.x, with each major version adding features that either other languages have, or new features that extend the language.

If you are familiar with other programming languages, then most of Dart will be familiar to you. However, there are some unique language features that make Dart stand out. Dart is an object-oriented language that also has garbage collection. What this means is that you do not have to worry (as much) about cleaning up memory (There are some classes that you will need to dispose of when finished). Although Dart is a single-inheritance language (meaning a class can only directly subclass one parent), it can achieve a form of multiple inheritance through the use of mixins. The following sections will cover the basics of the Dart language.

> Note: This chapter is not meant to be an exhaustive, detailed description of Dart but to give you enough information to write your Flutter applications (that would require a whole book).

# Structure

This chapter covers the following topics:

- Variables
- Control flow
- Functions
- Comments
- Imports
- Classes
- Enums
- Extensions
- Concurrency
- Exceptions

# Objectives

At the end of this chapter, you will have a solid understanding of Dart and will be able to use it to build Flutter applications. You will learn about variables for storing values, control flow for executing functions, and functions for building smaller executable code segments. Object-oriented programming with classes and enums and more advanced topics. Additionally, you will learn how to run code in the background and how to handle exceptions.

# Variables

One of the most important aspects of any language is the ability to store data in memory. This is done through variables. Dart is a type of safe language. It ensures that the variables match the type they are defined as. In Dart, you can declare a variable with the **var** keyword. This means the data stored in the variable can change, but it does not specify the type of data the variable holds. When you assign a value to a var variable it will then have that type. To do that you would declare it with a type. Dart provides some built-in types.

# Built-in types

Dart has types that are similar to other languages. These are:

- **Numbers**: int and double. Integers are whole numbers while doubles have fractional values
- **Strings**: Defined with single or double quotes

- **Booleans**: Bool—true or false
- **Sets**: Unique list of items
- **List**: List of one type
- **Maps**: Key/value pairs
- **Null**: An empty value
- **Object**: Top-level class that all classes subclass
- **Enum**: Enumeration of specific values
- **Iterable**: Used in for loops—an interface for classes that can retrieve each value
- **Never**: For functions that always throw an exception
- **Dynamic**: Usually used for JSON parsing—can be any value
- **Void**: The value is never used—used as a return type

Number variables store integers and double values. Strings are typically defined with single quotes but can also use double quotes, (you will get a lint error if you use double quotes as it is recommended that you use single). Booleans are crucial for controlling the flow of your program, while sets and maps are excellent for storing collections of items. The null value is used to indicate that a variable does not currently hold a valid value. The Object class is the root of the Dart class hierarchy. All classes implicitly inherit from Object if no other superclass is specified. Enums are used to define a type with a fixed set of possible values. The Iterable interface is implemented by collections like lists, which provide methods for iterating their elements. Many classes implement the Iterable interface, making them useful in for loops.

The Never type is less common; it indicates that an expression will never complete, typically because it throws an exception. You will probably never use it. It indicates that an expression will never finish, usually when it will be throwing an exception. The dynamic type is often used in JSON parsing when the exact types of the data are unknown. It allows you to check the type at runtime before using the values. The void type is used as the return type of a function to indicate that the function does not return a value.

Dart also has some more unique types:

- **Records**: Create lightweight anonymous classes without defining them.
- **Runes**: An integer representing a Unicode code point of a string.

Records allow you to create immutable objects on the fly, combining multiple values. They are useful for functions that return multiple results. Records are a newer part of Dart. You can create a record variable in several ways. The first and most simple is to surround a set of values in parentheses like:

```
var myData = (first:'Fred', last: 'Smith');
```

This creates a **myData** record with two fields: **first** and **last**. You can also return a record from a function. This allows you to return multiple values. For example:

```
(bool, String) processString(String name) {
  return (true, name);
}
```

If you want to return a result and the value of the function, records are something you could use. However, if you just use return types, the user of the function will not know what those types are for. A better way would be:

```
({bool result, String name}) processString(String name) {
  return (result: true, name: name);
}
```

Here you are giving names to the variables.

Runes represent Unicode code points, which are the numerical values assigned to characters in the Unicode standard. Unicode is a universal character encoding system that enables consistent representation of text across different platforms and languages. The characters package in Dart provides tools for working with individual characters and their Unicode representations.

Note: Dart uses the convention of using an underscore before a variable name to indicate that the variable is private. This applies to functions as well. The compiler will enforce this so that only the class defining it will be able to use it.

There is also the **late** keyword. This allows you to tell the compiler that the variable will be initialized later in the program. But be careful! If you define a variable as late and try to use it before it has been initialized, your application will crash.

You can also define a variable as a **const** variable. This says that it will never change and is useful for defining strings and numbers that you will use through-out your application. In fact, the Dart linter will recommend using const for widgets that do not change.

Dart also uses generics. This is a way to reuse code for different types of variables. For example, the built-in **List** class can be used for any type. It is defined as: **List<T>** where **T** is any type.

You can also use the **typedef** keyword to define an alias for a type. For example:

```
typedef StringList = List<String>;
```

This defines a new type called **StringList**, which is just a list of strings.

# Null safety

In Dart 2.12, null safety was introduced. This feature allows you to safely use variables that can either be null or not and to check their state. This feature solves a lot of crashes in earlier programs. Dart 3.0 became 100% null safe, with all types being non-nullable by default and requiring the **?** after a type to signify nullability. It helps solve the problem of null pointer exceptions. This occurs when a variable is accessed before it has been set. This has caused many crashes in programs in the past. With this update, the compiler ensures you do not use a nullable variable incorrectly. To declare a variable as nullable, simply append a question mark at the end of the variable type.

For example:

`String? name;`

When you use this variable, you have to use the question mark, like the following code:

```
void printNameLength(Simple simple) {
  print(simple.name?.length);
}
Class Simple {
  String? name;
  int age = 1;
}
Simple simple = Simple();
printNameLength(simple);
```

You can also use the **??** operator. This allows you to check for a null result:

`print(simple.name ?? 'No name');`

If you know a variable is not null, you can append it with the **!** character, like this:

`print(simple.name!);`

Be careful though as this will crash your application if it is null.

# Control flow

At the heart of programming is the ability to decide what to do based on the values of variables. This is done through control flow. Dart has some of the same control flow keywords as other languages. As your function executes, it may need to make decisions based on the value of a variable. The following keywords let you make decisions and perform different actions based on those values.

# Branches

There are two types of branching keywords: **if** and **switch**. If is usually used to check one statement at a time while a switch is used to check many different types.

## If

The **if** keyword is used to check if a condition is true or false. If you want to perform additional checks you can use the **else if** or **else** keywords. For example:

```
if (showWidget()) {
  MyWidget();
} else if (showOtherWidget()) {
  MyOtherWidget();
} else {
  NormalWidget();
}
```

This code first checks the value of the **showWidget** function. If it is true, then **MyWidget** is used. If not, it checks the next **else if**. If that value is true, then **MyOtherWidget** is used, otherwise, the **NormalWidget** is used.

## Switch

A switch will look something like the following code:

```
var type = 'File';
switch (type) {
  case 'File':
      print('The type is a File');
  case 'Directory:
      print('The type is a Directory);
  case 'Image:
      print('The type is an Image);
  default:
      print('Unknown type');
}
```

This checks for the type to be any of the following strings. Use the **default** keyword to catch any type other than the ones provided. Another way to use a switch is with an expression:

```
final result = switch (expression) {
  pattern1 => expression1,
  pattern2 => expression2,
```

```
  // ... more patterns and expressions
  _ => defaultExpression // Optional default case
};
```

This is a concise way to get a value based on the expression.

# Loops

Loops are used for going through a list of items or conditions. There are two types of loops provided which are for and while.

The most common type of for loop uses a variable for incrementing. For example:

```
for (var counter = 0; counter < 5; counter++) {
  print('counter is $counter');
}
```

This **for** loop creates the **counter** variable and prints the statement: **'counter is $counter'** where **$counter** is the value of **counter**. Another example of a for loop without an index is the for-in type of loop:

```
List<String> fruits = ['apple', 'banana', 'orange'];

for (String fruit in fruits) {
  print(fruit);
}
```

This does not need an index and avoids any indexing errors (starting at 0 vs 1 or going past the end of the list). The next type of loop is the while. It comes in two flavors. The first looks like this:

```
while (shouldContinue()) {
  print('Continuing...');
}
```

This will call the **shouldContinue** function and print the statement as long as that condition is true. The other flavor looks like this:

```
do {
  print('Continuing...');
} while (shouldContinue());
```

This does the conditional check after the print statement.

**Note: That this will always run at least once as the check is done at the end.**

For both branches and loops you can use two other keywords: **break** and **continue**. These keywords allow you to change the flow. If you use **break**, it will exit out of the flow. If you use **continue**, it will skip to the next iteration.

# Functions

Functions are a set of codes that can be reused. They are defined by:

```
returnType function name (type variable name)
```

The **returnType** is the value that the function will return. If you do not want to return a value, you can use the **void** keyword. The function name is just the name you want to call the function (Note: No spaces are allowed in names). After the parentheses, you define a list of variables with a type and the name of the variable.

Functions can also be defined with what is called the **arrow syntax**. If you have a one-line definition for a function, you can use the following syntax:

```
returnType function name (type variable name) => somefunction();
```

Parameters come in three different configurations:

- **Plain**: A type followed by a variable name.
- **Named**: Surround with brackets: {}. This allows callers to prefix the call with the name of the parameter.
- **Optional parameter:** Surround with: []. This allows callers to omit the parameter.

# Main function

All Dart and Flutter applications start with the main function:

```
void main() {
  print('Hello World!');
}
```

This is the entry point to the application. You can make the main function asynchronous by adding the **async** keyword. (Discussed in a later chapter).

You can also assign functions to variables. This allows you to execute the function in another function.

# Anonymous functions

Anonymous functions look like regular functions but do not have a name. They are mostly used as the last parameter to a function. Here is an example:

```
const list = ['apples', 'bananas', 'oranges'];
final upperCaseList = list.map((item) {
  return item.toUpperCase();
});
```

The section of code that starts with **(item) {** is the anonymous function.

# Comments

To help yourself and other developers, it is a good idea to comment on your code. This helps you when you come back later and wonder why you did something. Or, for other developers to help them know why you created this code. There are three different types of comments:

## Single line comments

Use two forward slashes like: **//**. This can be anywhere on a line but everything after these are part of a comment and are not code. For example, here is a single-line comment before a **MaterialApp** widget:

```
// The top level Flutter widget
return const MaterialApp(
```

## Multi-line comments

If you want multi-line comments, surround the code with **/\*** and **\*/**. Anything within these two comment endpoints is treated as a comment and can cover multiple lines. Here is a multi-line comment:

```
/**
 * This is the State for the MainApp
 * Used to display the main app
 */
class _MainAppState extends State<MainApp> {
```

## Documentation comments

The third type is a documentation comment. This comment uses three forward slashes like: **///**. This allows you to create comments that can be generated by a tool for stand-alone documentation. Here is an example of documentation comments:

```
/// This is the main entry point for Flutter
/// Use the runApp method to start your app
void main() {
  runApp(const MainApp());
}
```

# Imports

The **import** keyword is used to bring in a file or a library to your current file. To use another file or another package, you have to import the file that defines the classes you are using. For example:

```
import 'package:flutter/material.dart';
```

This imports the **material** library. Now you can use all of the Material widgets. If you have conflicting imports, you can use the **as** keyword and give it another name. This happens when two files have functions or classes with the same name. Notice in the following example, that both packages define **Element**:

```
import 'package:lib1/lib1.dart';
import 'package:lib2/lib2.dart' as lib2;

// Uses Element from lib1.
Element element1 = Element();

// Uses Element from lib2
lib2.Element element2 = lib2.Element();
```

This allows you to prefix a variable with the **lib2** name. You can also show and hide different elements from a library, by adding the **show** or **hide** keywords after the import statement.

```
import 'package:lumberdash/lumberdash.dart' show putLumberdashToWork;
```

This is for the **lumberdash** logging library and only shows the **putLumberdashToWork** function. By using show, you only bring in certain functions instead of importing the whole file. The **hide** keyword hides certain functions that may cause a conflict or are not needed. Usually, you will not need these keywords.

# Classes

A class is a blueprint or template for creating objects. It defines a set of attributes (data members) and methods (functions) that the objects of that class will possess. In Dart, classes can only inherit from a single class, but they can use mixins (described below), to get around that. Here is an example of a simple class:

```
class Simple {
  final String name;
  final int id;

  Simple({required this.name, required this.id});

  void printName() {
      print('Name is $name with id: $id');
  }
}
```

This **Simple** class has two fields named **name** and **id**. Since they are final, they need to be initialized in a constructor. There is a function named **printName** that just prints the **name** and **id**. Note that this string uses interpolation, which means you can put variables inside of strings if prefixed with a dollar sign. If you want to use more complex information, you would surround the expression with a dollar sign and left and right brackets, like: **${}**. In the following example, the variables cannot be null. If you want a variable to be null you would add a question mark after the type, like:

```dart
class Simple {
  final String name;
  int? id;

  Simple(this.name, this.id);

  void setId(int id) {
    this.id = id;
  }

  void printName() {
      print('Name is $name with id: $id');
  }
}
```

In this example the **id** field is nullable. If the **setId** method is not called, when **printName** is called it will print **id: null**.

# Constructors

The preceding example used a constructor that took a name and set the name variable to whatever was passed in when the class was created. You can also create named constructors. For example:

```dart
class Simple {
  final String name;
  int? id;

  Simple({required this.name, this.id});

  void setId(int id) {
    this.id = id;
  }

  void printName() {
    if (id != null) {
      print('Name is $name with id: $id');
    } else {
      print('Name is $name');
    }
```

```
}
final simple = Simple(name: 'Simple');
```

Notice the brackets in the constructor. As you can see on the last line, you need to use the name of the variable followed by a colon and then the value. Notice the **required** keyword before this .name. If the variable is final, you will need the **required** keyword.

To make a subclass of **Simple**, you would extend that class with the **extends** keyword.

```
class NotSoSimple extends Simple {
  final String description;
  static const int age = 10;

  NotSoSimple({required String name, required this.description}) :
super(name: name);

}
```

**NotSoSimple** adds description and age fields and passes the name to its parent. You can also override fields or methods. This class subclasses Simple and overrides the **printName** method:

```
class NotSoSimple extends Simple {
  final String description;

  NotSoSimple({required String name, required this.description}) :
super(name: name);

  void printDescription() {
    print('Description is $description');
  }

  @override
  void printName() {
    print('Name is $name with description: $description');
  }
}
```

Notice the **@override** before the **printName** function. This tells the compiler that this method overrides the function of the super class.

# Mixins

Mixins are like interfaces in other languages except that they can also provide functionality. They cannot, however, extend any other class or have constructors. They can provide functionality that many other classes can use. Here is a simple example:

```
mixin Animal {
```

```dart
  void run() {
    print('Running');
  }
}

class Dog with Animal {
  void bark() {
    print('Barking');
  }
}
```

While the **Dog** class provides the **bark** method, it also inherits the run method from the **Animal** class. If you need a class to have several different types, mixins are a great way to do that.

Earlier you saw the description field in the **NotSoSimple** class. This field is known as an **instance variable** and is associated with a specific instance of a class. What if you need a field or method that belongs to the class itself, rather than to any specific instance of the class? These are known as **static variables** and **methods**.

```dart
class NotSoSimple extends Simple {
  final String description;
  static const int age = 10;

  NotSoSimple({required String name, required this.description}) :
super(name: name);

  static void printAge() {
    print('Age is $age');
  }

  @override
  void printName() {
    print('Name is $name with description: $description');
  }
}
print(NotSoSimple.age);
NotSoSimple.printAge();
```

Now **NotSoSimple** has a static age. Notice that it cannot be changed and you can use it by accessing the name of the class and then the field, like: **NotSoSimple.age**. You can also call the static **printAge** method.

# Enums

Enums (or enumerations) are a special kind of class that have a fixed set of constant values. They are very useful when you want to have a class field that has a fixed set of values. This is very helpful when using switch statements as your editor will tell you if you are missing any values, you should be testing for. Here is an example that specifies all the file types, your application might handle:

```
enum FileType {
  any,
  media,
  image,
  video,
  audio,
  custom,
}
```

**FileType**, is a simple list of file types. Instead of defining constants with values like 0, 1, 2, etc., you can use actual names. You would use **FileType** like:

```
final currentFileType = FileType.any
```

You can even have fields in an enum, like the example below:

```
enum ChooseEnum {
  mySelf(name: 'Myself'),
  someoneElse(name: 'Someone else'),
  both(name: 'Both myself and someone else');

  const ChooseEnum({required this.name});

  final String name;
}
```

The second **enum**, **ChooseEnum**, has a name field. This is useful when you need to store values along with the enum. If you need to know the position of the enum, you can use the index getter. This will give you the index (position) of the enum value within the list of values. To get all the enum values, you would use **FileType.values**.

# Extensions

Extension methods allow you to extend a class. If you do not have the ability to change the source of a class, you can extend it with your own methods. For example, you can extend the String and int classes with extra functionality.

```
extension NumberParsing on String {
  int parseInt() {
```

```
      return int.parse(this);
   }
}
print('92'.parseInt());
```

To create an extension, use the **extension** keyword, the name of your extension, the keyword **on,** and then the class you would like to extend. Then enter any methods you like.

# Concurrency

While Flutter is a single-threaded framework, Dart supports the idea of isolates. An isolate is an independent unit of execution that runs in its own memory space and has a single thread of control. In Flutter, there is always the main isolate where the UI is rendered. When you run a Dart program, the Dart runtime runs an event loop where tasks are added to the event queue to be run. These tasks can be UI tasks, user input, disk IO, or network requests. In Flutter, you usually do not have to worry about isolates. Flutter can handle tasks quickly enough that it seems like they are being executed simultaneously. If you do not try to run too many tasks at once, you should be ok. How do you know what is too much? If your UI starts slowing down or stopping altogether, then you may need to investigate restructuring your code or using another isolate.

# Async/Await

Dart uses two keywords to handle asynchronous code. The **async** keyword, to mark a method as asynchronous, and the **await** keyword to wait for a result. The **await** keyword can only be used inside of a method marked with the **async** keyword. To fetch data from the internet, you will need to do this asynchronously. This can be done by creating methods that return a **Future**.

```
Future<MovieResponse?> getTrendingMovies() async {
    return _movieRepository. getTrendingMovies();
}

void main() async {
  final response = await getTrendingMovies();
}
```

In this example, the **getTrendingMovies** method returns a **Future<MovieResponse?>**. By adding the **async** keyword you mark this method as returning a future value. In the **main** function, you **await** the result. This calls the method and does not return until it is finished. You will learn more about Futures in later chapters.

# Streams

Streams are asynchronous and provide values over time. This could be useful in a chat application where you might be waiting on other users to add their comments and then the stream would inform you of that change. Events will continue until you close the stream. One piece of code would create the stream and another would listen to those events. In addition to data, streams can send errors.

Streams come in two types: Single subscription and broadcast streams. As the name implies, a single subscription allows only one listener and does not produce events until a listener is attached and stops sending when the listener detaches. A broadcast stream, on the other hand, produces events even if there are no listeners. Broadcast streams are good for things like mouse events that you can use and then discard.

# Exceptions

Error handling is very important in any program. Dart uses **Exception** and **Error** classes to indicate that there is a problem. Flutter or your code can throw an Exception and if you do not catch it, your application will crash. One difference Dart has from other programming languages is that Dart can throw any object, not just an **Exception** or **Error**. However, you will usually create classes that implement Exception. If one of your methods throws an exception, it is very important that you document it, as Dart only has unchecked exceptions. This means that the compiler will not tell you if your code does not catch a thrown exception. To catch an exception, you would wrap the code that could throw an exception with a try/catch bracket. The following is a simple class that throws an exception when the **throwException** method is called. It takes a required name but does not require an **id**. The **printName** method simply prints out the values of the class's fields.

```dart
class Simple {
  final String name;
  int? id;

  Simple({required this.name, this.id});

  void setId(int id) {
    this.id = id;
  }

  void throwException() {
    throw Exception('This is an exception');
  }

  void printName() {
    if (id != null) {
      print('Name is $name with id: $id');
```

```
    } else {
      print('Name is $name');
    }
  }
}

final simple = Simple(name: 'Simple');
try {
  print(simple.printName());
  simple.throwException();
} catch (exception) {
    print('Exception Thrown $exception');
}
```

In this example, Simple has a **throwException** method. When **simple.throwException()** is called, the **exception** is caught and **Exception Thrown** is printed. In this example, we used the **catch** keyword, but you can also use **on Exception catch** to catch a **specific** type of exception. If you need to catch multiple exceptions and then run some cleanup code, you can use the **finally** keyword. This allows you to run some code after any catch code is run.

Errors represent a serious problem that cannot be recovered from. This is usually thrown from the system, but your code can throw it too. Examples include **OutOfMemoryError** and **StackOverflowError**.

# Conclusion

This has been a crash course in Dart and you might feel overwhelmed. Use this as a reference as you go through the book. You now have a solid understanding of the Dart programming language, and this will help you in writing Flutter applications.

In the next chapter, you will learn all about Flutter's basic widgets and finally get to writing your first application.

# Join our book's Discord space

Join the book's Discord Workspace for Latest updates, Offers, Tech happenings around the world, New Release and Sessions with the Authors:

**https://discord.bpbonline.com**

CHAPTER 3

# Building the Movie App

## Introduction

In this chapter, you will dive into Flutter development by creating your first app. This chapter guides you through the essential steps of creating a new app, demystifying widgets, and how State works in Flutter. In this chapter, you will build a full-fledged movie app showcasing Flutter's power and versatility. This app will allow users to discover trending movies, explore detailed information, and watch trailers. Note that while the examples in this book are demonstrated on a Mac, they also apply to Windows. When discussing Windows-specific features, we will switch to that platform.

## Structure

The chapter covers the following topics:

- Creating the movie app
- Widgets
- Stateless and stateful widgets
- Hot reload and debugging
- Movie app UI
- Movie architecture
- First steps of the movie app

# Objectives

By the end of this chapter, you will have a comprehensive understanding of how to create a Flutter app, what widgets are, and how to build and debug your app. You will also have a good understanding of the movie app and what you will be building.

# Creating the movie app

There are several ways to create a Flutter project. Flutter comes with its own command-line program called **flutter**. When you installed Flutter, a command-line program was installed in the directory where you installed Flutter. This command-line tool allows you to do many things. You can create, build, and run Flutter projects. There are also several tools built into the flutter tool. You also use this tool to upgrade your version of Flutter. Here are a few popular commands:

- **doctor**: Check for any errors in the installation of Flutter.
- **config**: Configure Flutter settings.
- **upgrade**: Upgrade to the latest version of Flutter.
- **build**: Build a Flutter app.
- **clean:** Delete the build and `.dart_tool` directories.
- **run**: Run your Flutter app.
- **devices**: List of connected devices.
- **install**: Install the Flutter app on a device.
- **create**: Create a new Flutter project.

To create a new project, use the **create** command after typing in **flutter**. An example is as follows:

```
flutter create --platforms=macos,windows,ios,android,web --org=com.bpb.
movies .
```

There are additional options, such as specifying the language used to build Android or iOS apps, as shown:

```
--ios-language= objc, swift
--android-language= java, kotlin
```

You can even specify a template. The default template is app, but you can create all of the types as follows:

```
--template=app, module, package, plugin, plugin_ffi, skeleton
```

While creating projects from the command line is straightforward, using an IDE like **Visual Studio Code (VS Code)** or Android Studio simplifies the process even further. You will see how to create a new project from VS Code or Android Studio.

# Visual Studio Code

In this chapter, we will be using Android Studio, but if you are more comfortable with **VS Code** you can use it. If you want to use Android Studio, you can skip this section. VS Code is a lightweight and fast app. This section gives a step-by-step explanation of how to create a new project in VS Code.

The steps are as follows:

1.  Open up VS Code and then press *F1* or *Shift+Cmd+P*.

2.  You should see a text field. Type in **flutter new**. Select the first item, as shown in the following figure:

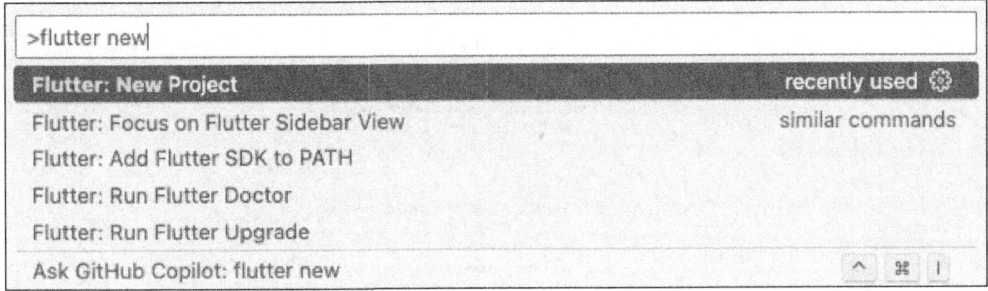

*Figure 3.1*: *New project*

3.  Next, choose the **Application** template, as shown in the following figure:

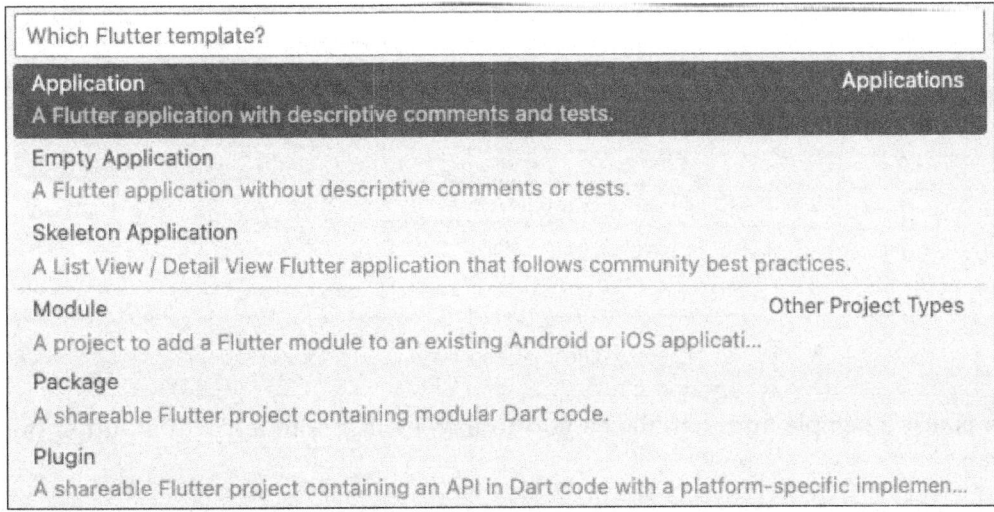

*Figure 3.2*: *Application template*

4.  Enter a **Project Name**. We will be using the name **movies** for this project. Refer to the following figure:

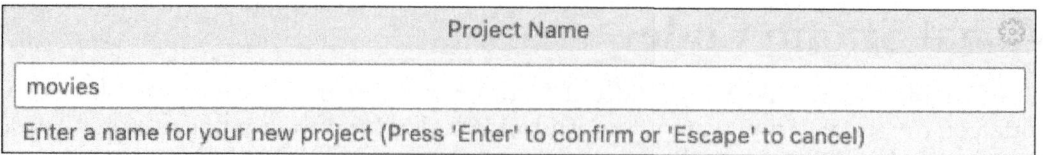

**Figure 3.3**: *Project name*

5.   This will create a new project and open the **main.dart** file, which contains the code for a sample counter app. The screen is as follows:

```
EXPLORER                    ...     main.dart ×
∨ MOVIES                            lib >  main.dart
> .dart_tool                        1    import 'package:flutter/material.dart';
> .idea                             2
> android                                Run | Debug | Profile
> ios                               3    void main() {
∨ lib                               4      runApp(const MyApp());
   main.dart                        5    }
> linux                             6
> macos                             7    class MyApp extends StatelessWidget {
> test                              8      const MyApp({super.key});
> web                               9
> windows                           10     // This widget is the root of your application.
 .gitignore                         11     @override
 .metadata                          12     Widget build(BuildContext context) {
! analysis_options.yaml             13       return MaterialApp(
 movies.iml                         14         title: 'Flutter Demo',
 pubspec.lock                       15         theme: ThemeData(
! pubspec.yaml                      16           // This is the theme of your application.
 README.md                          17           //
                                    18           // TRY THIS: Try running your application with "flutter run". You'll see
                                    19           // the application has a purple toolbar. Then, without quitting the app,
                                    20           // try changing the seedColor in the colorScheme below to Colors.green
                                    21           // and then invoke "hot reload" (save your changes or press the "hot
                                    22           // reload" button in a Flutter-supported IDE, or press "r" if you used
                                    23           // the command line to start the app).
                                    24           //
                                    25           // Notice that the counter didn't reset back to zero; the application
                                    26           // state is not lost during the reload. To reset the state, use hot
                                    27           // restart instead.
                                    28           //
                                    29           // This works for code too, not just values: Most code changes can be
                                    30           // tested with just a hot reload.
                                    31           colorScheme: ColorScheme.fromSeed(seedColor: Colors.deepPurple),
                                    32           useMaterial3: true,
                                    33         ), // ThemeData
                                    34         home: const MyHomePage(title: 'Flutter Demo Home Page'),
                                    35       ); // MaterialApp
                                    36     }
                                    37   }
                                    38
```

**Figure 3.4**: *VS Code files*

This is just a sample app that allows you to increment a counter with a button on the screen.

Pressing the small run button (shown in *Figure 3.5*) will launch the app on your Mac. The output is as follows:

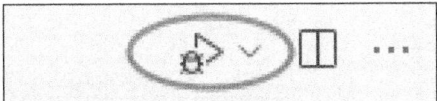

*Figure 3.5*: *Run buttons*

*Figure 3.6*: *First app*

# Android Studio

Android Studio, developed by *Google* with assistance from *JetBrains* (the creators of IntelliJ), is another excellent IDE for Flutter development.

The steps for app development using Android Studio are as follows:

1.  Open Android Studio and open the **File** menu by navigating to **File | New | New Flutter Project...**, as shown in the following figure:

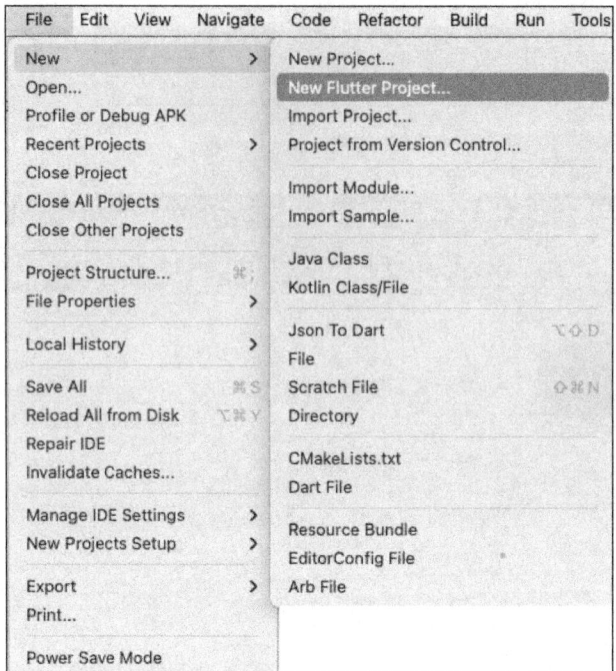

**Figure 3.7**: *New project menu*

2.  Next, choose **Flutter** from the **Generators** section on the left. Make sure your **Flutter SDK path** is set and press **Next**.

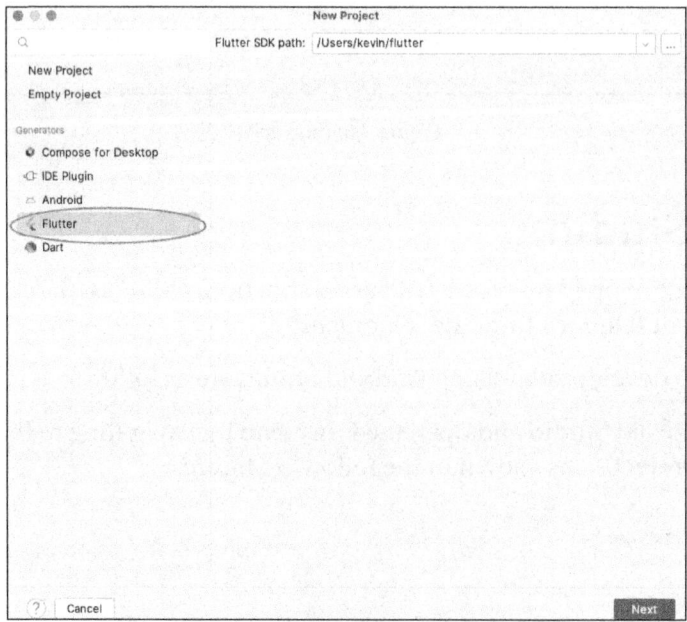

**Figure 3.8**: *New project*

3.  Next, enter **movies** as the **Project name**. You can modify the **Project location** if needed. Provide a brief description and your organization name (typically in reverse domain name notation: **com.mycompany** for **mycompany.com**). Unlike VS Code, Android Studio allows you to specify the organization, ensuring correct app settings for Android and iOS. By default, all platforms are selected, as shown in *Figure 3.9*.

4.  Uncheck any you do not intend to support. Finally, press the **Create** button.

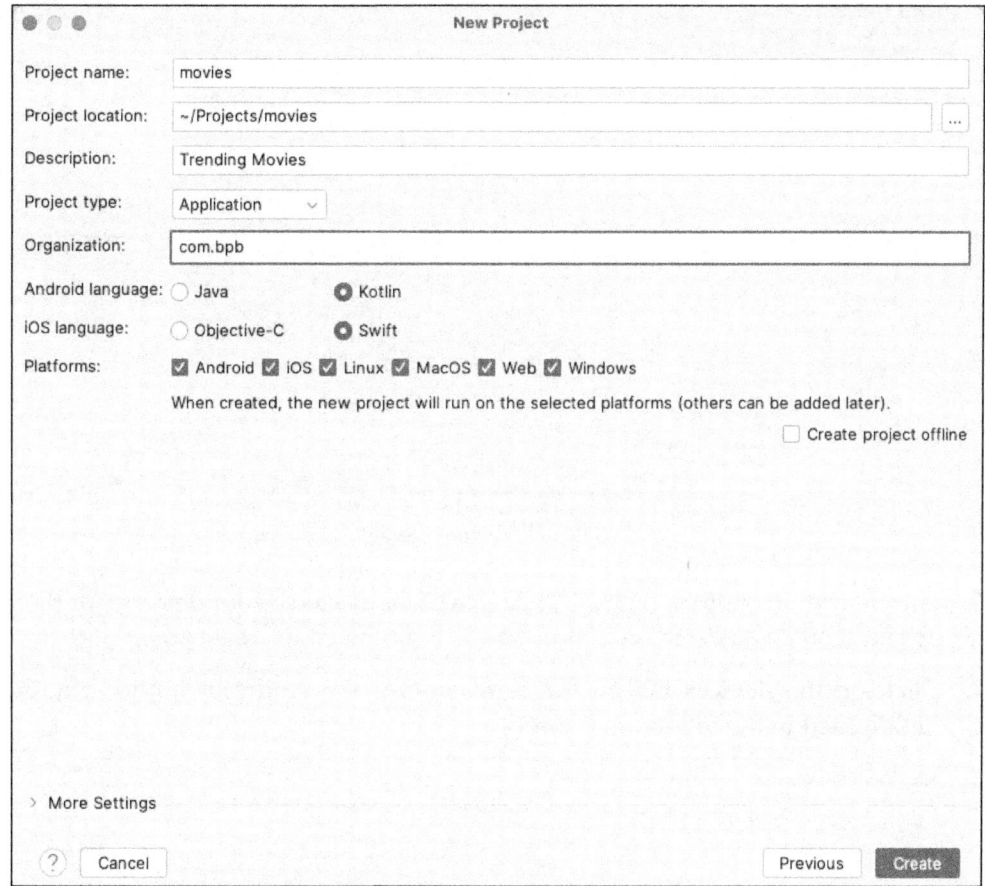

*Figure 3.9*: *New project screen 2*

5.  You should now see the same counter app created earlier in VS Code. (*Figure 3.4*) Congratulations on building your first Flutter app.

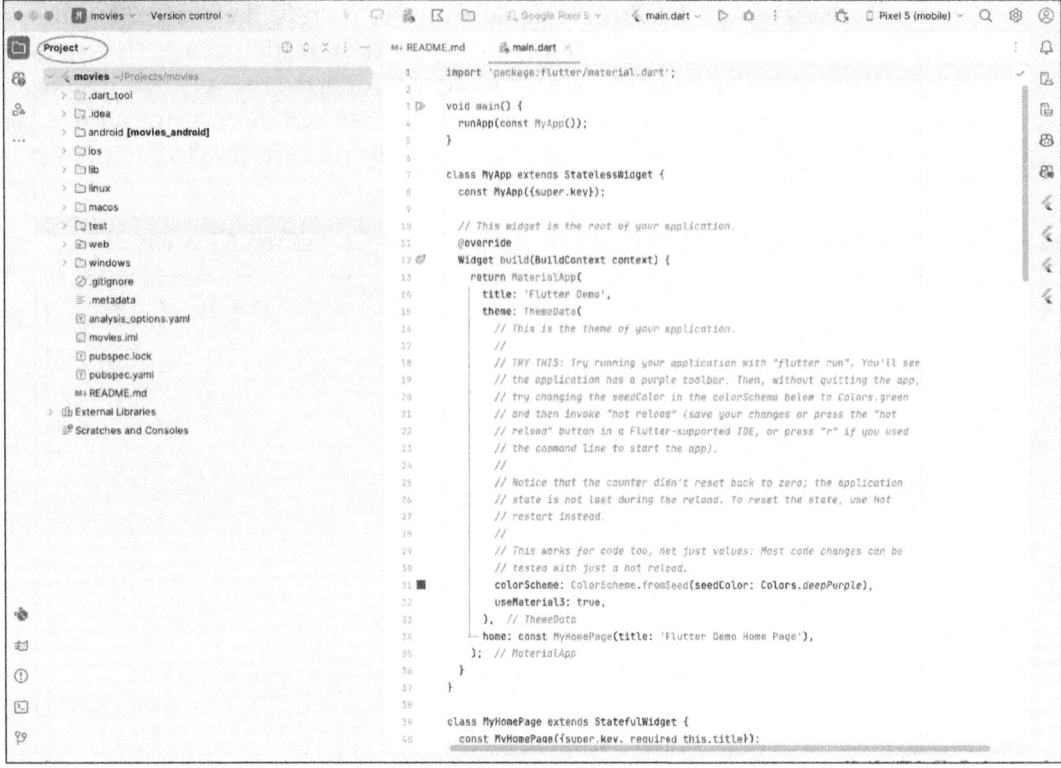

*Figure 3.10: Android Studio*

6. You can run the app on a physical device (if connected), your desktop, or the web. To run it on an Android emulator, you will first need to create one.

7. Click on the devices tab on the right side of the Android Studio window, as highlighted in the following figure:

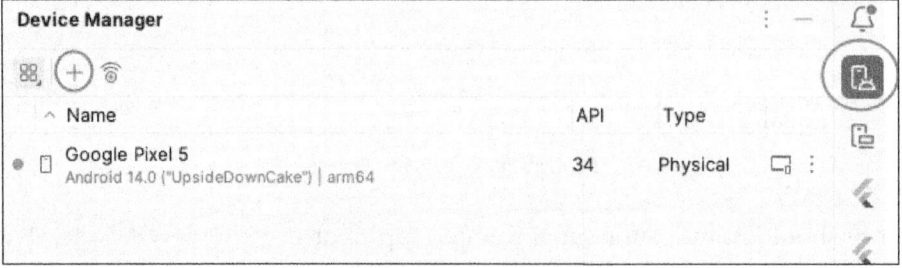

*Figure 3.11: Device manager*

8. Click the plus (+) icon in the top left corner, as highlighted in *Figure 3.11*.

9. Choose a **Phone** type, as shown in *Figure 3.12*. Here we have selected the **Pixel 8**. Click on the **Next** button.

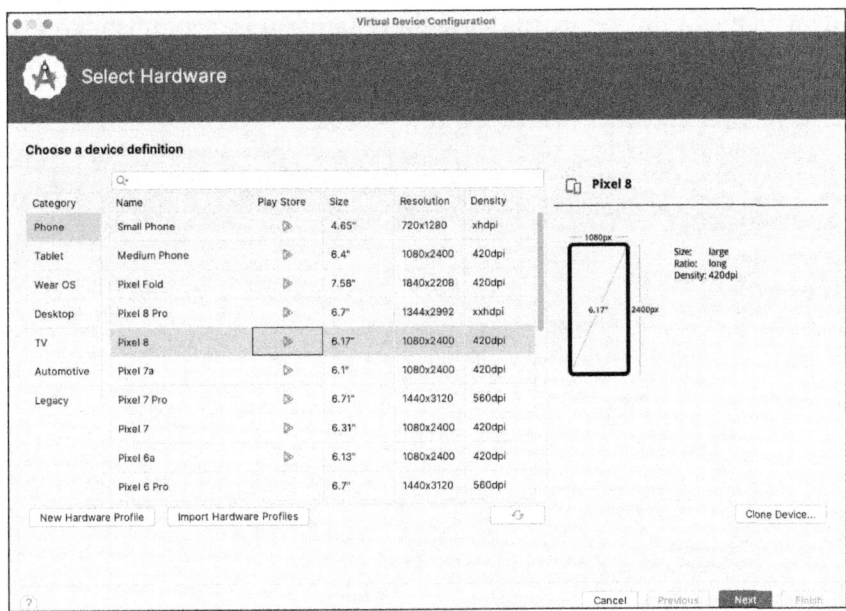

**Figure 3.12**: *Select hardware*

10. Choose one of the API images. It is recommended to choose a newer one, but not an experimental or privacy image. You may have to download the image by pressing the **Download** button. Once downloaded, select **Next**. The following figure shows the output window of this step:

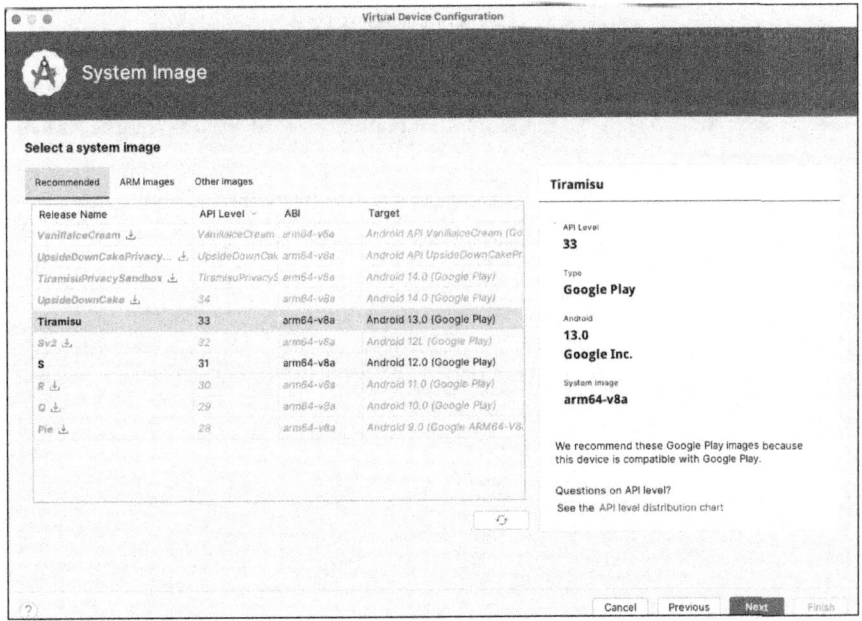

**Figure 3.13**: *Select image*

11. Enter a name for the device (or leave the default). It is recommended to change the advanced settings, so click the **Show Advanced Settings** button, as shown in the following figure:

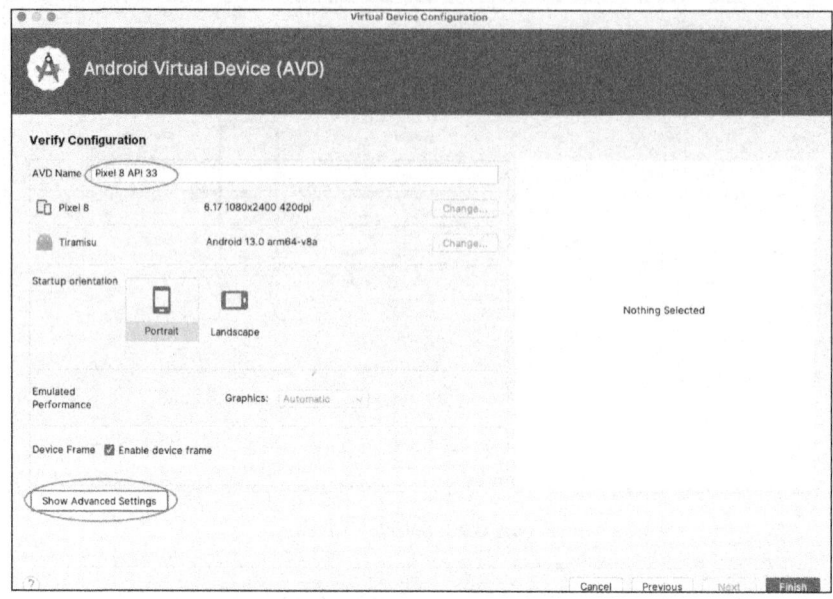

*Figure 3.14*: *Virtual device*

12. Change the **MB** to **GB** for both storage settings and enter **4**, as shown in *Figure 3.15*. This is not required, but emulators run out of storage. Press **Finish**.

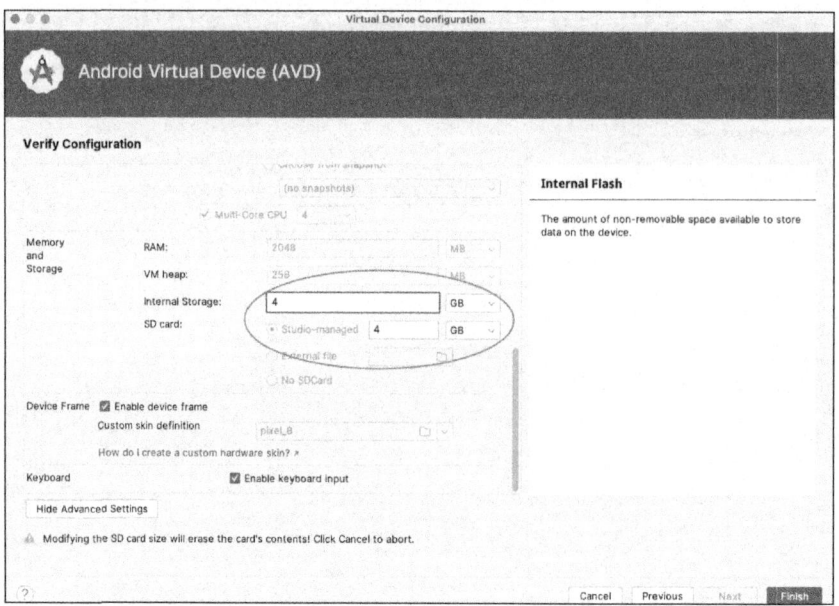

*Figure 3.15*: *Advanced settings*

13. You should see your new device in the **Device Manager** list, as shown in the following figure. Press the play button on the right to start the emulator.

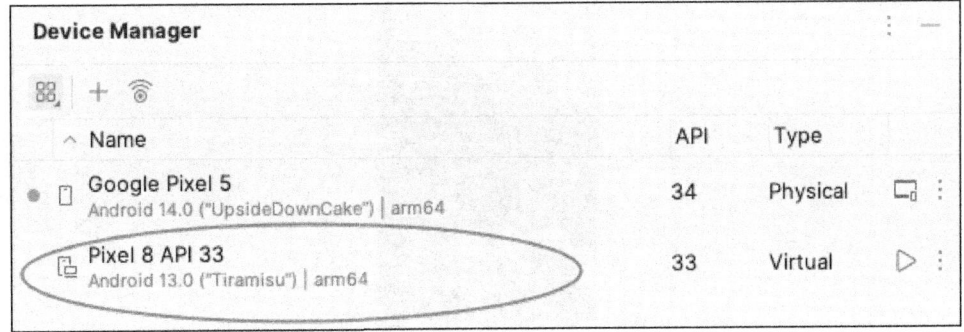

*Figure 3.16: New device*

14. In the top right corner of the window, select the dropdown next to the debug symbol and select a device to run on, as shown in the following figure:

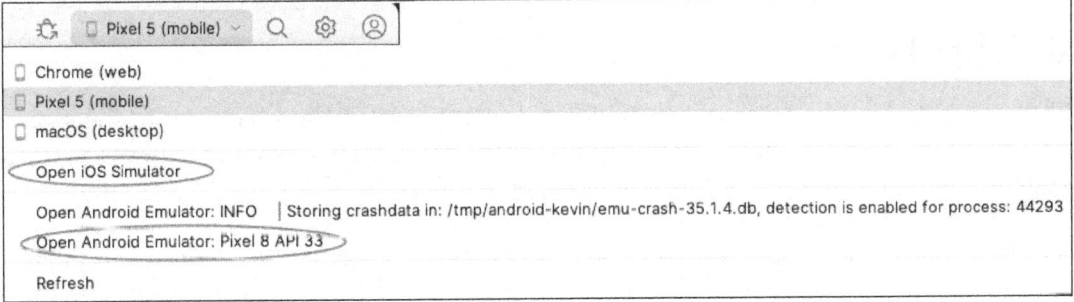

*Figure 3.17: Run menu*

15. You can choose an iOS simulator, Android emulator, Chrome (web) or macOS desktop. Once you have chosen your device, you can run by pressing the run button, in the following figure:

*Figure 3.18: Run buttons*

16. **main.dart** is the file that will be run. You should see your emulator, and then your app will run.

*Figure 3.19: Emulator*

# Widgets

Flutter is a declarative UI that uses widgets. Widgets are UI classes drawn to the screen and are meant to have one or more child widgets. This creates a tree of widgets to form your screen. You usually start with layout-type widgets like Column, Row, Container, or a higher-level widget like Scaffold. You then add child widgets until the screen is built out. First, decide how you want your screen to look, and then add widgets from the top down. Usually, you will start with a column and then put rows in the column. The rows can contain text, checkboxes, images, or any other widget. You do not have to follow the same procedure, but it is a good way to start. Besides these basic widgets, there are also lists, grids, and some fancy widgets. Other developers have built their own widgets that you can use by importing their packages. To see all of Flutter's widgets, go to their widget catalog: **https://docs.flutter.dev/ui/widgets**.

# Stateless and stateful widgets

In addition to the widgets that are included with Flutter, when you create your app, you need to decide if you want to create either stateless or stateful widgets. Just as the name implies, one widget has a state that can be changed, and one does not. Stateless widgets are immutable. They can only show the information passed to them and cannot change these values. Stateful widgets are useful because they can hold state. For example, when you have a text field, you need to keep track of the text controller, which holds the text the user has entered. This requires your widget to be a stateful widget.

If you look at `main.dart` in your current project, you can see everything you need for a simple project. This project will run on all platforms and will work without any changes.

You have the following:

- **main()**: Starting function of any app.
- **runApp()**: Starts Flutter.
- **MyApp**: An example of a stateless widget. You can name your widgets anything you want.
- **MaterialApp**: A starting point that allows you to use widgets with a Material Design.
- **ThemeData**: Set up your color scheme.
- **MyHomePage**: An example of a stateful widget.
- **Scaffold**: Holder for drawers, bottom sheets, and app bars.
- **App bar**: Top title section.
- **Center**: Center one child widget.
- **Column**: A vertical column of widgets.
- **Row**: A horizontal row of widgets.
- **Text**: Display non-editable text.

As you can see, the `MyHomePage` widget is a stateful widget because it has a `_counter` field that is used for updating. When the button is pushed, this value is incremented, and the widget is rebuilt. `MyApp` is stateless because it does not change.

# Hot reload and debugging

One of the best features of Flutter is its ability to perform a hot reload or hot restart. This means that once you have started your app on a device, you can change the code in your editor, hit hot reload, and your app is updated without the need to rebuild and re-install the app. This saves a lot of time. The difference between the two is that hot reload keeps the screen where it is and just reloads any code that has changed, whereas hot restart restarts the app from the very beginning. This is useful if you have made major changes because, in that case, a hot reload will not work.

# Movie app UI

In this section, you will be developing a movie app. This app will use the popular **The Movie Database** (**TMDB**) API to get trending and popular movies. You will be able to see the cast, description, and trailers from the movie. In addition, beautiful movie poster images will be shown. The following are some of the Figma (a popular design app) designs, along with the steps:

1. The first section is the home screen, as shown in *Figure 3.20*. This shows a carousel of trending movies and has a list of trending, popular, and top-rated movies. The user can click on a movie, and they are taken to the details screen.

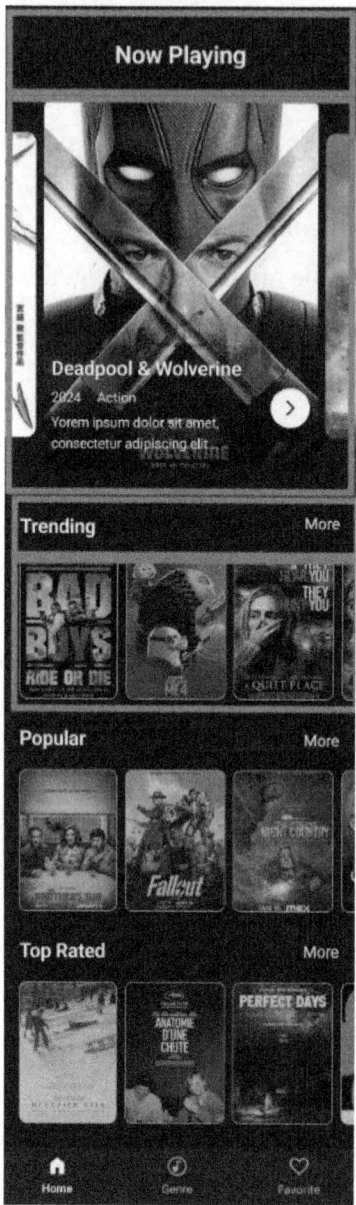

*Figure 3.20: Home screen*

2. The details screen is next, as shown in *Figure 3.21*. This shows an image of the film, an overview, some buttons to favorite, rate, and share, a list of trailers, and a list of the cast.

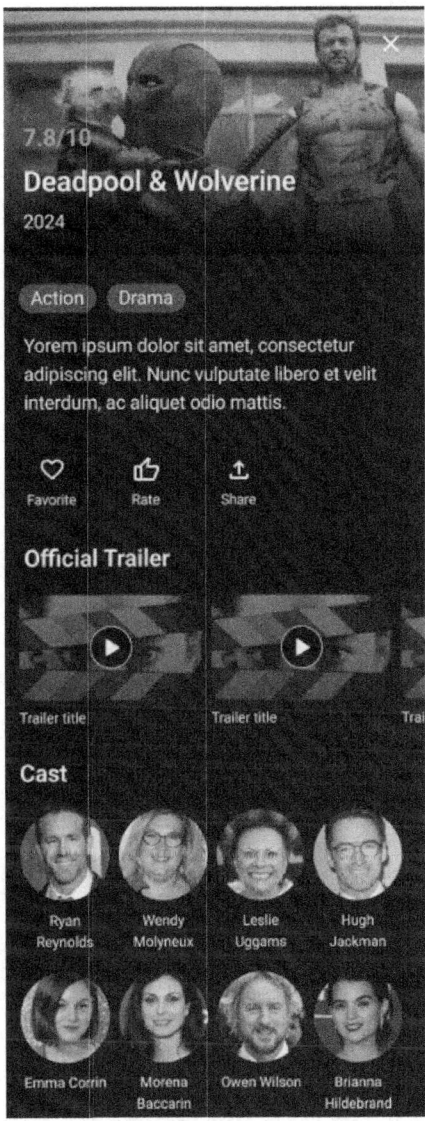

*Figure 3.21: Details screen*

3.  The next section is the **Genre** screen, as shown in *Figure 3.22*. This screen allows you to search by name and genre.

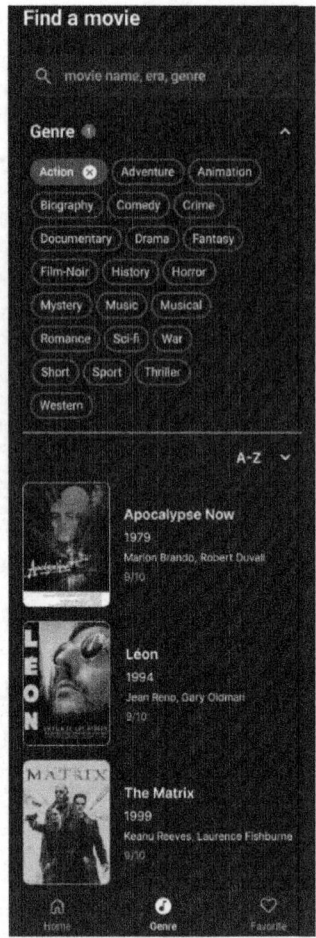

*Figure 3.22: Genre screen*

# Movie architecture

There are a lot of architectures out there, but the important thing to keep in mind when selecting an architecture is that you should create code that is simple to use, test, and update. Use libraries that you like and are easy to use. A typical architectural pattern is clean architecture.

# Clean architecture

Clean architecture is a software design philosophy that promotes the separation of concerns and prioritizes the independence of a system's core business logic from its external details (like frameworks, databases, and UI). It is a way of structuring your codebase to make it more testable, maintainable, and flexible over time. Try to make your classes as independent as possible. The following are some areas that clean architecture covers:

- **Layering**: Layer components into distinct layers. Common layers are:
  - o Domain/Entities for core business logic and models
  - o Use cases for application logic
  - o **Interface adapters**: Controllers, gateways and presenters
  - o **Frameworks and drivers**: UI, Database, devices
- **Dependency rule**: This rule states that higher-level components (domain/logic) should not depend on lower-level components like UI, frameworks, or databases.
- **Abstraction**: Create interfaces to be able to swap out components without affecting the whole application. This is very useful in testing.
- **Testability**: Writing single-responsibility components makes it easier to test.

# SOLID

**SOLID stands for: (S) Single-Responsibility Principle, (O) Open-Closed Principle, (L) Liskov Substitution Principle, (I) Interface Segregation Principle, and (D) Dependency Inversion Principle**. The explanation for each is:

- **Single-Responsibility Principle**: Each component should have a single, well-defined responsibility.
- **Open-closed Principle:** Software entities (classes, modules, functions, etc.) should be open for extension, but closed for modification.
  - o **Open for extension**: This means that you should be able to add new features or behaviors to a software entity without changing its existing code. This is often achieved through inheritance, interfaces, or other extensibility mechanisms.
  - o **Closed for modification**: The entity's core functionality should remain stable and unchanged. Modifying existing code can introduce bugs and break existing dependencies, so it should be avoided as much as possible.
- **Liskov Substitution Principle**: It states that objects of a superclass should be replaceable with objects of its subclasses without affecting the correctness of the program. In other words, if a program uses a superclass, it should be able to use objects of any subclasses without any unexpected behavior.
- **Interface Segregation Principle**: No client should be forced to depend on methods they do not use. Instead of having large, monolithic interfaces, create smaller, more focused interfaces that are specific to the classes needs.
- **Dependency Inversion Principle**:
  - o High-level components (like business logic or policies) should not be directly tied to the specific implementation details of lower-level components (like utility functions or database access).

○ Both high-level and low-level components should depend on abstractions, such as interfaces or abstract classes. This is a bit complicated, but you should know the terminology.

# Folder structure

In this section, we will use different folders to represent different areas of the app. The folder structure is as follows:

**data/**
⊠— **database/**
    ⊠— **models/**
⊠— **models/**
⊠— **repository/**
⊠— **sources/**
**network/**
**router/**
**ui/**
⊠— **screens/**
⊠— **themes/**
⊠— **widgets/**
**utils/**

As you move through the chapters, you will create these sections. For example, when you are in the networking chapter, you will create the files to access the network. You will also need to create models for the networking portion.

# First steps of the Movie app

Now that you know more about architecture, it is time to clean up the app. Since you want a movie app and not the default counter app, you need to delete the code generated when you created the project. Open **main.dart** in Android Studio and delete the **MyApp** and **MyHomePage** widgets. Only the **main** method should be present. You will see an error in the main because **MyApp** does not exist. Add the following code:

```
class MainApp extends StatefulWidget {
  const MainApp({super.key});

  @override
  State<MainApp> createState() => _MainAppState();
}

class _MainAppState extends State<MainApp> {

  @override
  Widget build(BuildContext context) {
```

```
  return const MaterialApp(
    title: 'Movies',
    debugShowCheckedModeBanner: false,
    home: MainScreen(),
  );
}
}
```

Now, change **MyApp** to **MainApp**. You will notice that the main screen shows an error as you have not yet created the **MainScreen** widget. This code creates a stateful widget, starts with a **MaterialApp** widget, has a **title** of **Movies**, does not show the debug banner, and has a child of **MainScreen**. In the left-hand project window, create a new **ui** folder under **lib**, as shown in the following figure:

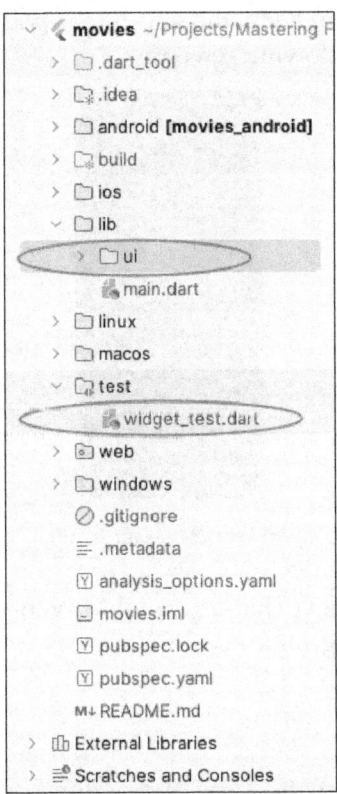

*Figure 3.23: Project list*

In the **ui** folder, create a new file called **main_screen.dart**. Delete the widget_test.dart file. Then add the following code to **main_screen.dart**:

```
import 'package:flutter/material.dart';

class MainScreen extends StatefulWidget {
  const MainScreen({super.key});
```

```
  @override
  State<MainScreen> createState() => _MainScreenState();
}

class _MainScreenState extends State<MainScreen> {
  @override
  Widget build(BuildContext context) {
    return const Placeholder();
  }
}
```

This code creates a stateful widget and returns a **Placeholder** widget. As its name implies, it is an excellent widget for filling the screen with a widget showing something that should go in that space. Return to **main.dart** and add the import for the main screen. Run your app, and you should see the following screen:

*Figure 3.24: Main screen*

This will prepare you for the next chapter, in which you will learn more about different widgets and start implementing some screens.

# Conclusion

In this chapter, you created your first app and are on your way to creating an excellent movie app. You also gained a solid understanding of widgets and the differences between stateless and stateful widgets. You learned about the advantages of hot reloading and learned a lot about different architectures.

In the next chapter, you will learn the basic widgets needed to build an app. You will learn about all the files created during the project creation. Then, you will learn in detail some of the important building blocks of a Flutter app. Finally, you will build the movie home screen.

# CHAPTER 4
# Basic
# Widgets

## Introduction

In this chapter, we cover most of the basic Flutter widgets, from rows to columns, text, and images. You will learn how to build a full screen from the top down. It is also important to learn about the file structure of a Flutter app and what all the files and folders mean. We will also look at the other building blocks of a Flutter app. Then, you will build the home screen for the movie app.

## Structure

The chapter covers the following topics:

- Flutter project structure
- Scaffold, AppBar, and NavigationBar
- Containers, rows, and columns
- Text, images, and icons
- Buttons and input fields
- Build the movie home screen

# Objectives

By the end of this chapter, you will have a solid understanding of Flutter widgets and will have built the home screen for your movie app. You will understand how the file structure of a Flutter app is laid out and what all the files in a project are for. You can create your own screen by using Scaffolds, columns, and rows and then populate them with buttons and text fields. Finally, you will put that knowledge into practice by building the home screen of the movie app.

# Flutter project structure

In the previous chapter, you created your first app. Now it is time to learn what all the files and folders mean. One of the most important files is **pubspec.yaml**.

## pubspec.yaml

The **pubspec.yaml** file defines your project and all the packages and plugins you will need for your app. Open up **pubspec.yaml**. **YAML Ain't Markup Language (YAML)** is an easy-to-read file that has a field, a colon, and then a value. One of the key aspects of YAML files is the indentation. You start at the left side, add a field name, and child elements are indented in two spaces. Ensure that it is spaces and not tabs. Not three spaces, but two. If you get it wrong, the build will not work.

## Pubspec fields

The elements under the field are as follows:

- **name**: At the top is the **name** field. Here you can put the name of the project.

- **description**: This describes your app. Go ahead and change this to describe your app. I put in **Select your favorite movies and watch them later**, but you can use anything.

- **publish_to**: URL to publish. Currently, it is set to **none**. If you want to publish your project to **pub.dev**, you will need to remove this line.

- **version**: This is just the current version of your app. Update it every time you send out a new version.

- **environment**: Define the Dart SDK and Flutter version. This is very important. Normally you will not change this unless a major Flutter version comes out and you support it. Right now, it is set to: **'>=3.3.4 <4.0.0'**. This means that it supports Flutter versions 3.3.4 up to (but not including) 4.0.0. So, every time you run **flutter upgrade**, Flutter's version increases and as long as the version number is between these two numbers, you can just rebuild and run your app. Note that this YAML file supports plain Dart projects as well. To tell the system that you are using Flutter, you need to add it as a dependency.

- **dependencies**: Define the packages and plugins to use in the app.

The following:

```
flutter:
  sdk: flutter
```

tells the build system to include the Flutter SDK. Next are the packages and plugins that your app uses. Currently, only the **cupertino_icons** package is provided. This is a set of icons for use on the iOS platform. Try adding the material icons pages by adding the following:

```
material_symbols_icons: ^4.2719.3
```

below **cupertino_icons**. Make sure it is indented two spaces. Next, click on **Pub get** at the top of the file. Now you can use the Material Design icons. Finally, there are the **dev_dependencies**. These are used for builders and other libraries that are needed during the development phase of your project. For writing unit tests, use the following:

```
flutter_test:
  sdk: flutter
```

For integration tests, use the following:

```
integration_test:
  sdk: flutter
```

At the very end is the Flutter-specific area. Here, you can set the flag to use Material Design, as follows:

```
uses-material-design: true
```

After that, you would have an **assets** section where you would define the assets for your app.

# Lints

Flutter uses the **flutter_lints** package to check for valid code. This is a very useful feature that allows the system to catch errors as well as code style errors. To add the **flutter_lint** package, open up **pubspec.yaml** and add the following under the **dev_dependencies** section below:

```
flutter_test:
  flutter_lints: ^2.0.0
```

Click on the **Pub get** button in the window (or use the command). Next, open up **analysis_options.yaml**. This file is where you put all of your lint settings. We have one lint we want to add, and that is to require the full package name for imports. There are several settings for this. Under the rules section add the following (make sure it is indented two spaces from the rules section):

```
avoid_relative_lib_imports: true
always_use_package_imports: true
prefer_relative_imports: false
```

Now, whenever you add an import, lint will suggest adding the full package name.

# lib folder

The most important folder is the **lib** folder. This is where your dart files reside. You can put them in nested folders however you like.

# Folders

There are several other folders at the top level. Most are platform-specific. For example, the **android** folder contains all the files needed to run on an Android device. You will normally not need to change these files except to add things like Android icons. **iOS** is for the iPhone, **macOS** is for the Mac, **windows** for Windows, etcetera. For unit tests, use the **test** folder, and for integration tests, use **integration_test.** There is no **assets** folder, but if you want to add files for your app, you must create this folder and add files you can load into your app in that directory.

# Scaffold, AppBar, and NavigationBar

In this section, we will look at Scaffold, AppBar, and NavigationBar.

## Widgets

The Flutter team likes to say that everything is a widget. That includes UI elements that do not draw anything independently but just lay out their child widgets. While all these widgets are just widgets, they have different purposes.

## Scaffold

Starting at the very top is the Scaffold. A Scaffold is a Material Design widget that lays out a full screen. It has the following parameters:

- **appBar**: A toolbar for a title, actions, and a navigation menu.
- **body**: This widget will be displayed in the middle, taking up the rest of the screen.
- **floatingActionButton**: A small button that floats at the bottom right of the screen.
- **bottomNavigationBar**: A bar at the bottom of the screen for navigating between screens.
- **drawer**: A side menu tied to the AppBar. A menu that slides in from the left or right.

All these items are optional except for the body, which is your content. A Scaffold is also needed to show snackbars, which are temporary floating message windows that display errors or messages.

# AppBar

The AppBar is useful for showing the page title, having a menu for options, and a back button. Note that the AppBar is useful for mobile devices and not as useful on the desktop or web. Having more room allows other ways of displaying information. The FloatingActionButton is mostly seen on Android platforms but can also be used on iOS. It is useful for creating new items but can be used for almost anything. Some nice packages do things like explode the button into more items.

# BottomNavigationBar

The BottomNavigationBar is very useful when your app has three or four screens. The navigation bar allows the user to switch between the screens by clicking a button at the bottom. You will be using this for the movie app. Note that this does not mean you cannot have more than four screens. You can easily go to other screens from those three or four screens, or you can have a final screen of options that shows a list of other screens.

# Drawer

Some apps use a drawer to display a menu of other options. Although its design has fallen out of favor among designers, some apps still use it.

# Snackbar

A snackbar is a small floating window that shows a message for a short time, usually for errors. You must have a Scaffold as a parent to show a snackbar.

# Containers, rows, and columns

Some layout widgets you can use are containers, rows, and columns. A container holds one child widget, which you can decorate with a background color, set a width and height, and other options.

# Container

A container allows you to surround your widget with the following:

- **Background color**: Provide a background color.
- **Padding**: Pad the interior before showing the widget.

- **Alignment**: Align widgets to different sides of the container.
- **Decoration**: Add all kinds of decorations, like rounded borders.
- **Width and height**: Set the size of the widget.
- **Transform**: Transform the container with a matrix. This is a powerful way to rotate, translate, or scale the container.

The following is an example of a small circle with text inside of the middle:

```
Container(
 width: 16,
 height: 16,
  decoration: const BoxDecoration(
 shape: BoxShape.circle,
     color: Colors.red,
                     ),
 child: Center(
 // Center the text
 child: Text(
   '1',
   ),
  ),
 )
```

As you can see, the **Container** is very powerful.

# Column

You will probably be using the **Column** widget frequently as it allows you to layout a list of items in a vertical format. Looking at the design image of the home page of the movie app, you would start with a **Column** and then add different widgets to build the screen. The following is an example **Column**:

```
Column(
    mainAxisAlignment: MainAxisAlignment.start,
    crossAxisAlignment: CrossAxisAlignment.start,
    mainAxisSize: MainAxisSize.min,
    children: [
      Text('Hello')
    ]
)
```

A Column has four main components:

- **mainAxisAlignment**: How the widgets are aligned going down. Left, right or center.

- **crossAxisAlignment**: How the widgets are aligned going across. Left, right or center.

- **mainAxisSize**: Take up a minimum or maximum height. Fill the screen or not.

- **children**: Add a list of child widgets.

There are also a few lesser-used parameters like:

- **textDirection**: Direction of the text. This will be left to right or right to left.

- **verticalDirection**: Defaults to down.

- **textBaseline**: Align text based on alphabetic characters or ideographic characters.

- **clipBehavior**: Allows for clipping if content overflows.

It is important to set the `mainAxisSize`, as a `Column` defaults to max. The following are the `mainAxisAlignment` values:

- **start**: Left aligned.

- **end**: Right aligned.

- **center**: Center widgets.

- **spaceBetween**: Evenly add free space between the widgets.

- **spaceAround**: Add free space at the ends.

- **spaceEvenly**: Add free space at the ends and in between.

The `crossAxisAlignment` is similar but different. It has the following:

- **start**: Left aligned.

- **end**: Right aligned.

- **center**: Center widgets.

- **stretch**: Require widgets to fill the cross axis.

- **baseline**: Align along the baseline of widgets. Usually used with text.

# Rows

Rows lay their children horizontally. This is ideal for widgets that go across the screen. Rows have the same parameters as a `Column` but have a horizontal direction. The following is an example `Row`:

```
Row(
    mainAxisSize: MainAxisSize.max,
    children: [
      Text(text),
      const Spacer(),
      TextButton(
```

```
              onPressed: () {},
              child: Text(
                'More',
              ),
            ),
        ],
    );
```

Here we have a **Text** widget, a **Spacer** (to fill up extra space and push the button to the right), and a **TextButton**. This makes up a row that fills up the width of the screen.

# Text, images, and icons

Text, images, and icons are a few of the most used widgets.

# Text

**Text** is for static text that is shown on the screen. The **Text** widget has many parameters:

- **data**: String value.
- **Style**: **TextStyle** information on color, font, and size.
- **strutStyle**: Sets the minimum line height (not used much).
- **textAlign**: How the text is aligned horizontally.
- **textDirection**: Left to right, or right to left.
- **Locale**: Set the user's language and country. Should be rarely used as there is a current global Locale.
- **softWrap**: If true, the text should break when needed in a space.
- **overflow**: If the text overflows its drawing area, what should happen? This will depend on the following command:
  - **clip**: Just cut off the text
  - **fade**: Fade the text
  - **ellipsis**: Add ... to the end of the text
  - **visible**: Render text outside of the box
- **textScaler**: How text should be scaled for better readability (not used much).
- **maxLines**: Useful for specifying whether the text should be a specific number of lines or if set to null, as many lines as needed.
- **semanticsLabel**: mostly used for accessibility purposes, but some testing systems use semantics to find text fields.

- **textWidthBasis**: A way of measuring the width of one or more lines.

- **textHeightBehavior**: How to apply a style's height (not used much).

- **selectionColor**: Color of text when selected.

There are many fields, but you will probably only use the actual text and a style. There are times when `maxLines` come in handy, but in general, this is a pretty easy widget to use.

The following is a simple example:

```
Text('My Favorites', style: TextStyle(fontSize: 24,
  fontWeight: FontWeight.w600,
  color: Colors.white))
```

# Images

Flutter uses the `Image` widget to display images. This widget can handle images from several sources:

- Local assets directory
- Internet
- File
- Memory
- **ImageProvider**: Class used to return an image

There are several parameters for creating an image. The most important ones are as follows:

- **Width and height**: Define the size of the image

- **Color**: color to be blended with each pixel

- **Opacity**: Animation for handling opacity

- **Fit**: Very important for sizing. Uses the *BoxFit* enum with:

  o **fill**: Fills the target but distorts the aspect ratio

  o **contain**: As large as possible inside of the target

  o **cover**: As small as possible while covering the target

  o **fitWidth**: Full width (height is adjusted)

  o **fitHeight**: Full height (width is adjusted)

  o **none**: Center and not resized

  o **scaleDown**: Center and scale down if needed

You can use static constructors for the different types like: `Image.file`, `Image.network`, and `Image.asset`. The following is a simple asset image:

```
Image.asset('assets/cat.png')
```

For network images, you might have something as follows:

```
Image.network(
    'url',
    width: 120,
    height: 98,
    fit: BoxFit.fill)
```

# Icons

Icons are a way to show standard images without having to create them yourselves. There are the **cupertino_icons** or the material design icons. Inside the **material_symbols_ icons** package is a file named **symbols.dart**. This has all the icons available. If you go to **https://fonts.google.com/icons**, you will see a page as follows:

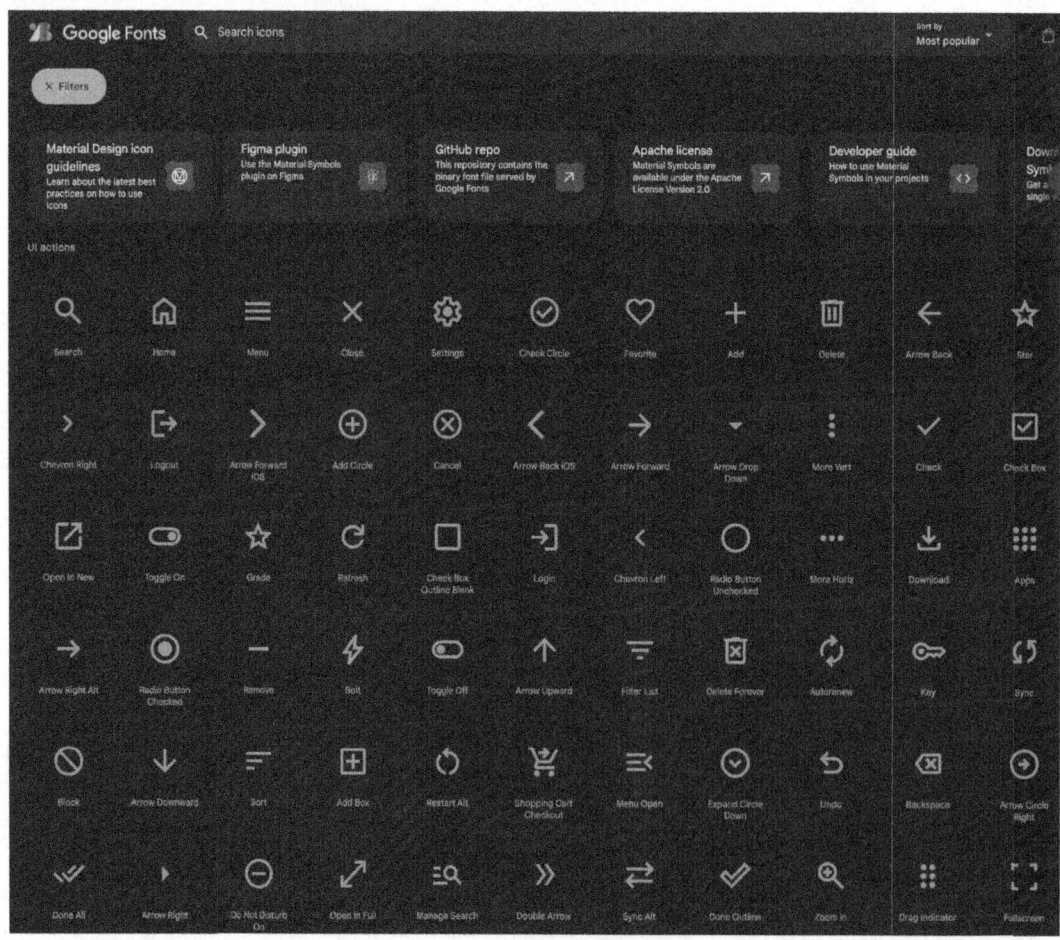

*Figure 4.1: Material icons*

Many common icons are needed for an app. **Close, Arrow Back** button icons, and more. On this page, you can easily search for an icon that will meet your needs. The following is an example of a search icon (the first icon in the list above):

```
const Icon(Icons.search, color: Colors.white,)
```

Many times, you will use these icons inside of an **IconButton**  class. This provides a click listener for the icon. Also, notice the **const** before the **Icon**. Android Studio and Flutter lints will remind you to use const before any widget that does not use any dynamic content.

# Buttons and more

In this section, we will learn about widgets like buttons, selection, chips, DatePicker, and more.

# Buttons

Buttons are an essential part of a UI. They allow the user to select and perform an action. There are many types of buttons:

- **IconButton**: For showing an icon
- **TextButton**: A button with text, no decoration
- **ElevatedButton**: Adds dimension to a button
- **FilledButton**: Fill a button with a color
- **OutlinedButton**: Rounded corner outline
- **FloatingActionButton**: Floating button.
- **SegmentedButton**: Checkable sections

These are some of the more common buttons. There is now an ExtendedFloatingActionButton that allows you to have text along with the icon.

# Selection

In addition to buttons, there are other widgets that allow you to select. The most common is the Checkbox. Note that this is just the box, not the text. Usually, you will have these two widgets together.

# Chips

Chips are a newer widget and there are several different types:

- **InputChip**: For attribute information. Contains an icon, text, and close button
- **ChoiceChip**: Are selectable and have a checkmark when selected

- **FilterChip**: Represent filters have an icon and text
- **ActionChip**: Allow the user to start an action by clicking on the chip

You will be using the `FilterChip` class to select genres when searching for movies.

# DatePicker

This widget allows you to create a popup window for selecting a date. A sample popup is as follows:

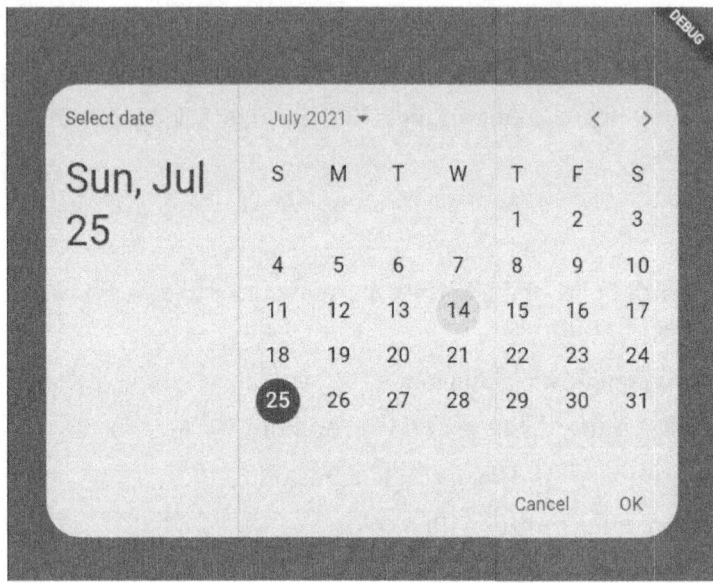

*Figure 4.2*: *DatePicker*

An example is as follows:

```
DatePickerDialog(
        restorationId: 'date_picker_dialog',
        initialEntryMode: DatePickerEntryMode.calendarOnly,
        initialDate: DateTime.fromMillisecondsSinceEpoch(arguments! as
int),
        firstDate: DateTime(2021),
        lastDate: DateTime(2022),
);
```

# PopupMenuButton

A menu that is usually tied to a button and shown when the user selects it. An example is as follows:

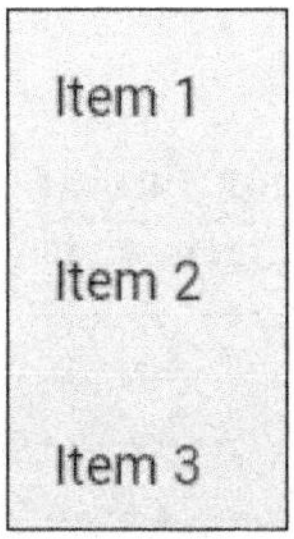

Item 1

Item 2

Item 3

*Figure 4.3*: *PopupMenuButton*

The following is an example:

```
PopupMenuButton<String>(
   initialValue: 'Item 1',
   onSelected: (String item) {
      setState(() {
          selectedItem = item;
      });
   },
   itemBuilder: (BuildContext context) => <PopupMenuEntry<String>>[
      const PopupMenuItem<String>(
         value: 'Item 1',
           child: Text('Item 1'),
         ),
      const PopupMenuItem<String>(
          value: 'Item 2',
            child: Text('Item 2'),
          ),
      const PopupMenuItem<String>(
          value: 'Item 3',
            child: Text('Item 3'),
          ),
   ],
 )
```

# Radio button

Another common widget is the radio button. It will look like something as follows:

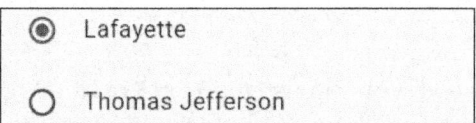

*Figure 4.4*: *Radio buttons*

# Slider

This widget is less common but useful for allowing the user to visually pick values. It has minimum and maximum values. It will look as follows:

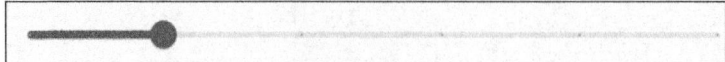

*Figure 4.5: Slider*

# Switch

A visual way to turn something on or off. It has two states, on and off, and will look like this:

*Figure 4.6: Switch*

# TimePicker

Like the DatePicker, the TimePicker allows the user to choose a specific time, as shown in the following figure:

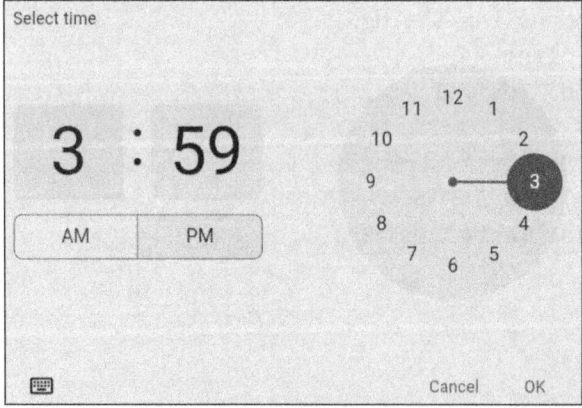

*Figure 4.7: TimePicker*

# Text input

To allow the user to enter text, you can use the **TextField** widget. A **TextField** requires a **TextEditingController**, which means it needs to be inside of a **StatefulWidget**. A **TextEditingController** holds the value of the text the user entered. To update the text in the field, you need to update the controller's text value. If you do not supply a controller, one will be created for you. The easiest way to create and destroy a controller is in the **initState** and **destroy** methods of a **State** class. The code is as follows:

```
class LoginDialog extends StatefulWidget {

  const LoginDialog({super.key});

  @override
  State createState() => _LoginDialogState();
}

class _LoginDialogState extends State<LoginDialog> {
  late TextEditingController emailTextController;

  @override
  void initState() {
    super.initState();
    emailTextController = TextEditingController(text: '');
  }

  @override
  void dispose() {
    emailTextController.dispose();
    super.dispose();
  }
}
```

Then, to use a **TextField**, you would do something as follows:

```
TextField(
    keyboardType: TextInputType.emailAddress,
    onSubmitted: (value) {},
    controller: emailTextController,
),
```

There are several options for TextFields, as follows:

- **controller**: Holds the text value.
- **focusNode**: Used to focus or unfocused where the user is adding text.
- **undoController:** Keeps track of the changes. Allows listening to changes and undoing/redoing those changes.
- **decoration—inputDecoration**: Lots of options for changing the border, labels, icons, styles etcetera.
- **keyboardType**: Useful for email, number, dates, password, and phone.
- **textCapitalization**: Can automatically capitalize words, sentences, or characters.

- **Style**: Input text style.
- **textAlign**: Align text to different sides of the container.
- **maxLines**, **minLines**: Min/max lines.
- **maxLength**: Maximum number of characters.
- **onChanged:** Listener for every time a user updates the text.
- **onSubmitted**: Listener for the final entry.

There are many more fields that can be used, but these are the main ones that you will generally use.

# Build movie app screens

In the previous chapter, you saw a design for the home screen. The following is that figure with sections drawn in red:

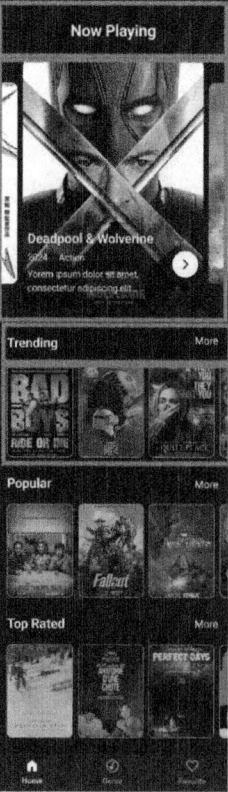

*Figure 4.8: Home screen*

If you look at the overall design, you can see that there is a column of rows. The column goes down while the rows go across. Inside your lib folder, create two new folders. Inside the **ui** folder, create **screens,** and then inside of that folder, create a **home**. Next, create the **home_screen.dart** file inside of that folder. Next, add the following:

```
import 'package:flutter/material.dart';

class HomeScreen extends StatefulWidget {
  const HomeScreen({super.key});

  @override
  State<HomeScreen> createState() => _HomeScreenState();
}

class _HomeScreenState extends State<HomeScreen> {
  @override
  Widget build(BuildContext context) {
    return const Placeholder();
  }
}
```

This adds a screen with another placeholder. Return to **main_screen.dart** and change **Placeholder()** with **HomeScreen()**. Import the home screen, then hot reload the app, and you should see the same thing as before. Next, add the **Now Playing** headline. Inside of **HomeScreen**, replace **Placeholder()** with the following:

```
    return Scaffold(
      body: Column(
        children: [
          Text('Now Playing')],
      ),
    );
```

Press hot reload. You will see:

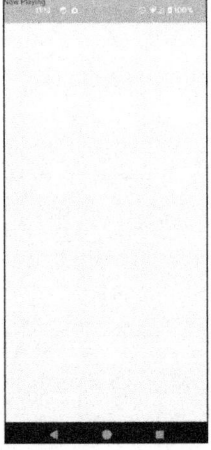

*Figure 4.9: Title*

As you can see, the title is in the status area. By default, Flutter draws to the whole screen. To avoid this, you must ensure you draw in a safe area. One shortcut in Android Studio is to use option-return on a widget. This will bring up a menu, as shown in the following figure:

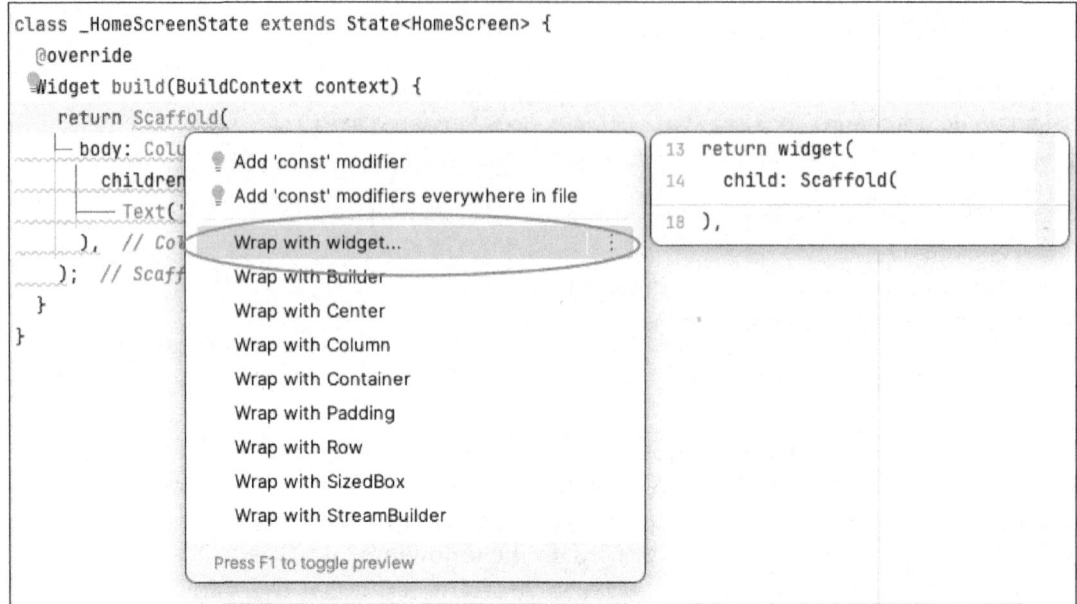

*Figure 4.10: Wrap menu*

Click on the **Column** widget and select **Wrap with widget...** Then type **SafeArea**. You should see the following:

```
    return SafeArea(
      child: Scaffold(
        body: Column(
          children: [
            Text('Now Playing')],
        ),
      ),
    );
```

Hot reload. Now it looks as follows:

*Figure 4.11: SafeArea*

To make the text bigger, you need to change the text style. We also want to center it. How would you do that? One very convenient widget is the **Align** widget. Change the text to the following:

```
const Align(
    alignment: Alignment.center,
    child: Text('Now Playing'))
```

Hot reload, and you should see it in the center. It looks too close to the top. Maybe add some padding?

Option-return on the **Text** widget and select the **Wrap with Padding...** option. It will default to 8 pixel margins. We want to have some vertical spacing. Specifically, 16 pixels on the top and 24 at the bottom. Change the padding to the following:

**const EdgeInsets.fromLTRB(0, 16.0, 0, 24)**

The **left, top, right, bottom (LTRB)** is the order that the values are in. Hot reload, and it should look better. Notice that with hot reload, we can design our screen as we go. This saves a lot of time. Now for the style. The screenshot is from the Figma app, which is a design tool that designers use. When we click on the **Now Playing** title, we see that it is Roboto semibold 24. We will cover fonts in a different chapter, but for now, we want the font to be bold and 24 pixels tall. After the **Now Playing** text, add the following:

**, style: TextStyle(fontSize: 24, fontWeight: FontWeight.w600)**

The weights for fonts range from 100 to 900. The higher the number, the bolder the text. Hot reload. The screen will be as follows:

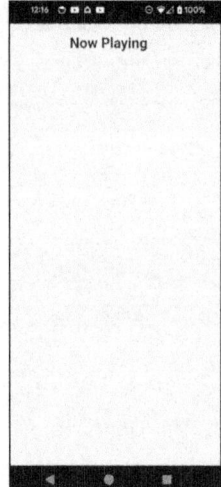

*Figure 4.12*: *Centered title*

You have a title, but if you compare it to the design, the background is black, and the text is white. To get a background color, you can use a **Container**. Surround the column with a **Container** and set the **color** to **0xFF111111** like this:

```
Container(
        color: const Color(0xFF111111),
```

Now, the title is not visible. Change the color of the text style as follows:

```
, color: Colors.white
```

Hot reload. You should see the following:

*Figure 4.13*: *Colors*

Next, you will add some libraries to help with the carousel at the top. Open up **pubspec. yaml**, and after **material_symbols_icons** add:

```
card_swiper: ^3.0.0
cached_network_image: ^3.3.1
```

The first package adds a carousel, and the second is for caching network images. Press the **Pub get** button at the top. Next, in the **home** folder, create a new file named **home_screen_ image.dart**.

Add the following:

```
import 'package:cached_network_image/cached_network_image.dart';
import 'package:card_swiper/card_swiper.dart';
import 'package:flutter/material.dart';

const delayTime = 1000 * 10;
const animationTime = 1000;

const images = [
  'http://image.tmdb.org/t/p/w780/z1p34vh7dEOnLDmyCrlUVLuoDzd.jpg',
  'http://image.tmdb.org/t/p/w780/gKkl37BQuKTanygYQG1pyYgLVgf.jpg',
  'http://image.tmdb.org/t/p/w780/4xJd3uwtL1vCuZgEfEc8JXI9Uyx.jpg',
  'http://image.tmdb.org/t/p/w780/uuA01PTtPombRPvL9dvsBqOBJWm.jpg',
  'http://image.tmdb.org/t/p/w780/H6vke7zGiuLsz4v4RPeReb9rsv.jpg',
  'http://image.tmdb.org/t/p/w780/e1J2oNzSBdou01sUvriVuoYp0pJ.jpg',
  'http://image.tmdb.org/t/p/w780/hu40Uxp9WtpL34jv3zyWLb5zEVY.jpg',
  'http://image.tmdb.org/t/p/w780/pKaΛ8VvfkNfEMUPMiiuL5qSPQYy.jpg',
  'http://image.tmdb.org/t/p/w780/zK2sFxZcelHJRPVr242rxy5VK4T.jpg',
  'http://image.tmdb.org/t/p/w780/7qxG0zyt29BI0IzFDfsps62kbQi.jpg',
  'http://image.tmdb.org/t/p/w780/8Gxv8gSFCU0XGDykEGv7zR1n2ua.jpg',
  'http://image.tmdb.org/t/p/w780/zDi2U7WYkdIoGYHcYbM9X5yReVD.jpg',
  'http://image.tmdb.org/t/p/w780/cxevDYdeFkiixRShbObdwAHBZry.jpg',
  'http://image.tmdb.org/t/p/w780/uXUs1fwSuE06LgYETw2mi4JxQvc.jpg',
  'http://image.tmdb.org/t/p/w780/fdZpvODTX5wwkD0ikZNaClE4AoW.jpg',
  'http://image.tmdb.org/t/p/w780/d5NXSklXo0qyIYkgV94XAgMIckC.jpg',
  'http://image.tmdb.org/t/p/w780/sh7Rg8Er3tFcN9BpKIPOMvALgZd.jpg',
  'http://image.tmdb.org/t/p/w780/sHJ2OIgpcpSmhqXkuSWxZ3nwg1S.jpg',
  'http://image.tmdb.org/t/p/w780/upKD8UbH8vQ798aMWgwMxV8t4yk.jpg',
  'http://image.tmdb.org/t/p/w780/vfrQk5IPloGg1v9Rzbh2Eg3VGyM.jpg',
];
```

This sets some constants for the swiper animation and an array of images. Note that we are hard-coding the images that we will be using later in the book. When we get to the networking section, you will get these images directly from the network. Next, add the widget:

```
class HomeScreenImage extends StatelessWidget {
  @override
  Widget build(BuildContext context) {
    // 1
    final screenWidth = MediaQuery.of(context).size.width - 32;
    // 2
    return SizedBox(
      height: 374,
      // 3
      child: Swiper(
        autoplayDelay: delayTime,
        duration: animationTime,
        itemWidth: screenWidth,
        autoplay: true,
        // 4
        itemCount: images.length,
        itemBuilder: (BuildContext context, int index) {
          // 5
          return CachedNetworkImage(
            imageUrl: images[index],
            alignment: Alignment.topCenter,
            fit: BoxFit.fitHeight,
            height: 374,
            width: screenWidth,
          );
        },
      ),
    );
  }
}
```

This code will show a carousel of images. The steps are as follows:

1. Get the width of the screen.
2. Create a fixed height box of 374 pixels.
3. Use the **Swiper** widget for the carousel and set animation parameters.
4. Set the **itemCount** to the length of the array.
5. Use the **CachedNetworkImage** widget to show the image.

Back in the home screen, add **HomeScreenImage()**, after the Padding widget, and import the **home_screen.dart** file. You must stop and restart the app after adding a new plugin. You should see an automated carousel of images:

*Figure 4.14*: *Carousel*

The designs show a bottom navigation section that shows home, genre, and favorites buttons. These buttons will take the user to the three different screens that you will be creating. To create these, go into **main_screen.dart**. We need to replace the single call to the home screen with a **BottomNavigationBar**. This class handles the selection of screens and shows the proper one. Before the build method, add some new variables:

```
var index = 0;
final List<Widget> screens = <Widget>[];
```

This will keep track of the current index and the screens list will hold the three screens. Now add the **initState** method:

```
@override
void initState() {
  super.initState();
  screens.add(const HomeScreen());
  screens.add(const Placeholder());
  screens.add(const Placeholder());
}
```

Now change the build method to:

```
@override
  Widget build(BuildContext context) {
    return Scaffold(
      body: screens[index],
```

```
      bottomNavigationBar: BottomNavigationBar(
        items: const [
          BottomNavigationBarItem(icon: Icon(Icons.home), label: 'Home'),
          BottomNavigationBarItem(
              icon: Icon(Symbols.genres), label: 'Genre'),
          BottomNavigationBarItem(icon: Icon(Icons.favorite), label:
'Favorites'),
        ],
        currentIndex: index,
        onTap: (navIndex) {
          setState(() {
            index = navIndex;
          });
        },
      ),
    );
  }
```

The Scaffold will show the current screen based on the current index. The **BottomNavigationBar** holds **BottomNavigationBarItem** items that just show the icons and text. The **currentIndex** is for the screen index currently selected, and the **onTap** call will set that index only when the user selects it. You will notice that the **Symbols. genres** cannot be found. This is an icon found in the **material_symbols** library. Add the following to **pubspec.yaml**:

```
material_symbols_icons: ^4.2719.3
```

Click on Pub Get. Import the **symbols** package. Looking back at the design, you will see three sections named trending, popular, and top-rated movies. They all look the same, which means they are good candidates for custom widgets. Start by creating a title row. In the home folder, create a new file named **title_row.dart**. Add the following:

```
import 'package:flutter/material.dart';


// 1
typedef OnMoreClicked = void Function();


class TitleRow extends StatelessWidget {
  final String text;
  final OnMoreClicked onMoreClicked;
  const TitleRow({super.key, required this.text, required this.
onMoreClicked});


  @override
```

```
Widget build(BuildContext context) {
  // 2
  return Row(
    // 3
    mainAxisSize: MainAxisSize.max,
    children: [
      Padding(
        padding: const EdgeInsets.fromLTRB(16, 16.0, 0.0, 8.0),
        // 4
        child: Text(text, style: const TextStyle(fontSize: 20,
fontWeight: FontWeight.w600, color: Colors.white)),
      ),
      // 5
      const Spacer(),
      Padding(
        padding: const EdgeInsets.fromLTRB(16, 16.0, 8.0, 0.0),
        // 6
        child: TextButton(
          onPressed: onMoreClicked,
          child: const Text(
            'More',
            style: TextStyle(fontSize: 16, fontWeight: FontWeight.w400,
color: Colors.white),
          ),
        ),
      ),
    ],
  );
}
}
```

This code shows a row with the passed in text on the left and a **More** button on the far right. The steps are as follows:

1. Define a function that will be run when the **More** button is clicked.

2. Create a row with several children.

3. Have the row take up the full width.

4. Show the passed-in title.

5. Use a **Spacer** widget to push the button to the right.

6. Use a **TextButton** to show more text.

Back in home screen, after **HomeScreenImage()** add the following:

```
    TitleRow(
      text: 'Trending',
      onMoreClicked: () {
      },
    ),
```

Hot reload. You should now see the Trending row. Copy and paste the **TitleRow** two times and change the text to popular and top-rated. Hot reload, and you should see three titles in a row.

# Movie row

Now, add the scrollable horizontal row for each type of movie. Create a new **.dart** file in the **home** folder named **horiz_movies.dart**. Add the following:

```
import 'package:cached_network_image/cached_network_image.dart';
import 'package:flutter/material.dart';

class HorizontalMovies extends StatelessWidget {
  // 1
  final List<String> movies;

  const HorizontalMovies({required this.movies, super.key});

  @override
  Widget build(BuildContext context) {
    // 2
    return SizedBox(
      height: 142,
      // 3
      child: ListView.builder(
          scrollDirection: Axis.horizontal,
          itemCount: movies.length,
          itemBuilder: (context, index) {
            // 4
            return GestureDetector(
              onTap: () {},
              child: SizedBox(
                width: 100,
                height: 142,
                // 5
                child: CachedNetworkImage(
                  imageUrl: movies[index],
                  alignment: Alignment.topCenter,
                  fit: BoxFit.fitHeight,
```

```
                    height: 100,
                    width: 142,
                ),
              ),
          );
        }),
     );
   }
}
```

This code will display a horizontal list of images and allow the user to click on individual images. The steps are as follows:

1.  Pass in a list of movie URLs.

2.  Each movie will only be 142 pixels high.

3.  Use a **ListView** to show a horizontal list (**ListViews** will be covered in more detail in another chapter).

4.  Use a **GestureDetector** to capture a click (**GestureDetector** will be covered in more detail in another chapter).

5.  Show the image.

Back in the home screen, add the following after the first **TitleRow**:

```
const HorizontalMovies(movies: images,),
```

Hot reload. You should see at least a part of the images, but what are the yellow and black striped lines? What are the error messages in the console? Now, you will be learning some of the hard parts about Flutter. If you read the error message in the console, you will see the following:

**A RenderFlex overflowed by 87 pixels on the bottom.**

**The relevant error-causing widget was:**
  **Column Column:file:///.../Mastering%20Flutter/git/Mastering-Flutter/ Chapter4/final/movies/lib/ui/screens/home/home_screen.dart:21:16**

This is saying that the last item in the column went 87 pixels beyond the area on the screen. To fix this, you need some sort of scrollable widget. There is an easy fix for this issue. Simply wrap the top **Container** with the following:

**SingleChildScrollView**

Hot reload, and the error should be gone. You will encounter several of these types of errors as your Flutter career progresses. The following is what your screen should look like:

*Figure 4.15: Scrolling lists*

The project is starting to look like an actual program. Copy the **HorizontalMovies** widget after each **TitleRow** and hot reload. You should be able to scroll down and see the three lists. You can even scroll right on the list. That is it for the home screen for now. In upcoming chapters, we will clean up the screen and get actual data from the network.

# Conclusion

In this chapter, you learned about the structure of a Flutter app and most of Flutter's basic widgets. Although it was a lot of information, you now have a handle on the basics of Flutter. We will continue to learn more about themes and advanced widgets.

In the next chapter, you will learn about colors, typography, and material design. You will use these to create a theme that sets the color and typography for the whole app at once.

# CHAPTER 5
# Themes, Colors and Fonts

## Introduction

In this chapter, we will cover all the design elements that make up your app, from colors that provide a consistent color scheme to fonts that look great for your app. You will learn about Material Design, *Google's open-source design system*, which makes it easy to create a great-looking app. Finally, you will create your own theme that incorporates all these elements.

## Structure

The chapter covers the following topics:

- Colors
- Typography
- Material Design
- Google Fonts
- Themes

# Objectives

This chapter will help you understand colors, typography, Material Design, and themes and how to apply them to your app. You will create a color and text theme that you can use in your movie app. By the end of this chapter, you will be able to create your own theme and apply it to your apps. You will have a solid understanding of the design system that Flutter uses and will be able to navigate the different components of the system.

# Colors

In Flutter, a color is represented as a hexadecimal number made up of the red, green, blue, and alpha values of a color. Alpha is a number for setting the opacity of the color. **0xFF** means it is completely opaque, and the full color is shown. **0x00** means that it is fully transparent. You can set the opacity with the **withOpacity** method on a color:

```
var grey = Colors.grey.withOpacity(0.5);
```

This creates a grey color at a 50% transparent level. There are many predefined colors in Flutter. Not only are there traditional colors like red, blue, green, purple, etc., but there are values with different opacity levels. For example, **Color.white70** is a white with 70% opacity. You can use these colors in your app or create your own. To create your own, you can either create a new **Color** class with a hex value as follows:

```
const primaryRed = Color(0xFFC13437);
```

You could also use **Color** methods. These are extension methods:

- **fromARGB**: alpha, red, green, blue
- **fromRGBO**: red, green, blue, opacity

Red, green and blue use values from 0 to 255, while opacity is 0.0 to 1.0. Alpha is from 0 to 255. A lot of widgets can take a color parameter. The **Container** widget has a **color** parameter and looks as follows:

```
Container(
    color: Color(0xFF111111),
)
```

For **Text**, you need to set the **color** in the **TextStyle** class, and use the following code:

```
Text('Now Playing', style: TextStyle(fontSize: 24, fontWeight: FontWeight.
w600, color: Colors.white),)),
```

# Typography

Typography is the technique of arranging text on the screen using different fonts, font sizes, colors, line spacing, and letter spacing. Normally, you use typography in text with a **TextStyle** class. This class defines the different attributes that will be used to display the text. You can set the font size, font weight (bold), font, letter spacing, colors, and more. While you can set each text's style manually, it is usually easier to define it once and reuse it. You can create variables for those or set them in a theme (discussed below).

# Material Design

Material Design is a design system by *Google* created to help developers and designers build beautiful, usable, and consistent digital experiences across various platforms. Currently, three versions are available: Version one was released in 2014 and introduced its core principles. Version two was introduced in 2018, and updated versions one and three were released in 2021. Version three can use a dynamic color system that can adapt to the currently displayed color. While the material design was originally designed for Android, it can be used on many other platforms as well. *Google* uses it for its Android and web products. You can still use the Material Design system on iOS, but it will not have the iOS look and feel. However, designers today usually create designs made for the app and company and not tied to a particular platform. This way, they can design the app once and use it on multiple platforms. This could use the company's colors and a specific design for their app. Material Design is customizable, so you do not have to use the default colors and styles. Material Design is built into the Flutter framework and can be customized by providing a theme with all the colors, fonts, and styles needed for your app. This system has custom-built elements such as buttons, cards, dialogs, and other widgets that use this system.

To use Material Design, you will start your app using the **MaterialApp** widget. This allows you to provide a theme (for colors, fonts, and other styles) and a router (for page navigation). Many Material Design widgets require a parent Material widget like **MaterialApp**. If there is no Material parent, you can use the Material widget to wrap your widget.

# Google Fonts

Google Fonts for Flutter is a package that simplifies the process of using Google Fonts in your Flutter applications. It allows you to easily access a vast collection of free, open-source fonts from *Google* and integrate them seamlessly into your app's text elements. To see all the fonts provided by *Google*, go to **https://fonts.google.com/**. The fonts page would be displayed as follows:

*Figure 5.1: Google Fonts*

Currently, this page lists 1,644 font families. Many of these are for different languages. This page also allows you to filter the fonts to find the one that works for you. *Google* also has a special font family called **Noto** that has all the current languages available. For the movie app, we are going to be using the Roboto font.

The steps to add Google Fonts are as follows:

1. You can add the **google_fonts** package by using the following command line:
   **flutter pub add google_fonts**.
   It can also be added by opening up **pubspec.yaml** in your project and adding the following:
   **google_fonts: ^6.2.1**

2. Now, create a new folder for your theme. Inside of the **lib/ui** folder, create a folder named **theme**. Now, create a new file named **theme.dart**. Add the following:
   ```
   import 'package:flutter/material.dart';
   import 'package:google_fonts/google_fonts.dart';

   var roboto = GoogleFonts.roboto();
   ```
   This imports the **material.dart** and **google_font** packages.

3. Using the **GoogleFonts** class, use the **roboto** function to retrieve an instance of the Roboto **TextStyle**. Now, let us create some **textStyles** needed for the movie app. Add the following:

```
var largeTitle = roboto.copyWith(
  fontSize: 24,
  fontWeight: FontWeight.w600,
  color: Colors.white,
);
```

This creates a variable named **largeTitle** that uses **roboto**, a font size of 24, a weight of 600 (which is semibold), and a color of white. Font weights go from w100 (thin) to w900 (thick). Bold is considered a w700 weight, and normal is a w400 weight.

4. Now add the rest of your styles, using the following code:

```
var heading1 = roboto.copyWith(
  fontSize: 20,
  fontWeight: FontWeight.w600,
  color: Colors.white,
);
var heading2 = roboto.copyWith(
  fontSize: 18,
  fontWeight: FontWeight.w600,
  color: Colors.white,
);
var body1Regular = roboto.copyWith(
  fontSize: 16,
  fontWeight: FontWeight.w400,
  color: Colors.white,
);
var body1Bold = roboto.copyWith(
  fontSize: 16,
  fontWeight: FontWeight.w700,
  color: Colors.white,
);
var body2Regular = roboto.copyWith(
  fontSize: 14,
  fontWeight: FontWeight.w400,
  color: Colors.white,
);
var body2Bold = roboto.copyWith(
  fontSize: 14,
  fontWeight: FontWeight.w700,
  color: Colors.white,
```

```
);
var caption = roboto.copyWith(
  fontSize: 12,
  fontWeight: FontWeight.w400,
  color: Colors.white,
);
var body3Regular = roboto.copyWith(
  fontSize: 12,
  fontWeight: FontWeight.w400,
  color: Colors.white,
);
var body3Bold = roboto.copyWith(
  fontSize: 12,
  fontWeight: FontWeight.w700,
  color: Colors.white,
);
var verySmallText = roboto.copyWith(
  fontSize: 10,
  fontWeight: FontWeight.w400,
  color: Colors.white,
);
```

There are many fonts here, but these are the styles that the app's designer provided. There are large fonts for titles and smaller ones for movie cast members' names. Usually, font sizes do not go below 10 pixels, as they become very hard to read.

5. To use these fonts, you would replace the hard-coded styles used with these variables. Open up **home_screen.dart** and find the **Now Playing** text field. Replace the style with **largeTitle**. You will have to add the following import:

```
import 'package:movies/ui/theme/theme.dart';
```

This looks a lot cleaner. Having to constantly type large **TextStyles** can waste a lot of time.

6. What about colors? If you look above the **Now Playing** text, you will see **Color(0xFF111111)**. We can replace this with variables as well. In **theme.dart**, add the following colors to the top:

```
// Colors
const screenBackground = Color(0xFF111111);
const searchBarBackground = Color(0xFF1E1E1E);
const primaryButton = Color(0xFFD9D9D9);
const posterBorder = Color(0xFFB5A9A9);
const buttonGrey = Color(0xFF504F4F);
```

These are some named variables that you will be using in the app.

7. Now replace that color with **screenBackground**. The rest of the colors will be used in the app when you start building the different screens.

# Themes

When a visual or UI designer starts to design an app, they start with a set of colors, fonts, shapes, and icons. This makes up the theme of the app. With a theme, every screen should follow that design, making screens consistent for a beautiful app. Flutter provides a way to use those colors, fonts, shapes, and icons by providing a theme parameter for the **MaterialApp** widget. That parameter is a **ThemeData** class. This class holds all the information needed to define the elements of your app. When using widgets in your Flutter app, if you specify any formatting for that widget, it will override the system styling. If you do not specify any formatting, Flutter will use the current theme's settings.

There are many ways to create a **ThemeData** class. The easiest is to use **ThemeData. light(useMaterial3: true)** or **ThemeData.dark(useMaterial3: true).** This will use either the light or dark theme defined by Flutter. This sets the theme's brightness level and uses the other defaults. If you know the main color you want to use for your app, like blue, then you can use the following command:

```
ThemeData(
useMaterial3: true,

// Define the default brightness and colors.
colorScheme: ColorScheme.fromSeed(
seedColor: Colors.blue,
brightness: Brightness.dark,
),
```

Here, you specify a **seedColor** and Flutter creates a color scheme for you. You can set the brightness as well to either dark or light.

# Fully customized theme

If you want to customize your theme fully, you will set the following parameters:

- **colorScheme**: Colors for the theme.
- **textTheme**: Text styles.
- **appBarTheme**: Theme for the AppBar.
- **bottomNavigationBarTheme**: Theme for the bottom navigation bar.
- **snackBarTheme**: Theme for snackbars.
- **tabBarTheme**: Theme for tabs.
- **actionIconTheme**: The action icons like back, close and drawer icons.

- **textButtonTheme**: Theme for text buttons.
- **useMaterial3**: Flag for using the newer Material 3 design system. This is true by default.

# ColorScheme

As mentioned above, the easiest way to create a **ColorScheme** is to use the **fromSeed** method. In addition to the **seedColor**, you can set other colors. You can set the primary, **onPrimary** (the color drawn on top of primary), secondary, and others. We will create a color scheme later in the chapter. To learn more about **ColorSchemes** and create your own, visit the Material 3 website: **https://m3.material.io/styles/color/roles/color-roles**. There are two different types of color schemes: Static and dynamic. Static just means you set the color once and do not change it. Dynamic is when you want your screens to match a color from that screen.

# Material Theme Builder

To help with dynamic colors, use the Material Theme Builder. The steps to launch Material Theme Builder are as follows:

1. If you go to **https://www.figma.com/community/plugin/1034969338659738588/material-theme-builder,** you can launch Figma's Material Theme Builder. This allows you to set your colors and text fonts. The screen will be as follows:

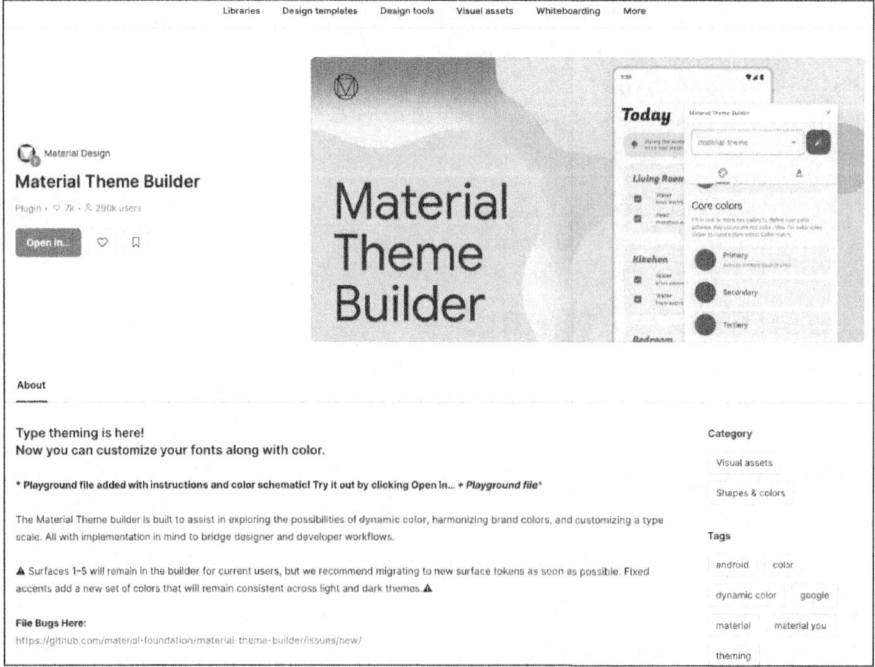

*Figure 5.2: Material Theme Builder*

2. Click on the **Open in...** button, and you will see the following:

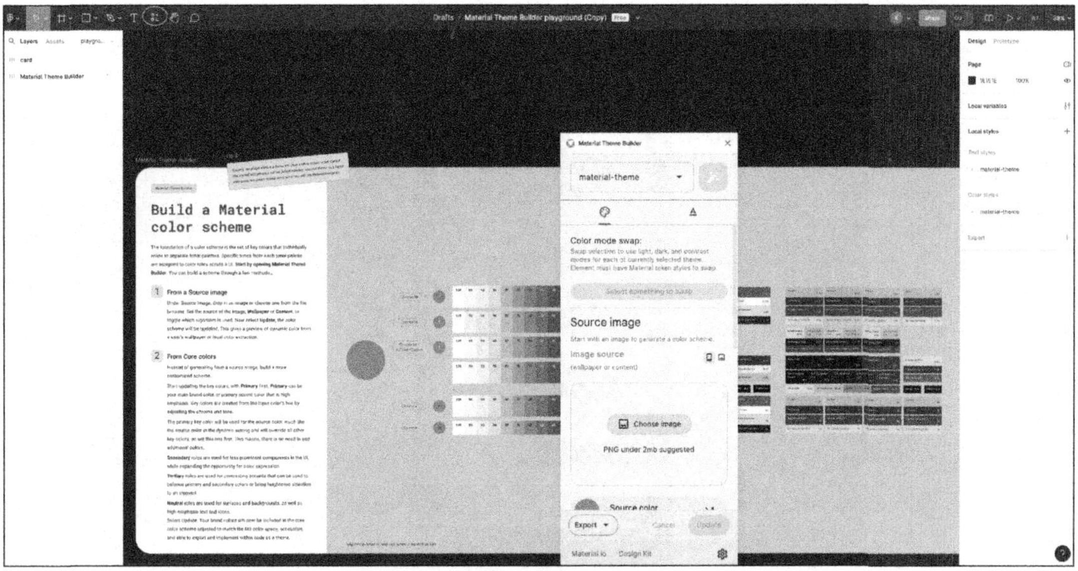

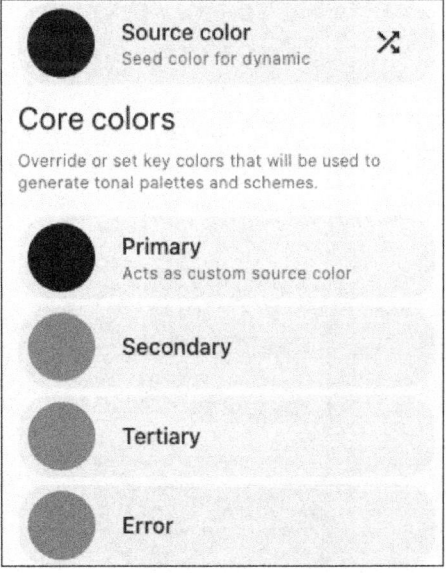

*Figure 5.3*: Color scheme

3. Click on the resources button, which is circled in red in *Figure 5.3*. This will bring up the Material Theme Builder dialog. Here, you can choose a color scheme in several different ways. If you select an image, it will create a color scheme based on that image. Or you can select your **Primary** colors, as shown in the following figure:

*Figure 5.4*: Core colors

4. Selecting any of the color rows will bring up the color picker, as follows:

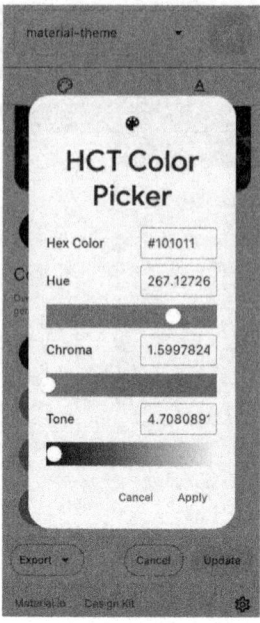

*Figure 5.5: Color picker*

5. Change the **Hue** to set the color, and then adjust the **Chroma** and **Tone** to get the exact color you want. To set a blue color, move the **Chroma** to the right and adjust the **Hue** towards blue, as shown in the following figure:

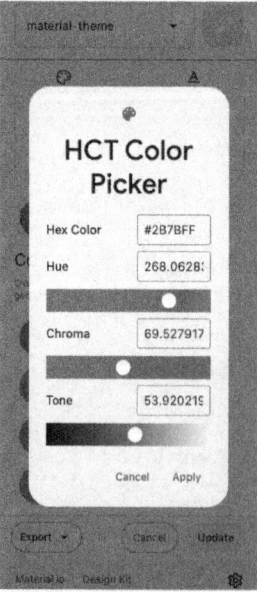

*Figure 5.6: Blue color picker*

6.  Once you have finished, click **Apply**. You can then export the design to Flutter by choosing the **Export** button as follows:

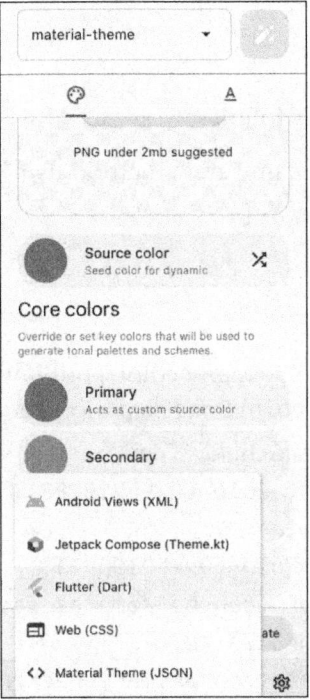

*Figure 5.7: Exporting*

7.  This will download a **material-theme.zip** file. Unzip the file, and you will find a **lib** directory with several files, as follows:
    *   **util.dart**: Creates the **TextTheme**.
    *   **theme.dart**: Creates some custom classes to store Figma's scheme colors.
    *   **main.dart**: Example usage of the theme.

While this is a nice tool for designing a color scheme, in this book, we will create our theme by hand so you can see all the different options available.

# Light vs dark

In **main.dart**, an interesting line of code, that gets the device's brightness, is as follows:

```
final brightness = View.of(context).platformDispatcher.platformBrightness;
```

You can then use a light or dark theme based on that brightness:

```
theme: brightness == Brightness.light ? theme.light() : theme.dark(),
```

This is a good way to change your theme based on the device's current brightness level.

> **Note: That this does not listen for changes in the brightness and will not change until the app is relaunched.**

# Creating a theme

The steps to create a theme are as follows:

1. Inside of **theme.dart**, create a new method using the following command:

```
ThemeData createTheme() {
  return ThemeData(
  );
}
```

2. The movie app does not use many colors, but if you wanted to set a color scheme, you would add it to the **colorScheme** parameter as follows:

```
colorScheme: ColorScheme.fromSeed(
  seedColor: const Color(0xFF2196F3),
  // Base blue color
  primary: const Color(0xFF2196F3),
  // Primary color (can be same as seed)
  onPrimary: Colors.white,
  // Text/icon color on primary background
  secondary: const Color(0xFF90CAF9),
  // Secondary color (lighter blue)
  onSecondary: Colors.black,
  // Background color (very light blue)
  surfaceContainerHighest: Colors.black,
  // Text/icon color on background
  surface: const Color(0xFFBBDEFB),
  // Surface color (cards, menus, etc.)
  onSurface: Colors.black,
  // Text/icon color on surface
  error: const Color(0xFFB00020),
  // Error color (red)
  onError: Colors.white,
  // Text/icon color on error background
  brightness: Brightness.light, // Overall brightness (light or
dark)
),
```

3. Here, we provide a seed color and a few other basic colors. Next, you will define the **textTheme** using the variables you created earlier. Add the following command:

```
textTheme: Typography.material2021().englishLike.copyWith(
        headlineLarge: heading1,
        headlineMedium: heading2,
        headlineSmall: body2Regular,
        titleLarge: largeTitle,
        titleMedium: heading2,
        titleSmall: body2Bold,
        bodyLarge: body1Regular,
        bodyMedium: body2Regular,
        bodySmall: body3Regular,
        labelLarge: body1Bold,
        labelMedium: body2Bold,
        labelSmall: caption,
    ),
```

4. This starts by copying the Material 2021 theme (remember that Material 3 was introduced in 2021) and then adds all the styles we defined earlier.

There are many more themes you can set. We will go over a few of the common themes. The first one is for the AppBar. The AppBar is the title section of an app. You can change the theme using the following:

```
appBarTheme: const AppBarTheme(
  backgroundColor: Colors.white, // App bar background color
  foregroundColor: Colors.black, // Text/icon color on app bar
),
```

You can also set the elevation, shadow color, surface tint color, shape, height, and many more. Next, set the theme for the bottom navigation bar. Add the following code:

```
bottomNavigationBarTheme: const BottomNavigationBarThemeData(
  backgroundColor: searchBarBackground,
  // Bottom nav background color
  selectedItemColor: Colors.white,
  // Selected item color
  unselectedLabelStyle: TextStyle(color: Colors.black),
  showUnselectedLabels: true,
  unselectedItemColor: posterBorder, // Unselected item color
),
```

Here, we set the background color to a dark color and set the selected color to white. There are a few other themes you can set that are not needed for the app, but you may find them useful in yours. There is a theme for the snackbar. You can customize it with the **SnackBarThemeData** class. For text buttons, there is the **TextButtonThemeData**, and for tab bars there is **TabBarTheme**.

Now that you have your theme set up, it is time to add it to your app. Open up `main.dart` and add the following:

```
theme: createTheme(),
```

The code should be added after home: `MainScreen()`.

# iOS

So far, we have only talked about running the app on Android. Now, we will try this on an iOS simulator. If you do not have a Mac, you can skip this section and just continue to test on your device.

# Xcode

The steps are as follows:

1.  Open up Xcode. The first thing you want to do is make sure you have a simulator. From the **Window** menu, select **Devices and Simulators**, as shown in the following figure:

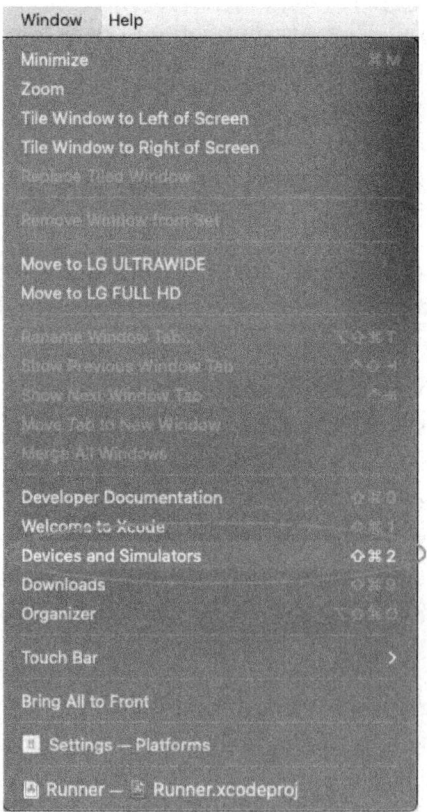

***Figure 5.8**: Window menu*

2. You should see the following screen:

*Figure 5.9*: *Simulators*

3. Click on the plus button in the bottom left. Enter a name and select a device. Press **Create**. The create screen is as follows:

*Figure 5.10*: *Create simulator*

4. You should now see the following screen:

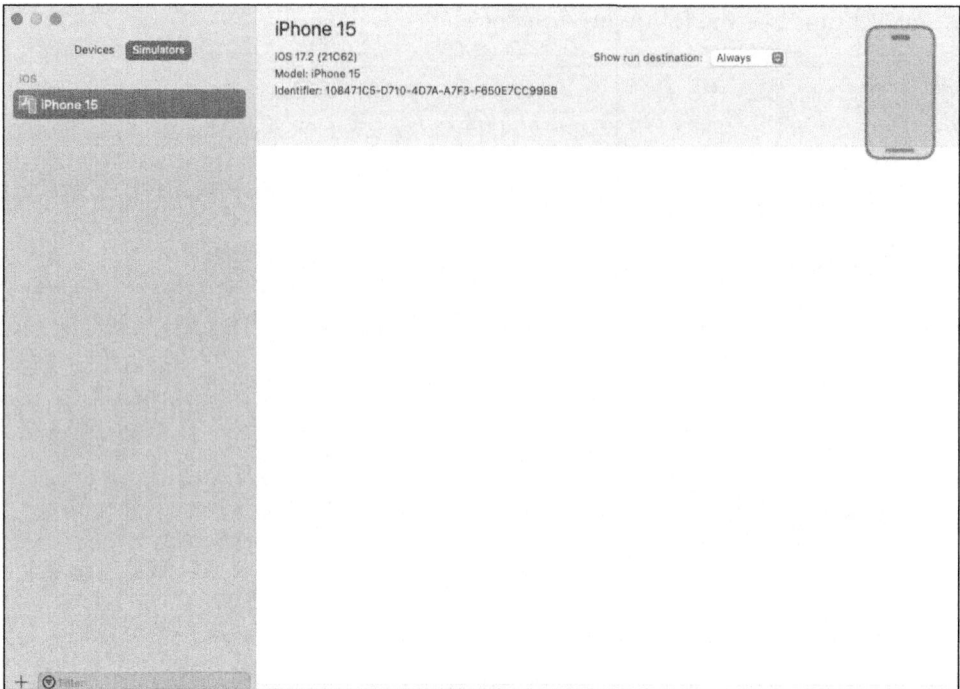

*Figure 5.11*: Simulators

5. Next, open the **Simulator** tool, as shown in the following figure:

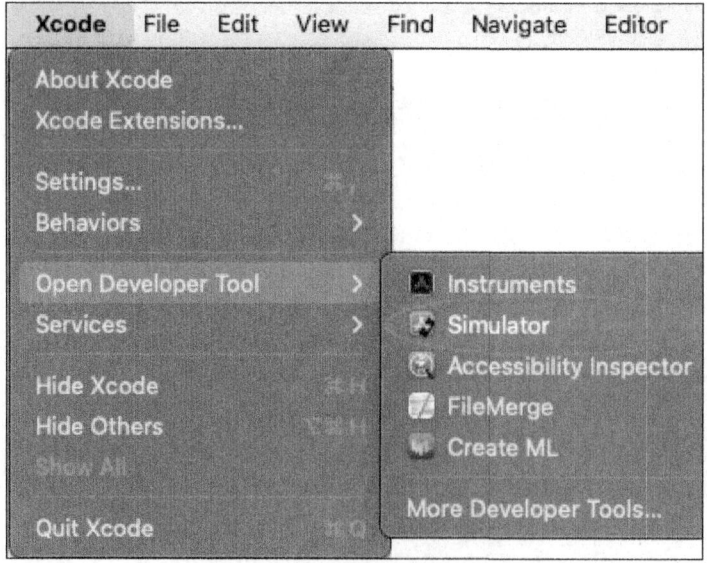

*Figure 5.12*: Simulator tool

6. The simulator will be generated as follows:

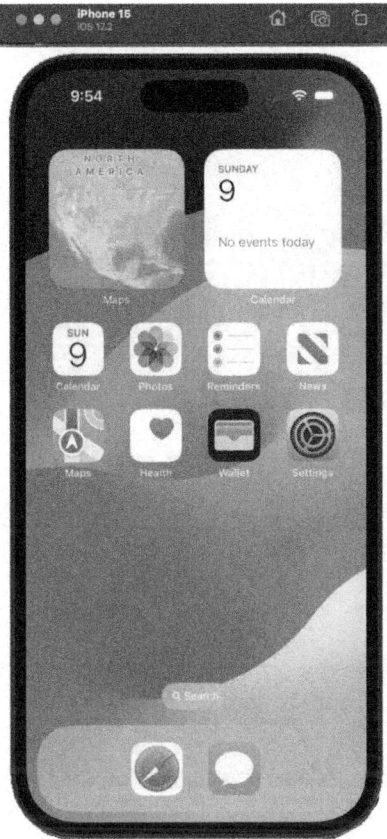

*Figure 5.13: iOS simulator*

7. In Android Studio, select the device drop-down and select **Open iOS Simulator**, as shown in the following figure:

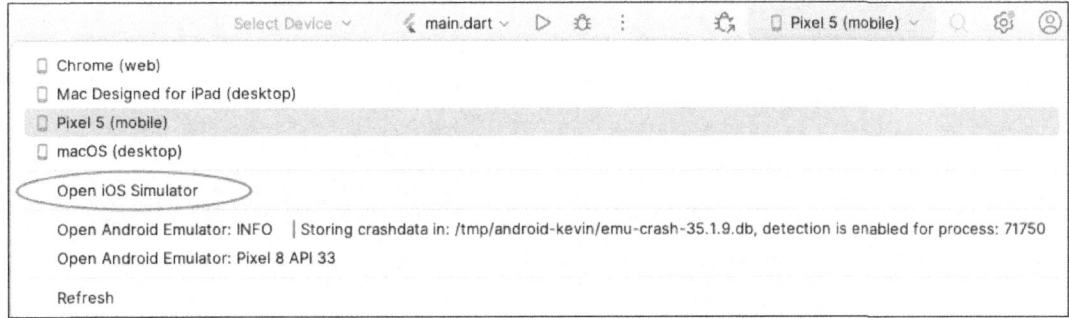

*Figure 5.14: Device picker*

If everything is set up properly, your simulator should show up.

Press the green run button. You should now see the following:

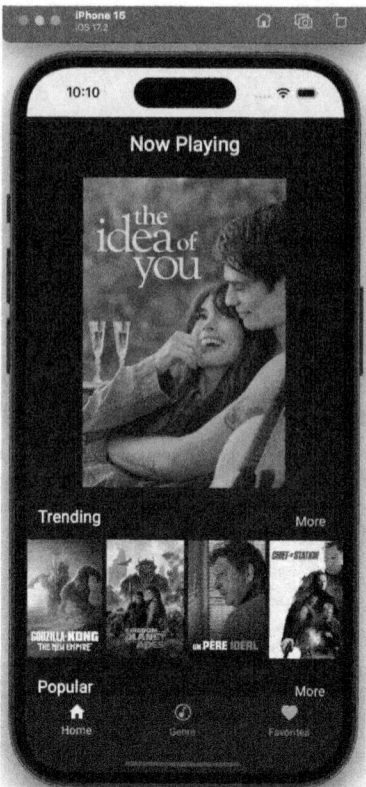

*Figure 5.15: App on iOS simulator*

If you do not like that simulator, you can choose another. The steps to do so are as follows:

1. In the simulator, select **Open Simulator** from the **File** menu, as shown in the following figure:

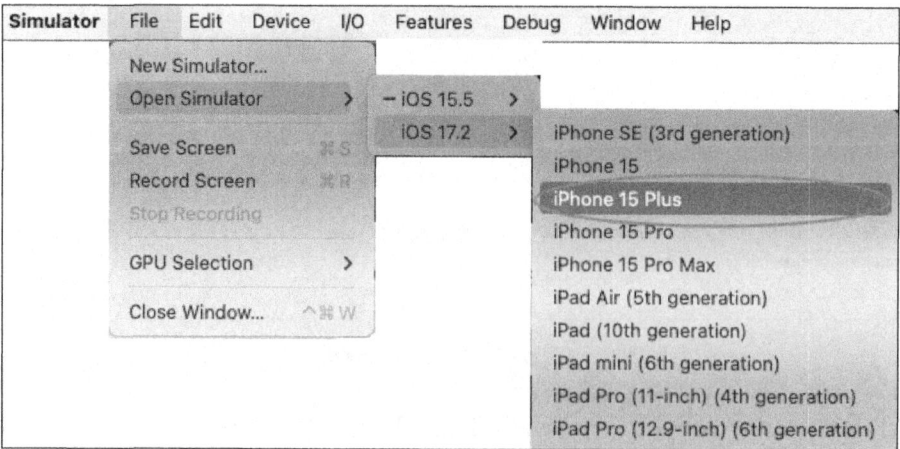

*Figure 5.16: Changing devices*

2. Your simulator list may be different. Stop the current build in Android Studio, select the new device, and run again.

Running on iOS can often have issues and being able to solve these issues is important.

Open up Xcode and your project. You can find your project in the **ios** folder, as shown in the following figure:

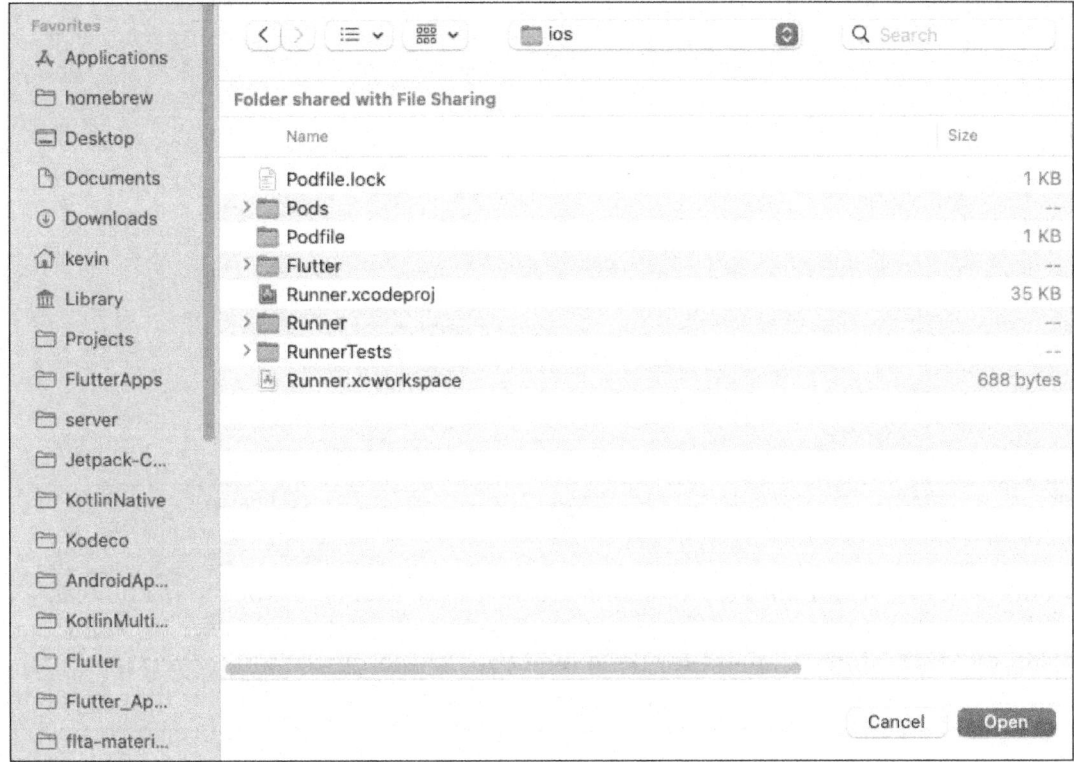

*Figure 5.17*: *Project chooser*

Click on **Open**. This will open the **Runner.xcodeproj** file. Once the project is open, select the **Runner** folder on the left, as selected in the following figure:

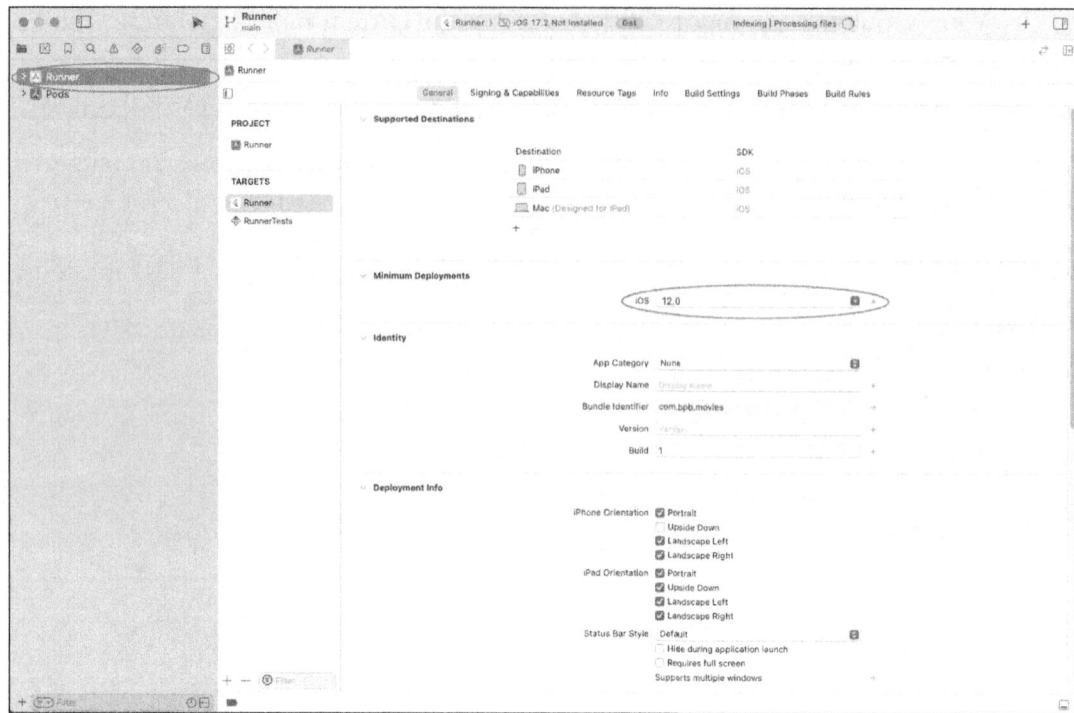

*Figure 5.18: Xcode project*

Notice that the **Minimum Deployments** are set to **12**. This is one of the main areas for setting up your iOS or macOS app. Notice that the **App Category** is set to **None**. You could set this to **Entertainment** for the movie app. You can usually run everything from the Android Studio, but some things are easier to see in Xcode. Explore the different tabs. Some are harder to understand than others but luckily you do not need to change most of them.

# Conclusion

In this chapter, you learned about what makes up the design of an app: Colors and typography. You use those to create a theme throughout your app for a consistent UI. You can also access tools like the Google Fonts page and the Material Theme builder, which will help design your app.

In the next chapter, you will learn about state management, a key aspect of building Flutter apps. You will also learn about some very nice packages for handling state. The genre screen will also be created, completing your second screen.

# CHAPTER 6

# State Management Fundamentals

## Introduction

In this chapter, you will learn all about state management in Flutter. State management is an important topic in Flutter and must be understood to write Flutter apps properly. You will learn about the built-in state management of Flutter as well as how to use third-party packages for handling global states.

## Structure

The chapter covers the following topics:

- Understanding state in Flutter
- Local versus app state
- Built-in state
- State management with packages
- Immutable state
- Riverpod
- Genre screen

# Objectives

This chapter will help you understand state and how to use it in Flutter. You will learn about many different packages that help with state management and will use the **Riverpod** package to set up state in the app. You will know how to use **Riverpod** to provide data to other screens and you will build out the genre screen. You will start using **Riverpod** to create your first provider for the movie images. You will learn about saving selection state when you use Flutter's chip classes for genre selection.

# Understanding state in Flutter

State is any data used in an app that can change over time and update the UI of the app. In Flutter, the UI is designed to update whenever any state changes. Remember that there are two types of widgets: Stateless and stateful. Stateless widgets are given data to display but do not change themselves, while stateful widgets contain their own state and can update it to update the widget. Stateful widgets use the **setState** method to signal the Flutter system that it needs to be redrawn. Use the **setState** method as low as possible in the widget tree; otherwise, the whole screen will be redrawn. In other words, if you have a widget in the middle of the screen, if that widget is stateful, it can just redraw itself when its state changes. This is also an example of why you want to put your widgets into their own classes. This will allow the Flutter system to only draw those items that have changed.

# Local versus app state

Local state is data specific to a single widget and typically managed within that widget's class. That class is a type of **StatefulWidget**. For example, if you use a **FilterChip** widget, you will need to save the selection state of the widget. This needs to be saved in a **StatefulWidget**.

App state is data that is shared between multiple parts of your app, like user preferences, authentication status, or shopping cart contents. Various state management techniques are available for handling app state. We will use the **Riverpod** package to allow the app-wide state to be shared among all of the screens. If you have a networking package, you do not want to re-create it on every screen. Using a package to create the library once and share it among screens is very helpful.

# Built-in State

If you look at **MainApp** in **main.dart**, you can see that it is made up of a **StatefulWidget** and a state. The **State** class is where you will store your data and build your UI. When the widget needs to be rebuilt, Flutter will create a new widget but keep a copy of the state so that your data is not lost. The **State** class has a widget parameter that lets you access its parent widget. It also keeps track of its lifecycle. The state class has a few important methods: **initState** (called once to initialize data), **destroy** (free up resources when done), **setState** (notify the system that the widget needs to be rebuilt), and **build** (return a widget to display).

# InheritedWidget

**InheritedWidget** is a Flutter widget that passes state down the widget tree without sending it through parameters. It stores the state in the **BuildContext**. Typical subclasses of this class have a **static of** method, that when passed in a **context**, will return that value. The following is an example of a widget that implements the **InheritedWidget** method:

```
static InheritedWidgetSubclass of(BuildContext context) {
  final result =
      context.dependOnInheritedWidgetOfExactType< InheritedWidgetSubclass
>();
  return result!;
}
```

The **dependOnInheritedWidgetOfExactType** method retrieves the stored value. This widget is not used much.

# State management with packages

In Flutter, you can just use stateful widgets to manage the state, but there are many packages out there that provide a lot of functionality. The following are a few that will be covered:

- Provider
- Riverpod
- **Business Logic Component (BLoC)**
- GetIt
- Redux
- MobX

Why would you want to use another package? If you have data that you want to share among all the widgets below the main widget, you would normally have to pass that data down the tree via parameters. This is known as **lifting the state**. A design pattern for moving the ownership of state as high as possible. This can be difficult if you have more than one parameter. These packages provide a way to set data in one location and retrieve it anywhere in a widget tree. No more parameters.

# Provider

**Provider** is a third-party package from *Google* but is in maintenance mode. It was originally developed by the author of Riverpod (who recommends using Riverpod). It is described as a wrapper around **InheritedWidget**. **InheritedWidget** is a Flutter widget that is useful for allowing child widgets to access state that has been defined higher up, without passing that state down via parameters. It uses the **BuildContext dependOnInheritedWidgetOfExactType** method to find instances. The **Provider** package has several classes that provide classes that can be used by widgets lower down in the tree. The basic class is the **Provider** class. This class has a **create** parameter where you would create your class once and a **child** parameter for your child widget. An example is:

```
Provider(
  create: (_) => MyModel(),
  child: ...
)
```

This creates the **MyModel** class once and returns a widget in the child parameter.

Another provider is called **ChangeNotifierProvider** and is useful for updating the widget when its value changes. This class has a **value** parameter instead of a **create** parameter. It uses the built-in Flutter **ChangeNotifier** class. An example would be:

```
class Counter extends ChangeNotifier {
  int _counter = 0;

  int get counter => _counter;

  void increment() {
    _counter++;
    notifyListeners();
  }
  void decrement() {
    _counter--;
    notifyListeners();
  }
}
```

This takes the sample Flutter apps **counter** variable and puts it in a class that holds that state. Whenever the **increment** or **decrement** methods are called, the **counter** gets modified and listeners are notified of the change. You would use the **ChangeNotifierProvider** as follows:

```
ChangeNotifierProvider(
    create: (context) => Counter(),
    child: const MyApp(),
  ),
```

If you have multiple providers, the provider has the **MultiProvider** widget, which takes an array of providers.

# BloC

**BLoC** is a package designed to make it easy to implement this design pattern. The idea behind this pattern is to separate the UI from the business logic. The UI takes actions from a user that are sent to a **cubit** (a class that stores state). This **cubit** takes that action, converts it to a new state, and then sends that state out for the UI to consume. **BloC** is a nice pattern but requires a lot of code to implement. You can find more information about **BloC** at **https://pub.dev/packages/bloc**.

# GetIt

**GetIt** is a service locator package (that is, dependency injection). While **GetIt** is not a state management solution, it provides dependency injection functionality like other packages. You would use it as follows:

```
final getIt = GetIt.instance;
getIt.registerSingleton<AppModel>(AppModel());
```

Then, to use it in the UI, apply the following code:

```
MaterialButton(
  child: Text("Update"),
  onPressed: getIt<AppModel>().update    // given that your AppModel has a
method update
),
```

You can find **GetIt** at **https://pub.dev/packages/get_it**.

# Redux

Redux comes in two packages: **Redux** for Dart and **flutter_redux** for Flutter (that uses Redux).

Redux has three principles:

- **Single source of truth**: Your state is stored in an object tree in one place.

- **State is read-only**: State objects are immutable and can only be changed by actions that create a new state.

- **Changes are made with pure reducers**: These functions take a state and an action and produce a new state.

In the **flutter_redux** package, there is a **StoreProvider** that takes a store you have created and a **child** widget. There is a **StoreConnector** that provides a **converter** function and a builder that has a callback. That callback will dispatch an action to the store. The flow is as follows:

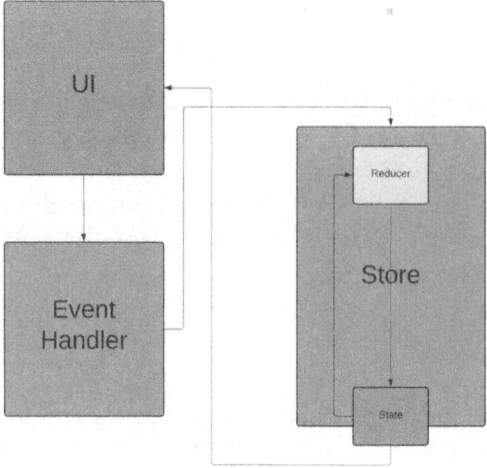

*Figure 6.1: Redux data flow*

# MobX

**MobX** is a state management library that uses the concepts of observables, actions, and reactions. It is like Redux. Actions are like the reducer, and observable is where you store your data. It has a code generator that can create some of the boilerplate code for you. You can find MobX at **https://pub.dev/packages/mobx**. You would mark a value with the **@ observable** annotation and an action with **@action** on a function. A class would use the store mixin, and the generator would create the store class needed in your widget tree. You can use the **Observer** widget to listen to changes in your store.

# Immutable state

Many libraries talk about the importance of immutability. The reason is that if you have state that can be changed by any class, you will eventually encounter bugs where one class changes the state and another class has a different instance of that state. Which one is correct? Will different parts of your app behave differently, or will it just crash? One of the downsides of a class that cannot have its data changed is that you have to create a new copy each time to update its state. There is a library that helps with that, and we will cover that library in a later chapter.

# Riverpod

**Riverpod** is another third-party package written by the same author as **Provider**. **Riverpod** is an anagram of provider. The author has learned from his experience with the provider and has created an excellent package. You can find more information about **Riverpod** at **https://riverpod.dev/**. We will be using this package for the movies app. It is like **Provider** but also has a generator so that you can use its annotation capabilities to generate code. **Riverpod** has several custom widgets that you will subclass to give you access to the provided data. These classes provide easy access to all the shared resources you have created. Another advantage is that you do not have to define your resources in the same file as your UI. **Riverpod** also handles asynchronous requests and can cache the result.

**Riverpod** is defined as a reactive caching framework for Flutter/Dart. It can handle asynchronous calling with error handling. Riverpod uses reference classes that allow you to listen for changes in data. The main reference class is **WidgetRef**. This class has several important methods:

- **watch(provider)**: Given a provider, update the widget when the provider changes.
- **listen(provider)**: Listen to changes in a provider and perform an action.
- **read(provider)**: Used to get the value of the provider and not listen to changes.

Both the watch and listen methods should be used inside of the build method. Read is usually used for other methods when you need to get the value of the provider and perform some action.

We will use the **Riverpod** package for dependency injection and, in part, for state management. To add **Riverpod**, you need to add several packages. Open **pubspec.yaml** and add the following:

```
flutter_riverpod: ^2.5.1
# the annotation package containing @riverpod
riverpod_annotation: ^2.3.5
```
Next, add two packages under the dev_depenencies section:

```
build_runner: ^2.4.8
riverpod_generator: ^2.4.0
riverpod_lint: ^2.3.5
```

Comment out the overrides:
```
#dependency_overrides:
#   analyzer: 5.13.0
```
Click on **Pub get**.

Here are what the packages are for:

- **flutter_riverpod**: Main **Riverpod** package.
- **riverpod_annotation**: Provides annotation used by the code generator.
- **build_runner**: This is a Flutter package used by other packages to create source code for you. Riverpod generator uses this to create **Riverpod** files.

- **riverpod_generator**: Package used to generate **Riverpod** code.

- **riverpod_lint**: Linter that checks for **Riverpod** issues.

In order to use **Riverpod**, you will need to wrap the **MainApp** in a **ProviderScope**. The **ProviderScope** stores the state of all providers. Open up **main.dart** and change **runApp** to:

```
runApp(const ProviderScope(child: MainApp()));
```

Then, import the **Riverpod** package. To use **Riverpod**, you need to define some providers. Inside the **lib** directory, create a new file named **providers.dart**. We will be moving the images list into the **providers.dart** file. Add:

```
import 'package:riverpod_annotation/riverpod_annotation.dart';

part 'providers.g.dart';

@riverpod
List<String> movieImages(MovieImagesRef ref) => [
// TODO add Images
];
```

This imports the **riverpod_anotation** file and uses the part keyword. This keyword will import the **providers.g.dart** file. This does not exist yet and will be generated by **Riverpod**. Next replace the TODO with:

```
'http://image.tmdb.org/t/p/w780/z1p34vh7dEOnLDmyCrlUVLuoDzd.jpg',
'http://image.tmdb.org/t/p/w780/gKkl37BQuKTanygYQG1pyYgLVgf.jpg',
'http://image.tmdb.org/t/p/w780/4xJd3uwtL1vCuZgEfEc8JXI9Uyx.jpg',
'http://image.tmdb.org/t/p/w780/uuA01PTtPombRPvL9dvsBqOBJWm.jpg',
'http://image.tmdb.org/t/p/w780/H6vke7zGiuLsz4v4RPeReb9rsv.jpg',
'http://image.tmdb.org/t/p/w780/e1J2oNzSBdou01sUvriVuoYp0pJ.jpg',
'http://image.tmdb.org/t/p/w780/hu40Uxp9WtpL34jv3zyWLb5zEVY.jpg',
'http://image.tmdb.org/t/p/w780/pKaA8VvfkNfEMUPMiiuL5qSPQYy.jpg',
'http://image.tmdb.org/t/p/w780/zK2sFxZcelHJRPVr242rxy5VK4T.jpg',
'http://image.tmdb.org/t/p/w780/7qxG0zyt29BI0IzFDfsps62kbQi.jpg',
'http://image.tmdb.org/t/p/w780/8Gxv8gSFCU0XGDykEGv7zR1n2ua.jpg',
'http://image.tmdb.org/t/p/w780/zDi2U7WYkdIoGYHcYbM9X5yReVD.jpg',
'http://image.tmdb.org/t/p/w780/cxevDYdeFkiixRShbObdwAHBZry.jpg',
'http://image.tmdb.org/t/p/w780/uXUs1fwSuE06LgYETw2mi4JxQvc.jpg',
'http://image.tmdb.org/t/p/w780/fdZpvODTX5wwkD0ikZNaClE4AoW.jpg',
'http://image.tmdb.org/t/p/w780/d5NXSklXo0qyIYkgV94XAgMIckC.jpg',
'http://image.tmdb.org/t/p/w780/sh7Rg8Er3tFcN9BpKIPOMvALgZd.jpg',
'http://image.tmdb.org/t/p/w780/sHJ2OIgpcpSmhqXkuSWxZ3nwg1S.jpg',
'http://image.tmdb.org/t/p/w780/upKD8UbH8vQ798aMWgwMxV8t4yk.jpg',
'http://image.tmdb.org/t/p/w780/vfrQk5IPloGg1v9Rzbh2Eg3VGyM.jpg',
```

This is the list of all movie images. Now remove the list from **home_screen_image.dart**. In order to generate the **providers.g.dart** file, you will use Flutter's **build_runner** app. Open the terminal in Android Studio and run:

```
dart run build_runner build
```

Your output will look like this:

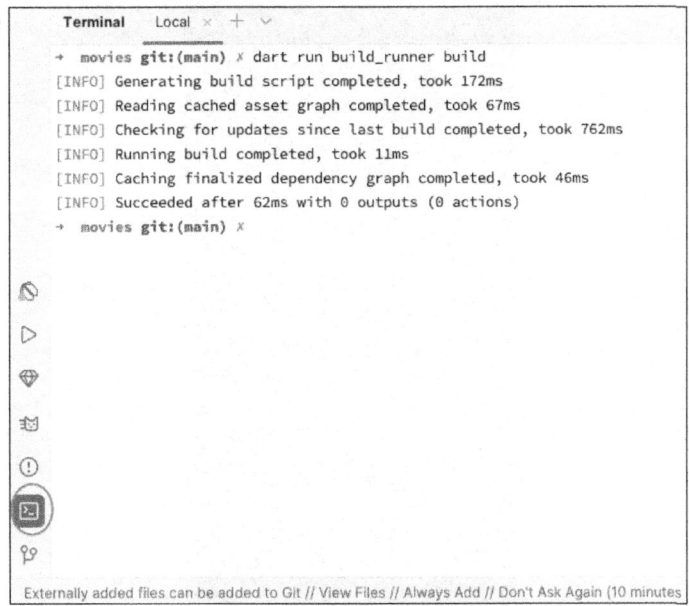

*Figure 6.2: build_runner*

Now that the provider file is ready, it is time to fix the errors that show up. Inside of **home_screen_image.dart**, add the flutter_riverpod import:

```
import 'package:flutter_riverpod/flutter_riverpod.dart';
```

and then change the type of **HomeScreenImage** to **ConsumerWidget**. This is a Riverpod stateless widget. Next change the build method to:

```
Widget build(BuildContext context, WidgetRef ref) {
```

This adds the **WidgetRef** parameter. Right after this add:

```
final images = ref.watch(movieImagesProvider);
```

This uses the **WidgetRef** to read the provider created by **Riverpod** and return the list of movie strings. Do the same thing with the home screen and **VerticalMovieList**. You should not see any errors. Hot reload and make sure everything works.

# Genre screen

It is time to create the **Genre** screen. This screen will allow users to search for a movie by genre or title. Here is the design of the screen:

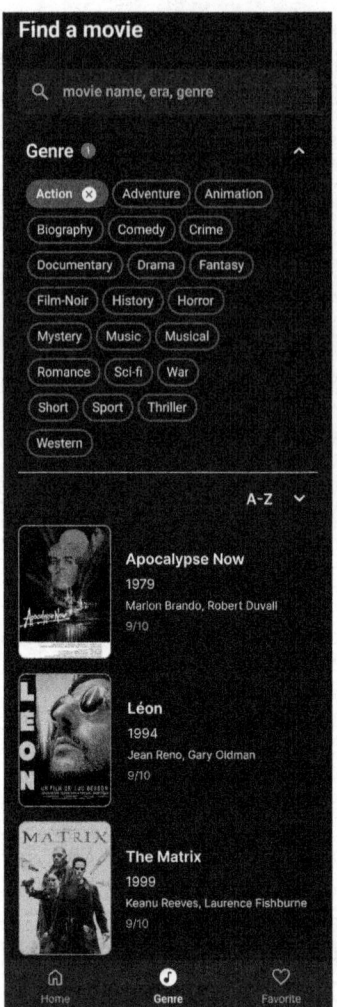

*Figure 6.3: Genre design*

Start by creating a new folder in the **ui/screens** directory, named **genres**. Inside that folder, create a new dart file named **genre_screen.dart**. Add the following:

```dart
import 'package:flutter/material.dart';
import 'package:flutter_riverpod/flutter_riverpod.dart';


class GenreScreen extends ConsumerStatefulWidget {
  const GenreScreen({super.key});

  @override
  ConsumerState<GenreScreen> createState() => _GenreScreenState();
}
```

```
class _GenreScreenState extends ConsumerState<GenreScreen> {
  @override
  Widget build(BuildContext context) {
    return Placeholder();
  }
}
```

Notice that this class uses a new **ConsumerStatefulWidget** class from the **Riverpod** package. This widget gives us access to provider references that allow us to retrieve our shared classes. **_GenreScreenState** extends **ConsumerState,** which is another **Riverpod** class. Open the **main_screen** and replace the second placeholder with the **GenreScreen**. Now run the app and click on the **Genre** screen. It will look the same, but you can now work on it while it shows the following:

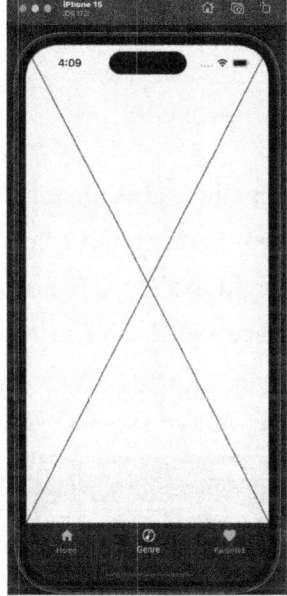

*Figure 6.4*: *Genre screen*

Inside of **GenreScreen**, replace the **Placerholder()** with the following:

```
// 1
SafeArea(
    // 2
    child: Container(
      color: screenBackground,
      // 3
      child: Column(
          mainAxisSize: MainAxisSize.max,
          mainAxisAlignment: MainAxisAlignment.start,
```

```
        crossAxisAlignment: CrossAxisAlignment.start,
        children: [
          // 4
          Row(
            mainAxisSize: MainAxisSize.max,
            children: [
              Padding(
                padding: const EdgeInsets.fromLTRB(16, 16.0, 0.0, 24.0),
                child: Text('Find a Movie',
                    style: Theme.of(context).textTheme.titleLarge),
              ),
            ],
          ),
        ]),
      ),
  );
```

Here is an explanation of the code:

1.  Use **SafeArea** to draw below the status area.

2.  Use a **Container** to show our background color.

3.  Use a **Column** set at max height to show a list of items.

4.  Use a **Row** to display items across the screen.

As we build this screen, we will create code that will change later as we add more items. Hot reload (or hot restart if that does not work), and you should see the following:

*Figure 6.5*: Genre with title

This is a good way to build a screen. Slowly add one item at a time to make sure it works by performing a hot reload. If you try to build the whole thing at once and it does not work, you cannot be sure what is causing the problem.

Next, we need a search text field. Add a new file called **genre_search_row.dart** in the **genres** folder. Start with the following:

```
import 'package:flutter/material.dart';
import 'package:flutter_riverpod/flutter_riverpod.dart';

import 'package:movies/ui/theme/theme.dart';

typedef OnSearch = void Function(String searchString);

class GenreSearchRow extends ConsumerStatefulWidget {
  final OnSearch onSearch;

  const GenreSearchRow(this.onSearch, {super.key});

  @override
  ConsumerState<GenreSearchRow> createState() => _GenreSearchRowState();
}

class _GenreSearchRowState extends ConsumerState<GenreSearchRow> {
  // TODO: Add variables

  // TODO Add init and dispose

  @override
  Widget build(BuildContext context) {
    return Row(mainAxisSize: MainAxisSize.max, children: [
        // TODO: Add TextField
    ]);
  }
}
```

The only unique item here is the **OnSearch typedef**. This defines a function that will receive a **searchString**.

1. When the user clicks on the search icon or hits the done button on the keyboard, a **searchString** will be sent to the owner of the **onSearch** function. Replace the first **TODO** with the following:

   ```
   late TextEditingController movieTextController;
   final FocusNode textFocusNode = FocusNode();
   ```

   This creates a **TextEditingController** for controlling the text the user inputs.

2. The **FocusNode** is an easy way for the user to start typing in the text field. Next, create the **initState** and dispose methods. These are needed as a one-time initialization and disposal. Replace the second **TODO** with the following:

```
@override
void initState() {
  super.initState();
  movieTextController = TextEditingController(text: '');
}

@override
void dispose() {
  movieTextController.dispose();
  super.dispose();
}
```

Whenever you use a text controller, you need to dispose of it in the **dispose** method.

3.  The **TextField** widget has a lot of options, and this one will use lots, so we will add them slowly. Replace **// TODO: Add TextField** with:

```
Expanded(
  child: Padding(
    padding: const EdgeInsets.only(left: 16.0, right: 16.0),
    child: TextField(
      style: const TextStyle(color: Colors.white),
      focusNode: textFocusNode,
      keyboardType: TextInputType.text,
      // TODO Add More
    ),
  ),
)
```

This just wraps the **TextField** with some padding and by using the **Expanded** widget, fill the row. The input type is text.

4.  Replace the **TODO** with the following code:

```
        enableSuggestions: false,
        autofocus: false,
// 1
        onSubmitted: (value) {
          widget.onSearch(value);
        },
// 2
        controller: movieTextController,
        autocorrect: false,
// 3
        decoration: InputDecoration(
```

```
                        filled: true,
                        focusColor: searchBarBackground,
                        focusedBorder: null,
                        enabledBorder: null,
                        fillColor: searchBarBackground,
                        border: OutlineInputBorder(
                          borderRadius: BorderRadius.circular(20),
                          borderSide: BorderSide.none,
                        ),
                        hintText: 'movie name, genre',
                        hintStyle: body1Regular.copyWith(color:
posterBorder),
// 4
                        suffixIcon: IconButton(
                          onPressed: () {
                            movieTextController.clear();
                          },
                          icon: const Icon(Icons.close, color: Colors.
white,), // Close icon
                        ),
// 5
                        prefixIcon: IconButton(
                          icon: const Icon(Icons.search, color: Colors.
white,),
                          onPressed: () {
                            widget.onSearch(movieTextController.text);
                          },
                        ),
                      ),
```

5.  The steps are as follows:

    a.  When the user hits the return key, call the **onSearch** method with the current search text.

    b.  Use the text controller we created earlier.

    c.  Create an **InputDecoration** that creates a nice rounded rectangle around the text field.

    d.  Create a clear icon at the end so that the text can be reset.

    e.  Create a search icon that will call the **onSearch** method.

6.  Back in **genre_screen.dart**, add the following after the row:

```
                  GenreSearchRow((searchString) {
                  }),
```

Perform a hot reload. You should see the following screen:

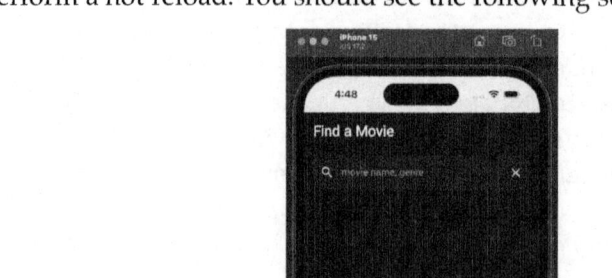

*Figure 6.6*: *Search Field*

# Genre section

Now, we will examine one of the most complicated, but exciting sections. This section will show a list of genres for the user to choose when they search. Start by adding a new package named **auto_size_text**. This package will expand and shrink text to fit better on the screen.

The steps to add the package are as follows:

1. Open **pubspec.yaml** and add the following code:

   ```
   auto_size_text: ^3.0.0
   ```

2. Click on **Pub get**. Create a new file named **genre_section.dart** in the **genres** folder. Add the following code:

   ```
   import 'package:auto_size_text/auto_size_text.dart';
   import 'package:collection/collection.dart';
   import 'package:flutter/material.dart';
   import 'package:flutter_riverpod/flutter_riverpod.dart';

   import 'package:movies/ui/theme/theme.dart';
   // 1
   class GenreState {
     final String genre;
   ```

```
    final bool isSelected;

    GenreState({required this.genre, required this.isSelected});
  }

  // 2
  typedef OnGenresSelected = void Function(List<GenreState>);
  typedef OnGenresExpanded = void Function(bool);

  // 3
  class GenreSection extends ConsumerStatefulWidget {
    final bool isExpanded;
    final List<GenreState> genreStates;
    final OnGenresExpanded onGenresExpanded;
    final OnGenresSelected onGenresSelected;

    const GenreSection(
        {required this.genreStates,
          required this.isExpanded,
          required this.onGenresExpanded,
          required this.onGenresSelected,
          super.key});

    @override
    ConsumerState<GenreSection> createState() => _GenreSectionState();
  }

  class _GenreSectionState extends ConsumerState<GenreSection> {
    @override
    Widget build(BuildContext context) {
      return Placeholder();
    }
  }
```

  a. **GenreState** is a class that holds the name of the genre and whether it is selected.

  b. These two functions are for when the genre is selected and the section is expanded.

  c. **GenreSection** is the widget. It is passed in the fields needed to display itself.

3. Now add the following method below build:

```
    List<Widget> getGenreChips() {
      return widget.genreStates.mapIndexed((index, element) {
```

```
      final genreState = widget.genreStates[index];
      return FilterChip(
        backgroundColor: searchBarBackground,
        selectedColor: buttonGrey,
        label: AutoSizeText(genreState.genre,
            style: Theme.of(context).textTheme.labelSmall),
        selected: widget.genreStates[index].isSelected,
        onSelected: (selected) {
          setState(
              () {
            widget.genreStates[index] = GenreState(
                genre: genreState.genre,
                isSelected: !widget.genreStates[index].
isSelected);
            widget.onGenresSelected(getSelectedGenres());
          },
        );
      },
    );
  }).toList();
}
```

4.  This method will return a list of **FilterChip** (a Flutter widget). **FilterChip** has checkmarks next to them if they are selected. Next, add the following:

```
List<GenreState> getSelectedGenres() {
  return widget.genreStates.where((e) => e.isSelected).toList();
}

int totalSelected() {
  return getSelectedGenres().length;
}
```

The first method will return a list of genres that have been selected. The last method just returns a total of the selected genres.

5.  Now replace the **Placeholder** widget with:

```
    final genreChips = getGenreChips();
    return ExpansionPanelList(
      expandIconColor: Colors.white,
      expansionCallback: (int index, bool expanded) {
        setState(() {
          widget.onGenresExpanded(expanded);
```

```
        });
      },
      children: [
        ExpansionPanel(
          isExpanded: widget.isExpanded,
          backgroundColor: screenBackground,
          headerBuilder: (BuildContext context, bool isExpanded) {
            // TODO Add Chips
        )
      ],
    );
```

This code will call the **getGenreChips** method to get a list of chips. The **ExpansionPanelList** widget will expand and contract when the user selects an arrow. The **expansionCallback** will be called, and we will call **onGenresExpanded** with the value to have the section updated.

6.  The **ExpansionPanel** is where the chips will live. Replace the **TODO** with:

```
                return Padding(
                    padding: const EdgeInsets.only(left: 16.0, top: 16),
                    child: Row(
                      children: [
// 1
                        Text('Genres',
                            style: Theme.of(context).textTheme.
headlineLarge),
                        const SizedBox(width: 8),
// 2
                        Container(
                          width: 16,
                          height: 16,
                          decoration: const BoxDecoration(
                            shape: BoxShape.circle,
                            color: Colors.red,
                          ),
                          child: Center(
                            // Center the text
                            child: Text(
                              totalSelected().toString(),
                              style: verySmallText,
                            ),
```

```
                      ),
                    )
                  ],
                ),
              );
            },
            body: Padding(
              padding: const EdgeInsets.only(left: 16.0, right: 16),
              child: Row(
                mainAxisAlignment: MainAxisAlignment.spaceBetween,
// 3
                children: genreChips,
              )
            ),
```

This will show the list of Genre chips that the user can select to choose which genres they are interested in.

1.  **Genre title**: Create the Title for the screen.

2.  A small red circle with a number of selected genres. This will be the count of selected genres.

3.  Chips. This is the list of chips to display.

7.  Back in **GenreScreen**, add the following after the genres list:

    ```
    final expandedNotifier = ValueNotifier<bool>(false);
    ```

8.  After **GenreSearchRow** add:

    ```
                    ValueListenableBuilder<bool>(
                        valueListenable: expandedNotifier,
                        builder: (BuildContext context, bool value,
    Widget? child) {
                            return GenreSection(
                              genreStates: genres,
                              isExpanded: value,
                              onGenresExpanded: (expanded) {
                                expandedNotifier.value = expanded;
                              },
                              onGenresSelected: (List<GenreState> states)
    {},
                            );
                        }),
    ```

9. **ValueListenableBuilder** is another Flutter widget that will rebuild just its child when its value changes. This will change when the user expands the **Genres** section. Do a hot restart (not reload). You should see the following screen:

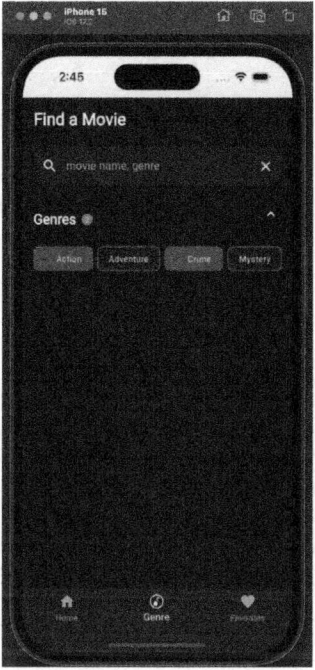

*Figure 6.7: Genres section*

# Sorting

The next item is a divider and a sort drop-down. The steps to add it are as follows:

1. Inside of **GenreScreen**, add a divider after the **ValueListenableBuilder**:

   ```
   const Divider(),
   ```

2. Create a new folder under the **lib** folder named **utils**. Add a new file named **utils.dart** then add the following code:

   ```
   import 'package:flutter/material.dart';

   Widget addVerticalSpace(double amount) {
     return SizedBox(height: amount);
   }

   Widget addHorizontalSpace(double amount) {
     return SizedBox(width: amount);
   }
   enum Sorting {
   ```

```
aToz(name: 'A-Z'),
zToa(name: 'Z-A'),
rating(name: 'Rating'),
year(name: 'Year');

const Sorting({required this.name});

final String name;
}
```

This adds two methods that just return a **SizedBox**. This is a helper method. The sorting enum will display its name in a drop-down.

3. Now add a new file named **sort_picker.dart** in then **genres** folder. Add the following:

```
import 'package:collection/collection.dart';
import 'package:flutter/material.dart';
import 'package:flutter_riverpod/flutter_riverpod.dart';

import 'package:movies/utils/utils.dart';

typedef OnSortSelected = void Function(Sorting);

class SortPicker extends ConsumerStatefulWidget {
  final OnSortSelected onSortSelected;

  const SortPicker({required this.onSortSelected, super.key});

  @override
  ConsumerState<SortPicker> createState() => _SortPickerState();
}

class _SortPickerState extends ConsumerState<SortPicker> {
  Sorting selectedSort = Sorting.aToz;

  @override
  Widget build(BuildContext context) {
    return Placeholder();
  }
}
```

The **OnSortSelected typedef** is used to return to the caller the user selected sort value. This sets up the **SortPicker** class and has a variable for managing the selected sort. Now replace **Placeholder** with:

```
return Row(
  children: [
    const Spacer(),
    Text(
```

```
        selectedSort.name,
        style: Theme.of(context).textTheme.labelLarge,
      ),
// 1
      addHorizontalSpace(16),
// 2
      PopupMenuButton<Sorting>(
        icon: const Icon(
          Icons.arrow_drop_down,
          color: Colors.white ,
        ),
// 3
        onSelected: (Sorting value) {
          widget.onSortSelected(value);
        },
        itemBuilder: (BuildContext context) {
// 4
          return Sorting.values
              .mapIndexed<PopupMenuItem<Sorting>>((int index, Sorting
sort) {
// 5
              return CheckedPopupMenuItem<Sorting>(
                checked: selectedSort == sort,
                value: sort,
                onTap: () {
                  setState(() {
                    selectedSort = sort;
                  });
                },
                child: Text(sort.name),
              );
          }).toList();
        },
      ),
    ],
  );
```

1. **addHorizontalSpace** is a utility method for adding a bit of space.

2. **PopupMenuButton** is a Flutter widget for showing a popup menu.

3. When an item is selected, call the callback.

4. Use the **mapIndexed** collection method to return a widget for each sorting item.

a. `CheckedPopupMenuItem` is another Flutter widget that has a checkbox when selected.

`mapIndexed` is a collection method that is a helpful way to iterate over all items in a list and provide an index. By going through the Sorting enum values, we create a checked popup for each item. When the user selects a sorting popup menu, the selected sort is set and the widget is rebuilt. Note that you need to call **toList** on **mapIndexed** in order for this to work.

1. Hot restart. The screen will be as follows:

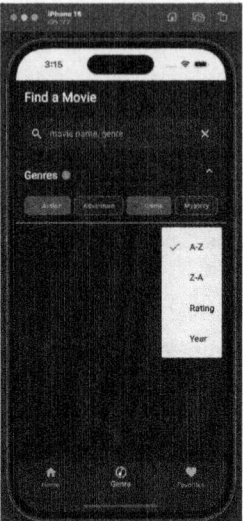

*Figure 6.8: Sort picker*

# Movie list

Now, we will add the section for the list of movies shown after a search. Note that we will not be using live data until the networking chapter. The movie list will be a widget that can be reused. For reusable widgets, create a widgets folder under the **lib/ui** folder. Then, create a new file named **movie_row.dart**. This class will display a row with a movie image, title, and release date (The title and release date will be added when we have actual movie data in later chapters).

The steps are as follows:

1. Add the following code:

```
import 'package:auto_size_text/auto_size_text.dart';
import 'package:cached_network_image/cached_network_image.dart';
import 'package:flutter/material.dart';

import 'package:movies/utils/utils.dart';
```

```
class MovieRow extends StatelessWidget {
  final String movie;
  const MovieRow({super.key, required this.movie});

  @override
  Widget build(BuildContext context) {
    // TODO
  }
}
```

We will use the AutoSizeText widget to have long titles fit properly. Now replace TODO with:

```
    if (movie.isNotEmpty) {
// 1
      return GestureDetector(
        onTap: () => {},
        child: Padding(
          padding: const EdgeInsets.all(8.0),
          child: SizedBox(
            height: 140,
// 2
            child: Row(
              mainAxisSize: MainAxisSize.max,
              children: [
                addHorizontalSpace(16),
// 3
                SizedBox(
                  height: 142,
                  width: 100,
// 4
                  child: CachedNetworkImage(
                    imageUrl: movie,
                    alignment: Alignment.topCenter,
                    fit: BoxFit.cover,
                    height: 142,
                    width: 100,
                  ),
                ),
                addHorizontalSpace(16),
// 5
                Column(
```

```
                        mainAxisSize: MainAxisSize.min,
                        mainAxisAlignment: MainAxisAlignment.end,
                        crossAxisAlignment: CrossAxisAlignment.start,
                        children: [
                          const Spacer(),
// 6
                          AutoSizeText(
                            'Title',
                            maxLines: 1,
                            minFontSize: 10,
                            style: Theme.of(context).textTheme.labelLarge,
                            overflow: TextOverflow.ellipsis,
                          ),
                          addVerticalSpace(4),
                          Text(
                            '1979',
                            style: Theme.of(context).textTheme.bodyMedium,
                          ),
                          addVerticalSpace(4),
                        ],
                      ),
                    ],
                  ),
                ),
              ),
            );
        } else {
          return Container();
        }
      }
```

a. Use a **GestureDetector** for taps on the full row.

b. Create a row that takes up the full width.

c. Create a box of a fixed size.

d. Use **CachedNetworkImage** to display the image.

e. Use a **Column** for the title and release date.

f. Use **AutoSizeText** to fit the text.

2. Now, create **vert_movie_list.dart** in the **widgets** folder. For now, this file will only show a few movies, as anything more will cause errors. These errors will be

addressed in the next chapter with more advanced widgets. Add the following code:

```
import 'package:flutter/material.dart';
import 'package:movies/utils/utils.dart';

import '../ui/screens/home/home_screen_image.dart';
import 'movie_row.dart';

typedef OnMovieTap = void Function(int movieId);

class VerticalMovieList extends StatelessWidget {
  final List<String> movies;
  final OnMovieTap onMovieTap;

  const VerticalMovieList({
    super.key,
    required this.movies,
    required this.onMovieTap,
  });

  @override
  Widget build(BuildContext context) {
    return Column(
      children: [
        MovieRow(
          movie: images[0],
        ),
        addVerticalSpace(10),
        MovieRow(
          movie: images[1],
        ),
      ],
    );
  }
}
```

3. The **OnMovieTap typedef** is used to notify the caller that the user tapped on this movie item. This just shows two images from our list of URLs. Now add the following in **GenreScreen** after **SortPicker**:

```
VerticalMovieList(movies: [], onMovieTap: (movieId) {},),
```

4. For now, we are just passing in an empty list of movies as the **VerticalMovieList** class just has two hard-coded strings. Perform a hot reload. The screen would be as follows:

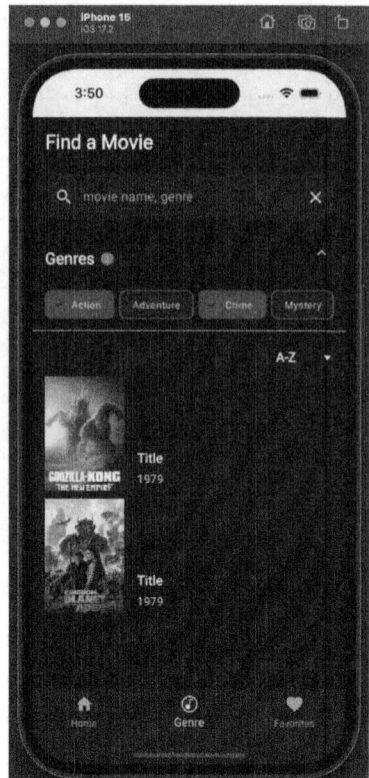

*Figure 6.9: Vertical images*

While this uses fixed data, later chapters will use live data from the internet.

# Conclusion

In this chapter, you learned about state management and some of the great packages available for helping maintain your state. You should understand local and app states and how the built-in state handling works. You should also understand the importance of an immutable state. You have built up the genre screen and learned more about some of the hidden widgets like ValueListenableBuilder, PopupMenuButton, and CheckedPopupMenuItem.

In the next chapter, you will learn some of the more advanced widgets that will overcome the limitations of row and column, like ListView and GridView which open up new possibilities for displaying information.

# CHAPTER 7
# Advanced Widgets

## Introduction

In this chapter, you will learn about advanced Flutter widgets and how to use them in your movie app. This will allow you to show more information on the screen as well as show that data in different ways. These are essential widgets that are used in Flutter apps. Widgets for showing large numbers of other widgets are critical for most apps.

## Structure

The chapter covers the following topics:

- ListView
- Expanded
- Stack
- IndexedStack
- LayoutBuilder
- GridView
- Table
- Card

- BottomSheets
- Slivers
- Movie trailers

# Objectives

You will learn about the more advanced widgets that Flutter provides. These widgets require more setup but can do some amazing things. As you learn about these widgets, you will build out the movie app with them. By the end of the chapter, you will know how to show horizontal and vertical lists of data, grids of data, and how to stack widgets. You will also have a solid understanding of slivers.

# ListView

In the last chapter, you used a column to display some movie titles. If your screen was a bit smaller or you added one more item, you would have seen a striped line with the message about overflow. This happens when your widget overflows the area it can draw. To avoid that problem, you need a widget that can scroll. **ListView** is one of the main widgets that are used to display a list of items either horizontally or vertically. You will use the same class and just change the orientation field if you want to show them horizontally. **ListView** has several different constructors you can use to display your list, as follows:

- **ListView**: Default constructor. Uses a children parameter for a fixed list of widgets.
- **ListView.builder**: Uses two key fields **itemCount** (number of items) and **itemBuilder** (used to return an item for a specific index).
- **ListView.separated**: Like a builder but puts dividers between each row.
- **ListView.custom**: Uses a **childrenDelegate** that is like a builder, returning items for a given index. Delegates provide a lot more power than just using a builder.

You will probably use either the builder or the separated constructors the most. They are flexible and easy to use.

All these methods take a **ScrollController** as a parameter. You do not have to pass one in, but if you do not, one will be created for you. A scroll controller will allow you to jump or animate to a specific position in the list. Vertical lists are the default. If you want a horizontal list, you will pass the following:

```
scrollDirection: Axis.horizontal
```

The builder and separated constructors take a builder parameter that looks as follows:

```
builder: (BuildContext context, int index) {}
```

Here, the index is the index value in your list of items to show. To see how **ListView** works, we will convert the **VerticalMovieList** Column to use a **ListView** that can handle a scrolling list of movies. Open **vert_movie_list.dart** and replace the column in the build method with the following:

```
return ListView.builder(
  itemCount: movies.length,
  itemBuilder: (context, index) {
    return MovieRow(
      movie: movies[index],
    );
  },
);
```

Now, return to **genre_screen.dart** and update the call to:

```
VerticalMovieList(movies: images, onMovieTap: (movieId) {},),
```

This will send the whole list of movies to the widget. Hot reload. You will probably see a white screen with lots of errors in the console. You will see the following error message a lot:

**Vertical viewport was given unbounded height.**

This means that one or several widgets do not give a fixed height and try to take up an infinite height, which causes this error. How do we solve this? We will use the **Expanded** widget.

# Expanded

The **Expanded** widget tries to take up as much width or height as its row or column will allow. **Expanded** only works in these two widgets. Wrap the **ListView** call in an **Expanded** and hot reload. The following code uses an **Expanded** widget to fill the column and then a **ListView** with the list of movies:

```
return Expanded(
  child: ListView.builder(
    itemCount: movies.length,
    itemBuilder: (context, index) {
      return MovieRow(
        movie: movies[index],
      );
    },
  ),
);
```

Here is what we have so far. Notice that you can scroll the list of movies, as shown in the following figure:

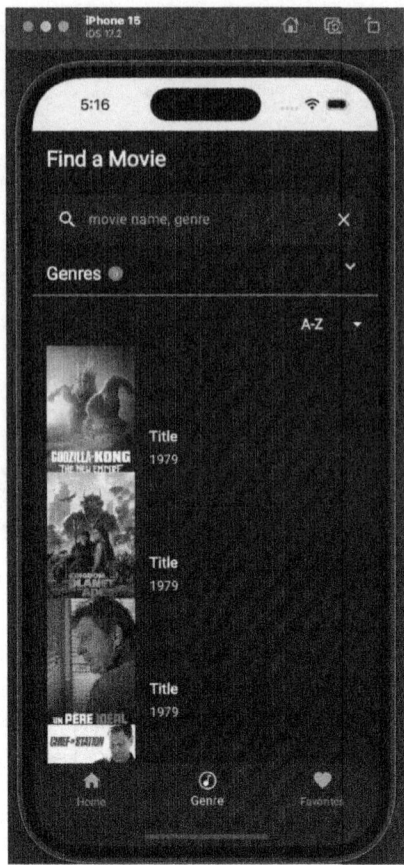

***Figure 7.1***: *ListView*

Now, open **horiz_movies.dart**. In *Chapter 4, Basic Widgets* (Adding a movie row), you added a **ListView** to this class. Here, you can see that it is a horizontal list and uses the movies list passed in. The code for this is as follows:

```
// 1
SizedBox(
    height: 142,
    child: ListView.builder(
// 2
        scrollDirection: Axis.horizontal,
// 3
        itemCount: movies.length,
// 4
        itemBuilder: (context, index) {
          return GestureDetector(
            onTap: () {},
```

```
              child: SizedBox(
                width: 100,
                height: 142,
                child: CachedNetworkImage(
                  imageUrl: movies[index],
                  alignment: Alignment.topCenter,
                  fit: BoxFit.fitHeight,
                  height: 100,
                  width: 142,
                ),
              ),
            );
          }),
      );
```

The description of the code is as follows:

1. This shows a horizontal list of movies at a fixed height of 142 pixels.

2. Make this a horizontal list.

3. Set the item count to the number of movies.

4. Use the **itemBuilder** to return a 100x142 movie image.

# Stack

A **Stack** widget displays its children, with the first one in the list displayed at the bottom. The advantage of this widget is you can use the **Positioned** widget to place items on top of each other or on different sides of the stack's box. The **Positioned** widget takes the top, left, bottom, and right position parameters. These are pixels from the top and left. You can also use the **Align** widget, which has an alignment parameter that can be **topCenter**, **topLeft**, **topRight**, **centerXXX**, and **bottomXXX**. The detail page will use the stack to show text on top of an image. A Stack with an image would be created by using the following code:

```
Stack(children: [
    Align(
        alignment: Alignment.topCenter,
        child: CachedNetworkImage(
                imageUrl: imageUrl,
                alignment: Alignment.topCenter,
                fit: BoxFit.fitWidth,
                height: 200,
              width: screenWidth,
```

```
            ),
          ),
  ]),
```

This will show an image in the top center of the stack. If you add additional images or text, they will lay on top of this image. This is useful for our detail page, where we want to display the movie details above the image.

# IndexedStack

A **IndexedStack** widget is like a stack but displays only one child at a time. It is useful as a paging widget that allows the user to display different pages when they click on a controlling widget. It would look as follows:

```
IndexedStack(
                index: _selectedIndex,
                children: [widget1, widget2, widget3],
            )
```

Another widget would change **_selectedIndex** to have the stack change.

# LayoutBuilder

If you ever need to know how big an area is to draw in, then **LayoutBuilder** is a great widget. It uses a builder parameter that passes in a **BoxConstraints**. Then, based on the constraints of min and max, width, and height, you decide whether to show different layouts or just size a widget to the max width or height. This is perfect for when you have a fixed size and want to put an image inside. Just use a **SizedBox** with the constraints, max width, or height. These constraints are the parent's constraints and are useful if you need to do any custom layouts. You could use one layout for tablets and another for phones using the **maxWidth** field. The following is a small example:

```
@override
Widget build(BuildContext context) {
  return MaterialApp(
    debugShowCheckedModeBanner: false,
    home: Scaffold(
      body: Center(
        child: LayoutBuilder(builder: (context, constraints) {
          if (constraints.maxWidth > 600) {
            return Row(children: [Text('Wide Screen')]);
          } else {
            return Column(children: [Text('Narrow Screen')]);
          }
        }),
```

```
      ),
    ),
  );
}
```

You can see that we check the **maxWidth**, and if it is greater than 600 (which usually signifies a tablet), we show a different layout than if it is smaller than 600 (like on a phone).

# GridView

**GridView** takes lists to the next level. They allow you to display items both horizontally and vertically. There are also ways to display a fixed set of columns or to even stagger mixed widths and heights. Grids work a bit differently in that they take a delegate, which is of type **SliverGridDelegate** (Slivers will be talked about in upcoming sections), and describe how the rows and columns will be set. Like list views, grids have several constructors, as follows:

- **GridView**: Default constructor.

- **GridView.builder**: Use a builder to return a widget.

- **GridView.count**: Display items with a fixed count of cross-axis items.

- **GridView.extend**: Each item has a maximum cross-axis size.

- **GridView.custom**: Roll your own Grid. There are no defaults; you must provide all parameters.

Open up **genre_section.dart** and scroll to the last row. Here, we just showed a list of about four chips. To display more, we will be using a **GridView**. Replace the Row with the following:

```
child: GridView.builder(
                shrinkWrap: true,
// 1
                itemCount: genreChips.length,
// 2
                gridDelegate:
// 3
                    const SliverGridDelegateWithMaxCrossAxisExtent(
                        maxCrossAxisExtent: 100,
                        crossAxisSpacing: 16,
                        childAspectRatio: 1.5,
                        mainAxisSpacing: 0),
// 4
                itemBuilder: (BuildContext context, int index) {
```

```
        return genreChips[index];
      },
    ),
```

This uses the builder constructor with several parameters, as follows:

1.  **itemCount** is the total number of items.

2.  **gridDelegate** describes how the grid will be laid out.

3.  This delegate lays out its children with a width of 100, 16 pixels of vertical space, and an aspect ratio of 1.5 (set the cross-axis height as a ratio of the width).

4.  Return an item at the given index.

Back in **genre_screen.dart**, update the list of genres to include the full list, as follows:

```
GenreState(genre: 'Action', isSelected: false),
GenreState(genre: 'Adventure', isSelected: false),
GenreState(genre: 'Crime', isSelected: false),
GenreState(genre: 'Mystery', isSelected: false),
GenreState(genre: 'War', isSelected: false),
GenreState(genre: 'Comedy', isSelected: false),
GenreState(genre: 'Romance', isSelected: false),
GenreState(genre: 'History', isSelected: false),
GenreState(genre: 'Music', isSelected: false),
GenreState(genre: 'Drama', isSelected: false),
GenreState(genre: 'Thriller', isSelected: false),
GenreState(genre: 'Family', isSelected: false),
GenreState(genre: 'Horror', isSelected: false),
GenreState(genre: 'Western', isSelected: false),
GenreState(genre: 'Science Fiction', isSelected: false),
GenreState(genre: 'Animation', isSelected: false),
GenreState(genre: 'Documentation', isSelected: false),
GenreState(genre: 'TV Movie', isSelected: false),
GenreState(genre: 'Fantasy', isSelected: false),
```

Do a hot restart as a reload will not re-run the **initState** method. The following figure shows a grid of columns and rows:

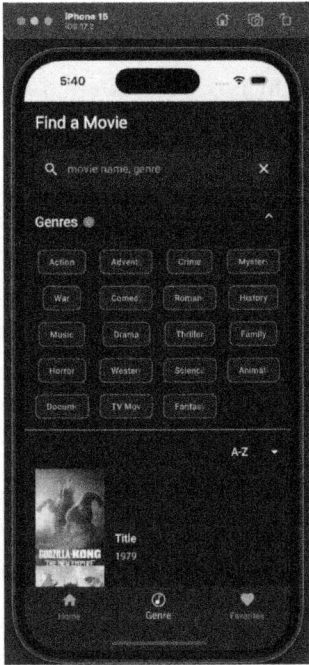

**Figure 7.2**: *GridView*

As you can see, there are four columns and five rows. If the screen changes sizes (like on the web), it will expand to fill the area.

# Table

Tables are great for data that needs to be displayed in columns and rows. You can set each column width, and have a border. A **Table's** children are a list of **TableRow** widgets. Each row can contain a normal widget or a **TableCell** widget. **TableCell** can control the alignment of the widget it contains. One of the differences between a **GridView** and a **Table** is that a **GridView** tries to size its columns and rows based on its widgets, while a **Table** forces its widgets to fit into the size of the column. The following is an example:

```
@override
Widget build(BuildContext context) {
  return MaterialApp(
    debugShowCheckedModeBanner: false,
    home: Scaffold(
// 1
      body: Table(
// 2
        border: TableBorder.all(),
// 3
```

```
        columnWidths: const <int, TableColumnWidth>{
          0: IntrinsicColumnWidth(),
          1: FlexColumnWidth(),
          2: FixedColumnWidth(64),
        },
        defaultVerticalAlignment: TableCellVerticalAlignment.middle,
// 4
        children: <TableRow>[
// 5
          TableRow(
            children: <Widget>[
              Text('Row 1: Column 1'),
// 6
              TableCell(
                verticalAlignment: TableCellVerticalAlignment.top,
                child: Text('Row 1: Column 2'),
              ),
              Text('Row 1: Column 3'),
            ],
          ),
          TableRow(
            decoration: const BoxDecoration(
              color: Colors.grey,
            ),
            children: <Widget>[
              Text('Row 2: Column 1'),
              Text('Row 2: Column 2'),
              Center(
                child: Text('Row 2: Column 2'),
              ),
            ],
          ),
        ],
      )));
  }
```

This will be displayed as shown in the following figure:

| Row 1: Column 1 | Row 1: Column 2 | | Row 1: Column 3 |
|---|---|---|---|
| Row 2: Column 1 | Row 2: Column 2 | | Row 2: Column 2 |

*Figure 7.3: Card*

The code uses several widgets that are needed for a Table: TableRow for rows and TableCells or other widgets for the individual items. The code is described by the following:

1. Start with the **Table** widget.

2. You can specify a **border** if needed. This can specify the color, line width, and border radius.

3. You can specify different column widths. Either fixed or sized for the included widgets.

4. The children should have a list of **TableRow**.

5. Each **TableRow** can have a list of table columns. The number of widgets should match the number of columns.

6. Besides regular widgets, you can use a **TableCell** to add more formatting.

Of course, tables are great for data that you would use in a spreadsheet, but they can be used if you want fixed columns.

# Card

Cards have rounded borders with elevations. They are useful for having sections stand out from the rest of the layout. You can add a child widget that can also contain other widgets. For example:

```
Card(
  child: Column(
    children: [
      Text('Title of Object'),
      Text('Description of Object')
    ],
  ),
)
```

You can set the **color**, **shadowColor**, **surfaceTintColor**, **elevation**, and **shape**. The following is an example of a ticket card:

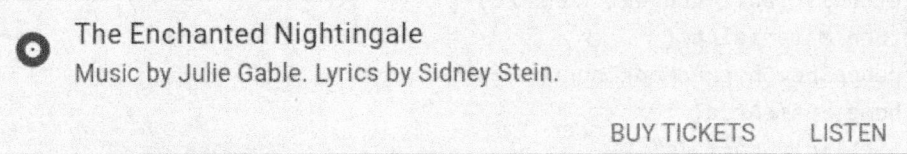

*Figure 7.4: Card*

Apart from the default constructor (which builds an elevated card), you can use **Card. filled** for a filled card and **Card.outlined** for an outline card.

# BottomSheets

As the name implies, BottomSheets are information items that are on the bottom of the screen. There are two kinds: Persistent and modal. Persistent sheets will stay in place, while modal sheets force the user to interact with the sheet until it is dismissed. These sheets can be animated and can have a drag handle. To show a bottom sheet, you would use the **showBottomSheet** method, and in the builder function, you would return a widget. You can change the background color using the **backgroundColor** parameter. A **BottomSheet** might look as follows:

*Figure 7.5*: *BottomSheet*

The code is as follows:

```
@override
Widget build(BuildContext context) {
  return MaterialApp(
    debugShowCheckedModeBanner: false,
    home: SafeArea(
      child: Scaffold(
        body: TextButton(
          child: Text('Show Me'),
          onPressed: () {
```

// 1

```
        showModalBottomSheet(
          context: context,
// 2
          builder: (BuildContext context) {
            return Container(
              height: 300,
              child: Column(
                mainAxisAlignment: MainAxisAlignment.center,
                children: [
                  Text(
                    'This is a BottomSheet',
                    style: TextStyle(fontSize: 24),
                  ),
                ],
              ),
            );
          },
        );
      },
    ),
  ),
  ),
  );
}
```

This code shows a modal bottom sheet when the user presses the text button.

# Slivers

Slivers are scrollable widgets and can be used in lists of slivers. You need to use a **CustomScrollView** as a parent widget and then add slivers to the slivers list parameter. There are many different types of slivers, as follows:

- **SliverList**: Displays a linear list of items.

- **SliverGrid**: Displays a 2D array of children.

- **SliverAppBar**: A material design app bar that integrates with a **CustomScrollView** and allows the bar to change while scrolling other items.

- **SliverToBoxAdapter**: A sliver that contains a single box widget. Useful for converting slivers to a widget that conforms to a regular type of widget.

- **SliverPadding**: Adds padding around another sliver.

The first sliver you will use is **SliverPadding**. You will create your own sliver widget to create a divider. In the widgets folder, create a new file named **sliver_divider.dart**. Add the following:

```dart
import 'package:flutter/material.dart';

import 'package:movies/ui/theme/theme.dart';

class SliverDivider extends StatelessWidget {
  const SliverDivider({super.key});

  @override
  Widget build(BuildContext context) {
    return const SliverPadding(
      padding: EdgeInsets.only(
          left: 16, top: 8, right: 16, bottom: 8),
      sliver: SliverToBoxAdapter(
        child: Divider(
          color: primaryButton,
          thickness: 1.0,
        ),
      ),
    );
  }
}
```

Since this widget returns a **SliverPadding**, it is itself a sliver. The **SliverToBoxAdapter** class converts the widgets below to sliver (in this case, just a regular divider).

Open up **genre_screen.dart**. We are going to convert some of the items into slivers. Find the first Row. Before the row, add the following:

```dart
Expanded(
child: CustomScrollView(
  slivers: [
    SliverList(
      delegate: SliverChildListDelegate(
        [
```

Remove the **Row** and **GenreSearchRow** and replace it with the following:

```dart
Padding(
padding:
    const EdgeInsets.fromLTRB(16, 16.0, 0.0,
24.0),

    child: Text('Find a Movie',
        style: Theme.of(context).textTheme.
titleLarge),
      ),
```

```
                GenreSearchRow((searchString) {
                }),
              ],
            ),
          ),
```

Change the **Divider** to **SliverDivider** and import the widget. You will next need to fix the number of parentheses and brackets at the end. This is good practice as you will do this many times. The following is what the ending of the widget looks like:

```
            ],
          ),
        ),
      ],
    ),
  ),
);
}
}
```

Dealing with parentheses is one area that gets messy with widgets. However, the more you break your widgets up into their own classes, the smaller each class will be and the easier it will be to read. Hot reload your app to make sure it still works. You should get an error, and it should look as follows:

**A RenderViewport expected a child of type RenderSliver but received a child of type _RenderMergeableMaterialListBody.**

Any idea what this means? If you have a list of slivers and one of them is not one, you will get this message. That means one of the widgets is not a sliver. It looks like **VerticalMovieList** uses an **Expanded** (which can only be in a row or column) and a **ListView**. Let us change that. Open up **vert_movie_list.dart** and change *Expanded* and the **ListView.builder** (up to the itemBuilder) to the following:

```
return SliverList(
  delegate: SliverChildBuilderDelegate(
    childCount: movies.length,
    (BuildContext context, int index) {
```

Open **genre_section.dart** and add the following before the **ExpansionPanelList**:

```
return SliverList(
  delegate: SliverChildListDelegate(
    [
```

Remove the return before the **ExpansionPanelList.** Fix the ending parentheses. Next, open up **sort_picker.dart**. Add a new parameter, as follows:

**final bool useSliver;**

Replace the constructor with the following:

```
const SortPicker({required this.useSliver, required this.onSortSelected,
super.key});
```

Replace the line: **Widget build(BuildContext context) {** with the following:

```
Widget build(BuildContext context) {
  if (widget.useSliver) {
    return SliverToBoxAdapter(
        child: buildRow()
    );
  } else {
    return buildRow();
  }
}

Widget buildRow() {
```

```
Back in genre_screen.dart, add the following:
```

```
                    useSliver: true,
```

The code provides the parameter to the **SortPicker**. Perform a hot restart, and the code should work. The following shows the **Genres** screen with the list of movies and the new **SliverList**:

*Figure 7.6: Genre screen*

You can now scroll through the list of movies and see all the movies on the list.

# Movie trailers

One area that needs work is the ability to show videos. In the case of the movie app, the ability to show movie trailers. These are short videos that showcase the movie. To show a video from *YouTube*, we will use a plugin called **pod_player**. Open up **pubspec.yaml** and add the following:

```
pod_player: ^0.2.2
```

Select pub get. In the **ui/screens** folder, create a new folder named **videos**. Then, create a new dart file named **video_page.dart**. Then add the following:

```dart
import 'package:flutter/material.dart';
import 'package:flutter_riverpod/flutter_riverpod.dart';
import 'package:pod_player/pod_player.dart';

class VideoPage extends ConsumerStatefulWidget {
  final String movieVideo;

  const VideoPage(this.movieVideo, {super.key});

  @override
  ConsumerState<VideoPage> createState() => _VideoPageState();
}

class _VideoPageState extends ConsumerState<VideoPage> {

  late final PodPlayerController podPlayerController;

  @override
  Widget build(BuildContext context) {
    return Placeholder();
  }
}
```

Here, the only new code is the **PodPlayerController**. This class is a controller for the **PodVideoPlayer** widget from the **pod_player** plugin. Since this variable is defined as a late variable, we need to initialize it using the **initState** method. First, we need to create a utility method for building a *YouTube* video URL. Open up **utils.dart** and add the following:

```dart
String youtubeUrlFromId(String videoId) {
  return 'https://www.youtube.com/watch?v=$videoId';
}
```

This is a simple method that just concatenates the video id to the URL. Back in **video_page.dart**, add the following before the **build** method:

```
  @override
  void initState() {
    super.initState();
// 1
    final playVideoFrom = PlayVideoFrom.youtube(
      youtubeUrlFromId(widget.movieVideo),
    );
// 2
    podPlayerController = PodPlayerController(
        playVideoFrom: playVideoFrom,
        podPlayerConfig: const PodPlayerConfig(autoPlay: false))
      ..initialise();
  }

  @override
  void dispose() {
// 3
    podPlayerController.dispose();
    super.dispose();
  }
```

These two methods, **initState** and dispose of, set up and dispose of the video controller:

1.  Use the new utility method to get the URL and create a **PlayVideoFrom** class to pass to the controller.

2.  Create the controller passing in the video URL class and config.

3.  Dispose of the controller when done.

Next, add a method to get the video player. Use the following code:

```
Widget getVideoPlayer(BuildContext context) {
  return Scaffold(
    appBar: AppBar(
      backgroundColor: screenBackground,
      leading: BackButton(
        color: Colors.white,
        onPressed: () {},
      ),
      centerTitle: false,
      title: Text('Back', style: Theme.of(context).textTheme.
headlineMedium),
    ),
    body: Container(
      width: double.infinity,
```

```
        height: double.infinity,
        color: screenBackground,
        child: Column(
          mainAxisSize: MainAxisSize.max,
          crossAxisAlignment: CrossAxisAlignment.center,
          children: [
            Expanded(
              child: PodVideoPlayer(
                  controller: podPlayerController,
                  matchVideoAspectRatioToFrame: true,
                  ),
              ),
          ],
        ),
      ),
    );
}
```

At the bottom of the method is the **PodVideoPlayer**, use the controller and a flag to match the video's aspect ratio to the screen. Now replace the build method with the following:

```
@override
Widget build(BuildContext context) {
  SystemChrome.setPreferredOrientations([
    DeviceOrientation.portraitUp,
    DeviceOrientation.portraitDown,
    DeviceOrientation.landscapeLeft,
    DeviceOrientation.landscapeRight,
  ]);
  return getVideoPlayer(context);
}
```

The **SystemChrome** class is useful for changing the orientation of the device. Here, we change the device orientation to allow landscape and then return the video player. Return to **main_screen.dart** and change the last **Placerholder** with the following:

```
screens.add(VideoPage('QwW5RD02uJo'));
```

This calls the video page with a *YouTube* key that is a trailer for a *Kung Fu Panda* movie. Stop the app (When you have plugins that have device-specific code, you must rebuild your app and you cannot hot reload). Restart the app and click on the **Favorites** button.

**Note: That we are just using this page to show the video but will be replacing it with favorites later.**

The device will turn to landscape, as shown in the following figure:

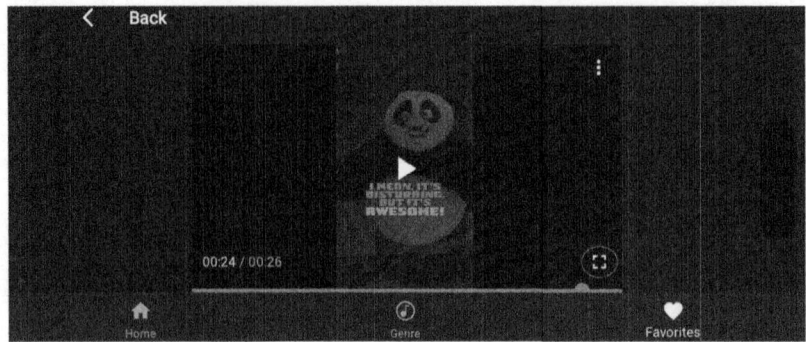

*Figure 7.7*: *Video screen*

If you press the expand button, you will see the window expand to full screen. However, this depends on the video that you are playing. This specific video was built for phones in portrait mode, as shown in *Figure 7.8*:

*Figure 7.8*: *Fullscreen*

In the chapter on the web and desktop, we will use a different package to show videos for the web.

# Conclusion

In this chapter, you learned a lot about the more advanced widgets like ListView, GridView, Table, BottomSheets, and Slivers. You were able to update the app to use these advanced widgets to show more items. You also created a video page and were able to show a video trailer for a movie.

In the next chapter, you will learn about navigation and routing. This is a very important topic that will allow you to switch between different screens. You will use a specific package to push screens on a stack and pop them off when returning.

# CHAPTER 8

# Navigation and Routing

## Introduction

In this chapter, you will learn about how Flutter apps navigate between pages. You will also learn about the built-in Navigator widget in Flutter and a newer way to handle navigation with Navigator 2.0. In addition, you will learn about packages that make navigation easier, and use one of the packages to hook up the movie app to allow the user to move among the pages of the app.

## Structure

The chapter covers the following topics:

- Navigator widget
- Named routes
- Deep linking
- Bottom navigation
- GoRouter and AutoRoute
- Connecting the movie app

# Objectives

By the end of this chapter, you will understand how the old Navigator and the new Navigator work. You will also have an understanding of deep linking and several navigation packages. You will set up AutoRoute as the navigation package and start creating routes. Finally, you will build up the movie details page, learn how to create a route and use navigation to go there.

# Navigator widget

Navigation is the ability to go from one screen to another. In Flutter, the system uses a stack to push screens to the front and to pop them when the user is done with that screen. It is important to understand how the old and new system works before using some of the packages that will make the process even easier.

Any app needs the ability to transition from one page to another and then back. Flutter uses the Navigator widget. These pages are called routes in Flutter. Routing consists of just pushing and popping pages. Navigator 1.0 was used before Flutter 1.22 and has some serious disadvantages, as follows:

- The route stack is not exposed to the developer (Makes it hard to replace pages).
- Navigator does not update the web URL path (for web apps).
- Does not handle the back button on Android devices well.

In Flutter 1.22 the Router API (or Navigator 2.0) was introduced. The advantages of the Router API are as follows:

- Exposes the Navigator's page stack.
- Is backward compatible with Navigator 1.0.
- Handles the back button on Android devices.
- Allows nested Navigators.
- Deep linking and web URLs are handled.

# Navigator

The **Navigator** widget has an array of pages. A Page is an abstract class that has a name and argument. The most common page subclass used is MaterialPage. The **pages** field is the list of pages that can be shown in an application. You can change the items in the page list when your app changes so that different pages are shown. There are a few important methods, as follows:

- **push(context, route)**: Push a new route/page to the stack.

- **pushNamed(context, routeName, arguments)**: Find the route with the given name and push it onto the stack.

- **pop(context)**: Pop the current, top-level page off the stack, showing the next page on the stack.

There is also a **onPopPage** callback parameter. This is a function that takes a route and result value, as follows:

```
typedef PopPageCallback = bool Function(Route<dynamic> route, dynamic
result);
```

This function must call **route.didPop** and update the list of pages to not include that route/page. The following is an example of an **onPopPage** usage:

```
MaterialApp(
    ...
    home: Navigator(
      pages: [],
      onPopPage: (route, result)=>route.didPop(result),
    ),
)
```

The pages list would be filled with a list of MaterialPages with a **MaterialPage** that looks as follows:

```
MaterialPage(
      key: ValueKey('MovieListing'),
      child: MovieListingScreen(),
    )
```

You could put some logic to return different pages, but that is messy and does not work well for large amounts of screens and complex logic.

# Router

The Router widget is a page dispatcher that wraps a Navigator class. To use deep linking, you will need to use the Router widget. Here is what the flow looks like for the Router API (*Figure 8.1*):

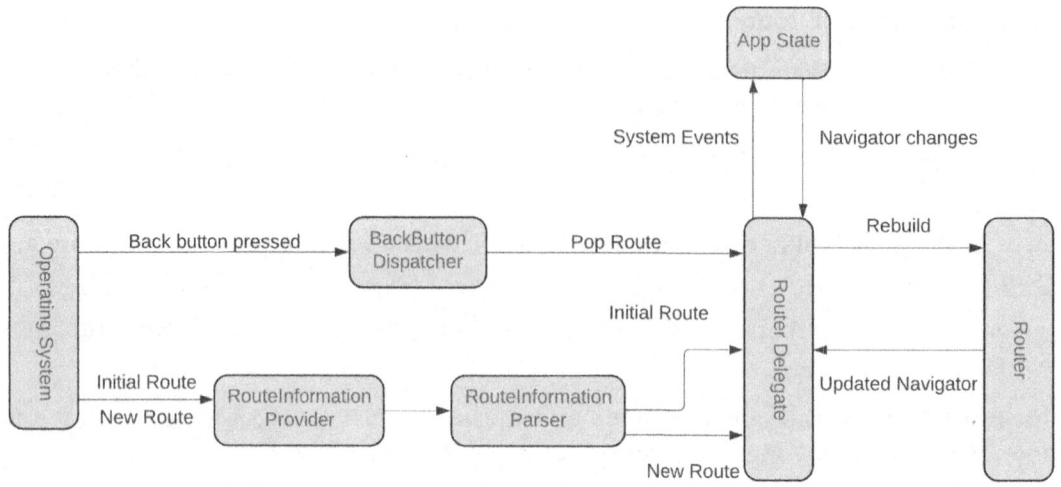

*Figure 8.1: Router API*

This shows some of the important classes involved with navigation. We will be using a package to handle this and make it easier, but it is important to understand how the Flutter system works.

# RouterDelegate

The **RouterDelegate** responds to app state and route changes and builds a new **Navigator** with an updated list of pages.

The **RouterDelegate** class has a few methods, listed as follows:

- **setInitialRoutePath**: Given a class with the route, configure the router.
- **setRestoredRoutePath**: Given a class, restore the route state.
- **setNewRoutePath**: Set a new route path given the data class.
- **popRoute**: Remove the current page from the stack.

# RouterInformationParser

The **RouterInformationParser** is an abstract class that acts as a delegate between the router widget and the route information provided by the system. It is responsible for parsing the route information into a configuration object that can be understood by the **RouterDelegate**. The **RouterInformationParser** transforms **RouteInformation** values into a user-defined class.

The **RouteInformationParser** class has three methods, as follows:

- **parseRouteInformation**: Parse a **RouteInformation** parameter and return a data class.

- **parseRouteInformationWithDependencies**: Has an extra **BuildContext** parameter.

- **restoreRouteInformation**: Given the data class, return a **RouteInformation** instance.

# RouteInformationProvider

The **RouteInformationProvider** provides the app's current route and notifies listeners of any changes. It will be used by the Router widget to determine which screen to display. It is also used to monitor changes in the route and notify listeners.

The **RouteInformationProvider** class has just one method:

- **routerReportsNewRouteInformation**: As this class is a **ValueListenable**, you can take this new information and notify users of the change.

# MaterialApp

The **MaterialApp** class can either be provided as a router class or individual parameters. Here are some parameters associated with navigation:

- **navigatorKey**: Global Key tied to the Navigator.

- **initialRoute**: Starting route (String-based).

- **navigatorObservers**: List of listeners to navigation events.

- **onUnknownRoute**: Uses a function that takes a RouteSettings instance and returns a Route to handle unknown routes.

- **onNavigationNotification**: Nofication callback listener.

- **routes**: Map of route names and WidgetBuilders.

One of the nice features about a global Navigator key is that you can use it anywhere to navigate to other pages. However, you can also just use **Navigator.of(context)** to get the current Navigator. You could use the key if you had multiple Navigators. To use a global key, you would define it as:

```
final navigatorKey = GlobalKey<NavigatorState>();
```

You would then add it to the MaterialApp and other pages could push a page as follows:

```
navigatorKey.currentState?.pushNamed("newRoute");
```

The second method is to use the **MaterialApp.router** method. It takes the following parameters:

- **routeInformationProvider**: Provides route information for the router widget.

- **routeInformationParser**: Parses route information into a class.

- **routerDelegate**: Main class for handling routing.

- **routerConfig**: This can be used in place of the other parameters. Contains all the above elements.

- **backButtonDispatcher**: Handles back button actions. There are two provided classes you can use (or create your own): **ChildBackButtonDispatcher** and **RootBackButtonDispatcher**. The root dispatcher is the default. The child dispatcher is for handling back button presses from a parent.

You will normally use the **router** method with packages as they have a **config** class you can use which makes it easier to set up.

# Named routes

The **Navigator** class uses the **pushNamed** method to push a string route onto the stack. These are called named routes as you give them a string name. Other classes can use this string to go to that page. Another way to define routes is with the route's parameter to **MaterialApp**. It looks as follows:

```
class MyApp extends StatelessWidget {
  const MyApp({Key? key}) : super(key: key);

  @override
  Widget build(BuildContext context) {
    return MaterialApp(
      debugShowCheckedModeBanner: false,
// 1
      routes: {
        'DetailPage': (context) => DetailPage()
      },
// 2
      home: Page1(),
    );
  }
}

// 3
class Page1 extends StatelessWidget {
  @override
  Widget build(BuildContext context) {
    return TextButton(onPressed: () => Navigator.pushNamed(context,
'DetailPage'), child: Text('Details'));
  }
```

```
}

// 4
class DetailPage extends StatelessWidget {
  @override
  Widget build(BuildContext context) {
    return TextButton(onPressed: () => Navigator.pop(context), child:
Text('Return'));
  }
}
```

Here we have the **MyApp** and two pages: **Page1** and **DetailPage**. The following is a detailed explanation:

1. Define the routes based on a string key value.

2. Start with **Page1**.

3. **Page1** just shows a button that when clicked, pushes the **Detail** page by its route name.

4. The detail page just pops the detail page from the stack and returns to **Page1**.

You can also pass in arguments. This would look as follows:

```
Navigator.pushNamed(context, 'DetailPage', arguments: 'Test'),
```

Then, in the **DetailPage** class, you would retrieve the arguments with the **ModalRoute** class as follows:

```
    final String args = ModalRoute.of(context)!.settings.arguments as
String;
    return TextButton(onPressed: () => Navigator.pop(context), child:
Text(args));
```

You can also return data from a page. When you call the pop method, you can pass the result as the last parameter. Here is an example:

```
class Page1 extends StatefulWidget {

  @override
  State<Page1> createState() => _Page1State();
}

class _Page1State extends State<Page1> {
  String textMessage = 'Details';
  @override
  Widget build(BuildContext context) {
// 1
```

```
    return TextButton(onPressed: () async {
      textMessage = await Navigator.pushNamed(context, 'DetailPage',
arguments: 'Test') as String;
      setState(() {
      });
    }, child: Text(textMessage));
  }
}

class DetailPage extends StatelessWidget {
  @override
  Widget build(BuildContext context) {
// 2
    final String args = ModalRoute.of(context)!.settings.arguments as
String;
// 3
    return TextButton(onPressed: () => Navigator.pop(context, 'Result'),
child: Text(args));
  }
}
```

Here we have converted the **Page1** class to a **StatefulWidget** and have a string message. The explanation of the code is as follows:

1. Make the **onPressed** method an **async** method and **await** the results. Update the state when finished.

2. Get the passed in arguments.

3. Return the results when popping the screen.

# Deep linking

Another way to use routes is through deep linking. A deep link is a URL that points to a specific page in an app. Just like on a web page, clicking on a URL in an email or webpage can take the user to a page in an app if the app is installed on their phone. Once the app receives the deep link, the router needs to figure out which page to go to. A URL looks as shown in *Figure 8.2*:

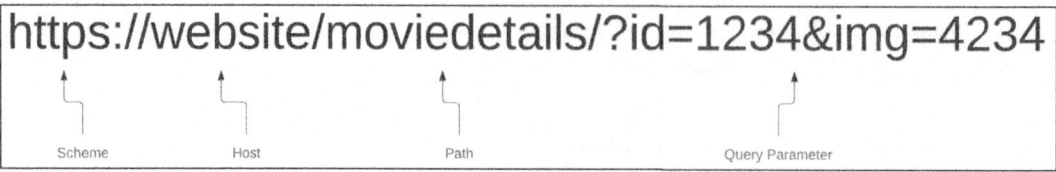

*Figure 8.2: URLs*

A URL is made up of a scheme (usually https), a host name (a specific website), a path to the page, and a set of query parameters (after a ?).

# Custom schemes

In addition to the **https** scheme, on mobile, you can create your own scheme. For example, we could create a scheme called **movieapp**. This would look as follows:

```
movieapp://moviedetails/?id=1234
```

This only works on mobiles. On Android, this is called a deep link while on iOS, it is called a custom URL. This scheme needs to be defined in Android's **AndroidManifest. xml** and iOS's **info.plist** files. This is an easy way to set up a link but comes with some downsides:

- Anyone can use the same scheme.
- You have to have the app installed for this to work.

If you want to use an **https** scheme for deep linking, you need to own the host site. These links are called App Links on Android and Universal Links on iOS. There is also host verification that is performed by Android and iOS devices.

# Android deep links

To handle deep links on Android, you will need to add an entry in the **AndroidManifest. xml** file. The entry code is as follows:

```
<intent-filter android:autoVerify="true">
  <action android:name="android.intent.action.VIEW" />
  <category android:name="android.intent.category.DEFAULT" />
  <category android:name="android.intent.category.BROWSABLE" />

  <data android:scheme="https" />
  <data android:host="yourDomain.com" />
</intent-filter>
```

For custom schemes, add the following code:

```
<meta-data
    android:name="flutter_deeplinking_enabled"
    android:value="true" />
<intent-filter android:autoVerify="true">
  <action android:name="android.intent.action.VIEW" />
  <category android:name="android.intent.category.DEFAULT" />
  <category android:name="android.intent.category.BROWSABLE" />

  <data android:scheme="yourScheme" />
```

```
<data android:host="yourDomain.com" />
</intent-filter>
```

You would add this intent filter to an Activity that would handle the https scheme. For Flutter, it would go to the Flutter **MainActivity** (a subclass of **FlutterActivity**) that is created for you. You can also set a path if you want your app to handle just a specific area of a URL. To find out more about the possible data values you can visit: **https://developer. android.com/guide/topics/manifest/data-element**

## Verifying a domain

To use URLs with your own domain, you need to create a file named **assetlinks.json**. The file will look as follows:

```
[{
  "relation": ["delegate_permission/common.handle_all_urls"],
  "target": {
    "namespace": "android_app",
    "package_name": "com.bpb.movieapp",
    "sha256_cert_fingerprints":
    ["FF:2A:CF:7B:DD:CC:F1:03:3E:E8:B2:27:7C:A2:
E3:3C:DE:13:DB:AC:8E:EB:3A:B9:72:A1:0E:26:8A:F5:EC:AF"]
  }
}]
```

You will need to use your own **package_name** and **sha25** value. You can create the sha value by using:

```
keytool -list -v -keystore <path-to-keystore> -alias <key alias>
-storepass <store password> -keypass <key password>
```

You then need to store this file at:

```
<webdomain>/.well-known/assetlinks.json
```

When you have everything setup on your website, you can use the tester at **https:// developers.google.com/digital-asset-links/tools/generator**.

## Testing Android

To test links on Android you will need to test from the command line. You will use the **adb** command that is located in **android/platform-tools/** folder. Make sure your path is set or just type in the full path. For **https** links, you would use:

```
adb shell am start -a android.intent.action.VIEW \
  -c android.intent.category.BROWSABLE \
  -d https://yourDomain.com \
  <package name>
```

For custom schemes use:

```
adb shell am start -a android.intent.action.VIEW \
  -c android.intent.category.BROWSABLE \
  -d yourScheme://yourDomain.com \
  <package name>
```

You can also email yourself the link on the phone and test that way. For https links, you will get a dialog on Android asking if you want to show the link with a web browser or your app. This is normal and will go away if you have the **android:autoVerify="true"** setting in your manifest and your website is set up properly.

# iOS deep links

For iOS, the process is different and requires you to modify the **info.plist** file. You can do this in Xcode, Android Studio, or a text editor. The first thing you need to do is add the Universal Link Capability. In Xcode, click on the **Runner** target, then the **Signing & Capabilities** tab, and then press the **Capability** button, as shown in the following figure:

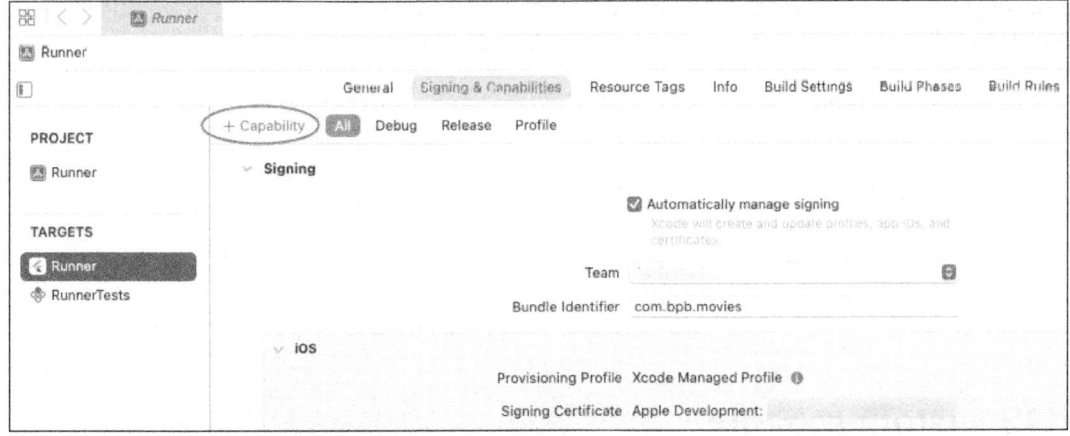

*Figure 8.3: Add Capability*

You will see the following dialog:

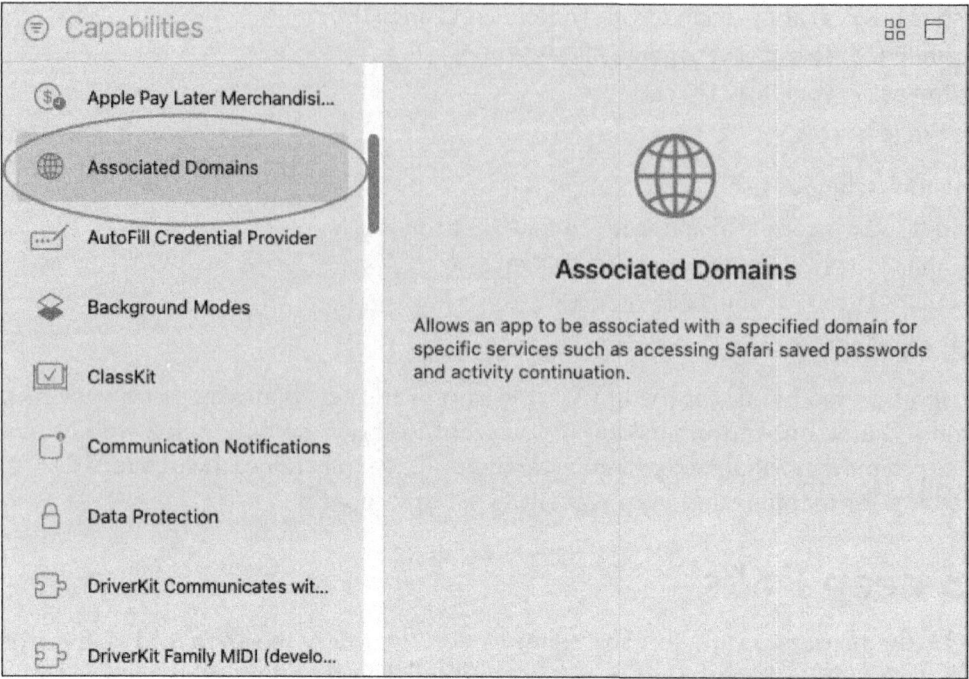

*Figure 8.4*: *Associated Domains*

Double-click the **Associated Domains**. In the **Domains** text area, change the link to applinks:<your domain>, as shown in the following figure:

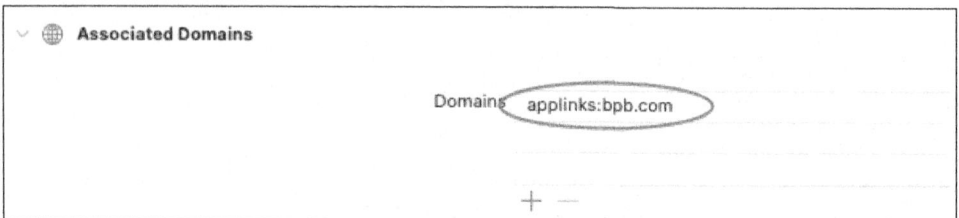

*Figure 8.5:* *Associated Domains link*

# iOS custom scheme

The steps to create a custom scheme are as follows:

1. For a custom scheme, you will need to edit the **info.plist** file. In the files pane, click on **Info**, as shown in *Figure 8.6*:

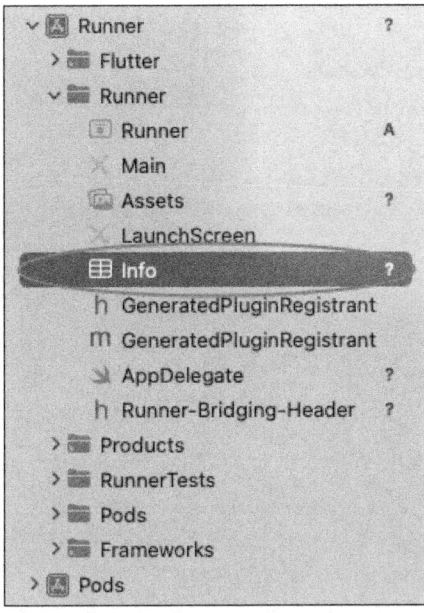

*Figure 8.6: Info.plist*

2.  Then in the table click on the first plus icon to bring up a list of types, as shown in the following figure:

| Key | | Type | Value |
|---|---|---|---|
| ∨ Information Property List | ⊕ | Dictionary ⌄ | (17 items) |
| Default localization | ⌄ | String | $(DEVELOPMENT_LANGUAGE) |
| Bundle display name | ⌄⊕⊖ | String | Movies |
| Executable file | ⌄ | String | $(EXECUTABLE_NAME) |
| Bundle identifier | ⌄ | String | $(PRODUCT_BUNDLE_IDENTIFIER) |
| InfoDictionary version | ⌄ | String | 6.0 |
| Bundle name | ⌄ | String | movies |
| Bundle OS Type code | ⌄ | String | APPL |
| Bundle version string (short) | ⌄ | String | $(FLUTTER_BUILD_NAME) |
| Bundle creator OS Type code | ⌄ | String | ???? |
| Bundle version | ⌄ | String | $(FLUTTER_BUILD_NUMBER) |
| Application requires iPhone environment | ⌄ | Boolean | YES |
| Launch screen interface file base name | ⌄ | String | LaunchScreen |
| Main storyboard file base name | ⌄ | String | Main |
| > Supported interface orientations | ⌄ | Array | (3 items) |
| > Supported interface orientations (iPad) | ⌄ | Array | (4 items) |
| CADisableMinimumFrameDurationOnPhone | ⌄ | Boolean | YES |
| Application supports indirect input events | ⌄ | Boolean | YES |

*Figure 8.7: Add Item*

3.  Type URL types to find the entry, as shown in the following figure:

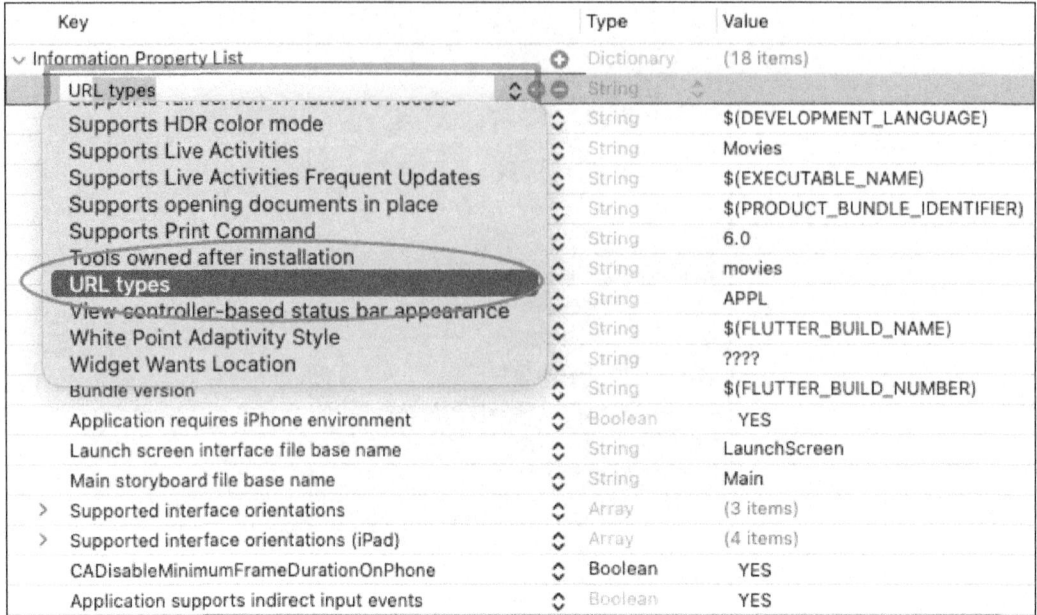

*Figure 8.8: URL types*

4.   Next, click on the plus icon and choose **URL Schemes**, as shown in *Figure 8.9*:

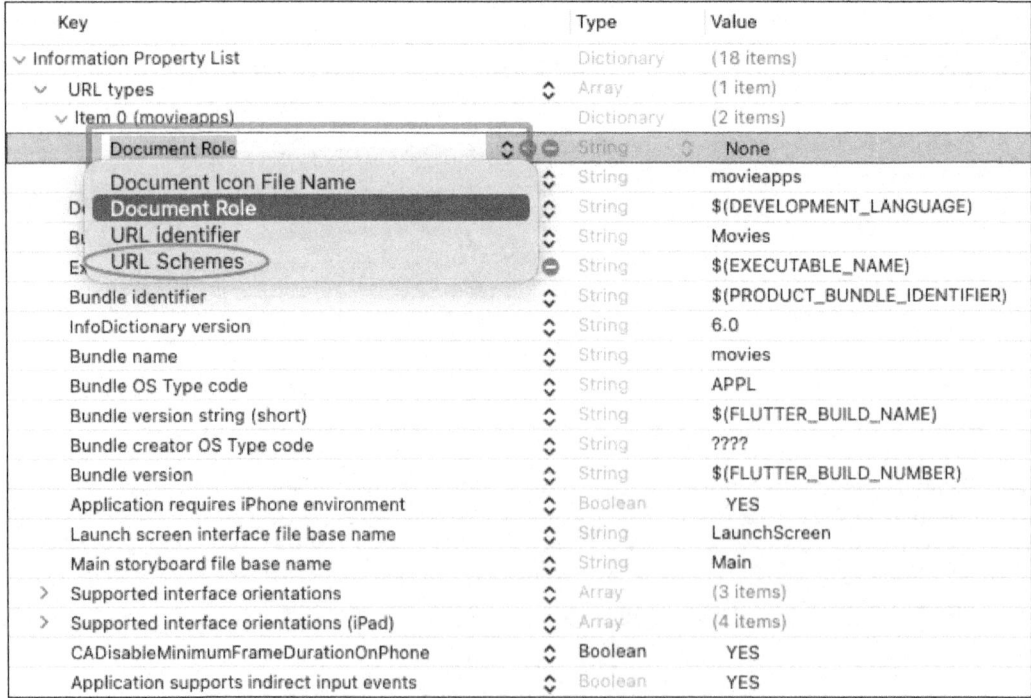

*Figure 8.9: URL scheme*

5.  Next, add your URL scheme and Identifier. Here we have added **movieapps** as the scheme and **URL Identifier** (*Figure 8.10*).

| Key | | Type | Value |
|---|---|---|---|
| ∨ Information Property List | | Dictionary | (18 items) |
| ∨   URL types | ⌄ | Array | (1 item) |
| ∨     Item 0 (movieapps) | | Dictionary | (2 items) |
| ∨       URL Schemes | ⌄ | Array | (1 item) |
|         Item 0 | | String | movieapps |
|       URL identifier | ⌄ ⊕ ⊖ | String ⌄ | movieapps |
|     Default localization | ⌄ | String | $(DEVELOPMENT_LANGUAGE) |

***Figure 8.10**: Final Scheme*

6.  In Android Studio you can open the `info.plist` file and it will look as follows:

```xml
<?xml version="1.0" encoding="UTF-8"?>
<!DOCTYPE plist PUBLIC "-//Apple//DTD PLIST 1.0//EN" "http://www.apple.com/DTDs/PropertyList-1.0.dtd">
<plist version="1.0">
<dict>
    <key>CFBundleURLTypes</key>
    <array>
        <dict>
            <key>CFBundleURLSchemes</key>
            <array>
                <string>movieapps</string>
            </array>
            <key>CFBundleURLName</key>
            <string>movieapps</string>
        </dict>
    </array>
```

***Figure 8.11**: info.plist*

7.  After the array, add the following entry:

```
<key>FlutterDeepLinkingEnabled</key>
<true/>
```

This enables Flutter Deep linking (although it may interfere with some packages).

# iOS verification

iOS verification is similar to but different than Android. You need to create a file named: **apple-app-site-association** (no extension). The file will look as follows:

```
{
  "applinks":{
    "apps":[

    ],
```

```
    "details":[
      {
        "appIDs":[
          "TeamID.BundleID"
        ],
        "components":[
          {
            "/":"/movies",
            "comment":"Matches URL with a path /movies"
          },
          {
            "/":"/moviedetails/*",
            "comment":"Matches URL with path that starts with /
moviedetails/"
          }
        ]
      }
    ]
  }
}
```

Use your Team ID and add all the paths you use. Note that iOS requires adding supported paths. The file needs to reside at:

```
https://yourDomain.com/.well-known/apple-app-site-association.
```

**Testing iOS URLs**

To test iOS URLs you will use the command line but with Apple command line tools. For https links, type the following:

```
xcrun simctl openurl booted https://yourDomain.com/path
```

Make sure you have setup XCode properly so that you can run this command. You can also use the full path:

```
/usr/bin/xcrun
```

For custom schemes type the following:

```
xcrun simctl openurl booted yourScheme://yourDomain.com/path
```

# Bottom navigation

One of the simplest ways to navigate is with the bottom navigation widget. You saw this in **main_screen.dart**. Add the following:

```
@override
Widget build(BuildContext context) {
```

```
  return Scaffold(
    body: screens[index],
    bottomNavigationBar: BottomNavigationBar(
      items: const [
        BottomNavigationBarItem(icon: Icon(Icons.home), label: 'Home'),
        BottomNavigationBarItem(
            icon: Icon(Symbols.genres), label: 'Genre'),
        BottomNavigationBarItem(icon: Icon(Icons.favorite), label:
'Favorites'),
      ],
      currentIndex: index,
      onTap: (navIndex) {
        setState(() {
          index = navIndex;
        });
      },
    ),
  );
}
```

This is a widget that is at the bottom of the screen and contains three to five items. You use the **BottomNavigationBarItem** class to define an icon and label. When a button is selected, the **onTap** method is called. Usually, you need to change the current index, but you can perform additional actions if needed. A newer Material 3 navigation widget is the **NavigationBar** class. Open up **main_screen.dart** and change the **bottomNavigationBar** code to the following:

```
NavigationBar(
      destinations: const [
        NavigationDestination(icon: Icon(Icons.home), label: 'Home'),
        NavigationDestination(icon: Icon(Symbols.genres), label:
'Genre'),
        NavigationDestination(icon: Icon(Icons.favorite), label:
'Favorites'),          ],
      selectedIndex: index,
      onDestinationSelected: (navIndex) {
        setState(() {
          index = navIndex;
        });
      },
    ),
```

This is similar to a **BottomNavigationBar** but uses the keyword **destinations** and then uses **NavigationDestination** instances. **currentIndex** is now **selectedIndex** and **onTap** is now **onDestinationSelected**. One key difference is that you will need to change the theme to change colors of the text and icons. In addition to the **NavigationBar** class, Material provides the **NavigationRail** class. This widget is used on the left or right side of the screen to navigation between a small amount of items. Open up **theme.dart** and add the following after **appBarTheme**:

```
navigationBarTheme: NavigationBarThemeData(
    backgroundColor: searchBarBackground,
    labelTextStyle: WidgetStateTextStyle.resolveWith((Set<WidgetState>
states) {
        // If the item is selected, use primary color; otherwise, use
your desired unselected color
        if (states.contains(WidgetState.selected)) {
          return TextStyle(color: Colors.white);
        }
        return TextStyle(color: posterBorder); // Unselected color
    }),
    iconTheme: WidgetStateProperty.all<IconThemeData>(
        IconThemeData(color: Colors.white)),
    indicatorColor: posterBorder),
```

This will set the background, icon, and the text color. The tricky part is the **WidgetStateTextStyle.resolveWith** method. This just returns a different text style depending on if the widget is selected or not.

# GoRouter and AutoRoute

You may have noticed that navigating with a router is not that easy. That is why there are several packages out there that help with this. We will cover two popular packages: GoRouter (recommended by *Google*) and AutoRoute (recommended by the author). Both of them are easy to use.

# GoRouter

The **GoRouter** package is maintained by *Google*. It is the recommended package to use for routing and is a good package. The steps to use **GoRouter** are as follows:

1. To use **GoRouter** you would create code to define your routes:

```
import 'package:go_router/go_router.dart';

// GoRouter configuration
final _router = GoRouter(
  routes: [
```

```
    GoRoute(
      path: '/',
      builder: (context, state) => MainScreen(),
    ),
  ],
);
```

This defines one main path, using the URL-like string '/'. That starting path will show the **MainScreen** widget.

2. To use the router, you would change the **MaterialApp** call using the following code:

```
Widget build(BuildContext context) {
    return MaterialApp.router(
      routerConfig: _router,
    );
  }
```

Both **GoRouter** and **AutoRoute** use the **routerConfig** parameter (remember that this parameter provides the dispatcher and provider classes).

3. GoRouter's routes can have child routes as follows:

```
GoRoute(
  path: '/',
  builder: (context, state) {
    return MainScreen();
  },
  routes: [
    GoRoute(
      path: 'details',
      builder: (context, state) {
        return MovieDetails();
      },
    ),
  ],
)
```

4. You can even pass parameters such as:

```
GoRoute(
  path: '/details/:id,
  builder: (context, state) => const MovieDetails(id: state.
pathParameters[id]),
),
```

You can find documentation on GoRouter at **https://pub.dev/packages/go_router**. There are a lot of other options but since we will use the **AutoRoute** package for the app, you can investigate more about the package at the URL provided above.

# AutoRoute

We found the **AutoRoute** package a bit easier to use. The routes are similar to **GoRouter**, but **AutoRoute** uses code generation to make the process a bit smoother. The steps to install the **AutoRoute** package are as follows:

1. Open **pubspec.yaml** and add the following dependency:
   ```
   auto_route: ^8.2.0
   ```

2. Then in the **dev_dependencies** section, add the following:
   ```
   auto_route_generator: ^8.0.0
   ```

3. Perform a Pub Get. Next, create a **router** folder under the **lib** folder. Then create the file **app_routes.dart**. Then add the following:
   ```
   import 'package:auto_route/auto_route.dart';

   import 'package:movies/ui/main_screen.dart';
   import 'package:movies/ui/screens/genres/genre_screen.dart';
   import 'package:movies/ui/screens/home/home_screen.dart';
   import 'package:movies/ui/screens/videos/video_page.dart';


   part 'app_routes.gr.dart';

   @AutoRouterConfig()
   class AppRouter extends _$AppRouter {

     @override
     List<AutoRoute> get routes => [
       AutoRoute(path: '/', initial: true, page: MainRoute.page,
   children: [
         AutoRoute(path: 'home', page: HomeRoute.page),
         AutoRoute(path: 'Genre', page: GenreRoute.page),
         AutoRoute(path: 'favorites', page: FavoriteRoute.page),
       ]),

     ];
   }
   ```

The part declaration will be the file generated by **AutoRoute**. The **@ AutoRouterConfig()** annotation tells the generator to create the **_$AppRouter** class. The routes getter returns one top-level route named **MainRoute** with three children of **HomeRoute**, **GenreRoute,** and **FavoriteRoute**.

4. To generate the route page classes, we need to add some annotations to those classes. First, open **home_screen.dart** and add the following before the class definition:

```
@RoutePage(name: 'HomeRoute')
```

You will need to import the **auto_route** package for this. For **genre_screen.dart** add:

```
@RoutePage(name: 'GenreRoute')
```

and for video_page.dart add:

```
@RoutePage(name: 'VideoPageRoute')
```

5. For the favorites page, create a new folder in the screens folder named **favorites**. Create a new file named **favorite_screen.dart**. Add a placeholder widget, as follows:

```
import 'package:auto_route/auto_route.dart';
import 'package:flutter/material.dart';
import 'package:flutter_riverpod/flutter_riverpod.dart';

@RoutePage(name: 'FavoriteRoute')
class FavoriteScreen extends ConsumerStatefulWidget {
  const FavoriteScreen({super.key});

  @override
  ConsumerState<FavoriteScreen> createState() => _
FavoriteScreenState();
}

class _FavoriteScreenState extends ConsumerState<FavoriteScreen> {

  @override
  Widget build(BuildContext context) {
    return const Placeholder();
  }
}
```

6. In the terminal window run the builder command:

```
dart run build_runner build
```

This will generate all the routes for each page.

7. Open up **main.dart** and replace the **build** method with:

```
    @override
  Widget build(BuildContext context) {
// 1
    return AutoTabsScaffold(
```

```
          backgroundColor: screenBackground,
// 2
      routes: [
        HomeRoute(),
        GenreRoute(),
        FavoriteRoute(),
      ],
      bottomNavigationBuilder: (_, tabsRouter) =>
buildBottomBar(tabsRouter),
    );
  }

  Widget buildBottomBar(TabsRouter tabsRouter) {
// 3
    return NavigationBar(
      destinations: const [
        NavigationDestination(icon: Icon(Icons.home), label:
'Home'),
        NavigationDestination(icon: Icon(Symbols.genres), label:
'Genre'),
        NavigationDestination(icon: Icon(Icons.favorite), label:
'Favorites'),
      ],
// 4
      selectedIndex: tabsRouter.activeIndex,
      onDestinationSelected: (navIndex) {
        setState(() {
// 5
          tabsRouter.setActiveIndex(navIndex);
        });
      },
    );
  }
```

8. Instead of a regular Scaffold, this code uses the **AutoTabsScaffold** widget from the **AutoRoute** package. This has a routes parameter that lists the three routes we created earlier. The steps are as follows:

   a. Use the **AutoTabsScaffold** to create a Scaffold that handles routes.

   b. Return the list of routes.

   c. Return the **NavigationBar**.

   d. Use the tabsRouter's **activeIndex** field for the index.

   e. Set the **tabsRouter** active index.

9. Now that we have the router built, we need a way to provide the router to other pages. We need a Riverpod provider. Open up **providers.dart** and add the following:

```
import package:movies/router/app_routes.dart';
@Riverpod(keepAlive: true)
AppRouter appRouter(AppRouterRef ref) => AppRouter();
```

10. In the terminal window, run the builder command:

```
dart run build_runner build
```

This will generate the provider for the **AppRouter**.

11. Open up **main.dart** and replace **MainApp** with:

```
class MainApp extends ConsumerStatefulWidget {
  const MainApp({super.key});

  @override
  ConsumerState<MainApp> createState() => _MainAppState();
}

class _MainAppState extends ConsumerState<MainApp> {

  @override
  Widget build(BuildContext context) {
// 1
    final router = ref.watch(appRouterProvider);
// 2
    return MaterialApp.router(
// 3
      routerConfig: router.config(),
      title: 'Movies',
      debugShowCheckedModeBanner: false,
      theme: createTheme(),
    );

  }
}
```

Here, we convert **MainApp** to a **ConsumerStatefulWidget** (From Riverpod) so that we can have access to a ref class.

12. Then, follow these steps:

   a. Watch the **appRouterProvider**. This gives us access to our **AutoRoute** router.

   b. Use **MaterialApp.router** to provide a **routerConfig**.

   c.   The class that was built has a **config** method that will return a **RouterConfig** instance.

13.  Stop the app and restart. The app should look the same. Now, we are setup to add more pages and navigate back and forth.

# Connecting the movie app

So far you have not done any navigation other than going from one bottom navigation item to another. We have not built the other pages because there was no easy way to get to them. We will now build the movie details page. This page will show the details of a specific movie. It will show a large poster image, title, description, a row of icons, trailers, and the cast members. Here is the Figma design:

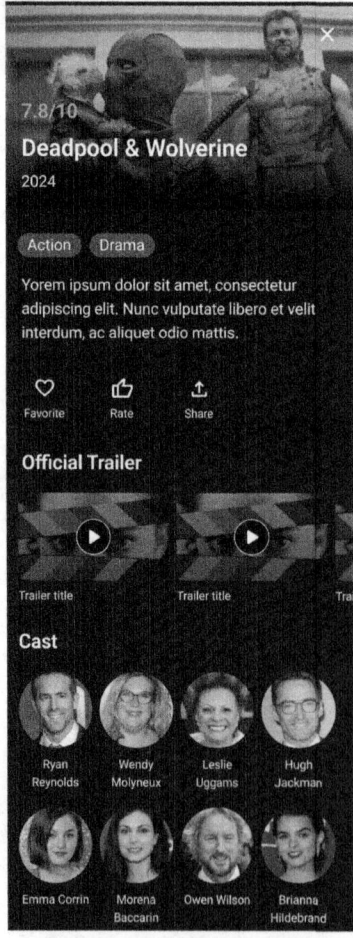

*Figure 8.12: Detailed design*

As you can see, this screen can be built from top to bottom. The steps are as follows:

1.  In the **ui/screens** folder, create a new folder named **movie_detail**. Inside this folder, create a **movie_detail.dart** file. Add the **MovieDetail** class:

```
import 'package:auto_route/auto_route.dart';
import 'package:flutter/material.dart';
import 'package:flutter_riverpod/flutter_riverpod.dart';

import ' package:movies/ui/theme/theme.dart';

@RoutePage(name: 'MovieDetailRoute')
class MovieDetail extends ConsumerStatefulWidget {
  final int movieId;

  const MovieDetail(this.movieId, {super.key});

  @override
  ConsumerState<MovieDetail> createState() => _MovieDetailState();
}

class _MovieDetailState extends ConsumerState<MovieDetail> {
  @override
  Widget build(BuildContext context) {
    // TODO Add Layout
  }
}
```

This defines the **MovieDetail** class to take a **movieId** as a parameter. At this point, the movie id will not be used until we get real data.

2.  We will hard-code a detail image for now. Add the **Scaffold** and **AppBar**:

```
return SafeArea(
    child: Scaffold(
      appBar: AppBar(
        backgroundColor: screenBackground,
        leading: BackButton(
          color: Colors.white,
          onPressed: () {
            context.router.maybePopTop();
          },
        ),
        centerTitle: false,
        title:
            Text('Back', style: Theme.of(context).textTheme.
headlineMedium),
```

```
        ),
      body: Container(
        color: screenBackground,
        child: Column(mainAxisSize: MainAxisSize.min, children: [
// TODO Add widgets
]),
      ),
    ),
  );
```

This will just have a back button and a **Column** for now.

3. Notice the BackButton's **onPressed** method. This calls for the following:

```
context.router.maybePopTop();
```

This will pop this screen off the stack and return to the calling page.

4. Return to **app_routes.dart** and add the following at the end of the list:

```
    AutoRoute(path:'/details/:movieId', page: MovieDetailRoute.page,
maintainState: false),
```

This provides the route as well as a path that can be used for deep linking.

5. In the terminal, run the following:

```
dart run build_runner build
```

This will build the route for the **MovieDetails** page.

6. Now we need to update a few files. Open up **utils.dart** and add:

```
typedef OnMovieTap = void Function(int movieId);
```

This defines a function that will return a movie ID when something is tapped.

7. Open **home_screen_image.dart** and add the following before the **build** method:

```
  final OnMovieTap onMovieTap;

  HomeScreenImage({super.key, required this.onMovieTap});
```

This constructor takes a **onMovieTap** field that we defined earlier.

8. To use this method, we need to surround the image with a **GestureDetector**. Wrap **CachedNetworkImage** with the following:

```
      return GestureDetector(
        onTap: () {
          onMovieTap(1);
        },
```

9. Back in **HomeScreen**, change the **HomeScreenImage** line with:

```
HomeScreenImage(onMovieTap: (id) {
   context.router.push(MovieDetailRoute(movieId: id));
}),
```

This adds the **onMovieTap** field.

10. AutoRoute adds an extension to the **BuildContext** class where you can access the router and push a new route. Here, we are pushing the **MovieDetailRoute** with the movie id. The **AutoRoute** generated code will use this route to push the **MovieDetail** screen on the stack. Perform a Hot Restart, then click on the top image. The screen will be as follows:

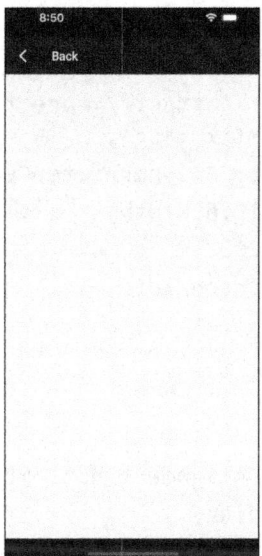

*Figure 8.13*: Detail one

This just shows the AppBar with the back button and an empty screen for now.

11. The first widget we will need to create is the detail image. Inside of the **movie_detail** folder create a new file named **detail_image.dart**. Add:

```
import 'package:flutter/material.dart';

class DetailImage extends StatelessWidget {
  const DetailImage({super.key});

  @override
  Widget build(BuildContext context) {
    return const Placeholder();
  }
}
```

12. Now, replace the placeholder with:

```
// 1
    final screenWidth = MediaQuery.of(context).size.width;
    return Padding(
      padding: const EdgeInsets.only(left: 8.0, right: 8),
      child: SizedBox(
        height: 200,
// 2
        child: Stack(children: [
          Align(
            alignment: Alignment.topCenter,
// 3
            child: CachedNetworkImage(
              imageUrl: 'https://image.tmdb.org/t/p/w780/
d5NXSklXo0qyIYkgV94XAgMIckC.jpg',
              alignment: Alignment.topCenter,
              fit: BoxFit.fitWidth,
              height: 200,
              width: screenWidth,
            ),
          ),
// 4
          Align(
            alignment: Alignment.bottomLeft,
            child: Padding(
              padding: const EdgeInsets.only(left: 24.0, bottom: 8),
              child: Column(
                mainAxisSize: MainAxisSize.min,
                mainAxisAlignment: MainAxisAlignment.start,
                crossAxisAlignment: CrossAxisAlignment.start,
                children: [
                  Text(
                    'Dune',
                    style: Theme.of(context).textTheme.
headlineLarge,
                  ),
                  addVerticalSpace(4),
                  Text(
                    '2024',
                    style: Theme.of(context).textTheme.bodyMedium,
```

```
                        ),
                  ],
                ),
              ),
            )
        ]),
      ),
  );
```

Here, we are using a **Stack** widget to show an image and overlay that with the title and year. We use the **Align** widget to position the image at the top center and the text in the bottom left of the 200 high box. A detailed explanation of key lines are as follows:

1. Use **MediaQuery** to get the width of the screen.

2. Use the **Stack** widget to wrap all of the widgets in the list on top of each other.

3. Show a hard-coded detail image.

4. Use the **Align** widget to position the text in the bottom left corner.

13. Back in **MovieDetail**, replace all the code below the **children: [** with:

```
              children: [
                Expanded(
                  child: CustomScrollView(slivers: [
                    SliverList(
                      delegate: SliverChildListDelegate([
                        Stack(children: [DetailImage()]),
                      ]),
                    ),
                  ]),
                )
              ],
            ),
          ),
        ),
  );
```

This wraps a **CustomScrollView** with an **Expanded** and uses a **SliverList**.

14. Right now, the stack just has our **DetailImage** widget. Hot restart.

You should see the following:

*Figure 8.14*: *Detail two*

15. The next row will be the genre chips. Since we wrote the genre screen earlier, we have a list of genres we can use. Open up **providers.dart** and **add**:

```
@riverpod
List<GenreState> genres(GenresRef ref) =>  [
  GenreState(genre: 'Action', isSelected: false),
  GenreState(genre: 'Adventure', isSelected: false),
  GenreState(genre: 'Crime', isSelected: false),
  GenreState(genre: 'Mystery', isSelected: false),
  GenreState(genre: 'War', isSelected: false),
  GenreState(genre: 'Comedy', isSelected: false),
  GenreState(genre: 'Romance', isSelected: false),
  GenreState(genre: 'History', isSelected: false),
  GenreState(genre: 'Music', isSelected: false),
  GenreState(genre: 'Drama', isSelected: false),
  GenreState(genre: 'Thriller', isSelected: false),
  GenreState(genre: 'Family', isSelected: false),
  GenreState(genre: 'Horror', isSelected: false),
  GenreState(genre: 'Western', isSelected: false),
  GenreState(genre: 'Science Fiction', isSelected: false),
  GenreState(genre: 'Animation', isSelected: false),
  GenreState(genre: 'Documentation', isSelected: false),
```

```
    GenreState(genre: 'TV Movie', isSelected: false),
    GenreState(genre: 'Fantasy', isSelected: false),
  ];
```

This will add a provider for genres.

16. In the terminal window run the builder command:

```
dart run build_runner build
```

17. Open up **genre_screen.dart** and remove the **initState** method and the genres list. Then in the build method after the images variable add:

```
final genres = ref.read(genresProvider);
```

18. Import the **providers.dart** file. In the **move_detail** folder create a new file **genre_row.dart**. This will show a list of genres for a particular movie. Add a simple **StatelessWidget** for showing a list of genres:

```
import 'package:flutter/material.dart';

import 'package:movies/ui/theme/theme.dart';
import 'package:movies/ui/genres/genre_section.dart';

class GenreRow extends StatelessWidget {
  final List<GenreState> genres;

  const GenreRow({super.key, required this.genres});

  @override
  Widget build(BuildContext context) {
    return Padding(
      padding: const EdgeInsets.only(left: 16.0, top: 24, bottom:
16),
      child: SizedBox(
        height: 34,
// 1
        child: ListView(
          scrollDirection: Axis.horizontal,
// 2
          children: genres
              .map((genre) => Container(
            margin: const EdgeInsets.only(right: 8),
            padding:
            const EdgeInsets.symmetric(horizontal: 8, vertical: 4),
// 3
            decoration: BoxDecoration(
```

```
              color: buttonGrey,
              borderRadius: BorderRadius.circular(12),
            ),
// 4
            child: Text(
              genre.genre,
              style: Theme.of(context)
                  .textTheme
                  .bodyLarge
                  ?.copyWith(color: Colors.white),
            ),
          ))
            .toList(),
        ),
      ),
    );
  }
}
```

This widget shows a horizontal list of grey-colored rectangles with the genre name inside. The description of key lines are as follows:

a.   A horizontal list.

b.   Use the **map** function of a list to generate a list of widgets (Note that you need to follow the map function with a **toList()** call or it will not work).

c.   Draw a grey rounded background.

d.   Display the genre name.

19.  Back in **movie_detail.dart**, add the provider for genres at the beginning of the build method:

```
final genres = ref.read(genresProvider);
```

20.  Import the **providers.dart** file. Then add the **GenreRow** class after the Stack:

```
GenreRow(genres: genres),
```

Here is what the screen looks like (*Figure 8.15*):

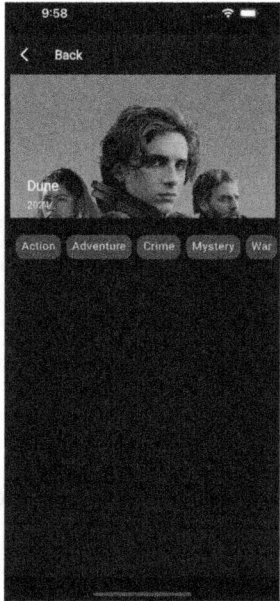

*Figure 8.15: Detail three*

While this shows all genres, we will change this once we have real data. The next row is the movie description.

21. Create a new file called **movie_overview.dart** in the **movie_detail** folder. Add the following:

```
import 'package:flutter/material.dart';

import 'package:movies/ui/theme/theme.dart';

class MovieOverview extends StatelessWidget {
  final String details;

  const MovieOverview({super.key, required this.details});

  @override
  Widget build(BuildContext context) {
    return Padding(
      padding: const EdgeInsets.fromLTRB(16, 0, 16, 24),
      child: Text(
        details,
        style: body1Regular,
      ),
    );
  }
}
```

This just shows a **Text** description. While we could have put this in the **detail** class, creating another class will make the overall readability of the class much better.

22. Add the **MovieOverview** class below **GenreRow** in **MovieDetails** with:

```
MovieOverview(details: 'Follow the mythic journey of Paul Atreides
as he unites with Chani and the Fremen while on a path of revenge
against the conspirators who destroyed his family. Facing a choice
between the love of his life and the fate of the known universe,
Paul endeavors to prevent a terrible future only he can foresee.'),
```

Your screen should now look as follows:

*Figure 8.16: Detail four*

23. The next row is the favorites row. For this app, we will only be implementing the favorite button and will give you the chance to implement the rate and share buttons on your own. Next, create a new file named **text_icon.dart** in the **ui/ widgets** folder. This widget will just show an **IconButton** and text below it. We will reuse this widget in several places, so it makes sense to add it to the **widgets** folder. Add the following code:

```
import 'package:flutter/material.dart';

import 'package:movies/utils/utils.dart';

class TextIcon extends StatelessWidget {
  final Text text;
```

```
    final IconButton icon;
    const TextIcon({super.key, required this.text, required this.
icon});

    @override
    Widget build(BuildContext context) {
      return Column(
        mainAxisSize: MainAxisSize.min,
        children: [
          icon,
          addVerticalSpace(4),
          text,
        ],
      )
      ;
    }
  }
}
```

This just uses a **Column** to show an **Icon** and **Text** widget.

24. Next, create a new file named **button_row.dart** in the **movie_detail** folder. Add:

```
import 'package:flutter/material.dart';

import 'package:movies/utils/utils.dart';
import 'package:movies/ui/widgets/text_icon.dart';

typedef OnFavoriteSelected = void Function();

class ButtonRow extends StatelessWidget {
  final bool favoriteSelected;
  final OnFavoriteSelected onFavoriteSelected;

  const ButtonRow({
    super.key,
    required this.favoriteSelected,
    required this.onFavoriteSelected,
  });

  @override
  Widget build(BuildContext context) {
    // TODO Add Row
  }
}
```

This will be a **Row** of three buttons.

25. Next, add the **Row**:

```
    return Padding(
      padding: const EdgeInsets.only(left: 16.0, top: 0, bottom:
32),
      child: Row(
        mainAxisAlignment: MainAxisAlignment.start,
        mainAxisSize: MainAxisSize.max,
        children: [
// 1
          TextIcon(
            text: Text(
              'Favorite',
              style: Theme.of(context).textTheme.labelSmall,
            ),
// 2
            icon: IconButton(
              onPressed: () {
                onFavoriteSelected();
              },
// 3
              icon: Icon(
                favoriteSelected ? Icons.favorite_outlined : Icons.
favorite_border,
                color: favoriteSelected ? Colors.red : Colors.white,
              ),
            ),
          ),
          addHorizontalSpace(32),
          TextIcon(
            text: Text(
              'Rate',
              style: Theme.of(context).textTheme.labelSmall,
            ),
            // TODO For you to implement
            icon: IconButton(
              onPressed: () {},
              icon: const Icon(
                Icons.thumb_up_alt_outlined,
                color: Colors.white,
              ),
            ),
```

```
          ),
          addHorizontalSpace(32),
          TextIcon(
            text: Text(
              'Share',
              style: Theme.of(context).textTheme.labelSmall,
            ),
            // TODO For you to implement
            icon: IconButton(
              onPressed: () {},
              icon: const Icon(
                Icons.ios_share,
                color: Colors.white,
              ),
            ),
          ),
        ],
      ),
    );
```

The last two icons have been left for you to implement. In this code, we performed the following functions:

    a.   Used the **TextIcon** widget for the favorite widget.

    b.   When the user selects the icon, call the **onFavoriteSelected** callback.

    c.   Show a different favorite icon depending on if it is selected.

26.  Back in **MovieDetail**, add a notifier as the first line in the **build** method for when the user selects the favorite icon:

```
final favoriteNotifier = ValueNotifier<bool>(false);
```

This is a widget that will rebuild just its child when the value changes.

27.  After the **MovieOverview** widget add the following code:

```
                ValueListenableBuilder<bool>(
                  valueListenable: favoriteNotifier,
                  builder:
                      (BuildContext context, bool value, Widget?
child) {
                    return ButtonRow(
                      favoriteSelected: favoriteNotifier.value,
                      onFavoriteSelected: () async {
                        if (favoriteNotifier.value) {
                          favoriteNotifier.value = false;
```

```
            } else {
              favoriteNotifier.value = true;
            }
          },
        );
      },
    ),
```

This listens for changes to the notifier, which is set in the **onFavoriteSelected** method. Hot reload and test the favorite button. Clicking on it should turn it red, as shown in *Figure 8.17*:

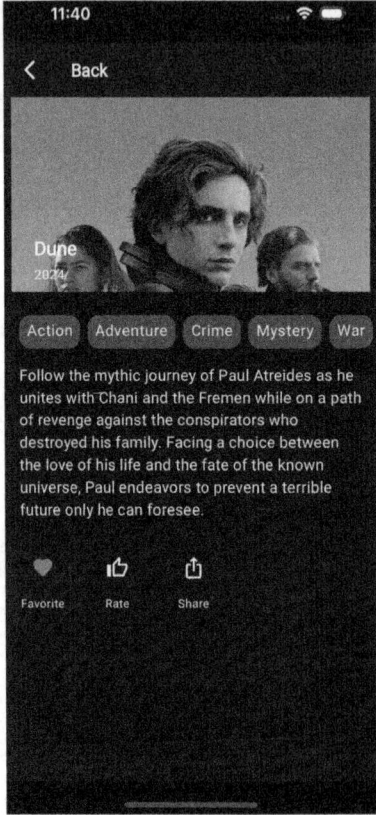

*Figure 8.17*: *Detail five*

28. The next section is the trailer section. This will show a horizontal list of movie trailers for the current movie. Open the **utls.dart** file and add:

```
typedef OnMovieVideoTap = void Function(String video);
```

This will be a callback function with the string of the video.

29. In the **movie_detail** folder create a new file named **trailer.dart**. Add:

```dart
import 'package:auto_size_text/auto_size_text.dart';
import 'package:cached_network_image/cached_network_image.dart';
import 'package:flutter/material.dart';
import 'package:flutter_riverpod/flutter_riverpod.dart';

import 'package:movies/utils/utils.dart';

class Trailer extends ConsumerStatefulWidget {
  final List<String>? movieVideos;
  final OnMovieVideoTap onVideoTap;

  const Trailer({this.movieVideos, required this.onVideoTap, super.
key});

  @override
  ConsumerState<Trailer> createState() => _TrailerState();
}

class _TrailerState extends ConsumerState<Trailer> {
  @override
  Widget build(BuildContext context) {
// TODO Add widgets
  }
}
```

30. Next, add the widgets at the TODO. The code is as follows:

```dart
// 1
    if (widget.movieVideos == null) {
      return Container();
    }
    return Padding(
      padding: const EdgeInsets.only(left: 16.0, right: 16),
// 2
      child: SizedBox(
        height: 120,
// 3
        child: ListView.builder(
          itemExtent: 166,
          scrollDirection: Axis.horizontal,
          // Ensure horizontal scrolling within the list
          itemCount: widget.movieVideos!.length,
          itemBuilder: (context, index) {
            final movieVideo = widget.movieVideos![index];
```

```
// 4
              return GestureDetector(
                onTap: () {
                  widget.onVideoTap(movieVideo);
                },
                child: Padding(
                  padding: const EdgeInsets.only(left: 4.0, right:
4.0),
                    child: SizedBox(
                      width: 166,
                      child: Column(
                        mainAxisAlignment: MainAxisAlignment.start,
                        crossAxisAlignment: CrossAxisAlignment.start,
                        mainAxisSize: MainAxisSize.min,
                        children: [
// 5
                          CachedNetworkImage(
                            httpHeaders: const {'Access-Control-Allow-
Origin': '*'},
                            imageUrl: movieVideo,
                            alignment: Alignment.topLeft,
                            // fit: BoxFit.fitWidth,
                            fit: BoxFit.fitHeight,
                            height: 98,
                            // width: 200,
                            // width: 142,
                          ),
// 6
                          AutoSizeText(
                            'Dune',
                            style: Theme.of(context).textTheme.
labelSmall,
                            maxLines: 1,
                            minFontSize: 10,
                            overflow: TextOverflow.ellipsis,
                          ),
                        ],
                      ),
                    ),
                  ),
```

```
        );
      },
    ),
  ),
);
```

This will display a horizontal list of trailer movies. Here is a description of the code:

  a.  First, check to make sure there were videos passed in. It is possible for some movies to not have trailers. A Container is used for an empty widget.

  b.  Make sure the height is fixed at 120 pixels.

  c.  Use a **ListView.builder** method where each item is 166 pixels high.

  d.  Use a **GestureDetector** to send the video to the callback.

  e.  Show the thumbnail image. The httpHeaders are to allow this to work on the web.

  f.  Show the text of the trailer below the image. This will contain real data in later chapters.

31. Back in **MovieDetails**, add the **Trailer** class below the favorite row:

```
Padding(
    padding: const EdgeInsets.only(
        left: 16, bottom: 8),
    child: Text('Trailers', style: Theme.
of(context).textTheme.headlineLarge),
    ),
    Trailer(
        movieVideos: ['https://img.youtube.com/vi/
U2Qp5pL3ovA/hqdefault.jpg'],
        onVideoTap: (video) {
            context.router
                .push(VideoPageRoute(movieVideo:
'U2Qp5pL3ovA'));                     },
    ),
```

After some padding, and the Trailers text, we hard-code the thumbnail image and the video URL for now. Hot restart. The detail screen now looks as follows:

*Figure 8.18: Detail six*

Click on the trailer and you should be taken to the video. You can change the orientation to display the video better. Click on the back arrow to return.

32. The last element is the cast list. This will be a grid with the avatars of each cast member. In the **widgets** folder, create a new file named **cast_image.dart**. Add:

```dart
import 'package:cached_network_image/cached_network_image.dart';
import 'package:flutter/material.dart';

import 'package:movies/utils/utils.dart';
import 'package:movies/ui/theme/theme.dart';
import 'package:auto_size_text/auto_size_text.dart';

class CastImage extends StatelessWidget {
  final String imageUrl;
  final String name;
  const CastImage({super.key, required this.imageUrl, required this.name});

  @override
  Widget build(BuildContext context) {
    // TODO Add widgets
  }
  // TODO Add getAvatar
}
```

This widget will take a URL for the image of the cast member and a name.

33. Now add the **getAvatar** method below the build method:

```
Widget getAvatar() {
    if (imageUrl.isNotEmpty) {
      return CircleAvatar(
          backgroundImage: CachedNetworkImageProvider(
            imageUrl,
            maxHeight: 76,
            maxWidth: 76,
          ));
    } else {
      return const CircleAvatar(
          backgroundColor: buttonGrey,
          child: Icon(Icons.person, size: 76.0, color: Colors.
black,));
    }
  }
```

This method uses a Flutter **CircularAvatar** widget to show an image in a circular shape. If there is no URL, show a grey circle.

34. Next, fill in the **build** method:

```
    return Column(
      mainAxisSize: MainAxisSize.min,
      crossAxisAlignment: CrossAxisAlignment.center,
      mainAxisAlignment: MainAxisAlignment.center,
      children: [
        SizedBox(
          width: 76,
          height: 78,
          child: getAvatar(),
        ),
        addVerticalSpace( 4),
        Align(
          alignment: Alignment.center,
          child: AutoSizeText(
            name,
            style: Theme.of(context).textTheme.labelSmall,
            maxLines: 1,
            overflow: TextOverflow.ellipsis,
          ),
```

```
      ),
    ],
  );
```

This is just a column with the avatar and the name below that.

35. Now that we have the widget for the image, we need a widget to show a grid of widgets. Create a new file in the **widgets** folder named **horiz_cast.dart**. Add:

```dart
import 'package:flutter/material.dart';
import 'package:flutter_riverpod/flutter_riverpod.dart';

import 'package:movies/ui/widgets/cast_image.dart';

class HorizontalCast extends ConsumerWidget {
  final List<String> castList;

  const HorizontalCast({required this.castList, super.key});

  @override
  Widget build(BuildContext context, WidgetRef ref) {
    return SliverPadding(
      padding: const EdgeInsets.only(left: 16.0, right: 16),
      sliver: SliverGrid(
        gridDelegate: const SliverGridDelegateWithMaxCrossAxisExtent(
            maxCrossAxisExtent: 100.0,
            mainAxisSpacing: 16,
            crossAxisSpacing: 16,
            mainAxisExtent: 100.0),
        delegate: SliverChildBuilderDelegate(((BuildContext context,
int index) {
          return CastImage(imageUrl: 'http://image.tmdb.org/t/p/
w780/BE2sdjpgsa2rNTFa66f7upkaOP.jpg', name: 'Timothée Chalamet');
        }, childCount: castList.length),
      ),
    );
  }
}
```

This widget uses a few slivers: **SliverPadding** and **SliverGrid**. It then returns the **CastImage** widget we created earlier with a hard-coded URL and name. We are hard-coding the main actor for now.

36. Back in **MovieDetails**, add the **HorizontalCast** widget after the **SliverList**. This is important: If you add it in the **SliverChildListDelegate** list it will not work. Add the following:

```dart
                    HorizontalCast(castList: ['', '']),
```

This will show two of the same cast members. Again, once we get real data, we will show all the cast members.

# DeepLink testing

Now that we have the details page finished, we need to test deep linking.

## Android

Open up **app/src/main/AndroidManifest.xml**. Here is the following code:

```
<intent-filter>
    <action android:name=»android.intent.action.MAIN»/>
    <category android:name="android.intent.category.LAUNCHER"/>
</intent-filter>
```

Add the following:

```
<meta-data
    android:name="flutter_deeplinking_enabled"
    android:value="true" />

<intent-filter android:autoVerify="true">
    <action android:name="android.intent.action.VIEW" />
    <category android:name="android.intent.category.DEFAULT" />
    <category android:name="android.intent.category.BROWSABLE"
/>

    <data android:scheme="movieapp" android:host="bpb.com"/>
</intent-filter>
```

This will add a custom scheme of **movieapp** to the Android app. Stop and rerun the Android app.

From the terminal, type the following:

```
adb shell 'am start -a android.intent.action.VIEW \
  -c android.intent.category.BROWSABLE \
  -d "movieapp://bpb.com/details/1"' \
com.bpb.movies/.MainActivity
```

This will send a message to the app to deal with the custom scheme **movieapp** and go to the **details** page.

## iOS

For iOS, make sure you follow the instructions above to add the associated domains and the custom scheme to the **info.plist**. Then in a terminal type:

```
xcrun simctl openurl booted 'movieapps://bpb.com/details/1
```

You will be able to see the details page.

# Conclusion

In this chapter, you learned about navigation and how to use it with just the Flutter widgets and with third-party packages. You now have the ability to navigate from page to page and control what the user sees. You built up the Movie detail page with lots of widgets to display different parts of the screen.

In the next chapter, you will learn about animations and transitions. You will learn about implicit and explicit animations as well as Hero animations and add page transitions to each page.

## Join our book's Discord space

Join the book's Discord Workspace for Latest updates, Offers, Tech happenings around the world, New Release and Sessions with the Authors:

**https://discord.bpbonline.com**

# CHAPTER 9

# Animations and Transitions

## Introduction

In this chapter, you will learn all about the built-in animations that Flutter provides, as well as some third-party packages for handling transitions and animations. You will start out with some of the easier pre-built animation widgets and then customize your own. Finally, you will build some amazing animations for the movie app.

## Structure

The chapter covers the following topics:

- Basic animation concepts
- Advanced animation techniques
- Animation widgets
- Custom animations
- Animation libraries and tools
- Movie app

# Objectives

By the end of this chapter, you will have a solid understanding for how animations work in Flutter. You will be able to build you own animations as well as create custom animations. You will understand how to create animations and where to put them. You will learn about third-party packages for animations. Your movie app will look great as you move from page to page.

# Basic animation concepts

Animations in Flutter are made up of a few different types of animations, including drawing-based, which uses graphics, and code-based, which focuses on widget layouts and styles. For code-based animations, there are two different types: implicit and explicit. Implicit animations are just animations that change the values of another widget, while explicit use an animation controller to **explicitly** tell it when and how to run.

# Implicit animations

Implicit animations give you less control than explicit animations but are easier to use. These widgets are of the type: **AnimatedXXXX**, where **XXX** could be a Container, opacity, positioning, padding, or any other attribute of a widget. All of these classes extend the **ImplicitlyAnimatedWidget** class. If Flutter does not have one already made for you, you can create your own. A very simple instance of an **AnimatedContainer** looks as follows:

```
AnimatedContainer(
    duration: const Duration(milliseconds: 2000),
    curve: Curves.easeInOut,
    decoration: BoxDecoration(
        color: selected ? Colors.blue : Colors.red,
        border: Border.all(
            color: Colors.black,
            width: 2,
        ),
    ),
    child: Container(),
),
```

There are two required parameters: duration, which defines how long the animation will run and the child, which will be the widget that is animated. This will show up as either a blue or red square that animates to the other color (*Figure 9.1*). Not shown is the **onTap** method that changes the selected value, causing the animation to start. It has a two-second duration and uses an easeInOut curve (explained as follows):

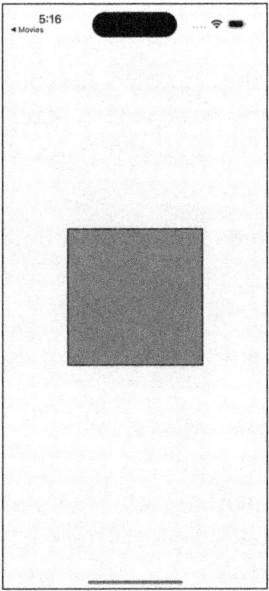

***Figure 9.1***: *AnimatedContainer*

Besides the color, you can animate the other properties of a container, like width and height. There are many more animated widgets. The following are a few examples:

- AnimatedAlign
- AnimatedOpacity
- AnimatedPadding
- AnimatedPositioned
- AnimatedSize
- AnimatedScale
- AnimatedRotation
- AnimatedSlide
- AnimatedIcon
- AnimatedCrossFade
- AnimatedSwitcher

These widgets modify their respective properties to change the underlying widget. Opacity will cause the widget to fade in and out. **AnimatedPositioned** is just like its **Positioned** widget and can only work inside of a **Stack** and move the widget inside of the Stack. Size and Scale animate the change in the size and scale of a widget. If you need to just perform one type of animation, then these widgets are a great solution. For more complex animations, you will need to use an implicit animation.

# Tween animations

If you cannot find an animation that does what you need and you want to change a property of a widget, you can use the **TweenAnimationBuilder** This widget uses a **Tween** class (like *in-between*) that has **begin** and **end** parameters for going from one property value to another.

The following is a **TweenAnimationBuilder** that animates the colors of a square:

```
TweenAnimationBuilder<Color?>(
          duration: const Duration(milliseconds: 2000),
          tween: ColorTween(begin: const Color(0xFF0D47A1), end: const
Color(0xFFB71C1C)),
          curve: Curves.easeInOut,
          builder: (context, value, child) {
            return Container(
              decoration: BoxDecoration(
                color: value,
                border: Border.all(
                  color: Colors.black,
                  width: 2,
                ),
              ),
            );
          },
        ),
```

This is similar to the previous example. Note that to use a **ColorTween**, we had to specify a nullable Color for the builder type. Another type of builder is with a double value that translates (or moves) a square across the screen. The code is as follows:

```
TweenAnimationBuilder<double>(
      duration: const Duration(milliseconds: 2000),
      tween: Tween(begin: 0.0, end: 1.0),
      child: Container(
        width: 120,
        height: 120,
        color: Theme.of(context).primaryColor,
      ),
      builder: (context, value, child) {
        return Transform.translate(
          offset: Offset(value * 200 - 100, 0),
          //angle: 0.5 * pi * value,
          child: child,
```

```
      );
    },
  ),
```

This just moves the square from the left side of the screen to the right side of the screen. If you use the child passed in the builder, you will improve performance as that entire widget tree does not have to be rebuilt each time.

# Advanced animation techniques

If you need to do more than the basics, you need to learn more advanced animation techniques. We will cover explicit animations, specifically the animation controller. These animations are a bit more complex but allow you to create amazing movement in your app.

# Explicit animations

Explicit animations give you more control over your animations but are a bit more complex. Explicit animations are named that way because you, or the user, tell it when to start and stop using an animation controller. If you want to handle multiple animations at the same time, you will need an animation controller.

# AnimationController

An **AnimationController** is a class that controls the progression of animations. It does this by producing a beginning and ending set of values for the duration of the animation. So, the longer the duration, the smaller the incremental values between the begin and ending values. The controller can also stop, forward, and reverse an animation. In order to use an **AnimationController**, you need to provide a **Ticker**. This ticker handles notifying listeners of new values on every frame. There are several mixins that provide this functionality and can be attached to a State class. There are two key mixins:

- **SingleTickerProviderStateMixin**: For a single controller.

- **TickerProviderStateMixin**: For multiple controllers.

We will be adding both an animation controller and the mixin to several classes to enable explicit animations. We will also need to change some classes to Riverpod classes to access movie information. To make the changes, make the following changes:

1.  Open **detail_image.dart**. Currently, the detail page has a hard-coded image. We will change that so that it will display the image passed in. In order to do that, we will need to change the class from a stateless widget to a stateful widget. Of course, we will use Riverpod's version: **ConsumerStatefulWidget**. Change the first two lines of the class to:

```
class DetailImage extends ConsumerStatefulWidget {
  final String movieUrl;
  DetailImage({required this.movieUrl, super.key});

  @override
  ConsumerState<DetailImage> createState() => _DetailImageState();
}

class _DetailImageState extends ConsumerState<DetailImage> with
SingleTickerProviderStateMixin {
```

2. Import the Riverpod package. Just add them **with SingleTickerProviderStateMixin,** and that functionality is automatically added. Next, change the hard-coded image URL to:

```
widget.movieUrl
```

3. Now that the **DetailImage** class is updated, open **movie_detail.dart** and make the following changes. As the first line in the build method add:

```
final movies = ref.read(movieImagesProvider);
```

4. Here we get the list of movies. Then change **DetailImage** line to:

```
Stack(children: [DetailImage(movieUrl: movies[widget.movieId])]),
```

5. To create an **AnimationController** you need to provide a duration and a **TickerProvider**. Now add the controller next:

```
late final AnimationController _controller = AnimationController(
  duration: const Duration(seconds: 2),
  vsync: this,
);
```

6. Here, **vsync** is for the **TicketProvider** and this refers to the **State** class with the mixin provided above. Add this as the first line in the **_DetailImageState** class. Just as you need to dispose of a **TextEditingController**, you need to dispose of an animation controller. Add the following to the state class:

```
@override
void initState() {
  super.initState();
  _controller.forward();
}

@override
void dispose() {
  _controller.dispose();
  super.dispose();
}
```

The forward method starts the controller, then when the widget is disposed of, dispose of the controller.

# Animation

Now, a controller by itself does not do anything. We need an animation. An animation is a very simple class that extends Listenable (used to notify listeners of changes), and has a status (dismissed, forward, reverse, or completed), and a value. Below the controller add the following:

```
late final Animation<double> _animation = CurvedAnimation(
  parent: _controller,
  curve: Curves.easeIn,
);
```

This is a curved animation. It just applies a curve to the animation and uses the controller we created above. Another way to create this animation is with the controller's **drive** method. For example:

```
late final Animation<double> _animation = _controller.
drive(CurveTween(curve: Curves.easeIn));
```

What we want is for the detail image to fade in when the detail page shows. To do that, we are going to use a **FadeTransition** widget. This animates the opacity of the widget (that is, fade). This widget requires a value for opacity and for that, we will use the animation we just created. What this does is that every time the controller changes its value, it will update the **FadeTransition** opacity and will slowly fade the image in. Now wrap the **CachedNetworkImage** with the following code:

```
FadeTransition(
         opacity: _animation,
```

Open up **home_screen_image.dart** and change the **onMovieTap** call to:

```
         onMovieTap(index);
```

Do a Hot Restart and go to the **detail** page. You should see the image slowly fade in. You can change the speed of the fade by changing the duration value of the controller.

# Curves

A curve is a mathematical function that defines the rate of change of an animation over time. It determines how the animated value (for example, position, size, opacity) progresses from its starting point to its ending point. If you do not use a curve, then all animations are linear, which may not feel natural. There are many pre-built curves in Flutter. Some examples are as follows:

- **bounceIn**: Oscillating Curve that grows.
- **bounceOut**: Oscillating Curve that shrinks.

- **bounceInOut**: Oscillating Curve that first grows and then shrinks.
- **elasticIn**: Oscillating Curve that grows and then overshoots its bounds.
- **elasticOut**: Oscillating Curve that shrinks and then overshoots its bounds.
- **elasticInOut**: Oscillating Curve that shrinks and then grows while overshooting its bounds.

# AnimatedBuilder

An **AnimatedBuilder** is a general-purpose widget for building an animation. This widget listens to changes in the animation and rebuilds its widget. It has a builder method that returns the widget to animate.

Here is an example:

```
AnimatedBuilder(
        animation: _animation,
        builder: (context, child) {
          return CircularProgressIndicator(value: _animation.value);
        },
      ),
```

This will draw a circular ring that starts at the top and goes clockwise around.

# Staggered animations

Staggered animations are a series of animations controlled by one animation controller. Each animation happens one after the other or they can overlap. An example of a staggered animation is one that shows a square that transforms into a circle. The example showcases the following output screen:

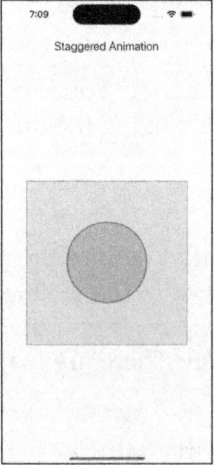

*Figure 9.2: Staggered animation*

The following is the example taken from the Flutter documentation. We will start with the definition of the class that has the animations and the controller:

```
class StaggeredAnimation extends StatefulWidget {
  const StaggeredAnimation({Key? key}) : super(key: key);

  @override
  State<StaggeredAnimation> createState() => _StaggeredAnimationState();
}

class _StaggeredAnimationState extends State<StaggeredAnimation>
    with SingleTickerProviderStateMixin {
  late AnimationController controller;
  late Animation<double> opacity;
  late Animation<double> width;
  late Animation<double> height;
  late Animation<EdgeInsets> padding;
  late Animation<BorderRadius?> borderRadius;
  late Animation<Color?> color;
}
```

Next, we initialize each of these animations:

```
  @override
  void initState() {
    super.initState();
// 1
    controller = AnimationController(
      duration: const Duration(milliseconds: 2000),
      vsync: this,
    );
// 2
    opacity = Tween<double>(
      begin: 0.0,
      end: 1.0,
    ).animate(
      CurvedAnimation(
        parent: controller,
        curve: const Interval(
          0.0,
          0.100,
          curve: Curves.ease,
        ),
      ),
    );
```

```
// 3
    width = Tween<double>(
      begin: 50.0,
      end: 150.0,
    ).animate(
      CurvedAnimation(
        parent: controller,
        curve: const Interval(
          0.125,
          0.250,
          curve: Curves.ease,
        ),
      ),
    );
// 4
    height = Tween<double>(begin: 50.0, end: 150.0).animate(
      CurvedAnimation(
        parent: controller,
        curve: const Interval(
          0.250,
          0.375,
          curve: Curves.ease,
        ),
      ),
    );
// 5
    padding = EdgeInsetsTween(
      begin: const EdgeInsets.only(bottom: 16),
      end: const EdgeInsets.only(bottom: 75),
    ).animate(
      CurvedAnimation(
        parent: controller,
        curve: const Interval(
          0.250,
          0.375,
          curve: Curves.ease,
        ),
      ),
    );
// 6
    borderRadius = BorderRadiusTween(
      begin: BorderRadius.circular(4),
```

```
      end: BorderRadius.circular(75),
    ).animate(
      CurvedAnimation(
        parent: controller,
        curve: const Interval(
          0.375,
          0.500,
          curve: Curves.ease,
        ),
      ),
    );
// 7
    color = ColorTween(
      begin: Colors.indigo[100],
      end: Colors.orange[400],
    ).animate(
      CurvedAnimation(
        parent: controller,
        curve: const Interval(
          0.500,
          0.750,
          curve: Curves.ease,
        ),
      ),
    );
  }
```

Here we have created the controller and each animation. An Interval has a beginning and end time. These are values that depend on the time of the controller. The following is a description of the steps:

1. Create an animation controller that lasts two seconds.

2. Define an opacity animation that goes from 0 to 0.10.

3. Create a width animation that goes from a width of 50 to 150 from time 0.125 to 0.250.

4. Create a height animation that goes from a height of 50 to 150 from time 0.250 to 0.375.

5. Create a padding animation that goes from a 16 to 75 from time 0.250 to 0.375.

6. Create a border animation that goes from a height of 4 to 75 from time 0.375 to 0.500.

7. Create a color animation that goes from indigo to orange from time 0.500 to 0.750.

Next is the **build** method. This has a **Scaffold** and when clicked starts the animation:

```
@override
Widget build(BuildContext context) {
  return Scaffold(
    appBar: AppBar(
      title: const Text('Staggered Animation'),
    ),
    body: GestureDetector(
      behavior: HitTestBehavior.opaque,
// 1
      onTap: () async {
        try {
          await controller.forward().orCancel;
          await controller.reverse().orCancel;
        } on TickerCanceled {
          // The animation got canceled, probably because we were
disposed.
        }
      },
      child: Center(
        child: Container(
          width: 300,
          height: 300,
          decoration: BoxDecoration(
            color: Colors.black.withOpacity(0.1),
            border: Border.all(
              color: Colors.black.withOpacity(0.5),
            ),
          ),
// 2
          child: AnimatedBuilder(
            builder: (BuildContext context, Widget? child) {
              return Container(
                padding: padding.value,
                alignment: Alignment.bottomCenter,
                child: Opacity(
                  opacity: opacity.value,
                  child: Container(
                    width: width.value,
                    height: height.value,
                    decoration: BoxDecoration(
                      color: color.value,
```

```
                    border: Border.all(
                      color: Colors.indigo[300]!,
                      width: 3,
                    ),
                    borderRadius: borderRadius.value,
                  ),
                ),
              ),
            );
          },
          animation: controller,
        ),
      ),
    ),
  );
}
```

The **AnimationBuider** returns a Container with several of the properties that we are changing in the animations. The animation starts when the container is clicked. The following is a description of the steps:

1. Make the **onTap** asynchronous so that the controller can start and then go backward.

2. Use the **AnimationBuider** to return the **Container** with all of the different animation values.

# Animation widgets

There are a few other animation widgets that we have not covered yet. The first one is the **AnimatedList**. This widget is used for animating items as they are inserted or removed from a list. Just like a **ListView**, it has an **itemBuilder** method. This method takes a context, index, and an additional animation parameter. This would look as follows:

```
final GlobalKey<AnimatedListState> _listKey =
GlobalKey<AnimatedListState>();
AnimatedList(
    key: _listKey,
      initialItemCount: movies.length,
      itemBuilder: (context, index, animation) {
        return buildItem(movies[index], animation); // Build each list
item
      },
    ),
```

When an item is removed from the list (and **setState** is called), you would then use the key to remove the item with an animation as follows:

```
// Remove the item from the data list
setState(() {
  movies.removeAt(index);
});

// Remove the item from the AnimatedList with animation
_listKey.currentState!.removeItem(
  index,
      (context, animation) => buildItem(removedItem, animation),
);
```

The next widget is the **AnimatedSwitcher**. This widget is for transitioning between widgets with an animation. It provides a cross-fade between the switching of widgets. It requires a duration and you can set the in and out curves.

**AnimatedPositioned** is an animated version of Position (which is used inside of a Stack). This widget will transition the widget in position over time.

# Hero animations

**Hero** widgets provide a transition between pages. Typically, you will have an image (you can have other types of widgets) that will be in a location on one screen and then animate to the new position on the next page. They are very easy to use, just wrap the widget in a Hero widget and give it an identical, unique, tag. This tag can be any object but it is important that they be unique. In the movie app, we will use Heros to wrap the movie images. On the home screen, there are duplicate images. For example, a movie might be in the Trending section as well as the Popular section. We will create a unique key based on the movie URL and the movie type. So, the movie tag will be '**movieUrl + movieType**'. This will create a unique tag.

The first task in creating Hero animations for the **movie** app is to separate the image into its widget. Make the following changes:

1.  In the **widgets** folder, create a new file called **movie_widget.dart**. Add the following:

    ```
    import 'package:cached_network_image/cached_network_image.dart';
    import 'package:flutter/material.dart';
    import 'package:flutter_riverpod/flutter_riverpod.dart';
    import 'package:movies/providers.dart';

    import 'package:movies/utils/utils.dart';
    // 1
    enum MovieType {
    ```

```
  trending,
  popular,
  topRated,
  nowPlaying
}
class MovieWidget extends ConsumerStatefulWidget {
// 2
  final int movieId;
  final String movieUrl;
  final OnMovieTap onMovieTap;
  final MovieType movieType;

  const MovieWidget(
      {required this.movieId,
      required this.movieUrl,
      required this.onMovieTap,
      required this.movieType,
      super.key});

  @override
  ConsumerState<MovieWidget> createState() => _MovieWidgetState();
}

class _MovieWidgetState extends ConsumerState<MovieWidget> {

  late String uniqueHeroTag;

  @override
  void initState() {
    super.initState();
// 3
    uniqueHeroTag = widget.movieUrl + widget.movieType.name;
  }

  @override
  Widget build(BuildContext context) {
    // TODO Add Image
  }
}
```

This is the start of a widget for displaying an image. It uses a string to create a unique tag from the movie URL and the movie type. The important lines are as follows:

a.  Define an enum for the different movie types.

b. The constructor takes the movie ID, URL, movie tap function, and movie type.

c. Create a unique tag.

2. Now add the image as follows:

```
return GestureDetector(
  onTap: () {
    widget.onMovieTap(widget.movieId);
  },
  child: Padding(
    padding: const EdgeInsets.all(8.0),
    child: SizedBox(
      width: 100,
      height: 142,
      child: Hero(
        tag: uniqueHeroTag,
        child: CachedNetworkImage(
          imageUrl: widget.movieUrl,
          alignment: Alignment.topCenter,
          fit: BoxFit.fitHeight,
          height: 100,
          width: 142,
        )
      ),
    ),
  ),
);
```

Here we are wrapping the image in a **Hero** widget with a unique tag. When the user taps on the image, the callback will be executed.

3. Open up **horiz_movies.dart**. Add the following and replace the constructor:

```
import ' package:movies/utils/utils.dart';
import ' package:movies/ui/widgets/movie_widget.dart';

class HorizontalMovies extends StatelessWidget {
  final MovieType movieType;
  final OnMovieTap onMovieTap;
  final List<String> movies;

  const HorizontalMovies(
      {required this.onMovieTap, required this.movies, required
this.movieType, super.key});
```

Just like the **MovieWidget**, we take a movie type and an **onMovieTap** function.

4.  Next, replace the code in the **itemBuilder** with the following:

```
return MovieWidget(movieId: index, movieUrl: movies[index],
onMovieTap: onMovieTap, movieType: movieType,);
```

This just uses the movie widget we just created and passes the index and that movie. We will be able to reuse this widget in other places.

5.  Now, open **home_screen.dart**. Change the name of the image variable to movies to better represent what they are:

```
final movies = ref.read(movieImagesProvider);
```

6.  Now change the three instances of **HorizontalMovies** with the following three calls:

```
            HorizontalMovies(movies: movies, onMovieTap:
onMovieTap, movieType: MovieType.Trending,),

            HorizontalMovies(movies: movies, onMovieTap:
onMovieTap, movieType: MovieType.Popular,),

            HorizontalMovies(movies: movies, onMovieTap:
onMovieTap, movieType: MovieType.TopRated,),
```

7.  Now add the function for **onMovieTap** after the build method:

```
void onMovieTap(int movieId) {
    context.router.push(MovieDetailRoute(movieId: movieId));
}
```

8.  Import the **movie_widget.dart** file. Now, we want the detail page to be the ending destination for our Hero. In order to do that, it needs to know the **hero** tag. This is another good example of using Riverpod's providers. Open up **providers.dart** and add:

```
final heroTagProvider = StateProvider<String>((ref) {
    return '';
});
```

9.  This creates a notifier provider class. In a terminal window run:

```
dart run build_runner build
```

This will allow classes to retrieve the current hero tag and for other classes to set that tag.

10.  Back in **detail_image.dart**, add the following line as the first line in the **build** method:

```
final heroTag = ref.watch(heroTagProvider);
```

11. This uses our provider to get the current **hero** tag. Now surround the **CachedNetworkImage** with:

```
child: Hero(
    tag: heroTag,
```

12. While we are changing things, open up **home_screen_image.dart** and add a **Hero**. Change the **images** variable to the following:

```
final movies = ref.read(movieImagesProvider);
```

13. Then, change the **itemCount** to:

```
itemCount: movies.length,
```

14. Change **onMovieTap** to:

```
ref.read(heroTagProvider.notifier).state =
movies[index] + 'swiper';
    onMovieTap(index);
```

15. This will set the hero tag to the movie URL plus the string swiper and pass in the index used. Wrap the **CachedNetworkImage** with a **Hero** like:

```
child: Hero(
    tag: movies[index] + 'swiper',
    child: CachedNetworkImage(
```

16. And the **imageUrl** as follows:

```
imageUrl: movies[index],
```

17. Open up **movie_widget.dart** and add the following as the first line in the **onTap** method:

```
ref.read(heroTagProvider.notifier).state = uniqueHeroTag;
```

This will set the current hero tag. Perform a Hot restart and click on either the main image or one of the images in the Trending list. Notice the animation when you click on the image and it transitions to the detail page.

The last place that needs a **Hero** is the **MovieRow** class:

1. Open up **movie_row.dart** and first change the widget to a **ConsumerWidget** (Riverpod's version of a StatelessWidget):

```
class MovieRow extends ConsumerWidget {
  final int movieId;
  final String movieUrl;
  final OnMovieTap onMovieTap;
  const MovieRow({required this.movieId, required this.movieUrl,
        required this.onMovieTap, super.key});
```

```
@override
Widget build(BuildContext context, WidgetRef ref) {
```

This adds a few new parameters, as follows:

- **movieId**: The id of the movie.
- **movieUrl**: The URL of the movie.
- **onMovieTap**: Tap function.

2.  Next, we need to create the hero tag. Replace:

```
if (movie.isNotEmpty) {
  return GestureDetector(
    onTap: () => {},
```

3.  with:

```
late String uniqueHeroTag = movieUrl + 'MovieRow';
if (movieUrl.isNotEmpty) {
  return GestureDetector(
    onTap: () {
      ref.read(heroTagProvider.notifier).state = uniqueHeroTag;
      onMovieTap(movieId);
    },
```

This will create a unique hero tag by adding the **MovieRow** string to the URL. It will then set the tag when tapping on the image.

4.  Next, wrap the **CachedNetworkImage** with a **Hero**:

```
child: Hero(
  tag: uniqueHeroTag,
  child: CachedNetworkImage(
    imageUrl: movieUrl,
```

The calling class is **VerticalMovieList**.

5.  Open up **vert_movie_list.dart** and change the images variable to:

```
final movies = ref.read(movieImagesProvider);
```

6.  And the call to **MovieRow** with:

```
movieId: index, movieUrl: movies[index], onMovieTap: onMovieTap,
```

Since we have modified **VerticalMovieList**, we need to modify its caller.

7.  Open up **genre_screen.dart**. Add the routes package:

```
import 'package:movies/router/app_routes.dart';
```

8. Change the **onMovieTap** to:

```
onMovieTap: (movieId) {
    context.router.push(MovieDetailRoute(movieId:
movieId));
},
```

Perform a Hot restart and click on a movie in the genre screen. All these Hero additions will cause the image to fly from its current position to the top of the screen on the detail page.

# Custom animations

If you want to create something truly unique that a traditional widget does not provide, you can use a **CustomPaint** and **CustomPainter** classes. The **CustomPaint** class provides a Canvas that you can use to draw lower-level graphics like lines, arcs, circles, and rectangles. The **Canvas** class is key to these types of animations. The **Canvas** class uses a few key classes and methods, listed as follows:

- **Paint**: This class is used for setting the color and style for drawing.
- **saveLayer**: This method sets a rectangle that will be drawn into.
- **restore**: This method restores the canvas to a state before the **saveLayer** call.
- **drawCircle, drawRect, drawArc, drawOval, drawPath, drawImage**: Drawing methods.
- **drawParagraph**: Draw text.
- **translate**: Shift the coordinate space.
- **scale**: Add a scale to the current transform.
- **clipRect, clipPath**: Set the clip region.

There are more methods, but these are some of the key ones.

A **CustomPaint** class looks as follows:

```
CustomPaint(
    child: myWidget(),
    foregroundPainter: foregroundPainter(),
    painter: MyPainter(),
)
```

The order of drawing is as follows:

- painter
- child
- foregroundPainter

So, there are three layers that are drawn. Both the painter and the **foregroundPainter** can be null. Here is an example of a CustomerPainter that draws a circle with a sun (*Figure 9.3*):

**Figure 9.3**: *CustomPainter*

The painter looks as follows:

```
class MyCustomPainter extends CustomPainter {
  @override
  void paint(Canvas canvas, Size size) {
    final paint = Paint()
      ..shader = RadialGradient(
        center: const Alignment(0.7, -0.6), // near the top right
        radius: 0.2,
        colors: [
          const Color(0xFFFFFF00), // yellow sun
          const Color(0xFF0099FF), // blue sky
        ],
        stops: const [
          0.4,
          1.0,
        ],
      ).createShader(Rect.fromCircle(
        center: Offset(size.width / 2, size.height / 2),
        radius: size.width / 2,
      ));

    canvas.drawCircle(
      Offset(size.width / 2, size.height / 2),
      size.width / 2,
      paint,
    );
```

```
  }

  @override
  bool shouldRepaint(MyCustomPainter oldDelegate) => false; // No need to
repaint
}
```

The **build** method is as follows:

```
  @override
  Widget build(BuildContext context) {
    return MaterialApp(
      home: Scaffold(
        appBar: AppBar(title: const Text("Custom Paint Example")),
        body: Center(
          child: CustomPaint(
            size: const Size(200, 200),
            painter: MyCustomPainter(),
          ),
        ),
      ),
    );
  }
```

Another popular widget is the **RotationTransition**. This will rotate another widget and uses an animation controller to define the animation. **ScaleTransition** is similar but scales a widget larger or smaller. Like the **ScaleTransition**, the **SizeTransition** widget changes the size of a widget along a horizontal or vertical axis.

# Animation libraries and tools

There are many different types of third-party animation packages. High-level packages like Lottie and Rive require you to define an animation with their tools and then run it in your app.

Lottie animations are JSON-based lightweight, scalable, and usable on multiple platforms. They can be interacted with by the user. You will have to pay to design the animations; however, free animations are available. You can produce Lottie animations using other tools like Adobe After Effects, Figma, etc. You can find it at **https://lottiefiles.com/**.

Rive Animations are similar to Lottie but require their own tool. You can find it at **https://rive.app/**. Rive considers its tools to be smaller and faster than Lottie's.

# Animation packages

There are many third-party packages that just perform animations. Some popular ones are as follows:

- **flutter_animate**: Adds many effects to widgets.
- **flutter_spinkit**: Loading animations
- **flutter_staggered_animations**: Used to add animations to lists and gridviews.
- **Funvas**: Create canvas-based animations based on time and math functions
- **simple_animations**: Easily implement custom animations for common use cases.
- **Spring**: A collection of 12 widgets based on spring animation effects.

We will use the **flutter_animate** package, which was written by the author of the Wonderous App, to perform some nice animations.

# Movie app

The first animation we will create is to modify the heart icon in the **ButtonRow** class to beat like a heart when the user clicks on it.

1. Open up **button_row.dart** and first convert the class to a **StatefulWidget**:

   ```
   class ButtonRow extends StatefulWidget {
     final bool favoriteSelected;
     final OnFavoriteSelected onFavoriteSelected;

     const ButtonRow({
       super.key,
       required this.favoriteSelected,
       required this.onFavoriteSelected,
     });

     @override
     State<ButtonRow> createState() => _ButtonRowState();
   }

   class _ButtonRowState extends State<ButtonRow> with
   TickerProviderStateMixin {
   ```

   The **TickerProviderStateMixin** allows this widget to handle multiple controllers. (Remember you use a **SingleTickerProviderStateMixin**).

2. Then add the animation variables:

   ```
   late AnimationController _sizeController;
   late Animation<double> _sizeAnimation;
   ```

```
late AnimationController _colorController;
late Animation<Color?> _colorAnimation;
```

3.  There is one animation controller for the size, one controller for the color and a size and color animation. Now initialize these variables:

```
@override
void initState() {
  super.initState();
// 1
  _sizeController = AnimationController(
    vsync: this,
    duration: Duration(seconds: 1), // Adjust pulse duration
  )..repeat(reverse: true); // Make animation repeat

// 2
  _sizeAnimation = Tween<double>(
    begin: 1.0, // Original size
    end: 1.5, // Scaled-up size
  ).animate(
    CurvedAnimation(parent: _sizeController, curve: Curves.
easeInOut),
  );
// 3
  _colorController = AnimationController(
    vsync: this,
    duration: Duration(seconds: 1), // Adjust color change
duration
  )..repeat(reverse: true);
// 4
  _colorAnimation = ColorTween(
    begin: Colors.white, // Starting color
    end: Colors.red, // Ending color
  ).animate(
    CurvedAnimation(parent: _colorController, curve: Curves.
easeInOut),
  );
}

@override
void dispose() {
  _sizeController.dispose();
```

```
    _colorController.dispose();
    super.dispose();
}
```

The size controller is a one second animation that repeats, and uses the size animation. The color controller is a one second animation that repeats, and uses the color animation. Here is an explanation:

a.  Create the size controller. Notice the repeat command.

b.  Create a size animation that starts at a scale of 1 and goes to 1.5.

c.  Create the color controller.

d.  Create a color animation that goes from white to red.

4.  From the **onPressed** method on, replace the icon:

```
                    widget.onFavoriteSelected();
                  },
                  icon: widget.favoriteSelected
                    ? AnimatedBuilder(
                        animation:
                          Listenable.merge([_sizeController, _
colorController]),
                        builder: (context, child) {
                          return Icon(
                            Icons.favorite_outlined,
                            size: 21 * _sizeAnimation.value,
                            color: _colorAnimation.value,
                          );
                        })
                    : Icon(
                        Icons.favorite_border,
                        color: Colors.white,
                      ),
```

If the widget is selected, show the heart animation, otherwise show a white outlined heart. This uses an **AnimatedBuilder** with two controllers. It uses the **merge** method from the **Listenable** class to return a list of controllers. Hot Reload and go into the **detail** page. Click on the favorite button and you will see the animation start.

5.  Now we can spice up the Genre Row and add some animation for sliding the row of genres in. Open up **genre_row.dart** and first convert the class to a **StatefulWidget**:

```
class GenreRow extends StatefulWidget {
  final List<GenreState> genres;

  const GenreRow({super.key, required this.genres});

  @override
  State<GenreRow> createState() => _GenreRowState();
}

class _GenreRowState extends State<GenreRow>
    with SingleTickerProviderStateMixin {
```

This uses a Single ticker mixin. Now add the needed variables:

```
  late AnimationController _controller;
  late Animation<Offset> _offsetAnimation;

  @override
  void initState() {
    super.initState();
    _controller = AnimationController(
      duration: const Duration(seconds: 2),
      vsync: this,
    )..forward(); // Start animation on initialization

    _offsetAnimation = Tween<Offset>(
      begin: const Offset(1.0, 0.0), // Start offscreen to the right
      end: Offset.zero, // End at the normal position
    ).animate(CurvedAnimation(
      parent: _controller,
      curve: Curves.elasticOut, // Use elastic curve for bounce
effect
    ));
  }

  @override
  void dispose() {
    _controller.dispose();
    super.dispose();
  }
```

6.  This creates a two second animation controller and an offset animation that will start on the right side of the screen and go to the left. The elasticOut curve will give it a bounce effect. Next, wrap the ListView with:

```
    child: SlideTransition(
      position: _offsetAnimation,
```

7.  Change the genres instance to:

    ```
    widget.genres
    ```

    Hot reload and you should see the row of genres animate from right to left.

# Flutter animate

The Flutter animate package (or **flutter_animate**) was written by the author of the Wonderous app, which is a showcase for Flutter apps and animations. You can find more information at: **https://flutter.gskinner.com/wonderous/**. To use the package, open **pubspec.yaml** and add:

```
flutter_animate: ^4.5.0
```

Perform a Pub get. Make the following changes:

1.  Now open up **movie_widget.dart**. Remember, that to use an animation controller, your state class needs to use a ticker mixin. Add the following to the end of the state class:

    ```
    with SingleTickerProviderStateMixin
    ```

    Then, add the following before the **uniqueTag** to create an animation controller with a two second duration. The code is as follows:

    ```
    bool animateImage = false;
    late final AnimationController _controller = AnimationController(
      duration: const Duration(seconds: 2),
      vsync: this,
    );
    Change the onTap method to:
        onTap: () {
          setState(() {
            ref.read(heroTagProvider.notifier).state = uniqueHeroTag;
            animateImage = true;
            _controller.forward();
          });
        },
    ```

    This removes the **onMovieTap** call so that we can start the animation by calling **_controller.forward()**.

2.  After the **CachedNetworkImage** widget add the following:

    ```
              .animate(
    ```

```
// 1
                    autoPlay: false,
// 2
                    controller: _controller,
// 3
                    onComplete: (controller) {
// 4
                      if (animateImage) {
                        animateImage = false;
                        widget.onMovieTap(widget.movieId);
                      }                             })
// 5
                  .scaleXY(begin: 1.0, end: 1.1, duration: 600.ms)
// 6
                  .then(delay: 600.ms)
// 7
                  .scaleXY(begin: 1.1, end: 1.0, duration: 600.ms),
```

Import the **flutter_animate** package. This uses flutter_animate's animate class. Here is an explanation of the steps:

a. Use the **autoPlay** parameter to make sure the animation does not start at first.

b. Set the controller.

c. Listen to the completion of the animation.

d. Reset the controller.

e. Scale the image up to 1.1 percent.

f. Wait for 600 milliseconds.

g. Scale the image back down to normal.

What this does is pulse the image before launching into the detail screen.

Hot Restart (reload may not work) and try clicking on a trending movie to see the animation.

## Custom routes

To add a transition animation between pages, the **AutoRoute** package has a custom route class that will allow you to add an animation. Open up **app_routes.dart**. Change the movie detail and video page route to:

```
CustomRoute(
  path: '/details/:movieId',
  page: MovieDetailRoute.page,
```

```
      maintainState: false,
      transitionsBuilder: TransitionsBuilders.slideBottom,
      durationInMilliseconds: 500,
    ),
    CustomRoute(
      page: VideoPageRoute.page,
      maintainState: false,
      transitionsBuilder: TransitionsBuilders.slideRight,
      durationInMilliseconds: 500,
    ),
```

The first transition will slide in from the bottom, the second transition will slide from the right. Do a Hot Restart (not reload). Try navigating to the detail page and click on the trailer.

# Conclusion

In this chapter, you learned about all the available Flutter animation widgets and how to use both implicit and explicit animations. There are many different types of animations and the possibilities are limitless. As well as the built-in animations, there are third-party animation packages that allow designers to use tools to create animations and you can use those in your apps. You learned about the important animation controller as well as the animation classes it uses to create animations for the movie app.

In the next chapter, you will learn about Futures and asynchronous programming, which will allow you to perform tasks in the background, load data, and then handle the result. This will set you up for handling networking and databases. You will also learn how to use networking libraries to retrieve data from the internet. This will allow us to finally get real movie data. You will also learn more about how to handle JSON data.

## Join our book's Discord space

Join the book's Discord Workspace for Latest updates, Offers, Tech happenings around the world, New Release and Sessions with the Authors:

**https://discord.bpbonline.com**

# CHAPTER 10

# Futures and Async/Await

## Introduction

In this chapter, you will learn about asynchronous programming and how to run code in the background. You will also learn about the classes that Flutter provides to handle concurrency for a responsive UI and widgets that handle these asynchronous classes. You will be able to load data in the background and update the UI when it is finished.

## Structure

The chapter covers the following topics:

- Concurrency in Flutter
- Futures
- Async/await
- Event loop
- FutureBuilder
- Streams
- StreamBuilder
- Isolates

# Objectives

By the end of this chapter, you will understand how to create asynchronous functions and use them in your apps. You will know when to use a Future and you will also understand the Dart keywords needed to use them. Finally, you will build out the favorites screen and use Futures, streams, and other asynchronous classes. You will be able to run tasks in the background without slowing down the user interface.

# Concurrency in Flutter

Concurrency is the ability of a language to process multiple tasks as if they were running simultaneously. This is important because if you have code running while the user is trying to use the screen, it will become unresponsive. The system must balance drawing the UI, handling user input, and background tasks. Typically, a program will run in one process but can run code on different threads. Dart is a bit different. Dart uses the concept of an isolate. An isolate is an independent execution unit with its own memory heap and event loop. Memory cannot be shared between isolates. This means the isolate does not have to worry about concurrency problems like other languages. In exchange for this feature, communicating between isolates is not easy. To communicate between isolates, messages must be sent through send and receive ports. Flutter uses one main isolate to run all code in. This includes an event loop to handle both regular UI work and asynchronous tasks. You create asynchronous tasks by defining a function that uses the **async** and **await** keywords. These keywords let the Dart system know that the code will run asynchronously.

# Futures

Futures are defined in Dart as an abstract class that represents a Future value. You will usually use Futures as a return value on a function. This is for functions that perform asynchronous operations. This might be a network call, a database operation, or a long computation. Instead of blocking the UI, you can define a method to return a value when it is done. While the **Future** class is mostly an interface, the implementation is complex. The main class is the **_Future<T>** class. This class has listeners and implements all of the Future class's functions. The Future class has a few important methods, listed as follows:

- **Future.value (value)**: Creates a Future with an already completed value.

- **Future.microtask (computation)**: Creates a Future that contains the result of the computation and is run as a microtask.

- **Future.delayed (duration, computation)**: Runs a computation after a delay.

- **Future.wait (List<Future>)**: Waits for all of the futures in the list to complete.

- **Future.then(function(value))**: Calls the function with the value when the Future is done.

- **Future.doWhile (bool action())**: Calls the action while the action returns true.
- **Future.asStream**: Converts the result to a stream.
- **Future.catchError(onError())**: Handles errors emitted by the Future.

A Future has several different states, as follows:

- **Incomplete**: Starting state. Future is waiting for a result.
- **StatePendingComplete**: Set when completed.
- **StateValue**: Completed and contains a value.
- **StateError**: Completed with an error and stack trace.

Normally you would use Futures as return values. Functions can return a Future without a type or with a specific type. You would use a Future without a type when you just want to indicate you are done but do not have a return value. For functions that return a result, you would create a function as follows:

```
Future<String> loadRemoteString() async {
    return network.getString();
}
```

# Async/await

**async** and **await** are Dart keywords that work with Futures. **async** is used after the definition of the function and marks the function as asynchronous. If you use this keyword, your function must return a Future. The **await** keyword is used inside a function and waits for the result of another function. It will not continue until the result has returned. This is important if you need to get a result before proceeding to the next call. You do not have to use the **await** keyword in your function; you can just return a Future. Remember, you can only use the **await** keyword inside an **async** function. The following is an example of an **async** function that retrieves data from the internet:

```
Future<String> _fetchData() async {
    final response = await http.get(Uri.parse('https://jsonplaceholder.
typicode.com/todos/1'));

    if (response.statusCode == 200) {
      final Map<String, dynamic> json = jsonDecode(response.body);
      _data = json.toString(); // Update state with the fetched data
      return _data;
    } else {
      throw Exception('Failed to load data');
    }
}
```

This class uses the built-in **http** package to await the result of a call to the internet and return a string result.

# Event loop

Most UI frameworks work with an event loop. This is a continually running system that listens for events and will continue until it gets an exit event. The event loop runs on a single thread, and anything slowing this event loop will make the UI seem unresponsive. The whole Flutter system is started by the **runApp** method, starting from the main method. Events are of the following types:

- **User interactions**: Pointer events (taps), Text input, and Focus.
- **Lifecycle events**: Events for widget lifecycle events.
- **System events**: Device orientation, battery, and platform channel events.

Once these events are handled, the system checks for micro tasks and executes them, and then the UI is rebuilt if needed. A microtask is a short, high-priority function that will be run after the current event loop's events but before any asynchronous tasks.

# FutureBuilder

**FutureBuilder** is a Flutter widget that uses a **Future** for data and then a builder callback to return a widget based on the future data. This widget looks as follows:

```
FutureBuilder(
      future: loadData(),
      builder: (context, snapshot) {
        if (snapshot.connectionState != ConnectionState.done) {
          return const NotReady();
        }
        return Placeholder();
      }
)
Future loadData() async {
      return Future.value(data);
}
```

The **FutureBuilder** has a **future** parameter, our **loadData** function, that returns a future and then a builder. This builder takes a context and a snapshot. snapshot is a class of type **AsyncSnapshot**. This class has three fields:

- **data**: When the future is finished, this field has the data.
- **error**: If there is an error, this field has the error.
- **connectionState**: Current state of the future.

The connection state has the following values:

- **none**: Null value.

- **waiting**: Operation is executing.

- **active**: Connected to an active data source, like a stream.

- **done**: Finished executing future.

The builder function can return different values depending on the connection state.

To demonstrate Futures, we will start by creating a view model class to do some of the logic for retrieving movies. This view model will return genres, favorites, and movies. Instead of just referring to movies by the URL, we need to create a class to hold all the information about a movie. To start out, you need to create a new set of folders in the **lib** directory.

1. First, create a **data** folder and then a **models** folder inside of the **data** folder. Inside the **model's** folder, create a new file named **movie.dart**. Add the following:

   ```
   class Movie {
     final int movieId;
     final String image;
     final String title;
     final String overview;
     final double popularity;
     final DateTime releaseDate;

     Movie({required this.movieId, required this.image, required this.
   title, required this.overview, required this.popularity, required
   this.releaseDate});

   }
   ```

   This holds the movie ID, image URL, title, overview (a description of the movie), popularity value (will come from the next chapter), and release date.

2. Next, in the **ui** folder, create a new file called **movie_viewmodel.dart**. Add the following:

   ```
   import 'package:movies/data/models/movie.dart';
   class MovieViewModel {
     late List<String> movieGenres;
     List<Movie> trendingMovies = [];
     List<Movie> topRatedMovies = [];
     List<Movie> popularMovies = [];
     List<Movie> nowPlayingMovies = [];
     List<Movie> allMovies = [];
   }
   ```

This contains a list of movie genres, trending, top-rated, popular, and now-playing movies. The final field holds all of the movies.

3.  Next, add the following methods:

```
Future setup() async {
   await Future.wait([setupConfiguration(), setupGenres(),
loadMovies()]);
}

Future setupConfiguration() async {
   // TODO add configuration
}

Future setupGenres() async {
   // TODO return list of genres
}
Future loadMovies() async {
 // TODO load movies
}
```

The setup method uses Future's **wait** method. Remember that this method will wait until all methods have finished. The **setupConfiguration** method will load in the movie configuration, the **setupGenres** method will load all genres, and the **loadMovies** method will load all movies.

4.  In the **setupGenres** method, add the following:

```
movieGenres = [
    'Action',
    'Adventure',
    'Crime',
    'Mystery',
    'War',
    'Comedy',
    'Romance',
    'History',
    'Music',
    'Drama',
    'Thriller',
    'Family',
    'Horror',
    'Western',
    'Science Fiction',
    'Animation',
    'Documentation',
```

```
    'TV Movie',
    'Fantasy',
];
```

This just sets a string list of genres. The next chapter will get the list from a server.

5. Next, we will implement the **loadMovies** method by setting the **allMovies** array to a list of hard-coded movies. For now, the only items that matter are the **movieId** and the image URL. For **loadMovies** add, the following:

```
allMovies = [
  Movie(
      movieId: 1,
      image:
      'http://image.tmdb.org/t/p/w780/
z1p34vh7dEOnLDmyCrlUVLuoDzd.jpg',
      title: 'Title',
      overview: 'Overview',
      popularity: 1.0,
      releaseDate: DateTime.now()),
    Movie(
      movieId: 2,
      image:
      'http://image.tmdb.org/t/p/w780/
gKkl37BQuKTanygYQG1pyYgLVgf.jpg',
      title: 'Title',
      overview: 'Overview',
      popularity: 1.0,
      releaseDate: DateTime.now()),
    Movie(
      movieId: 3,
      image:
      'http://image.tmdb.org/t/p/
w780/4xJd3uwtL1vCuZgEfEc8JXI9Uyx.jpg',
      title: 'Title',
      overview: 'Overview',
      popularity: 1.0,
      releaseDate: DateTime.now()),
    Movie(
      movieId: 4,
      image:
      'http://image.tmdb.org/t/p/w780/
uuA01PTtPombRPvL9dvsBqOBJWm.jpg',
```

```
            title: 'Title',
            overview: 'Overview',
            popularity: 1.0,
            releaseDate: DateTime.now()),
      Movie(
            movieId: 5,
            image:
            'http://image.tmdb.org/t/p/w780/H6vke7zGiuLsz4v4RPeReb9rsv.
jpg',
            title: 'Title',
            overview: 'Overview',
            popularity: 1.0,
            releaseDate: DateTime.now()),
      Movie(
            movieId: 6,
            image:
            'http://image.tmdb.org/t/p/w780/
e1J2oNzSBdou01sUvriVuoYp0pJ.jpg',
            title: 'Title',
            overview: 'Overview',
            popularity: 1.0,
            releaseDate: DateTime.now()),
      Movie(
            movieId: 7,
            image:
            'http://image.tmdb.org/t/p/w780/
hu40Uxp9WtpL34jv3zyWLb5zEVY.jpg',
            title: 'Title',
            overview: 'Overview',
            popularity: 1.0,
            releaseDate: DateTime.now()),
      Movie(
            movieId: 8,
            image:
            'http://image.tmdb.org/t/p/w780/
pKaA8VvfkNfEMUPMiiuL5qSPQYy.jpg',
            title: 'Title',
            overview: 'Overview',
            popularity: 1.0,
            releaseDate: DateTime.now()),
```

```dart
      Movie(
          movieId: 9,
          image:
          'http://image.tmdb.org/t/p/w780/
zK2sFxZcelHJRPVr242rxy5VK4T.jpg',
          title: 'Title',
          overview: 'Overview',
          popularity: 1.0,
          releaseDate: DateTime.now()),
      Movie(
          movieId: 10,
          image:
          'http://image.tmdb.org/t/p/
w780/7qxG0zyt29BI0IzFDfsps62kbQi.jpg',
          title: 'Title',
          overview: 'Overview',
          popularity: 1.0,
          releaseDate: DateTime.now()),
      Movie(
          movieId: 11,
          image:
          'http://image.tmdb.org/t/p/
w780/8Gxv8gSFCU0XGDykEGv7zR1n2ua.jpg',
          title: 'Title',
          overview: 'Overview',
          popularity: 1.0,
          releaseDate: DateTime.now()),
      Movie(
          movieId: 12,
          image:
          'http://image.tmdb.org/t/p/w780/
zDi2U7WYkdIoGYHcYbM9X5yReVD.jpg',
          title: 'Title',
          overview: 'Overview',
          popularity: 1.0,
          releaseDate: DateTime.now()),
      Movie(
          movieId: 13,
          image:
          'http://image.tmdb.org/t/p/w780/
cxevDYdeFkiixRShbObdwAHBZry.jpg',
```

```
          title: 'Title',
          overview: 'Overview',
          popularity: 1.0,
          releaseDate: DateTime.now()),
      Movie(
          movieId: 14,
          image:
          'http://image.tmdb.org/t/p/w780/
uXUs1fwSuE06LgYETw2mi4JxQvc.jpg',
          title: 'Title',
          overview: 'Overview',
          popularity: 1.0,
          releaseDate: DateTime.now()),
      Movie(
          movieId: 15,
          image:
          'http://image.tmdb.org/t/p/w780/
fdZpvODTX5wwkD0ikZNaClE4AoW.jpg',
          title: 'Title',
          overview: 'Overview',
          popularity: 1.0,
          releaseDate: DateTime.now()),
      Movie(
          movieId: 16,
          image:
          'http://image.tmdb.org/t/p/w780/
d5NXSklXo0qyIYkgV94XAgMIckC.jpg',
          title: 'Title',
          overview: 'Overview',
          popularity: 1.0,
          releaseDate: DateTime.now()),
      Movie(
          movieId: 17,
          image:
          'http://image.tmdb.org/t/p/w780/
sh7Rg8Er3tFcN9BpKIPOMvALgZd.jpg',
          title: 'Title',
          overview: 'Overview',
          popularity: 1.0,
          releaseDate: DateTime.now()),
```

```
      Movie(
          movieId: 18,
          image:
          'http://image.tmdb.org/t/p/w780/
sHJ2OIgpcpSmhqXkuSWxZ3nwg1S.jpg',
          title: 'Title',
          overview: 'Overview',
          popularity: 1.0,
          releaseDate: DateTime.now()),
      Movie(
          movieId: 19,
          image:
          'http://image.tmdb.org/t/p/w780/
upKD8UbH8vQ798aMWgwMxV8t4yk.jpg',
          title: 'Title',
          overview: 'Overview',
          popularity: 1.0,
          releaseDate: DateTime.now()),
      Movie(
          movieId: 20,
          image:
          'http://image.tmdb.org/t/p/w780/
vfrQk5IPloGg1v9Rzbh2Eg3VGyM.jpg',
          title: 'Title',
          overview: 'Overview',
          popularity: 1.0,
          releaseDate: DateTime.now()),
    ];
```

This is the same list of image URLs we had earlier but with movie IDs. When we get to the next chapter, we will load real data.

6. Next, add the **getTrendingMovies** method:

```
    Future<List<Movie>> getTrendingMovies(int page) async {
      if (trendingMovies.isEmpty) {
        trendingMovies = [
          allMovies[0],
          allMovies[2],
          allMovies[4],
          allMovies[6],
          allMovies[8],
          allMovies[10],
```

```
      allMovies[12],
    ];
  }
  return trendingMovies;
}
```

This method just sets the trending movies list to the even-numbered movies.

7. Do something similar for the **getPopular** method. Use the following code:

```
Future<List<Movie>> getPopular(int page) async {
  if (popularMovies.isEmpty) {
    popularMovies = [
      allMovies[1],
      allMovies[3],
      allMovies[5],
      allMovies[7],
      allMovies[9],
      allMovies[11],
      allMovies[13],
    ];
  }
  return popularMovies;
}
```

This just uses the even-numbered movies.

8. For top rated, add:

```
Future<List<Movie>> getTopRated(int page) async {
  if (topRatedMovies.isEmpty) {
    topRatedMovies = [
      allMovies[14],
      allMovies[16],
      allMovies[18],
      allMovies[1],
      allMovies[3],
      allMovies[5],
      allMovies[7],
    ];
  }
  return topRatedMovies;
}
```

9. For now, playing add the following code:

```
Future<List<Movie>> getNowPlaying(int page) async {
  if (nowPlayingMovies.isEmpty) {
    nowPlayingMovies = [
      allMovies[8],
      allMovies[10],
      allMovies[12],
      allMovies[14],
      allMovies[16],
      allMovies[18],
      allMovies[1],
    ];
  }
  return nowPlayingMovies;
}
```

Now we need to make the view model available to other classes. That means adding a provider in the providers' file.

10. Open up **providers.dart** and remove the **movieImages** and genres providers as these will come from the movie view model. Then add the following:

```
import 'ui/movie_viewmodel.dart';
@Riverpod(keepAlive: true)
Future<MovieViewModel> movieViewModel(MovieViewModelRef ref) async {
  final model = MovieViewModel();
  await model.setup();
  return model;
}
```

This creates a new view model and waits until the setup method has finished. Only when this is complete will the view model be available. Since this view model is not available right away, we have to use some functionality from Riverpod to handle this.

11. In the terminal window run the build runner command:

```
dart run build_runner build
```

This will create the movie view model provider. You will now have several errors in several files.

12. Open up **home_screen.dart** and in the **state** class, replace the first three lines in the **state** class with:

```
late MovieViewModel movieViewModel;
```

```
Future<List<List<Movie>>>? movieFuture;

@override
Widget build(BuildContext context) {
  final movieViewModelAsync = ref.watch(movieViewModelProvider);
  return movieViewModelAsync.when(
    error: (e, st) => Text(e.toString()),
    loading: () => const NotReady(),
    data: (viewModel) {
      movieViewModel = viewModel;
      return buildScreen();
    },
  );
}

Widget buildScreen() {
```

Import **Movie** and **MovieViewModel**. This uses Riverpod's **watch** method to get an asynchronous provider. We can then use the **when** method to check for the following three possible conditions:

- **error**: An error has occurred.
- **loading**: The asynchronous provider is still running.
- **data**: The provider is ready.

Notice that Android Studio does not know what the **NotReady** widget is. This is a very simple widget that just shows a circular progress bar.

13. In the **widgets** folder, create the file **not_ready.dart**. Add:

```
import 'package:flutter/material.dart';

class NotReady extends StatelessWidget {
  const NotReady({super.key});

  @override
  Widget build(BuildContext context) {
    return const Center(child: CircularProgressIndicator());
  }
}
```

We will reuse this widget a lot. Import that widget into **HomeScreen**. Now that we have the view model, we can use it in the **buildScreen** method.

14. Wrap the **SingleChildScrollView** widget (option-return on Mac and choose "wrap with widget") with a **FutureBuilder**. **FutureBuilder** needs a future. Replace child: *SingleChildScrollView* with:

```
        future: loadData(),
          builder: (context, snapshot) {
            if ((snapshot.connectionState != ConnectionState.active)
&&
                (snapshot.connectionState != ConnectionState.done))
{
                return const NotReady();
            }
            return SingleChildScrollView(
```

**loadData** has not been defined yet.

15. Scroll down to the bottom of the method and find the parentheses for the **SingleChildScrollView**. Change the comma to a semi-colon and add a right bracket '}'. The ending should look like:

```
            ],
          ),
        ),
      );
    },
  ),
);
```

16. Now, add the **loadData** method as the last method:

```
Future loadData() async {
  movieFuture ??= Future.wait([
    movieViewModel.getTrendingMovies(1),
    movieViewModel.getTopRated(1),
    movieViewModel.getPopular(1),
    movieViewModel.getNowPlaying(1)
  ]);
  return movieFuture;
}
```

This will wait until all futures have finished. This will get the first page of trending, top-rated, popular, and now-playing movies. If you scroll up, you will see errors with the **HorizontalMovies** widget.

17. Change the first **HorizontalMovies** to:

```
HorizontalMovies(movies: movieViewModel.trendingMovies,
    onMovieTap: onMovieTap,
    movieType: MovieType.trending,),
```

This uses the view models trending movies list.

18. Do the same for the other calls:

```
HorizontalMovies(movies: movieViewModel.popularMovies,
    onMovieTap: onMovieTap,
    movieType: MovieType.popular,),
```

19. Also add the following:

```
HorizontalMovies(movies: movieViewModel.topRatedMovies,
    onMovieTap: onMovieTap,
    movieType: MovieType.topRated,),
```

You will notice that you will get an error here as well. This is because **HorizontalMovies** expects a list of strings.

20. Open up **horiz_movies.dart** and change:

```
final List<String> movies;
```

to:

```
final List<Movie> movies;
```

21. Import the **movie.dart** file. Next, we see that **MovieWidget** needs work. Command-click on **MovieWidget** to open the file. Change the fields and constructor from:

```
final int movieId;
final String movieUrl;
final OnMovieTap onMovieTap;
final MovieType movieType;

const MovieWidget(
    {required this.movieId,
    required this.movieUrl,
    required this.onMovieTap,
    required this.movieType,
    super.key});
```

to:

```
final Movie movie;
final OnMovieTap onMovieTap;
final MovieType movieType;

const MovieWidget(
    {required this.movie,
    required this.onMovieTap,
    required this.movieType,
    super.key});
```

22. Import **movie.dart**. Next, change the creation of the unique hero tag to the following:

```
uniqueHeroTag = widget.movie.image + widget.movieType.name;
```

23. Then change the following:

```
imageUrl: widget.movieUrl,
```

to:

```
imageUrl: widget.movie.image,
```

and,

```
widget.onMovieTap(widget.movieId);
```

to:

```
widget.onMovieTap(widget.movie.movieId);
```

Now that **MovieWidget** has changed, **HorizontalMovies** needs to be updated.

24. Change the **MovieWidget** call to:

```
return MovieWidget(movie: movies[index], onMovieTap:
onMovieTap, movieType: movieType,);
```

The next change needed is the **genre_screen.dart** file. We need to integrate the view model and not use the list of movies or genres.

25. Open up **genre_screen.dart**, and replace:

```
@override
  Widget build(BuildContext context) {
    final images = ref.read(movieImagesProvider);
    final genres = ref.read(genresProvider);
```

with:

```
late MovieViewModel movieViewModel;
List<GenreState> genreStates = [];
List<Movie> currentMovieList = [];

@override
Widget build(BuildContext context) {
  final movieViewModelAsync = ref.watch(movieViewModelProvider);
  return movieViewModelAsync.when(
    error: (e, st) => Text(e.toString()),
    loading: () => const NotReady(),
    data: (viewModel) {
      movieViewModel = viewModel;
      buildGenreState();
      return buildScreen();
```

```
      },
    );
  }

  void buildGenreState() {
    genreStates.clear();
    for (final genre in movieViewModel.movieGenres) {
      genreStates.add(GenreState(genre: genre, isSelected: false));
    }
  }


  Widget buildScreen() {
```

26. Add all the imports. The beginning of the **build** method is just like **HomeScreen**. The only difference is the **buildGenreState** method. This just creates a list of genre states. Find the line:

```
      genreStates: genres,
```

and replace with:

```
      genreStates: genreStates,
```

and

```
      movies: images,
```

replace with:

```
      movies: currentMovieList,
```

As you can tell, when you make major refactoring changes like this, it can require changes to multiple files. Ideally, you will develop models before you write your app so you do not have to do major refactoring.

27. Now **VerticalMovieList** needs updating. Command-click to open up **VerticalMovieList**. Change the following:

```
    final List<String> movies;
```

to:

```
    final List<Movie> movies;
```

28. Import the **Movie** class. Change the **MovieRow** to:

```
        return MovieRow(
          movie: movies[index], onMovieTap: onMovieTap,
        );
```

We want to pass in the movie and not just the **id**. This way, the **MovieRow** class has access to all the **movie** data.

29. Now open **MovieRow**. Change:

```
final int movieId;
final String movieUrl;
final OnMovieTap onMovieTap;
const MovieRow({required this.movieId, required this.movieUrl,
required this.onMovieTap, super.key});
```

To:

```
final Movie movie;
final OnMovieTap onMovieTap;
const MovieRow({required this.movie, required this.onMovieTap,
super.key});
```

In the build method, change:

```
late String uniqueHeroTag = movieUrl + 'MovieRow';
if (movieUrl.isNotEmpty) {
  return GestureDetector(
    onTap: () {
      ref.read(heroTagProvider.notifier).state = uniqueHeroTag;
      onMovieTap(movieId);
    },
```

To:

```
String uniqueHeroTag = movie.image + 'MovieRow';
if (movie.image.isNotEmpty) {
  return GestureDetector(
    onTap: () {
      ref.read(heroTagProvider.notifier).state = uniqueHeroTag;
      onMovieTap(movie.movieId);
    },
```

Finally, change the following:

```
                    imageUrl: movieUrl,
```

to:

```
                    imageUrl: movie.image,
```

We are getting close to finishing. There are three more files that need changing.

30. Open **home_screen_image.dart**. Change:

```
final OnMovieTap onMovieTap;

HomeScreenImage({super.key, required this.onMovieTap});

@override
```

```
Widget build(BuildContext context, WidgetRef ref) {
  final movies = ref.read(movieImagesProvider);
```

to:

```
final MovieViewModel movieViewModel;
final OnMovieTap onMovieTap;

HomeScreenImage({required this.movieViewModel, required this.
onMovieTap, super.key});

@override
Widget build(BuildContext context, WidgetRef ref) {
```

31. We no longer need the movie list. Next, after autoplay: true, change the rest to:

```
        itemCount: movieViewModel.nowPlayingMovies.length,
        itemBuilder: (BuildContext context, int index) {
          final currentMovie = movieViewModel.
nowPlayingMovies[index];
          String uniqueHeroTag = '${currentMovie.image}swiper';
          return GestureDetector(
            onTap: () {
              ref.read(heroTagProvider.notifier).state =
uniqueHeroTag;
              onMovieTap(currentMovie.movieId);
            },
            child: Hero(
              tag: uniqueHeroTag,
              child: CachedNetworkImage(
                imageUrl: currentMovie.image,
                alignment: Alignment.topCenter,
                fit: BoxFit.fitHeight,
                height: 374,
                width: screenWidth,
              ),
            ),
          );
        },
      ),
    );
```

32. Return to **HomeScreen** and update the call to **HomeScreenImage**:

```
HomeScreenImage(movieViewModel: movieViewModel, onMovieTap:
(movieId) {
```

```
        context.router.push(MovieDetailRoute(movieId: movieId));
    }),
```

Now we just have the movie detail to fix.

33. Open up **movie_detail.dart**. Just like the other files, we need the view model. After **favoriteNotifier**, replace:

```
@override
  Widget build(BuildContext context) {
    final movies = ref.read(movieImagesProvider);
    final genres = ref.read(genresProvider);
```

with:

```
  late MovieViewModel movieViewModel;
  List<GenreState> genreStates = [];
  late Movie currentMovie;

  @override
  Widget build(BuildContext context) {
    final movieViewModelAsync = ref.watch(movieViewModelProvider);
    return movieViewModelAsync.when(
      error: (e, st) => Text(e.toString()),
      loading: () => const NotReady(),
      data: (viewModel) {
        movieViewModel = viewModel;
        currentMovie = movieViewModel.findMovieById(widget.movieId);
        buildGenreState();
        return buildScreen();
      },
    );
  }

  void buildGenreState() {
    for (final genre in movieViewModel.movieGenres) {
      genreStates.add(GenreState(genre: genre, isSelected: false));
    }
  }

  Widget buildScreen() {
```

34. Add any needed imports. Find **SliverChildListDelegate** and replace the following two lines with:

```
                    Stack(children: [DetailImage(movieUrl:
```

```
                    currentMovie.image)]),
                                GenreRow(genres: genreStates),
```

Hot restart and everything should look the same.

# Streams

Streams are a sequence of events that can have listeners to those events. Those events are delivered asynchronously. There are two types of streams: single and broadcast. Single streams can only be listened to by a single listener, while a broadcast stream can be listened to by multiple listeners. Be careful though, most streams are single streams. To get a broadcast stream, you can call the **asBroadcastStream** method on a stream to create a broadcast stream. This would look as follows:

```
final broadcastStream = stream.asBroadcastStream(
  onCancel: (controller) {
    print('Stream paused');
    controller.pause();
  },
  onListen: (controller) async {
    if (controller.isPaused) {
      print('Stream resumed');
      controller.resume();
    }
  },
);
```

You can create a regular stream in multiple ways:

- **StreamController**: If you have a **StreamController**, use the stream getter.
- **Factory methods**:
  - **Stream.fromIterable**: Returns a stream from a list.
  - **Stream.value**: Emit a single value and close.
  - **Stream.periodic**: Emit items at a specific interval.
  - **Stream.fromFuture**: Convert a Future to a stream that emits one value or an error.
- **Create a function that emits a stream**:

```
Stream<int> intStream(int to) async* {
  for (int i = 1; i <= to; i++) {
    yield i;  // Emit each value asynchronously
    await Future.delayed(Duration(seconds: 1)); // Optional delay
```

```
    }
  }
```

Streams are very useful when you have a widget that is listening for changes. For example, if you had a chat app, the screen would listen to a stream of chat messages. If you are listening for location updates or sensor data, many plugins provide this functionality. Google's Firebase database provides streams for the data from its servers.

To consume streams in a Flutter app, use a **StreamBuilder** widget or listen to the stream. The **listen** method is defined as follows:

```
StreamSubscription<T> listen(void onData(T event)?,
    {Function? onError, void onDone()?, bool? cancelOnError});
```

This method returns a **StreamSubscription** and takes an **onData** function that receives the event and optional **onError** and **onDone** methods. The **cancelOnError** flag will cancel the subscription on the first error. The **StreamSubscription** has a **cancel** method. You can also pause and resume the subscription.

# StreamBuilder

This widget takes a stream and a builder. The builder also listens for the connection state. An example is as follows:

```
StreamBuilder<List<Item>>(
        stream: getFavoriteStream(),
        builder: (context, snapshot) {
          if (snapshot.connectionState != ConnectionState.active) {
            return const NotReady();
          }
          return Scaffold();
      })
```

In place of the Scaffold, you would build out the widget with the items given in the snapshot. You would get a list of the current items by using: **snapshot.requireData**. This would be a list of the items returned in the stream. Note that this does not have to be a list. It can be any type of item.

To show how streams and **StreamBuilder** work, we will use them for the favorites screen. We will start with a few widgets needed for the favorite screen.

1. Start by creating a new file in the **data/models** folder named **favorite.dart**. This will hold information about a favorite item. Add the following:

```
class Favorite {
  final int movieId;
  final String image;
```

```
bool favorite;
final String title;
final String overview;
final double popularity;
final DateTime releaseDate;

Favorite({required this.movieId, required this.image, required
this.favorite, required this.title, required this.overview, required
this.popularity, required this.releaseDate});
}
```

This holds the movie ID, movie URL, whether it is a favorite or not, title, overview, popularity, and release date.

2. Next, create **favorite_row.dart** in the **widgets** folder. Add the following:

```
import 'package:auto_size_text/auto_size_text.dart';
import 'package:cached_network_image/cached_network_image.dart';
import 'package:flutter/material.dart';

import 'package:movies/data/models/favorite.dart';
import 'package:movies/utils/utils.dart';
import 'package:movies/ui/movie_viewmodel.dart';

class FavoriteRow extends StatelessWidget {
  final Favorite favorite;
  final MovieViewModel movieViewModel;
  final OnMovieTap onMovieTap;
  final OnFavoriteResultsTap onFavoritesTap;

  const FavoriteRow(
      {super.key,
      required this.favorite,
      required this.movieViewModel,
      required this.onMovieTap, required this.onFavoritesTap});

  @override
  Widget build(BuildContext context) {
  }
}
```

This takes a favorite, the movie view model, an **onMovieTap** method, and an **onFavoritesTap** method. This last method does not exist yet.

3. Open up **utils.dart** and add the following code:

```
typedef OnFavoriteResultsTap = void Function(Favorite favorite);
```

Add the import. Next, fill out the build method with:

```
// 1
    final screenWidth = MediaQuery.of(context).size.width;
    final textWidth = screenWidth - 132;
    final imageUrl = favorite.image;
    if (imageUrl.isNotEmpty) {
      return GestureDetector(
        onTap: () => onMovieTap(favorite.movieId),
// 2
        child: SizedBox(
          height: 148,
          child: Row(
            mainAxisSize: MainAxisSize.max,
            children: [
              addHorizontalSpace(16),
              SizedBox(
                height: 140,
                width: 100,
                child: CachedNetworkImage(
                  imageUrl: imageUrl,
                  alignment: Alignment.topCenter,
                  fit: BoxFit.cover,
                  height: 140,
                  width: 100,
                ),
              ),
              addHorizontalSpace(16),
// 3
              Stack(
                children: [
                  Positioned(
                    top: 8,
                    right: 8,
                    child: IconButton(
                      onPressed: () => onFavoritesTap(favorite),
                      icon: favorite.favorite ? const Icon(
                        Icons.favorite_outlined,
                        color: Colors.red,
                      ) : const Icon(
                        Icons.favorite_border,
```

```
                          color: Colors.white,
                    ),
                  ),
                ),
     // 4
                  Column(
                    mainAxisSize: MainAxisSize.min,
                    mainAxisAlignment: MainAxisAlignment.start,
                    crossAxisAlignment: CrossAxisAlignment.start,
                    children: [
                      const Spacer(),
                      Column(
                        mainAxisSize: MainAxisSize.min,
                        mainAxisAlignment: MainAxisAlignment.
     start,
                        crossAxisAlignment: CrossAxisAlignment.
     start,
                        children: [
                          SizedBox(
                            width: textWidth,
                            child: AutoSizeText(
                              'Title',
                              maxLines: 1,
                              minFontSize: 10,
                              style: Theme.of(context).textTheme.
     labelLarge,
                              overflow: TextOverflow.ellipsis,
                            ),
                          ),
                          addVerticalSpace( 4),
                          Text(
                            '1972',
                            style: Theme.of(context).textTheme.
     bodyMedium,
                          ),
                          addVerticalSpace( 4),
                        ],
                      ),
                    ]),
                ],
              ),
```

```
          ],
        ),
      ),
    );
  } else {
    return Container();
  }
}
```

These widgets perform the following functions:

a.  Use MediaQuery to get the width of the screen. Set the width of the text based on the screen width.

b.  Use some SizedBoxes to set the row to be 148 pixels high.

c.  Use a Stack to show the favorite icon at the top right.

d.  Create a Column for the text.

4.  Next, in the **widgets** folder, create a file named **vert_favorite_list.dart**. Add the following code:

```dart
import 'package:flutter/material.dart';

import 'package:movies/data/models/favorite.dart';
import 'package:movies/utils/utils.dart';
import 'package:movies/ui/movie_viewmodel.dart';
import 'favorite_row.dart';

class VerticalFavoriteList extends StatelessWidget {
  final List<Favorite> favorites;
  final MovieViewModel movieViewModel;
  final OnMovieTap onMovieTap;
  final OnFavoriteResultsTap onFavoritesTap;

  const VerticalFavoriteList(
      {super.key,
      required this.favorites,
      required this.movieViewModel,
      required this.onMovieTap,
        required this.onFavoritesTap,
      });

  @override
  Widget build(BuildContext context) {
    return SliverList(
```

```
      delegate: SliverChildBuilderDelegate(
        (BuildContext context, int index) {
          return FavoriteRow(
            favorite: favorites[index],
            movieViewModel: movieViewModel,
            onMovieTap: (id) {
              onMovieTap(id);
            },
            onFavoritesTap: (favorite) {
              onFavoritesTap(favorite);
            },
          );
        },
        childCount: favorites.length, // Number of items in the list
      ),
    );
  }
}
```

This uses a **SliverList** to show a list of **FavoriteRows**.

5. Open up **movie_viewmodel.dart**. We will be using streams for favorites. This will allow us to update the list of favorites in all areas. Add the following after **movieGenres**:

```
Stream<List<Favorite>>? favoriteStream = null;
List<Favorite>? favoriteList = null;
```

After the **loadMovies** method add the creation of the favorite list:

```
Stream<List<Favorite>> streamFavorites() {
  if (favoriteList == null) {
    favoriteList = [
      Favorite(
          movieId: 1,
          image:
              'http://image.tmdb.org/t/p/w780/
z1p34vh7dEOnLDmyCrlUVLuoDzd.jpg',
          favorite: false,
          title: 'Title',
          overview: 'Overview',
          popularity: 1.0,
          releaseDate: DateTime.now())),
      Favorite(
```

```
                movieId: 2,
                image:
                    'http://image.tmdb.org/t/p/w780/
gKkl37BQuKTanygYQG1pyYgLVgf.jpg',
                favorite: false,
                title: 'Title',
                overview: 'Overview',
                popularity: 1.0,
                releaseDate: DateTime.now()),
        Favorite(
                movieId: 3,
                image:
                    'http://image.tmdb.org/t/p/
w780/4xJd3uwtL1vCuZgEfEc8JXI9Uyx.jpg',
                favorite: false,
                title: 'Title',
                overview: 'Overview',
                popularity: 1.0,
                releaseDate: DateTime.now()),
        Favorite(
                movieId: 4,
                image:
                    'http://image.tmdb.org/t/p/w780/
uuA01PTtPombRPvL9dvsBqOBJWm.jpg',
                favorite: false,
                title: 'Title',
                overview: 'Overview',
                popularity: 1.0,
                releaseDate: DateTime.now()),
        Favorite(
                movieId: 5,
                image:
                    'http://image.tmdb.org/t/p/w780/
H6vke7zGiuLsz4v4RPeReb9rsv.jpg',
                favorite: false,
                title: 'Title',
                overview: 'Overview',
                popularity: 1.0,
                releaseDate: DateTime.now()),
    ];
  }
```

```
    favoriteStream = Stream.value(favoriteList!);
    return favoriteStream!;
}
```

This creates a list and then a stream using that list. However, what if we want to update a favorite item? We can update the list and when the stream is retrieved, the stream is updated.

6.  Add a new method:

```
void updateFavorite(Favorite favorite) {
    final index = favoriteList!
        .indexWhere((favItem) => favItem.movieId == favorite.
movieId);
    if (index != -1) {
      favoriteList![index] = favorite;
    }
}
```

This will find the favorite in the list and update it.

7.  Open up **favorite_screen.dart** in the **ui/favorites** folder. Replace the build method with:

```
late MovieViewModel movieViewModel;
List<Favorite> currentFavorites = [];
Sorting selectedSort = Sorting.aToz;
final valueNotifier = ValueNotifier<List<Favorite>>([]);

@override
Widget build(BuildContext context) {
  final movieViewModelAsync = ref.watch(movieViewModelProvider);
  return movieViewModelAsync.when(
    error: (e, st) => Text(e.toString()),
    loading: () => const NotReady(),
    data: (viewModel) {
      movieViewModel = viewModel;
      return buildScreen();
    },
  );
}

Widget buildScreen() {
```

8.  Add any needed imports. This uses the same method to retrieve the view model. Next, add the following to the **buildScreen** method:

```
    return SafeArea(
      child: StreamBuilder<List<Favorite>>(
// 1
        stream: getFavoriteStream(),
        builder: (context, snapshot) {
          if ((snapshot.connectionState != ConnectionState.active)
&& (snapshot.connectionState != ConnectionState.done)) {
            return const NotReady();
          }
          return Scaffold(
            body: Container(
              color: screenBackground,
              child: Column(
                mainAxisSize: MainAxisSize.min,
                mainAxisAlignment: MainAxisAlignment.start,
                crossAxisAlignment: CrossAxisAlignment.start,
                children: [
                  Expanded(
                    child: CustomScrollView(
                      slivers: [
// 2
                        SliverList(
                          delegate: SliverChildListDelegate(
                            [
                              Padding(
                                padding: const EdgeInsets.fromLTRB(
                                    16, 16.0, 0.0, 24.0),
                                child: Text('My Favorites', style:
Theme.of(context).textTheme.titleLarge),
                              ),
                            ],
                          ),
                        ),
// 3
                        SortPicker(
                            useSliver: true,
                            onSortSelected: (sorting) {
                              selectedSort = sorting;
                              sortMovies();
                            }),
```

```
// 4
                            VerticalFavoriteList(
                              favorites: snapshot.requireData,
                              movieViewModel: movieViewModel,
                              onMovieTap: (movieId) {
                                context.router
                                    .push(MovieDetailRoute(movieId:
movieId));
                              },
                              onFavoritesTap: (Favorite favorite) {
                                setState(() {
// 5
                                  favorite.favorite = !favorite.
favorite;
                                  movieViewModel.
updateFavorite(favorite);
                                });
                              },
                            )
                          ],
                        ),
                      ),
                    ],
                  ),
                ),
              );
            },
          ),
        );
```

Add any needed imports. The following is an explanation:

    a.   Call the **getFavoriteStream** method to return a stream of favorites.

    b.   Use a **SliverList** to show a scrolling list of widgets.

    c.   Use our **SortPicker** widget to allow sorting.

    d.   Use the **VerticalFavoriteList** widget we created earlier.

    e.   Update whether the movie is a favorite or not.

There are a few methods that have not been implemented yet. Let us add those next.

9.  Next, create the stream with the following:

    ```
    Stream<List<Favorite>> getFavoriteStream() {
        return movieViewModel.streamFavorites();
    }
    ```

10. Then, add the sort movies method. This just compares the titles, popularity, or release date.

    ```
    void sortMovies() {
      if (currentFavorites.isEmpty) {
        return;
      }
      currentFavorites = currentFavorites.sorted((a, b) {
        switch (selectedSort) {
          case Sorting.aToz:
            return a.title.compareTo(b.title);
          case Sorting.zToa:
            return b.title.compareTo(a.title);
          case Sorting.rating:
            return b.popularity.compareTo(a.popularity);
          case Sorting.year:
            return a.releaseDate.compareTo(b.releaseDate);
        }
      });
      valueNotifier.value = currentFavorites;
    }
    ```

    You will notice that there is an error in the sorted method. This method is an extension that is part of the collections package.

11. Open up **pubspec.yaml** and add:

    ```
    collection: ^1.17.1
    ```

12. Do a Pub get, return to **favorite_screen.dart**, and import the collection package. Finally, add the **removeFavorite** method:

    ```
    Future removeFavorite(Favorite favorite) async {
      setState(() {
        currentFavorites.remove(favorite);
      });
    }
    ```

    Perform a Hot Reload, and you should see the favorites screen with a list of movies. Try clicking on the heart. It should change to a filled heart.

# Isolates

As previously mentioned, Flutter runs in a single isolate. If you have a task that will take a long time, like syncing a local database with a remote database, using an isolate is your only solution. This will create a thread to do work. However, communicating with a running thread requires the use of Ports. Ports are used for communication between isolates with messages sent using a **SendPort** and **ReceivePort**. You will usually create a **ReceivePort** and use that port's **SendPort** to send to an isolate. That isolate can use the **SendPort** to send messages back to the caller. The caller will listen for messages on the **ReceivePort** using the **listen()** method. The following is a simple example:

```
import 'dart:isolate';

void main() async {
  final receivePort = ReceivePort();

  // Spawn a new isolate
  Isolate.spawn(isolateFunction, receivePort.sendPort);

  // Listen for messages from the isolate
  receivePort.listen((message) {
    print('Received: $message');
  });
}

void isolateFunction(SendPort sendPort) {
  sendPort.send('Hello from the isolate!');
}
```

The main function first creates the **ReceivePort**, then uses **Isolate.spawn** with a reference to a function and the send port. If you need to send more than just strings to an isolate, one way to handle this is to convert data classes to JSON strings, send them via the send port, and then de-serialize the JSON back into classes in the isolate. You can also pass arguments to an isolate. The following is an example of a function sending arguments to the isolate function:

```
final receivePort = ReceivePort();
final isolate = await Isolate.spawn<Map<String, dynamic>>(
  entryPoint,
  {
    'sendPort': receivePort.sendPort,
    'mapReference': <JSON string>
  },
  errorsAreFatal: true,
  debugName: 'RepositoryIsolate',
);
```

```
void entryPoint(Map<String, dynamic> arguments) async {
  final sendPort = arguments['sendPort'] as SendPort;
  final sharedMap = arguments['mapReference'] as Map<String, dynamic>;
}
```

You can only send primitives, Lists, Maps, Sets, and **SendPorts** via *SendPort's* **send** method. This uses the **Isolate.spawn** method with a **Map<String, dynamic>** (which is what JSON data is). The first parameter is the function, and the second is the map with a send port and the data. There are extra parameters that you can use for handling errors. There are also **onExit** and **onError** parameters. The **entryPoint** method gets the send port from the arguments and the data next (Note that you can name the function anything you want). Here is an example of listening to a receive port:

```
receivePort.listen((message) async {
  if (message is String) {
    // Process message
  }
  // When done, you can kill the isolate

  isolate.kill();

});
```

Remember that you cannot use fields or classes created outside of the isolate. You will have to create new instances of them. Some packages, like database handlers, do not like to have multiple instances of a database open at the same time, so be careful when choosing your database.

# Conclusion

In this chapter, you learned about asynchronous functions and how to use them in your apps. You used **Futures**, **FutureBuilder**, **StreamBuilder**, and the **async** and **await** keywords needed to use Futures. You learned about isolates and how they are useful. Finally, you refactored your movie app to use these features and added the Favorites screen to your movie app.

In the next chapter, you will use what you have learned in this chapter to retrieve data from the internet. You will use **Future** and **async** functions to download movie information to finally show real movie information in your movie app.

## Join our book's Discord space

Join the book's Discord Workspace for Latest updates, Offers, Tech happenings around the world, New Release and Sessions with the Authors:

**https://discord.bpbonline.com**

# CHAPTER 11
# Networking

## Introduction

In this chapter, you will learn all about networking and start using **The Movie Database** (**TMDB**) website to retrieve the latest movies. You will learn how to asynchronously download data and update the screen with new moves. You will learn about APIs and how to retrieve data from the internet using networking packages.

## Structure

The chapter covers the following topics:

- Networking
- TMDB
- JSON and serialization
- Data models
- Networking packages
- Dio package

# Objectives

By the end of this chapter, you will have a solid understanding of how to download data in the background and update the UI with that new information. You will understand the JSON format, how to create models for downloaded data, and how to put the data into those models. You will know how to work with networking APIs and write code to use them. You will also be able to use packages to create code to connect with APIs to download that data. You will also learn about consuming data from other sites.

# Networking

Cellular phones use WiFi and cellular data to handle networking. So far, the movie app only has icons, images, and videos. All the icons come from the Flutter framework, but the URLs we have used pull in images and videos from the internet. The cached network image library uses networking calls to download images in the background, and the **pod_player** package uses networking to play videos. Now, we will learn how to download data ourselves. We will still use a package to make things easier, but it is a lower-level package that allows us to download information from other sites. Not only can the package download images or videos, but the package allows us to download anything we want. Flutter comes with its own package for networking, but we will use a better third-party package. Most apps need to be able to retrieve data from the internet. This is a critical part of your app and should be written early in app development so that you can have data to use for your UIs.

# TMDB

We will be using the TMDB site to get information about movies. This site allows you to freely use it for personal use. If you decide to use the app commercially, you will need a paid account. You will need to create an account and be approved, so make sure you put in a valid email address when you sign up. Go to the TMDB site: **https://www.themoviedb.org/signup.** You will see a sign-up form, as shown in *Figure 11.1*. Enter all required information.

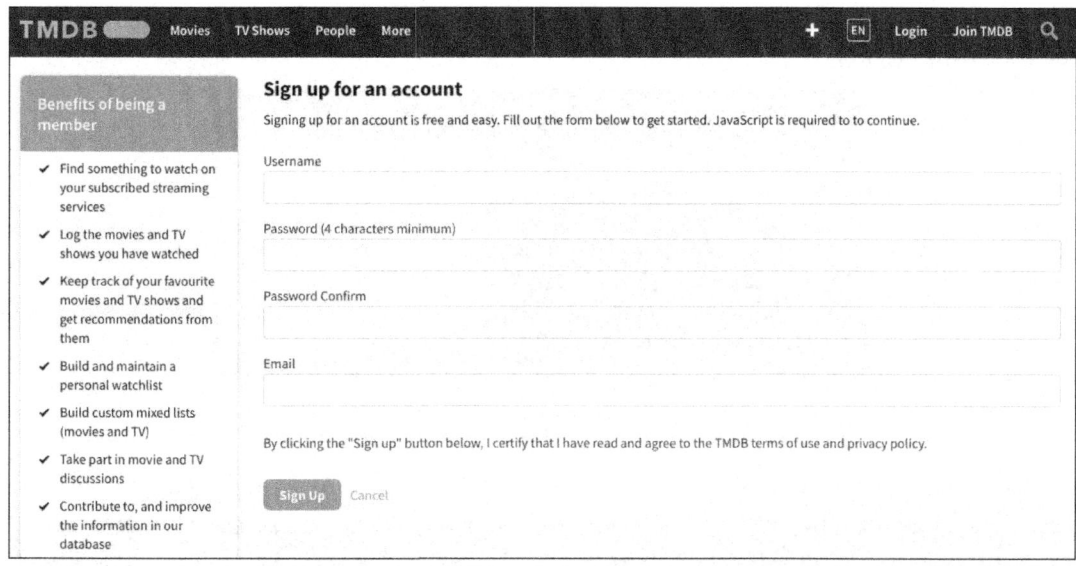

*Figure 11.1*: TMDB signup

Once you click on the signup button, you will receive an email to verify your email, and shortly, you will be accepted. Once you have been accepted, you will see your dashboard, as shown in *Figure 11.2*. Note that you are signing up for the TMDB site that anyone can use to view movies.

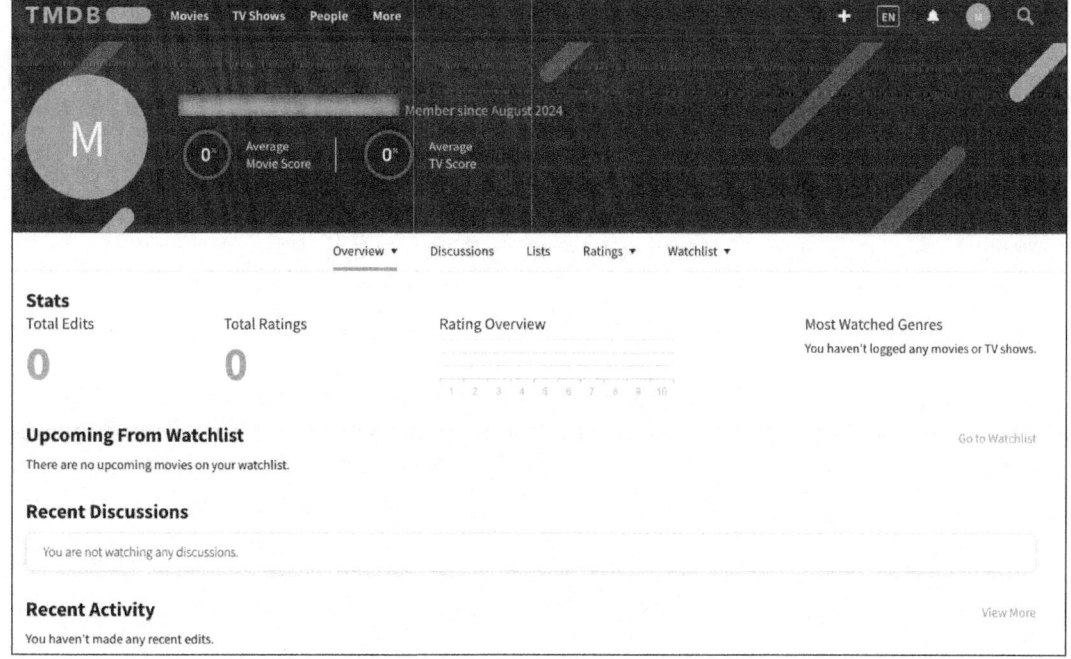

*Figure 11.2*: TMDB dashboard

To go to the developer section, choose the **More** link and then the **API** link, as shown in the following figure:

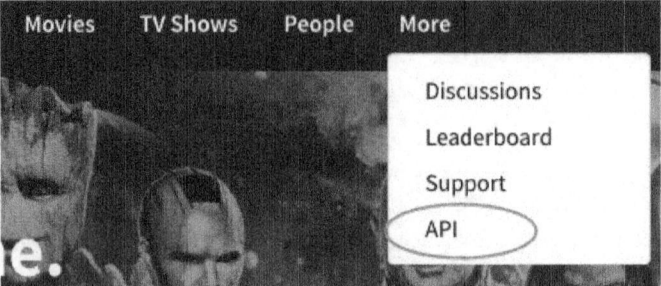

*Figure 11.3*: TMDB API Link

On the API site, you will need to create a developer API key. Click on the **Developer** link:

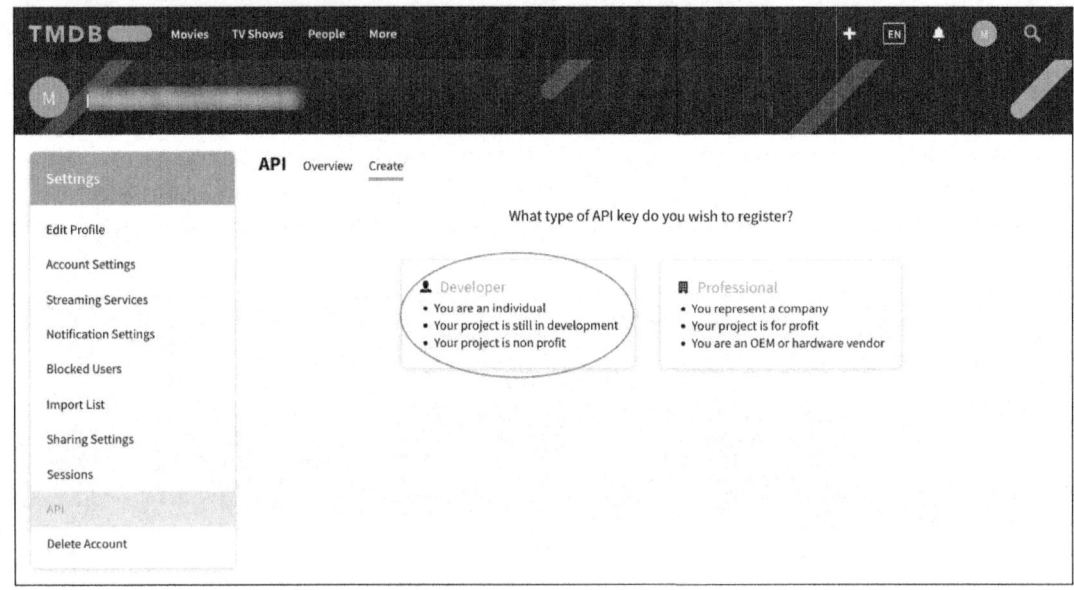

*Figure 11.4*: TMDB API Key

On the next page, choose **Mobile Application** for the type, give your app any name you want, and add an **Application URL**. The author is unsure whether this field needs a valid website, as they entered their website here. Finally, enter a summary and your information:

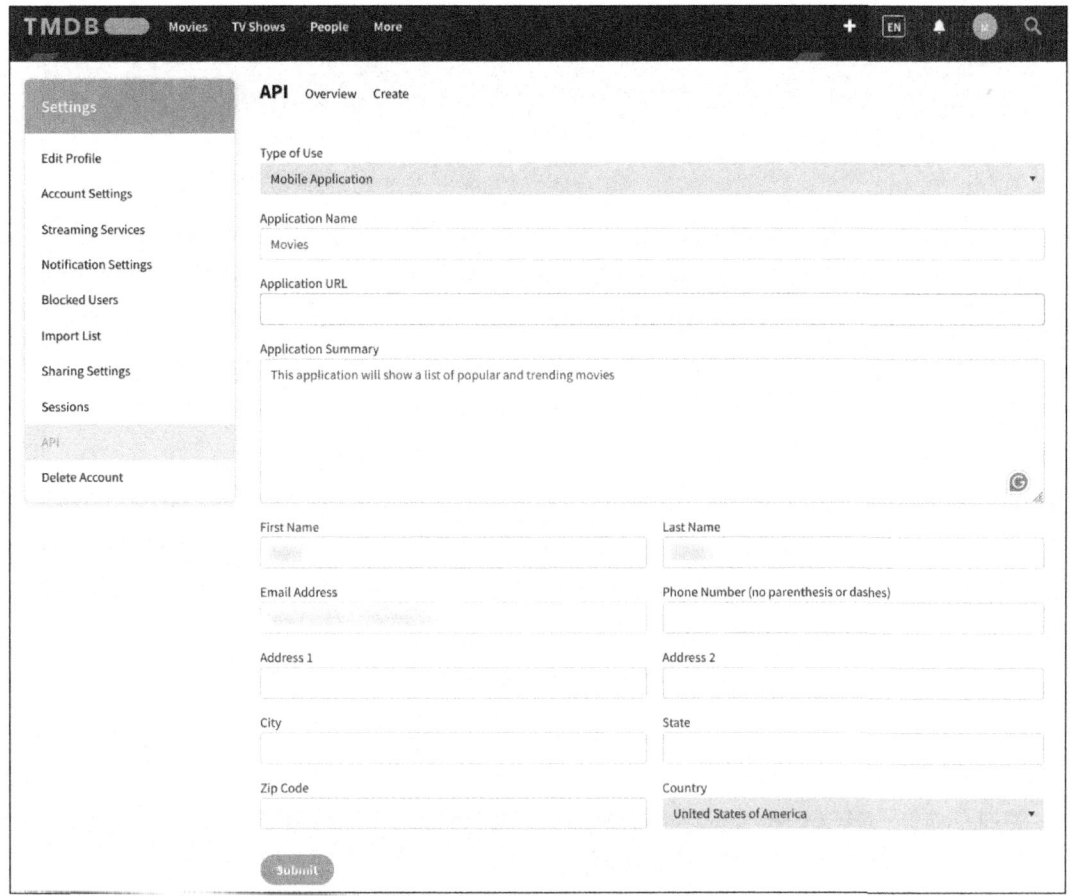

***Figure 11.5***: *TMDB API key application*

Once you select **Submit**, you will be taken to the API Key page, as shown in the following figure. Copy the API Key since you will need it later.

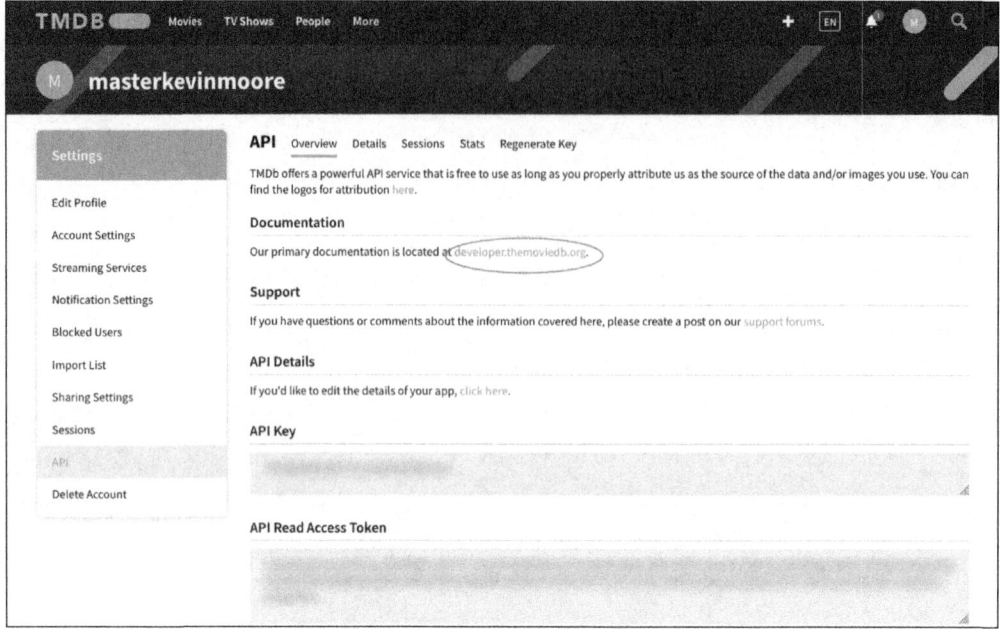

*Figure 11.6*: TMDB API key overview

Click on the *developer.themoviedb.org* link, and you will be taken to the **Getting Started** page, as shown in the following figure:

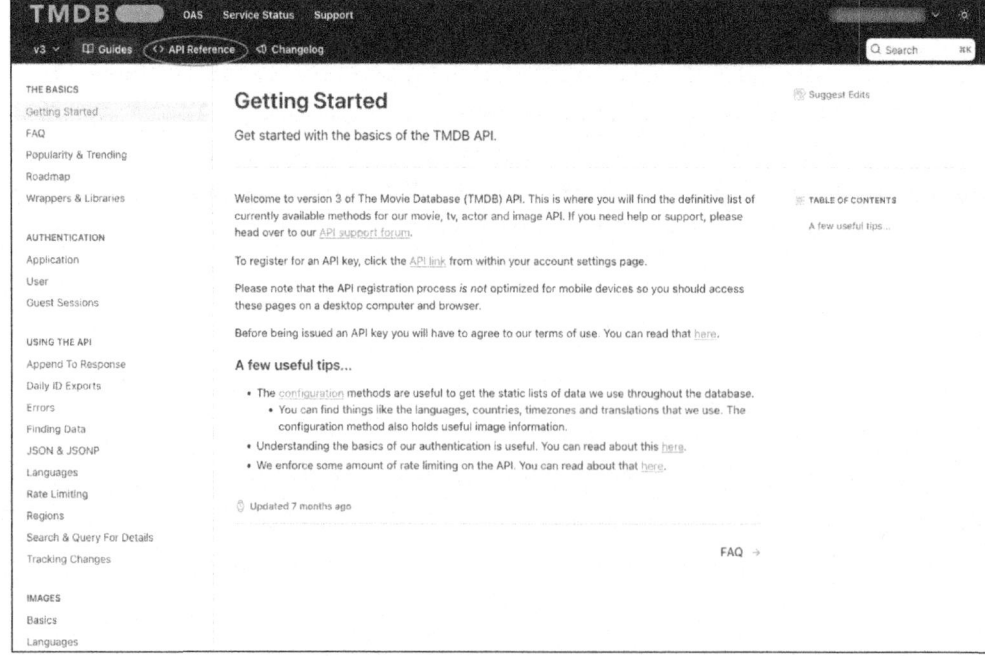

*Figure 11.7*: TMDB API reference

Next, click on the **API Reference** menu, as shown in the following figure:

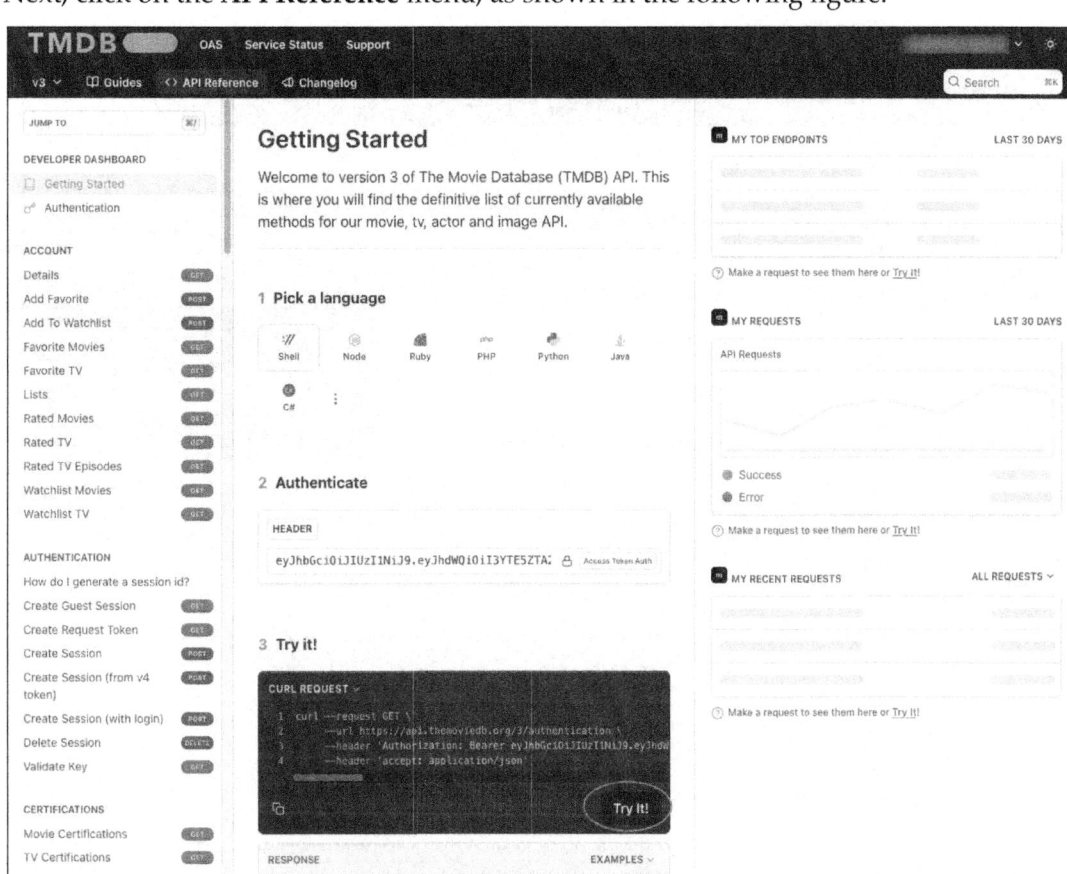

*Figure 11.8: TMDB Getting Started*

To make sure your key works, click on the **Try it!** *Button*. You should see a successful response as follows:

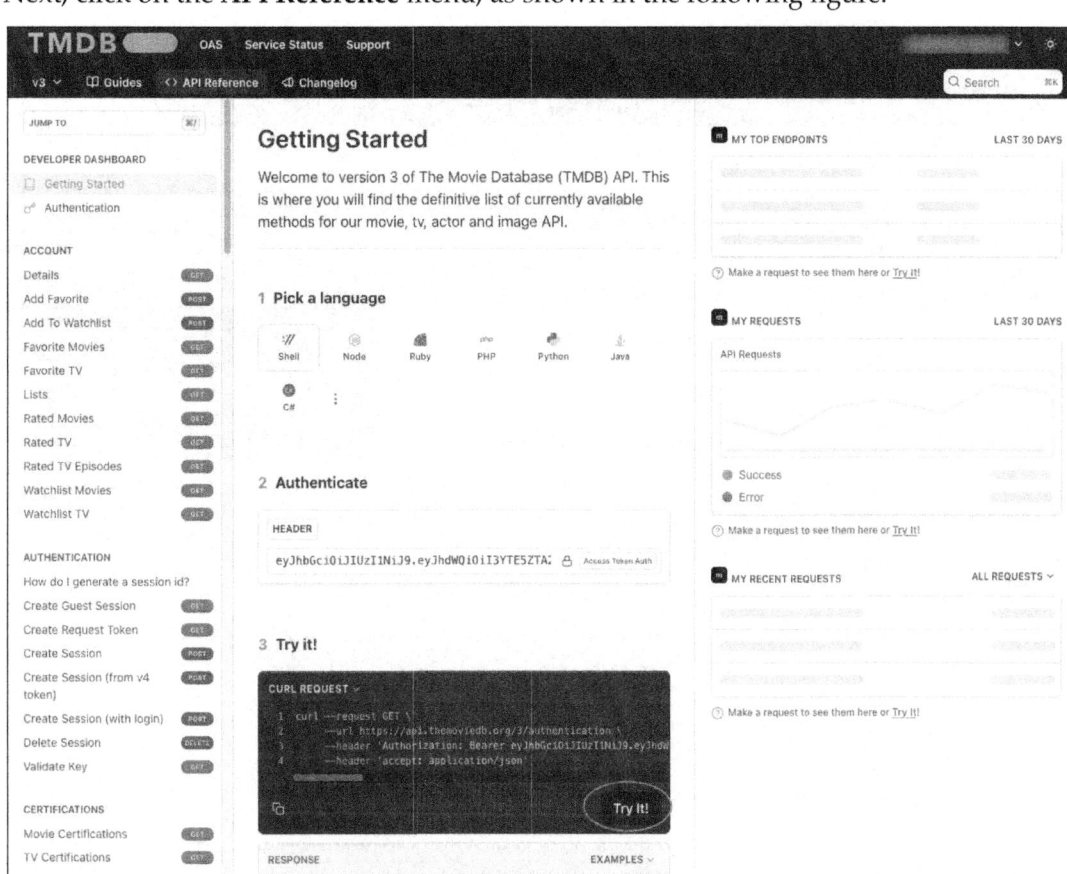

*Figure 11.9: Success response*

Scroll down the left list to the **Movie Lists** section and click on **Now Playing**. This will show the Now Playing API:

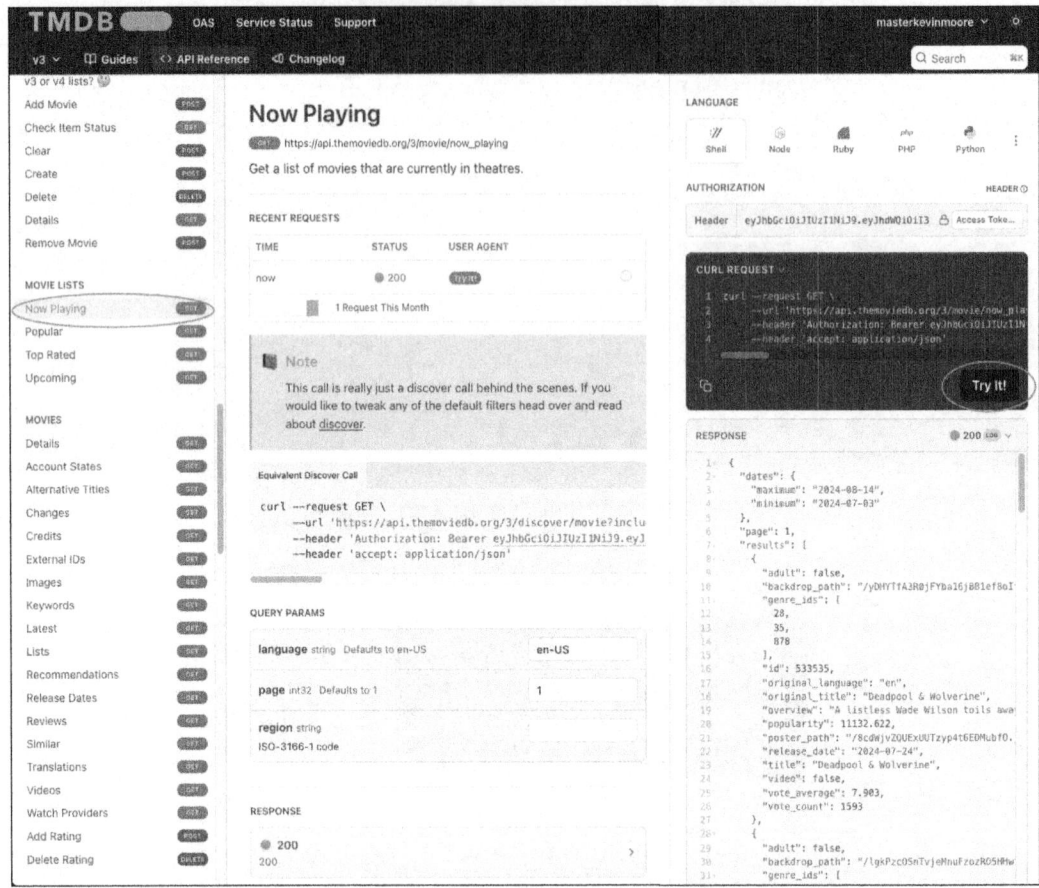

*Figure 11.10*: *TMDB Now Playing API*

Click on the **Try it!** *Button,* and you should see a response.

# JSON and serialization

The response above contains data in the **JavaScript Object Notation (JSON)** format. It is the most widely used format for **Representational State Transfer (REST)**-based APIs that servers provide. REST-based APIs are standardized ways for systems to communicate. These consist of stateless requests from a client to a server. That means that the server does not remember previous calls. Most servers return data in JSON format. JSON is easy to read and uses left "{" and right "}" brackets with key/value pairs. These values can have child entries as well. Dart and Flutter use JSON extensively. What you will typically do is read in JSON and convert it into class files so that your app can read that data easily. JSON supports a few data types listed as follows:

- **String**: A value surrounded by quotes
- **Number**: An integer value (No quotes)
- **Boolean**: True or false
- **null**: Empty value
- **Array**: A list of items using "[" "]"
- **Object**: A collection of key/value pairs

There is a hard and easy way to convert JSON to a class. While it is possible to treat JSON as just a long string and try to parse out the data, it is much easier to use a package that already knows how to do that. Flutter has a built-in package for decoding JSON, but in this chapter, you will use the **freezed**, **json_serializable** and **json_annotation** packages to help make the process easier.

Flutter's built-in **dart:convert** package contains methods like **json.decode()** and **json.encode()**, which converts a JSON string to a **Map<String, dynamic>** and back. While this is a step ahead of manually parsing JSON, you still have to write extra code that takes that map and puts the values into a new class.

The **json_serializable** package is useful because it can generate model classes for you according to the annotations you provide via the **json_annotation** package. **freezed** is even more powerful and allows you to create classes that handle both JSON serialization and deserialization and provides the following methods:

- **copyWith**: Allows you to create copies of a class by changing specific fields.
- **toString**: Creates a method that returns a string with all data values.
- **equals operator**: Provides equality. This is needed for adding classes to lists and maps.
- **hashCode**: Getter that provides a unique value for the class and its values. Needed for equals to work.
- **toJson**: Returns a JSON **Map<String, dynamic>**.
- **fromJson**: Converts a JSON map to this class.

Since **freezed** uses the **json_serializable** package, we will talk about **freezed**. Before looking at automated serialization, you must understand how to serialize JSON manually.

So, how do you go about writing code to serialize JSON yourself? Typical model classes have **toJson()** and **fromJson()** methods. The **toJson()** method helps to convert objects into JSON strings, and the **fromJson()** method helps to parse a JSON string into an object so you can use it inside the program. In an earlier chapter, you wrote the **Movie** class. The following is an example of what it would look like with the two new methods:

```
class Movie {
  final int movieId;
```

```dart
  final String image;
  final String title;
  final String overview;
  final double popularity;
  final DateTime releaseDate;

  Movie({required this.movieId, required this.image, required this.
title, required this.overview, required this.popularity, required this.
releaseDate});

  factory Movie.fromJson(Map<String, dynamic> json) {
    return Movie(
      movieId: json['movieId'],
      image: json['image'],
      title: json['title'],
      overview: json['overview'],
      popularity: json['popularity'],
      releaseDate: json['releaseDate'],
    );
  }

  Map<String, dynamic> toJson() {
    return <String, dynamic>{
      'movieId': movieId,
      'image': image,
      'title': title,
      'overview': overview,
      'popularity': popularity,
      'releaseDate': releaseDate,
    };
  }
}
```

Notice that we have to write every single field to create a new movie and convert it into a JSON map. This is a lot of work. With **freezed**, you will add annotations to the class and write it in a certain way to have it generate a lot of code for you.

1.  Start by adding the needed libraries to the **pubspec.yaml** file. Under the dependencies section, add the following:

    ```yaml
    intl: ^0.18.1
    json_annotation: ^4.8.1
    freezed_annotation: ^2.4.1
    ```

2. Under the **dev_dependencies** section, add:

```
json_serializable: ^6.7.1

freezed: ^2.4.7
```

The **intl** package is the Flutter internationalization package which has some date formatting utilities that we will be using. Both annotation packages have annotation classes that are needed for your models. The dev dependencies are used when running the builder. Do a Pub get. Now that we have these libraries, it is time to create the models for the movies. As you saw earlier, the TMDB website lists movies in JSON format. It looks as follows:

```json
{
  "dates": {
    "maximum": "2024-08-14",
    "minimum": "2024-07-03"
  },
  "page": 1,
  "results": [
    {
      "adult": false,
      "backdrop_path": "/yDHYTfA3R0jFYba16jBB1ef8oIt.jpg",
      "genre_ids": [
        28,
        35,
        878
      ],
      "id": 533535,
      "original_language": "en",
      "original_title": "Deadpool & Wolverine",
      "overview": "A listless Wade Wilson toils away in civilian life with
his days as the morally flexible mercenary, Deadpool, behind him. But when
his homeworld faces an existential threat, Wade must reluctantly suit-up
again with an even more reluctant Wolverine.",
      "popularity": 11132.622,
      "poster_path": "/8cdWjvZQUExUUTzyp4t6EDMubfO.jpg",
      "release_date": "2024-07-24",
      "title": "Deadpool & Wolverine",
      "video": false,
      "vote_average": 7.893,
      "vote_count": 1634
    },
```

```
  ],
  "total_pages": 167,
  "total_results": 3339
}
```

This just shows one entry, but the important parts are as follows:

- **page**: This shows which page is returned.

- **results**: This is the list of movies.

- In the brackets are all the details for the movie.

- **total_pages**: The total number of pages worth of movies the API could return. Useful for downloading the next page.

- **total_results**: This gives the total number of movies available.

# Data models

We will need to create a **movie** class that has this information in it. In the **data/models** folder, create a new file named **movie_results.dart**.

1. Start by adding the imports and parts as follows:

   ```
   import 'package:freezed_annotation/freezed_annotation.dart';
   import 'package:intl/intl.dart';

   part 'movie_results.freezed.dart';

   part 'movie_results.g.dart';
   ```

   This imports the freezed annotation and the international package. The part files will be created for you when you run the builder. The freezed file is for equality, and the g file is for JSON.

2. Next, add a helper function that helps override the serialization so that we can use dates instead of strings:

   ```
   // Parsing function to be used by @JsonKey
   DateTime? _parseDate(String? dateString) {
     if (dateString == null || dateString.isEmpty) {
       return null;
     }
     return DateFormat('yyyy-MM-dd').parse(dateString);
   }
   ```

   This just uses the **intl** package's **DateFormat** class to convert a string into a **DateTime** class.

3. Now add the class. Note that we are not using every single field that the data returns, just the most useful:

```
// 1
@freezed
// 2
class MovieResults with _$MovieResults {
// 3
  const factory MovieResults({
// 4
    @JsonKey(name: 'backdrop_path')
    String? backdropPath,
// 5
    required int id,
    @JsonKey(name: 'original_title')
    required String originalTitle,
    required String overview,
    @JsonKey(name: 'poster_path')
    String? posterPath,
    @JsonKey(name: 'media_type')
    String? mediaType,
    required bool adult,
    required String title,
    @JsonKey(name: 'original_language')
    required String originalLanguage,
    @JsonKey(name: 'genre_ids')
    required List<int> genreIds,
    required double popularity,
// 6
    @JsonKey(name: 'release_date', fromJson: _parseDate)
    DateTime? releaseDate,
    required bool video,
    @JsonKey(name: 'vote_average')
    required double voteAverage,
    @JsonKey(name: 'vote_count')
    required int voteCount,
// 7
  }) = _MovieResults;
// 8
  factory MovieResults.fromJson(Map<String, dynamic> json) =>
      _$MovieResultsFromJson(json);
}
```

Here, we are creating a `MovieResults` class. The with `_$MovieResults` is a mixin that will be generated by **freezed**. It uses a factory method to create the `MovieResults` class. The following is a description of the important elements:

1. Use the **@freezed** annotation to mark the class to be generated with freezed.

2. Use the generated **_$MovieResults** mixin.

3. Use a factory to create the class.

4. The **@JsonKey** annotation allows you to use one name for the field and another for the data it should be expecting. In Dart, you do not use underscores for field names.

5. If a field is not nullable, it needs the required keyword.

6. Use the **fromJson** annotation to specify a function to convert the field into a date.

7. The factory ends with an underscore class name. This is needed by freezed.

8. Use a factory for the **fromJson** method. Freezed will create the method.

4. In the terminal window, run the build runner command:

```
dart run build_runner build
```

You should now see the **.freezed.dart** and **.g.dart** files. Remember when you saw the JSON output there were fields for **total_pages** and **total_results**? We will need to write a class that has these fields. It will also contain a list of the movies.

5. In the same folder, create a new file named **movie_response.dart**. Add the following:

```
import 'package:freezed_annotation/freezed_annotation.dart';
import 'package:movies/data/models/movie_results.dart';

part 'movie_response.freezed.dart';

part 'movie_response.g.dart';

@freezed
class MovieResponse with _$MovieResponse {
  const factory MovieResponse({
    required int page,
    required List<MovieResults> results,
    @JsonKey(name: 'total_pages')
    required int totalPages,
    @JsonKey(name: 'total_results')
    required int totalResults
```

```
        }) = _MovieResponse;

    factory MovieResponse.fromJson(Map<String, dynamic>  json) =>
    _$MovieResponseFromJson(json);

    }
```

6.  In the terminal window, run the build runner command:

    ```
    dart run build_runner build
    ```

    Looking at the **Dart Analysis** tab in Android Studio, you will see some warnings on the JsonKey annotations. This warning does not understand how the classes are built, and if you want to remove those warnings, you can add the following to the **analysis_options.yaml** file underneath the last analyzer item:

    ```
    errors:
        invalid_annotation_target: ignore
    ```

Now, it is time to start using these models.

# Networking packages

Dart provides the **http** package. This provides basic functionality for accessing the internet. While it is perfectly fine to use this package, there are many others that provide functionality like logging, network timeouts, and response and request modification. Many web services that provide data use REST, a style for designing networked applications. It provides several different interfaces, as follows:

- **GET**: for retrieving information.
- **POST**: For creating new data.
- **PUT**: For updating existing data.
- **DELETE**: For deleting data.

Data is usually in JSON format but can also be in other formats, like XML. Since JSON is easy to use and is part of Dart and Flutter, we will use that format.

Many other packages provide a bit more functionality than the **http** package.

# Dio package

An **application programming interface (API)** is a set of rules that define how systems communicate. The TMDB website has APIs for talking to its movie database. We will use the Dio package because it is easy to use to talk to this database or set of APIs.

1.  Start out by adding the Dio package to the **pubspec.yaml**:

    ```
    dio: ^5.4.3+1
    ```

Perform a Pub get.

2. Next, create a new folder in the lib folder named **network**. Inside this folder, create a new file named **movie_api_service.dart**. Add the following:

```
import 'package:dio/dio.dart';

// 1
const String movieAPIUrl = 'https://api.themoviedb.org/3/';
// 2
const trendingUrl = 'trending/movie/week';
const nowPlayingUrl = 'movie/now_playing';
const topRatedUrl = 'movie/top_rated';
const popularUrl = 'movie/popular';
const pageParameterName = 'page';
const movieIdParameterName = 'movie_id';
const apiKeyParameterName = 'api_key';

class MovieAPIService {
  late final Dio dio;
  final showDebugInfo = false;
}
```

This defines several URLs needed for movies and then defines the class and a flag to show debug information. If you look at the Now Playing page on the TMDB website, you will see the following:

*Figure 11.11: TMDB Now Playing API*

The **https://api.themoviedb.org/3/** URL is called the **base** URL. All other URLs are made from this URL plus a specific location, like **movie/now_playing**. We will be concatenating these strings to make the full URL. We have defined a late field for the **Dio** class because we will initialize it later. The **showDebugInfo** is a flag for printing all the network calls. This is useful as it prints all the network calls to the console.

3. Add the following:

```
MovieAPIService() {
  configureDio();
```

```
  }

  void configureDio() {
    final options = BaseOptions(
      baseUrl: movieAPIUrl,
      connectTimeout: const Duration(seconds: 5),
      receiveTimeout: const Duration(seconds: 3),
    );
    dio = Dio(options);
    // TODO Add interceptors
  }
```

This creates options for Dio with the base URL and some timeouts for connecting and receiving data. We then create the **Dio** class with those options.

4. For the TODO, add the following:

```
    dio.interceptors.add(
// 1
      InterceptorsWrapper(
// 2
        onRequest: (RequestOptions options, RequestInterceptorHandler
handler) {
// 3
          final queryParameters = options.queryParameters;
          queryParameters[apiKeyParameterName] = apiKey;
          return handler.next(options);
        },
        onResponse: (Response response, ResponseInterceptorHandler
handler) {
          // Do something with response data.
          // If you want to reject the request with a error message,
          // you can reject a `DioException` object using `handler.
reject(dioError)`.
          return handler.next(response);
        },
// 4
        onError: (DioException error, ErrorInterceptorHandler
handler) {
          // Do something with response error.
          // If you want to resolve the request with some custom
data,
          // you can resolve a `Response` object using `handler.
```

```
    resolve(response)`.
            return handler.next(error);
        },
      ),
    );
  // 5
    if (showDebugInfo) {
      dio.interceptors.add(LogInterceptor(
        responseBody: true,
        // Whether to log the response body (can be large)
        error: true,
        // Whether to log errors
        request: true,
        // Whether to log requests
        requestHeader: true,
        // Whether to log request headers
        responseHeader: true, // Whether to log response headers
      ));
    }
```

This adds an **interceptor**. This will intercept all API calls both before, after, and when there is an error. You can handle errors in the **onError** callback and add the API key to each query in the **onRequest** callback. If you look at the **onRequest** call, you will see that we get the current query parameters map and add the API key. The **showDebugInfo** flag adds a logging interceptor to print out all API data. This helps when debugging problems. However, you should always turn this off before shipping a product. The major sections are as follows:

1.  Use an **InterceptorsWrapper** helper class. (Makes it easier to write)

2.  The **onRequest** method catches requests before they are made and can modify them.

3.  Get the current query parameters and add the API key.

4.  Handle errors. This is a good place to handle expired access tokens.

5.  Add a **LogInterceptor** to print API call information.

# API Security

You may have noticed that there is an error with the **apiKey** variable. We have not defined it yet because we do not want to put this key in our app. This would be a security problem if someone were to download your app and look at the source code. To get around this problem, you can use a library to store the information in a file that has not been checked into source control. One of these libraries is the **flutter_dotennv** package. This package will load the variable inside an invisible **.env** file in your root directory.

1.  Add the following to your **pubspec.yaml**:

    ```
    flutter_dotenv: ^5.1.0
    ```

2.  Now, in the root folder of your project, create a new file named **.env** (make sure you have a dot before the name; this makes it invisible on the system). If you have your files in git, add the **.env** file to your **.gitignore** file. You also need to add this to your list of assets so that it is included in your app.

3.  To do this, add the following as an assets section at the bottom of the **pubspec. yaml** file:

    ```
    assets:
      - .env
    ```

    Perform a Pub Get. Make sure that **assets** is indented properly underneath **uses-material-design**.

4.  In the **.env** file, add your key as follows:

    ```
    TMDB_KEY=''
    ```

    Add your key inside of the single quotes.

5.  Next, in the **movie_api_service.dart** file, after the **dio** field add the following:

    ```
    final String apiKey = dotenv.env['TMDB_KEY']!;
    ```

    Add the import:

    ```
    import 'package:flutter_dotenv/flutter_dotenv.dart';
    ```

    This will allow us to have the key just on our development machine. You could add it to a **continuous integration** (**CI**) machine as well, if needed. Now, you need to initialize **dotenv** to load the **.env** file.

6.  In **main.dart**, change the definition of the main function to:

    ```
    Future<void> main() async {
    ```

    Add the following before the **runApp** call:

    ```
    await dotenv.load(fileName: '.env');
    ```

    Add the import for **dotenv**.

# Trending movies

Now that we have the **dio** class configured, we need to write a method that will get the list of trending movies.

1. In the **movie_api_service.dart**, at the end of the class, add the following code:

```
Future<Response> getTrending([int page = 1]) async {
  final response =
  await dio.get(trendingUrl, queryParameters: {pageParameterName:
page});
  return response;
}
```

This method takes an optional page number that defaults to one. It then uses the trending URL (which is added to the base URL) and a page query. Changing the page number will get the movie results for that page.

Now that we have our movie API service, we need to add a provider so that other classes can use it.

2. Open up **providers.dart** and add:

```
@Riverpod(keepAlive: true)

MovieAPIService movieAPIService(MovieAPIServiceRef ref) =>
MovieAPIService();
```

3. Add the import for the **MovieAPIService** and then change the construction of the view model:

```
final model = MovieViewModel(movieAPIService: ref.
read(movieAPIServiceProvider));
```

4. Open **movie_viewmodel.dart** and add the service at the beginning of the class:

```
final MovieAPIService movieAPIService;
```

5. Add the movie API import. Add a constructor:

```
MovieViewModel({required this.movieAPIService});
```

6. In the terminal window, run the build runner command:

```
dart run build_runner build
```

# Logging

Since we could get errors, it would be nice to have the ability to log error messages. We will use the lumberdash library. Lumberdash and the color packages provide very nice logging capabilities and will print in color.

1. Open **pubspec.yaml** and add:

```
lumberdash: ^3.0.0

colorize_lumberdash: ^3.0.0
```

2. Do a Pub get and then open **main.dart**. At the top of the main function add:

```
   WidgetsFlutterBinding.ensureInitialized();
   putLumberdashToWork(withClients: [
     ColorizeLumberdash(),
   ]);
```

This will ensure that Flutter is initialized before configuring Lumber Dash.

# ViewModel

We can now use this service in the movie view model.

1. Open **movie_viewmodel.dart**. In the setup method, remove the **loadMovies** method. Go to **getTrendingMovies**.

2. Replace the method with the following:

```
// 1
   Future<MovieResponse?> getTrendingMovies(int page) async {
// 2
     final response = await movieAPIService.getTrending(page);
// 3
     if (response.statusCode == 200) {
// 4
       var movieResponse = MovieResponse.fromJson(response.data);
       trendingMovies = movieResponse.results;
       return movieResponse;
     } else {
// 5
       logError(
           'Failed to load movies with error ${response.statusCode}
and message ${response.statusMessage}');
       return null;
     }
   }
```

3. Then change the definition of **trendingMovies** to the following:

```
   List<MovieResults> trendingMovies = [];
```

Import the **MovieResponse** and **MovieResults** classes. Here, we perform the following steps:

1. Return a **MovieResponse**.

2. Call the service to get the trending movies.

3. Check the status code. This service always returns 200 for success.

4. Parse the JSON into a **MovieResponse** class.

5.   Otherwise, we have an error. Log the error.

Status codes are HTTP codes. Any codes in the 200-299 range are considered successful. Codes in the range of 400-499 are client errors, and 500-599 are server errors.

Warning: this will cause a lot of errors in our code that we will have to work through.

# Fixing errors

1.   Open **home_screen.dart**. You will need to change the definition of **movieFuture**:

```
Future<List<MovieResponse?>>? movieFuture;
```

2.   Import **MovieResponse**. Inside of **loadData**, change the call to:

```
movieFuture ??= Future.wait([
  movieViewModel.getTrendingMovies(1),
  // movieViewModel.getTopRated(1),
  // movieViewModel.getPopular(1),
  // movieViewModel.getNowPlaying(1)
]);
```

We will deal with the other calls later. Inside the **buildScreen** method, comment out the **HorizontalMovies** for the last two movie lists: popular and top-rated.

3.   Inside of **HorizontalMovies**, change the definition of movies to:

```
final List<MovieResults> movies;
```

4.   Inside of **MovieWidget** change the fields and constructor to:

```
final int movieId;
final String movieUrl;
final OnMovieTap onMovieTap;
final MovieType movieType;

const MovieWidget(
    {required this.movieId,
    required this.movieUrl,
    required this.onMovieTap,
    required this.movieType,
    super.key});
```

5.   Then change the hero tag to the following:

```
uniqueHeroTag = widget.movieUrl + widget.movieType.name;
```

6.   Then the **imageUrl** for **CachedNetworkImage** to:

```
imageUrl: widget.movieUrl,
```

7. Change **onMovieTap** call to the following:

```
widget.onMovieTap(widget.movieId);
```

The movie URL is contained in the **posterPath** field of the **MovieResults** class. However, this path is only a partial path. To create the full path, we must create a method to build this path.

8. Open **utils.dart** and add the following code:

```dart
import 'package:intl/intl.dart';
enum ImageSize {
  small,
  large
}
String getImageUrl(ImageSize size, String? path) {
  if (path == null) {
    return '';
  }
  switch (size) {
    case ImageSize.small:
      return 'http://image.tmdb.org/t/p/w154/$path';
    case ImageSize.large:
      return 'http://image.tmdb.org/t/p/w780/$path';
  }
}
final yearFormat = DateFormat('yyyy');
String youtubeImageFromId(String videoId) {
  return 'https://img.youtube.com/vi/$videoId/hqdefault.jpg';
}
```

This will build a URL from a base URL, a small size of 154 or a large size of 780, and a path. There is also a year formatter for the movie date and a method for getting a YouTube URL.

9. Back in **HorizontalMovies**, add the following as the first line in the **itemBuilder** section, replacing the current **MovieWidget**:

```dart
        final imageUrl = getImageUrl(ImageSize.small,
movies[index].posterPath);
        return MovieWidget(
          movieId: movies[index].id,
          movieUrl: imageUrl,
          onMovieTap: onMovieTap,
          movieType: movieType,
        );
```

Do a full hot restart. You will see the trending list but not the Swiper movies, as that uses the now playing list, which we commented out.

10. Open **movie_api_service.dart** and add the rest of the API calls:

```
Future<Response> getNowPlaying([int page = 1]) async {
    final response = await dio
        .get(nowPlayingUrl, queryParameters: {pageParameterName:
page});
    return response;
  }

  Future<Response> getTopRated([int page = 1]) async {
    final response =
        await dio.get(topRatedUrl, queryParameters:
{pageParameterName: page});
    return response;
  }

  Future<Response> getPopular([int page = 1]) async {
    final response =
        await dio.get(popularUrl, queryParameters:
{pageParameterName: page});
    return response;
  }
```

11. Back in **MovieViewModel**, change the other lists to **MovieResults**:

```
List<MovieResults> topRatedMovies = [];
List<MovieResults> popularMovies = [];
List<MovieResults> nowPlayingMovies = [];
```

12. Remove the **allMovies** variable and the **loadMovies** method. Replace **getPopular** with:

```
Future<MovieResponse?> getPopular(int page) async {
    final response = await movieAPIService.getPopular(page);
    if (response.statusCode == 200) {
      var movieResponse = MovieResponse.fromJson(response.data);
      popularMovies = movieResponse.results;
      return movieResponse;
    } else {
      logError(
          'Failed to load movies with error ${response.statusCode}
and message ${response.statusMessage}');
      return null;
    }
  }
```

13. Replace **getTopRated** with the following:

```
Future<MovieResponse?> getTopRated(int page) async {
  final response = await movieAPIService.getTopRated(page);
  if (response.statusCode == 200) {
    var movieResponse = MovieResponse.fromJson(response.data);
    topRatedMovies = movieResponse.results;
    return movieResponse;
  } else {
    logError(
        'Failed to load movies with error ${response.statusCode}
and message ${response.statusMessage}');
    return null;
  }
}
```

14. Replace **getNowPlaying** with:

```
Future<MovieResponse?> getNowPlaying(int page) async {
  final response = await movieAPIService.getNowPlaying(page);
  if (response.statusCode == 200) {
    var movieResponse = MovieResponse.fromJson(response.data);
    nowPlayingMovies = movieResponse.results;
    return movieResponse;
  } else {
    logError(
        'Failed to load movies with error ${response.statusCode}
and message ${response.statusMessage}');
    return null;
  }
}
```

15. Then, remove the **findMovieById** method.

    There are a few more errors.

16. Open **home_screen_image.dart**. Underneath the **currentMovie**, add the following:

```
final imageUrl =
    getImageUrl(ImageSize.large, currentMovie.
backdropPath);
```

17. Replace **uniqueHeroTag** with:

```
String uniqueHeroTag = '${currentMovie.posterPath}swiper';
```

18. Replace **onMovieTap** with:

```
onMovieTap(currentMovie.id);
```

19. Finally, replace **currentMovie.image** with:

```
imageUrl: imageUrl,
```

20. In **movie_detail.dart**, comment out **currentMovie** for now.

21. In HomeScreen, uncomment the calls in **loadData**. All errors should be gone, and you should be able to perform a hot restart. Do not click on a movie, as that will crash until we get the details page fixed.

# Movie details

To fix **movie_details**, we need the details for the movie that was selected. To do that, we need a new API call to get the details.

1. At the top of **movie_api_service.dart**, add a new URL for the details:

```
const movieUrl = 'movie';
```

2. After the **getPopular** method, add the following code:

```
Future<Response> getMovieDetails(int movieId) async {
  return dio.get('$movieUrl/$movieId');
}
```

This will get the details for a movie with the given ID. Now, we need to create a model for the movie details.

3. Inside of the data/models directory, add **genre.dart**. Add the following:

```
import 'package:freezed_annotation/freezed_annotation.dart';

part 'genre.freezed.dart';

part 'genre.g.dart';

@freezed
class Genre with _$Genre {
  const factory Genre({
    required int id,
    required String name,
  }) = _Genre;

  factory Genre.fromJson(Map<String, dynamic> json) =>
_$GenreFromJson(json);
}
```

```
@freezed
class Genres with _$Genres {
  const factory Genres({
    required List<Genre> genres,
  }) = _Genres;

  factory Genres.fromJson(Map<String, dynamic> json) =>
_$GenresFromJson(json);
}
```

This is just a model with an id and name. This will contain all the genres that the movie has.

4. Next, create **movie_details.dart**. Add the following:

```
import 'package:freezed_annotation/freezed_annotation.dart';

import 'package:movies/data/models/genre.dart';

part 'movie_details.freezed.dart';
part 'movie_details.g.dart';

@freezed
class MovieDetails with _$MovieDetails {
  const factory MovieDetails({
    @JsonKey(name: 'adult')
    required bool adult,
    @JsonKey(name: 'backdrop_path')
    required String backdropPath,
    @JsonKey(name: 'budget')
    required int budget,
    @JsonKey(name: 'genres')
    required List<Genre> genres,
    @JsonKey(name: 'homepage')
    required String homepage,
    @JsonKey(name: 'id')
    required int id,
    @JsonKey(name: 'imdb_id')
    required String imdbId,
    @JsonKey(name: 'origin_country')
    required List<String> originCountry,
    @JsonKey(name: 'original_language')
    required String originalLanguage,
    @JsonKey(name: 'original_title')
```

```
      required String originalTitle,
      @JsonKey(name: 'overview')
      required String overview,
      @JsonKey(name: 'popularity')
      required double popularity,
      @JsonKey(name: 'poster_path')
      required String posterPath,
      @JsonKey(name: 'release_date')
      required DateTime releaseDate,
      @JsonKey(name: 'revenue')
      required int revenue,
      @JsonKey(name: 'runtime')
      required int runtime,
      @JsonKey(name: 'status')
      required String status,
      @JsonKey(name: 'tagline')
      required String tagline,
      @JsonKey(name: 'title')
      required String title,
      @JsonKey(name: 'video')
      required bool video,
      @JsonKey(name: 'vote_average')
      required double voteAverage,
      @JsonKey(name: 'vote_count')
      required int voteCount,
  }) = _MovieDetails;

  factory MovieDetails.fromJson(Map<String, dynamic> json) =>
  _$MovieDetailsFromJson(json);
}
```

There is a lot here, but it contains all the necessary information.

5.  In the terminal window, run the build runner command:

    ```
    dart run build_runner build
    ```

6.  Back in **movie_viewmodel.dart**, add the **getMovieDetails** method at the bottom:

    ```
    Future<MovieDetails?> getMovieDetails(int movieId) async {
      final response = await movieAPIService.getMovieDetails(movieId);
      if (response.statusCode == 200) {
        try {
    ```

```
        return MovieDetails.fromJson(response.data);
    } catch (e) {
        logError('Failed to parse movie details with error $e');
        return null;
    }
} else {
    logError(
        'Failed to load movie details with error ${response.
statusCode} and message ${response.statusMessage}');
    return null;
}
}
```

This will just call the API service to get the movie details. Now, the **MovieDetails** class needs this information.

7.  In this class, remove the following lines:

    ```
    List<GenreState> genreStates = [];

    late Movie currentMovie;
    ```

8.  Along with the previous command, remove the **buildGenreState** method and the call to it. In the **buildScreen** method, before the **SafeArea** widget, add a **FutureBuilder** as follows:

    ```
    return FutureBuilder(
        future: loadData(),
        builder: (context, snapshot) {
          if (snapshot.connectionState != ConnectionState.done) {
            return const NotReady();
          }
          if (snapshot.hasError) {
            logMessage('Error: ${snapshot.error.toString()}');
            return Text(snapshot.error.toString());
          }
          final movieDetails = snapshot.data as MovieDetails?;
          if (movieDetails == null) {
            return const NotReady();
          }
    ```

You will need to fix the ending parentheses by adding the following at the end of the method:

```
    },
    );
```

9. At the bottom, add the following code:

```
Future loadData() async {
  return movieViewModel.getMovieDetails(widget.movieId);
}
```

This will return a Future that will have the **MovieDetails** in the **snapshot.data**. Instead of passing in parts to the other classes, we will just pass in the details class.

10. Update the **DetailImage** parameter and constructor to:

```
final MovieDetails details;
const DetailImage({required this.details, super.key});
```

11. After the **screenWidth** variable, add the following:

```
final imageUrl = getImageUrl(ImageSize.large, widget.details.
backdropPath);
```

12. Then change **widget.movieUrl** to **imageUrl**, and the hard-coded strings:

```
'Dune'
```

To:

```
widget.details.title,
```

```
'2024'
```

To:

```
yearFormat.format(widget.details.releaseDate)
```

13. Back in **MovieDetail**, change:

```
DetailImage(movieUrl: currentMovie.image)
```

To:

```
DetailImage(details: movieDetails)
```

14. Inside of **GenreRow**, change:

```
final List<GenreState> genres;
```

To:

```
final List<Genre> genres;
```

And **genre.genre** to **genre.name**.

15. After that, change the call in **MovieDetails** from:

```
GenreRow(genres: genreStates),
```

To:

```
GenreRow(genres: movieDetails.genres),
```

16. In **MovieOverview**, change:

```
final String details;
```

To:

```
final MovieDetails details;
```

17. Also, change the following:

```
        details,
```

To:

```
        details.overview,
```

In **MovieDetail** update the call to **MovieOverview** to:

```
        MovieOverview(details:movieDetails),
```

Hot restart. If you click on a movie, you should now see actual data on the movie. Your screen will look something as follows:

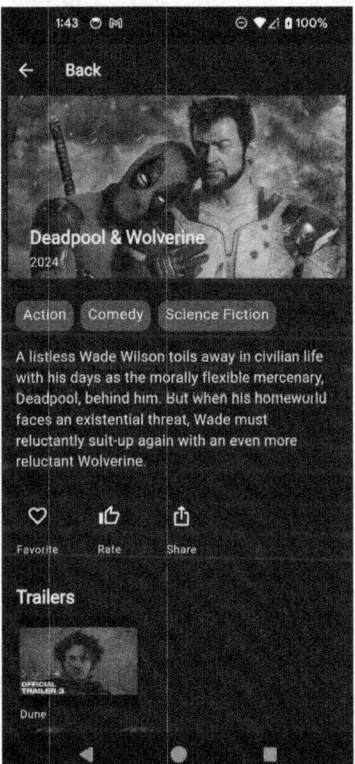

*Figure 11.12: Movie Details*

# Trailers and cast

Notice that there is still the hard-coded Trailer and cast members. TMDB has APIs for both movies and cast members.

1. Open up **MovieAPIService** and add the following video and credit constants:

```
const videosParameter = 'videos';
const creditsParameter = 'credits';
```

2. Now add the method to get the list of videos for a movie:

```
Future<Response> getMovieVideos(int movieId) async {
  return dio.get('$movieUrl/$movieId/$videosParameter');
}
```

3. Add the method to get the list of credits for a movie:

```
Future<Response> getMovieCredits(int movieId) async {
  return dio.get('$movieUrl/$movieId/$creditsParameter');
}
```

Now that we have these calls, we need the models to put them in.

4. In the **data/models** directory, add **movie_videos.dart**. Add the following code:

```
import 'package:freezed_annotation/freezed_annotation.dart';

part 'movie_videos.freezed.dart';
part 'movie_videos.g.dart';

@freezed
class MovieVideos with _$MovieVideos {
  const factory MovieVideos({
    @JsonKey(name: 'id')
    required int id,
    @JsonKey(name: 'results')
    required List<MovieVideo> results,
  }) = _MovieVideos;

  factory MovieVideos.fromJson(Map<String, dynamic> json) =>
_$MovieVideosFromJson(json);
}

@freezed
class MovieVideo with _$MovieVideo {
  const factory MovieVideo({
    @JsonKey(name: 'name')
    required String name,
    @JsonKey(name: 'key')
    required String key,
    @JsonKey(name: 'size')
```

```
      required int size,
      @JsonKey(name: 'official')
      required bool official,
      @JsonKey(name: 'published_at')
      required DateTime publishedAt,
      @JsonKey(name: 'id')
      required String id,
    }) = _MovieVideo;

    factory MovieVideo.fromJson(Map<String, dynamic> json) =>
    _$MovieVideoFromJson(json);
}
```

5.  Create the credits file: **movie_credits.dart**. The code is as follows:

```
import 'package:freezed_annotation/freezed_annotation.dart';

part 'movie_credits.freezed.dart';
part 'movie_credits.g.dart';

@freezed
class MovieCredits with _$MovieCredits {
  const factory MovieCredits({
    @JsonKey(name: 'id')
    required int id,
    @JsonKey(name: 'cast')
    required List<MovieCast> cast,
    @JsonKey(name: 'crew')
    required List<MovieCast> crew,
  }) = _MovieCredits;

  factory MovieCredits.fromJson(Map<String, dynamic> json) =>
  _$MovieCreditsFromJson(json);
}

@freezed
class MovieCast with _$MovieCast {
  const factory MovieCast({
    @JsonKey(name: 'adult')
    required bool adult,
    @JsonKey(name: 'gender')
    required int gender,
    @JsonKey(name: 'id')
    required int id,
```

```
    @JsonKey(name: 'name')
    required String name,
    @JsonKey(name: 'original_name')
    required String originalName,
    @JsonKey(name: 'popularity')
    required double popularity,
    @JsonKey(name: 'profile_path')
    required String? profilePath,
    @JsonKey(name: 'cast_id')
    int? castId,
    @JsonKey(name: 'character')
    String? character,
    @JsonKey(name: 'credit_id')
    required String creditId,
    @JsonKey(name: 'order')
    int? order,
    @JsonKey(name: 'job')
    String? job,
  }) = _MovieCast;

  factory MovieCast.fromJson(Map<String, dynamic> json) =>
_$MovieCastFromJson(json);
}
```

6. In the terminal window, run the build runner command:

```
dart run build_runner build
```

7. Add the following two methods to **MovieViewModel**:

```
Future<MovieVideos?> getMovieVideos(int movieId) async {
    final response = await movieAPIService.getMovieVideos(movieId);
    if (response.statusCode == 200) {
      try {
        return MovieVideos.fromJson(response.data);
      } catch (e) {
        logError('Failed to parse movie videos with error $e');
        return null;
      }
    } else {
      logError(
          'Failed to load movie videos with error ${response.
statusCode} and message ${response.statusMessage}');
      return null;
```

```
      }
    }

    Future<MovieCredits?> getMovieCredits(int movieId) async {
      final response = await movieAPIService.getMovieCredits(movieId);
      if (response.statusCode == 200) {
        try {
          return MovieCredits.fromJson(response.data);
        } catch (e) {
          logError('Failed to parse movie credits with error $e');
          return null;
        }
      } else {
        logError(
            'Failed to load movie credits with error ${response.
    statusCode} and message ${response.statusMessage}');
        return null;
      }
    }
```

8. Now, in **MovieDetail**, add the following underneath **movieViewModel**:

   ```
   MovieCredits? credits;
   MovieVideos? movieVideos;
   ```

9. Change the Trailer call to:

   ```
           movieVideos: movieVideos?.results,
   ```

10. Then, change the hard-code video to:

    ```
    VideoPageRoute(movieVideo: video));
    ```

11. Inside of Trailer, change:

    ```
      final List<String>? movieVideos;
    ```

    To:

    ```
      final List<MovieVideo>? movieVideos;
    ```

    Change:

    ```
            imageUrl: movieVideo,
    ```

    To:

    ```
            imageUrl: youtubeImageFromId(movieVideo.key),
    ```

12. Also, change **'Dune'** to:

    ```
    movieVideo.name
    ```

13. In **utils.dart**, change **OnMovieVideoTap** to:

```
typedef OnMovieVideoTap = void Function(MovieVideo video);
```

You will then need to change the video items.

14. In **VideoPage**, change the String to:

```
final MovieVideo movieVideo;
```

15. In **initState**, change the **youtubeUrlFromId** call to:

```
youtubeUrlFromId(widget.movieVideo.key),
```

16. Back in **MovieDetail**, add the following after the Trailer call:

```
Padding(
        padding: const EdgeInsets.only(left: 16, bottom: 16, top: 16),
    child: Text('Cast', style: Theme.of(context).textTheme.
headlineLarge),),
```

This will add a title of **Cast** below the trailer and before the cast.

17. Next, change the **HorizontalCast** call to:

```
HorizontalCast(castList: credits?.cast ?? []),
```

(Make sure to remove the const).

18. Add the following calls to the beginning of the **loadData** method:

```
credits = await movieViewModel.getMovieCredits(widget.movieId);
movieVideos = await movieViewModel.getMovieVideos(widget.
movieId);
```

Now, we have some errors in these widgets. We will need to change their parameters.

19. Next, open **HorizontalCast** and change **castList** to:

```
final List<MovieCast> castList;
```

20. Change the **CastImage** call to:

```
return CastImage(imageUrl: getImageUrl(ImageSize.small,
castList[index].profilePath), name: castList[index].name);
```

21. In the terminal window, run the build runner command:

```
dart run build_runner build
```

**(Note: You may have to add imports to the app_routes.dart file)**

Perform a hot reload, and you should see real trailers for the movie and the cast members, as shown in the following figure:

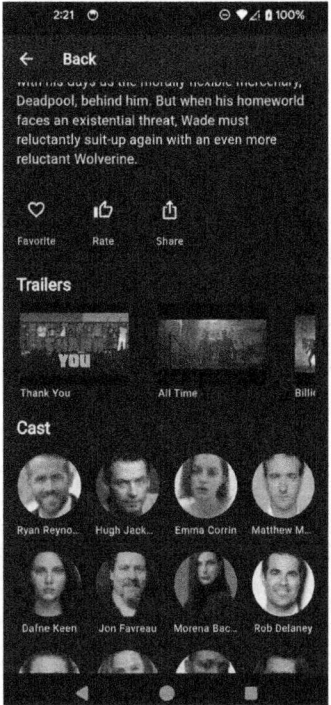

*Figure 11.13*: *Movie Details with Cast*

# Home screen image

Now that we have movie details on the detail screen, we need those details on the main home screen. Open **home_screen_image.dart**. Replace:

```
child: Hero(
  tag: uniqueHeroTag,
  child: CachedNetworkImage(
    imageUrl: imageUrl,
    alignment: Alignment.topCenter,
    fit: BoxFit.fitHeight,
    height: 374,
    width: screenWidth,
  ),
),
```

With the following:

```
child: Padding(
  padding: const EdgeInsets.all(8.0),
  child: Stack(children: [
    Align(
```

```
          alignment: Alignment.topCenter,
          child: Hero(
            tag: uniqueHeroTag,
            child: CachedNetworkImage(
              imageUrl: imageUrl,
              alignment: Alignment.topCenter,
              fit: BoxFit.fitHeight,
              height: 374,
              width: screenWidth,
            ),
          ),
        ),
      Align(
        alignment: Alignment.bottomLeft,
        child: Padding(
          padding: const EdgeInsets.only(left: 16.0),
          child: Column(
            mainAxisSize: MainAxisSize.min,
            mainAxisAlignment: MainAxisAlignment.start,
            crossAxisAlignment: CrossAxisAlignment.start,
            children: [
              Text(
                movieViewModel.nowPlayingMovies[index].title,
                style: Theme.of(context).textTheme.headlineLarge,
              ),
              addVerticalSpace(4),
              currentMovie.releaseDate != null
                  ? Text(
                      yearFormat.format(currentMovie.releaseDate!),
                      style: Theme.of(context).textTheme.bodyMedium,
                    )
                  : Container(),
              addVerticalSpace(4),
              Padding(
                padding:
                    const EdgeInsets.only(bottom: 8.0, right: 8.0),
                child: AutoSizeText(
                  movieViewModel.nowPlayingMovies[index].overview,
                  style: Theme.of(context).textTheme.bodyMedium,
                  maxLines: 3,
                  overflow: TextOverflow.ellipsis,
                ),
```

```
                        ),
                    ],
                ),
            ),
          )
      ]),
    ),
```

This will add the movie name, release year, and details to the main image, as shown in the following figure:

*Figure 11.14: Movie text*

# Final APIs

There are a few more APIs that we will use in later chapters. We will add them but not use them until later. The first one retrieves a list of genres.

1. In **movie_api_service.dart**, add the following constants:

```
const genreUrl = 'genre/movie/list';
const searchMovieUrl = 'search/movie';
const discoverMovieUrl = 'discover/movie';
```

```
const configurationUrl = 'configuration';
const queryParameterName = 'query';
const genreParameterName = 'with_genres';
```

2. Add the following code to the end of the class:

```
Future<Response> getGenres() async {
  final response = await dio.get(genreUrl);
  return response;
}
Future<Response> searchMovies(String query, [int page = 1]) async
{
  return dio
      .get(searchMovieUrl, queryParameters: {queryParameterName:
query});
}

Future<Response> searchMoviesByGenre(String genre, [int page = 1])
async {
  return dio.get(discoverMovieUrl,
      queryParameters: {genreParameterName: genre,
pageParameterName: page});
}

Future<Response> getMovieConfiguration() async {
  return dio.get(configurationUrl);
}
```

After the **getGenres** method, there is **searchMovies** to search by a query string, **searchMoviesByGenre** to search by genre, and finally, **getMovieConfiguration**, which will be used to get configuration information in a later chapter.

3. Now, update **MovieViewModel**. Replace:

```
late List<String> movieGenres;
```

With:

```
List<Genre>? movieGenres;
```

4. Replace **setupGenres** with:

```
Future setupGenres() async {
  final response = await movieAPIService.getGenres();
  if (response.statusCode == 200) {
    movieGenres = Genres.fromJson(response.data).genres;
  } else {
    logError(
        'Failed to load genres with error ${response.statusCode}
and message ${response.statusMessage}');
```

```
    }
}
```

This will get all of the current genres that the service supports.

5. At the end of the class add:

```
    Future<MovieResponse?> searchMoviesByGenre(String genres, int
page) async {
      final response = await movieAPIService.searchMoviesByGenre(genres,
page);
      if (response.statusCode == 200) {
        var movieResponse = MovieResponse.fromJson(response.data);
        return movieResponse;
      } else {
        logError(
            'Failed to load movies with error ${response.statusCode}
and message ${response.statusMessage}');
        return null;
      }
    }

    Future<MovieResponse?> searchMovies(String searchText, int page)
async {
      final response = await movieAPIService.searchMovies(searchText,
page);
      if (response.statusCode == 200) {
        var movieResponse = MovieResponse.fromJson(response.data);
        return movieResponse;
      } else {
        logError(
            'Failed to load movies with error ${response.statusCode}
and message ${response.statusMessage}');
        return null;
      }
    }
```

These two methods just implement the APIs for searching for movies.

# Genres

Now that **MovieViewModel** loads genres instead of strings, you need to change some of the genre screens.

1. Open **genre_screen.dart**. Add a ! character after the **movieGenres** in the **buildGenreState** method:

```
    for (final genre in movieViewModel.movieGenres!) {
```

2. Open **GenreState** and change the string to a **Genre**:

```
final Genre genre;
```

3. In **GenreSection**, change the **GridView** to:

```
child: GridView.builder(
    shrinkWrap: true,
    padding: const EdgeInsets.all(0.0),
    itemCount: genreChips.length,
    gridDelegate: const
SliverGridDelegateWithFixedCrossAxisCount(
        crossAxisCount: 3,
        crossAxisSpacing: 0,
        childAspectRatio: 2.2,
        mainAxisSpacing: 0),
```

4. Then, in **getGenreChips**, change the following:

```
final genreState = widget.genreStates[index];
```

To:

```
final genre = widget.genreStates[index].genre;
```

And:

```
label: AutoSizeText(genreState.genre.name,
```

To:

```
label: Text(genre.name,
```

And:

```
genre: genreState.genre,
```

To:

```
genre: genre,
```

Hot restart and test the Genre screen. As you can see, adding network calls required many changes. Ideally, you would write your networking code early on in your app work so you can design around the models instead of using strings, as we needed to do.

# Conclusion

In this chapter, you learned about APIs and networking packages. You also saw how to sign up for a service that provides an API and how to implement those APIs in code.

In the next chapter, you will learn about local storage and databases. These will allow you to store user information locally so that a network connection is not always needed and to save application settings.

# CHAPTER 12

# Local Storage and Databases

## Introduction

In this chapter, you will learn about storing information on the device. You will learn about storing data from simple key/value pairs to full databases and tables. This will allow you to save user information as well as cache data that does not need to be downloaded each time the app starts up.

## Structure

The chapter covers the following topics:

- SharedPreferences
- Saving genres
- Databases
- Movie configuration

## Objectives

By the end of this chapter, you will have a solid understanding of SharedPreferences and how to create local databases. You will learn how to create tables and database classes to interact with local files. You will save a user's genre selections to SharedPreferences and favorites to a local database. You will also download movie configuration and genre information and store them in the local database, caching that information for future sessions.

# SharedPreferences

So far, you have learned how to build UIs that display information but have not saved any information on the local device. When a user restarts your app, it will start the same way each time. If you wanted to have settings or preferences that a user could set, it would not do any good if it only lasted the lifetime of the current session. In this chapter, you will learn how to save those settings and movie information so that if there is no internet connection, those settings will still be available. There are many types of information you could save. You could save the current screen the user is on or their sorting preferences. In this chapter, you will save the user's favorites locally. Since these favorites cannot be stored on **The Movie Database** (**TMDB**) site, saving them locally is a good option. Of course, if the user uninstalls your app, they will lose any settings saved locally. For more permanent storage, you would need a server that would allow you to save that information. In *Chapter 15, Firebase*, you will learn about Firebase and how you can save that information in the cloud. There are several ways to save data locally. This is usually done using the local storage that phones provide. You could save the information in a file you create but that is pretty low-level and there are better ways to do it. Both iOS and Android have a way to save preferences as well as a built-in SQLite database that can be used to save data. We will cover both preferences and different ways to use databases.

There are many types of persistence, but one of the most basic is the notion of preferences, where you can save small amounts of data. This is called SharedPreferences on Android. If you are familiar with iOS, that class is called **UserDefaults**. These classes allow you to save very simple key/value pairs to the device. It is not meant to store large amounts of data; it is meant to store settings. This can be the current user's access token, name, settings values, or anything that can be stored as an int, String, double, or Boolean. We will be using the **shared_preferences** plugin. This plugin supports all platforms.

Next, we will create a **Prefs** class that will handle all interactions with the **shared_preferences** plugin:

1.  Open up **pubspec.yaml** and add:

    ```
    shared_preferences: ^2.2.3
    ```

2.  Click on Pub get.

3.  Next, create **prefs.dart** in the **utils** directory. Add the following:

    ```
    import 'package:shared_preferences/shared_preferences.dart';
    class Prefs {
      final SharedPreferences preferences;

      Prefs(this.preferences);
    ```

```
   // Add String methods
}
```

This is the **Prefs** class that takes an instance of the **SharedPreferences** class.

4.  Next, create two methods for storing and getting strings:

```
void setString(String key, String value) {
    preferences.setString(key, value);
}

String? getString(String key) {
    return preferences.getString(key);
}
```

Notice that the **set** method takes a key and a string value. The getter just needs the key. If it does not exist, a null value is returned.

5.  Add the remaining methods:

```
void setInt(String key, int value) {
    preferences.setInt(key, value);
}

int? getInt(String key) {
    return preferences.getInt(key);
}

void setBool(String key, bool value) {
    preferences.setBool(key, value);
}

bool? getBool(String key) {
    return preferences.getBool(key);
}

void setDouble(String key, double value) {
    preferences.setDouble(key, value);
}

double? getDouble(String key) {
    return preferences.getDouble(key);
}
```

This just creates getters and settings for int, Booleans, and Doubles.

6.  Open the **providers.dart** file in the **lib** directory. Add the following:

```
import 'package:movies/utils/prefs.dart';
import 'package:shared_preferences/shared_preferences.dart';
```

```
@Riverpod(keepAlive: true)
Future<SharedPreferences> sharedPrefs(SharedPrefsRef ref) =>
    SharedPreferences.getInstance();
```

(Make sure the imports are before the part statement). The first import is for the **prefs** file you just created. The last import is for the **SharedPreferences** plugin. The **@Riverpod** annotation tells the **Riverpod** generator to create a single **FutureProvider** for the **SharedProvider** plugin.

Since you created a nice class to make this package easier to use, you will use the **Prefs** class instead. This also makes testing easier. Add the following:

```
@Riverpod(keepAlive: true)
Future<Prefs> prefs(PrefsRef ref) async {
  final sharedPrefs = await ref.read(sharedPrefsProvider.future);
  return Prefs(sharedPrefs);
}
```

This will create a provider for the **Prefs** class.

7.  Open up the **Terminal** tab at the bottom left of Android Studio, as shown in the following figure:

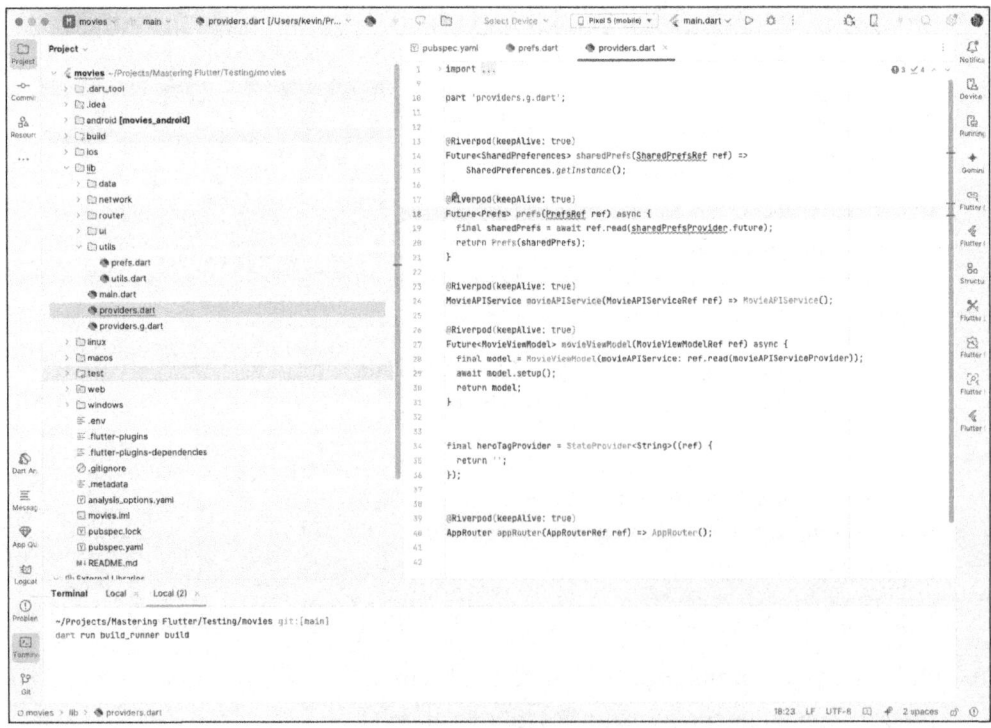

*Figure 12.1: Generating files*

8. Then type **dart run build_runner build**. This will run **build_runner** and will update the **providers.g.dart** file. You can have the **build_runner** running continuously by using the **watch** command instead of the **build**. Opening **providers.g.dart** file, you will see something as follows:

```
1   // GENERATED CODE - DO NOT MODIFY BY HAND
2
3   part of 'providers.dart';
4
5   // **************************************************************************
6   // RiverpodGenerator
7   // **************************************************************************
8
9   String _$sharedPrefsHash() => r'0ebc135ba0bea1685cfcb6d3e19119eec07a339a';
10
11  /// See also [sharedPrefs].
12  @ProviderFor(sharedPrefs)
13  final sharedPrefsProvider = FutureProvider<SharedPreferences>.internal(
14    sharedPrefs,
15    name: r'sharedPrefsProvider',
16    debugGetCreateSourceHash:
17        const bool.fromEnvironment('dart.vm.product') ? null : _$sharedPrefsHash,
18    dependencies: null,
19    allTransitiveDependencies: null,
20  );  // FutureProvider.internal
21
22  typedef SharedPrefsRef = FutureProviderRef<SharedPreferences>;
23  String _$prefsHash() => r'17cdb26eee576ff65fcfde9a84ac9146206202ba';
24
25  /// See also [prefs].
26  @ProviderFor(prefs)
27  final prefsProvider = FutureProvider<Prefs>.internal(
28    prefs,
29    name: r'prefsProvider',
30    debugGetCreateSourceHash:
31        const bool.fromEnvironment('dart.vm.product') ? null : _$prefsHash,
32    dependencies: null,
33    allTransitiveDependencies: null,
34  );  // FutureProvider.internal
35
36  typedef PrefsRef = FutureProviderRef<Prefs>;
37  String _$movieAPIServiceHash() => r'db9ab9b85429b927cb42da2dd05e3ebc092e5107';
38
39  /// See also [movieAPIServic
40  @ProviderFor(movieAPIService
41  final movieAPIServiceProvide
42    movieAPIService,
43    name: r'movieAPIServicePr
44    debugGetCreateSourceHash: const bool.fromEnvironment('dart.vm.product')
```

package:movies/providers.dart
String _$movieAPIServiceHash()

 movies

*Figure 12.2: Generated file*

This class has been created for you, so do not attempt to change it yourself. It will be overwritten the next time you run the builder. You do not need to worry about what is created. The most important variable is the **sharedPrefsProvider** variable. You can use this variable throughout your code to get an instance of the **SharedPreference** instance.

# Saving genres

A good way to use preferences is to save the selected genres. Since this is only needed on a per-phone basis, it is perfect for saving the user time. For example, if the user likes horror / romance films, pre-selecting those genres would save them time. The first thing we want to do is put the **GenreState** class into its file and add the freeze annotation.

Create the **GenreState** class:

1.  Open up **genre_section.dart** and remove the **GenreState** class.

2.  In the data/models folder, create a new file named **genre_state.dart**.

3.  Add the following:

```
import 'package:freezed_annotation/freezed_annotation.dart';

import 'package:movies/data/models/genre.dart';

part 'genre_state.freezed.dart';
part 'genre_state.g.dart';

@freezed
class GenreState with _$GenreState {
  const factory GenreState({
    required Genre genre,
    required bool isSelected,
  }) = _GenreState;

  factory GenreState.fromJson(Map<String, dynamic> json) =>
_$GenreStateFromJson(json);
}
```

4.  In the terminal, type:

```
dart run build_runner build.
```

5.  Open **genre_section.dart** and add the **GenreState** import.

6.  Open **genre_screen.dart** and add the **GenreState** import.

7.  Above the **GenreScreen** class, add the following constant before the class that will be used to save genres:

```
const String genreStringKey = 'GenreKey';
```

While we are in the genre class, we will be adding the ability to search for movies.

8.  Remove the **currentMovieList** variable.

9. Add the following variables:

```
String currentSearchString = '';
List<MovieResults> currentMovieList = [];
final moviesNotifier = ValueNotifier<List<MovieResults>>([]);
MovieResponse? currentMovieResponse;
Sorting selectedSort = Sorting.aToz;
```

The **currentSearchString** holds the string the user is searching for. As we no longer use the **Movie** class, the current movie list holds a list of **MovieResults**. The **currentMovieResponse** is the current list of movies based on the search a user made. Sorting starts with an A-Z sort, but the user can change that.

10. Inside the **buildGenreState** method, add the following call at the end of the method:

```
getSelectedGenres();
```

11. At the end of the class, add the import for the collection package:

```
void getSelectedGenres() async {
// 1
    final prefs = await ref.read(prefsProvider.future);
// 2
    final genreNameList = prefs.getString(genreStringKey)?.
split(',');
    if (genreNameList?.isNotEmpty == true) {
// 3
      for (final genreName in genreNameList!) {
// 4
        var genreState = genreStates
            .firstWhereOrNull((genre) => genre.genre.name ==
genreName);
        if (genreState != null) {
// 5
          final index = genreStates.indexOf(genreState);
          genreState = genreState.copyWith(isSelected: true);
          genreStates[index] = genreState;
        }
      }
    }
}
```

You will need to add the collection import for the **firstWhereOrNull** call. This method will get the genre settings from the preferences package. Note that the genres are stored as a single string, separated by commas. Here is a breakdown:

a. Get an instance of the **Prefs** class.

b. Get the genre string and split it into an array of genre names.

c. Go through each genre.

d. Find the genre state with that name.

e. Get the index and then make a copy with the selected value set.

This gets the genres, but how do you save them?

12. Before this method, add the following save method:

```
void saveSelectedGenres() async {
  final prefs = await ref.read(prefsProvider.future);
  final genreNameList = genreStates.map((state) => state.genre.name).
toList();
  prefs.setString(genreStringKey, genreNameList.join(','));
}
```

This will get the **Prefs** class and save the genres as a comma separated string.

13. Update the **GenreSearchRow** call:

```
GenreSearchRow((searchString) {
    currentSearchString = searchString;
    currentMovieResponse = null;
    FocusScope.of(context).unfocus();
    expandedNotifier.value = false;
    search();
  }),
```

This will take the **searchString** returned by the search row, close the keyboard (**unfocus** call), close the genre section, and start a search.

14. Since the **search** method does not exist yet, add the **search** method:

```
Future<List<MovieResults>?> search() async {
// 1
    if (currentSearchString.isEmpty && genreStates.isEmpty) {
      moviesNotifier.value = <MovieResults>[];
      return <MovieResults>[];
    }

// 2
    // 1st, search by title
    // Search through the list for the search string
    final pageNumber = (currentMovieResponse?.page == null)
        ? 1
```

```
          : (currentMovieResponse!.page + 1);
// 3
    if (currentSearchString.isNotEmpty) {
      currentMovieResponse =
          await movieViewModel.searchMovies(currentSearchString,
pageNumber);
      currentMovieList = currentMovieResponse!.results;
    }
// 4
    // 2nd Search by genre if there is no search string
    if (currentSearchString.isEmpty && genreStates.isNotEmpty) {
      final buffer = getGenreString();
      currentMovieResponse = await movieViewModel.
searchMoviesByGenre(
          buffer.toString(), pageNumber);
      currentMovieList = currentMovieResponse!.results;
      // 3rd Search through the movies to see if they match our
genres
// 5
    } else if (genreStates.isNotEmpty && currentMovieList.
isNotEmpty) {
      currentMovieList = currentMovieList.where((movie) {
        for (final selectedGenre in genreStates) {
          if (movie.genreIds.contains(selectedGenre.genre.id)) {
            return true;
          }
        }
        return false;
      }).toList();
    }
// 6
    sortMovies();
    return currentMovieList;
  }
```

The **search** method does several things. Here is a breakdown:

a.   Check to see if the search string and genre states are empty.

b.   Update the page number (There could be multiple pages of results).

c.   Perform the search using the search string.

d.   If the search string is empty and we have genres, do a search by genre.

    e.  If we have genres, go through the results and find movies that have those genres.

    f.  Sort the movies.

Now add the **getGenreString** and **sortMovies** methods.

15. Add the **getGenreString** method:

```
StringBuffer getGenreString() {
  final buffer = StringBuffer();
  genreStates.map((e) {
    if (e.isSelected) {
      if (buffer.isNotEmpty) {
        buffer.write('|');
      }
      buffer.write(e.genre.id);
    }
  }).toList();
  return buffer;
}
```

This method builds a **StringBuffer** that is a **|** delimited string. This is required by the movies API.

16. Add the **sortMovies** method:

```
void sortMovies() {
  if (currentMovieList.isEmpty) {
    return;
  }
  currentMovieList = currentMovieList.sorted((a, b) {
    switch (selectedSort) {
      case Sorting.aToz:
        return a.originalTitle.compareTo(b.originalTitle);
      case Sorting.zToa:
        return b.originalTitle.compareTo(a.originalTitle);
      case Sorting.rating:
        return b.popularity.compareTo(a.popularity);
      case Sorting.year:
        if (a.releaseDate != null && b.releaseDate != null) {
          return a.releaseDate!.compareTo(b.releaseDate!);
        }
    }
    return 0;
```

```
    });
    moviesNotifier.value = currentMovieList;
  }
```

This just returns a sorted list of movies. We now need a way to save the selected genres.

17. Find **onGenreSelected** and replace with:

```
onGenresSelected: (genres) {
  genreStates = genres;
  saveSelectedGenres();
  currentMovieResponse = null;
});
```

This will set the save the selected genres. Next, we need to save the selected sort value.

18. Find **SortPicker** and change the call to:

```
SortPicker(
    useSliver: true,
    onSortSelected: (sorting) {
      selectedSort = sorting;
      sortMovies();
    }),
```

This will re-sort the current movie list.

19. Change the call to **VerticalMovieList** with:

```
ValueListenableBuilder<List<MovieResults>>(
    valueListenable: moviesNotifier,
  builder: (BuildContext context, List<MovieResults> value,
        Widget? child) {
      return VerticalMovieList(
        movies: value,
        movieViewModel: movieViewModel,
        onMovieTap: (movieId) {
          context.router
              .push(MovieDetailRoute(movieId: movieId));
        },
      );
    },
  ),
```

This wraps the movie list with a **ValueListenableBuilder**. This will help performance by only updating this section if the list of movies changes. Notice that **VerticalMovieList** does not like those changes.

20. Open **vert_movie_list.dart** and remove the **onMovieTap typedef** as it already exists in utils. Import the **utils.dart** file.

21. Change the fields and constructor to the following:

```
final List<MovieResults> movies;
final MovieViewModel movieViewModel;
final OnMovieTap onMovieTap;

const VerticalMovieList(
    {super.key,
    required this.movies,
    required this.movieViewModel,
    required this.onMovieTap,
    });
```

Add any imports.

22. Change the call to **MovieRow** to:

```
return MovieRow(
  movie: movies[index],
  movieViewModel: movieViewModel,
  onMovieTap: (movie) {
    onMovieTap(movie.id);
  },
);
```

This passes the view model to **MovieRow**.

23. Open **movie_row.dart**. Change the fields and constructor to:

```
final MovieResults movie;
final MovieViewModel movieViewModel;
final OnMovieResultsTap onMovieTap;

const MovieRow({
  required this.movie,
  required this.movieViewModel,
  required this.onMovieTap,
  super.key,
});
```

Add any imports. Notice that we changed **onMovieTap** to **onMovieResultsTap**. That definition does not exist. We want to pass the **MovieResults** to the caller.

24. Open **utils.dart** and add:

```
typedef OnMovieResultsTap = void Function(MovieResults movie);
const Widget emptyWidget = SizedBox.shrink();
```

25. Back in **MovieRow**, change the first two lines in the build method with:

```
final imageUrl = getImageUrl(ImageSize.small, movie.posterPath);
final uniqueHeroTag = '${imageUrl}MovieRow';
if (imageUrl.isNotEmpty) {
```

26. Change **onMovieTap(movie.movieId)** to:

```
onMovieTap(movie);
```

27. Change the **imageUrl** parameter in **CachedNetworkImage** call to:

```
imageUrl: imageUrl,
```

Next, you need to put in real movie information in instead of just using the text *title* and *1979* for the title and year.

28. Replace the **Column** with:

```
Expanded(
  child: LayoutBuilder(
    builder: (BuildContext context, BoxConstraints
constraints) {
        return Column(
          mainAxisSize: MainAxisSize.min,
          mainAxisAlignment: MainAxisAlignment.end,
          crossAxisAlignment: CrossAxisAlignment.start,
          children: [
            const Spacer(),
            SizedBox(
              width: constraints.maxWidth,
              child: AutoSizeText(
                movie.title,
                maxLines: 3,
                minFontSize: 10,
                style: Theme.of(context).textTheme.labelLarge,
                overflow: TextOverflow.ellipsis,
              ),
            ),
            addVerticalSpace(4),
            movie.releaseDate != null
                ? Text(
```

```
                            yearFormat.format(movie.releaseDate!),
                            style: Theme.of(context).textTheme.
bodyMedium,
                        )
                      : Container(),
                  addVerticalSpace(4),
                ],
              );
            },
          ),
        ),
```

This wraps the column with **Expanded** and **LayoutBuilder** widgets. The **Expanded** widget makes the column as big as possible, and the **LayoutBuilder** gives us some sizes to work with. Specifically, we need the column's width. The **SizedBox** uses the **constraints. maxWidth** value from the LayoutBuilder.

Perform a hot reload. Press the **Genre** tab, type in a search query, select any genres, and press the search icon. You should see something like the following figure:

*Figure 12.3: Genre search*

# Databases

There are times when an internet connection is not available or when you want to store information locally. That is where on-device databases come in. By storing information locally, you can display information to the user without a connection or save information to be uploaded to the internet later when the connection is restored. Luckily, Flutter has many database options for you. We will cover some of the most popular databases and then we will use the drift database as the database for the movies app.

## SQLite

Both Android and iOS come with the built-in SQLite database. This is a self-contained, serverless SQL database engine. It is file based, very small, and efficient. It does not require any configuration and uses SQL. If you are familiar with SQL, you will understand how to use SQLite. However, because it is based on SQL, it can be hard for users who do not know that language. It is important to understand the basics of SQL. SQL stores data in tables that are made up of columns and rows. Each column is a specific data type, and each row is a record in that table. SQL comprises queries (getting information) and commands for adding, deleting, and updating data. For queries, you should use the **SELECT** command. This would look as follows:

```
SELECT name, address FROM Customers;
```

This command selects the **name** and **address** columns from the **Customers** table.

To add data, you would use the **INSERT** command as follows:

```
INSERT INTO Customers (NAME, ADDRESS) VALUES(value1, value2);
```

This makes a new row and inserts value1 into the **name** column and value2 into the **address** column.

To delete a row, use the **DELETE** command as follows:

```
DELETE FROM Customers WHERE id = 1;
```

This command searches for the row with an **id** of **1** and deletes that row.

To update a row, use the **UPDATE** command as follows:

```
UPDATE Customers SET phone='555-12345' WHERE id=1;
```

This will change the row's **phone** column to this value for the row with an **id** of **1**.

If you want to use SQLite by itself, you can use the sqlite3 package. You can find this package at: **https://pub.dev/packages/sqlite3**.

## Floor

Floor is a reactive SQLite abstraction that is inspired by the Android Room persistence library. This package requires a knowledge of SQL as you use query statements in the code which is mapped to classes. If you come from the Android world and like the Room database, you will be familiar with the setup of this library. This package requires the creation of entities, which are classes for storing information in tables. You then create a **data access object** (**DAO**) class for queries, insertions, updates, and deletions. Finally, you need to create a database class that extends the **FloorDatabase**. This class will hold all of the DAO classes. Here is an example of a **Person** entity:

```
import 'package:floor/floor.dart';

@entity
class Person {
  @primaryKey
  final int id;

  final String name;

  Person(this.id, this.name);
}
```

This uses the **@entity** annotation to mark this class as an entity. Because the plugin uses annotations, you must use the floor generator to create classes based on this annotation. To create a DAO, you would use something as follows:

```
import 'package:floor/floor.dart';

@dao
abstract class PersonDao {
  @Query('SELECT * FROM Person')
  Future<List<Person>> findAllPeople();

  @Query('SELECT name FROM Person')
  Stream<List<String>> findAllPeopleName();

  @Query('SELECT * FROM Person WHERE id = :id')
  Stream<Person?> findPersonById(int id);

  @insert
  Future<void> insertPerson(Person person);
}
```

To create the database, you would create a class as follows:

```
import 'dart:async';
import 'package:floor/floor.dart';
import 'package:sqflite/sqflite.dart' as sqflite;

import 'dao/person_dao.dart';
import 'entity/person.dart';

part 'app_database.g.dart'; // the generated code will be there
```

```
@Database(version: 1, entities: [Person])
abstract class AppDatabase extends FloorDatabase {
  PersonDao get personDao;
}
```

To use the generated classes, you would write code as follows:

```
final database = await $FloorAppDatabase.databaseBuilder('app_database.db').
build();

final personDao = database.personDao;
final person = Person(1, 'Frank');

await personDao.insertPerson(person);
final result = await personDao.findPersonById(1);
```

# Hive

Hive is a lightweight and fast key/value database written in Dart. You can also store annotated classes. Here is an example of a simple **box**:

```
var box = Hive.box('myBox');

box.put('name', 'David');

var name = box.get('name');
```

You can also create **BoxCollections**. This is just a collection of multiple boxes. Here is an example:

```
final collection = await BoxCollection.open(
    'MyFirstFluffyBox', // Name of your database
    {'cats', 'dogs'}, // Names of your boxes
    path: './', // Path where to store your boxes (Only used in Flutter /
Dart IO)
    key: HiveCipher(), // Key to encrypt your boxes (Only used in Flutter /
Dart IO)
  );

  // Open your boxes. Optional: Give it a type.
  final catsBox = collection.openBox<Map>('cats');

  // Put something in
  await catsBox.put('fluffy', {'name': 'Fluffy', 'age': 4});
  await catsBox.put('loki', {'name': 'Loki', 'age': 2});

  // Get values of type (immutable) Map?
  final loki = await catsBox.get('loki');
```

To store a class you would write a class as follows:

```
@HiveType(typeId: 0)
class Person extends HiveObject {

  @HiveField(0)
  String name;

  @HiveField(1)
  int age;
}
```

You would use this class as follows:

```
var box = await Hive.openBox('myBox');

var person = Person()
  ..name = 'Dave'
  ..age = 22;
box.add(person);

print(box.getAt(0)); // Dave - 22

person.age = 30;
person.save();
```

You can find Hive at **https://pub.dev/packages/hive**.

# Isar

If you are interested in a NoSQL database, then Isar is one of the best. It is very fast and works on most platforms. The author originally used it for the movies project and ran into trouble with the web. That part is still in development, so we chose drift. Isar uses annotations and a generator as well. Isar uses the **@collection** annotation for classes. One of the nice features of this database is that you can have references for other collections. Here is an example of an email and recipient class:

```
part 'email.g.dart';

@collection
class Email {
  Id id = Isar.autoIncrement; // you can also use id = null to auto
increment

  @Index(type: IndexType.value)
  String? title;

  List<Recipient>? recipients;

  @enumerated
```

```
  Status status = Status.pending;
}

@embedded
class Recipient {
  String? name;

  String? address;
}

enum Status {
  draft,
  pending,
  sent,
}
```

As you can see, it has IDs, indexes, embedded classes, and the ability to handle enumerations. To use the database, you will have to use the **path_provider** package and open the database as follows:

```
final dir = await getApplicationDocumentsDirectory();
final isar = await Isar.open(
  [EmailSchema],
  directory: dir.path,
);
```

You can then query emails:

```
final emails = await isar.emails.filter()
  .titleContains('awesome', caseSensitive: false)
  .sortByStatusDesc()
  .limit(10)
  .findAll();
```

In addition to queries, you can also insert and delete:

```
final newEmail = Email()..title = 'Amazing new database';

await isar.writeTxn(() {
  await isar.emails.put(newEmail); // insert & update
});

final existingEmail = await isar.emails.get(newEmail.id!); // get

await isar.writeTxn(() {
  await isar.emails.delete(existingEmail.id!); // delete
});
```

One of the features the author likes about this database is its powerful query language. The following are a few examples:

```
final importantEmails = isar.emails
  .where()
  .titleStartsWith('Important') // use index
  .limit(10)
  .findAll()

final specificEmails = isar.emails
  .filter()
  .recipient((q) => q.nameEqualTo('David')) // query embedded objects
  .or()
  .titleMatches('*university*', caseSensitive: false) // title containing
'university' (case insensitive)
  .findAll()
```

You can find Isar at **https://pub.dev/packages/isar**. As mentioned earlier, Isar would be a great database if you do not need it for the web.

# Drift

Drift is described as a reactive persistence library built on top of SQLite. You can find documentation for drift at **https://pub.dev/packages/drift** and **https://drift.simonbinder. eu/**. Drift is similar to other packages in that you need to create **Table** classes and annotate a **Database** class. It has a builder for these generated files. Drift's tables are a bit different. All table classes must extend the Table class, and you define fields with the **get** keyword. The following is an example table:

```
class TodoItems extends Table {
  IntColumn get id => integer().autoIncrement()();
  TextColumn get title => text().withLength(min: 6, max: 32)();
  TextColumn get content => text().named('body')();
  IntColumn get category =>
      integer().nullable().references(TodoCategory, #id)();
  DateTimeColumn get createdAt => dateTime().nullable()();
}
```

An ID field is defined as:

```
IntColumn get id => integer().autoIncrement()();
```

This defines a field named id that is an **IntColumn** and auto increments (automatically increments the id without you knowing what the next value should be). You can have text fields defined as a **TextColumn** and a date field defined as a **DateTimeColumn**. To create a Database, you create a class that extends to a Drift built class, similar to the way **freezed** creates its classes. The following is a sample:

```
@DriftDatabase(tables: [TodoItems, TodoCategory])
```

```
class AppDatabase extends _$AppDatabase {
}
```

The **_$AppDatabase** class will get generated for you. The **@DriftDatabase** annotation defines the tables.

# Movie configuration

TMDB has an API call that will get you information on all the image types and sizes. This API is at **https://api.themoviedb.org/3/configuration**. This API returns the base URL for images as well as the sizes. You build a URL for each image from the base URL and a size. Instead of hard coding the sizes and base URLs, you can download the configuration information and store it in a local database.

First, we need to create a UI model for the configuration, use the following steps:

1. Create a new file in the **data/models** folder named **movie_configuration.dart**.

2. Add the following:

```
import 'package:freezed_annotation/freezed_annotation.dart';

part 'movie_configuration.freezed.dart';
part 'movie_configuration.g.dart';

@freezed
class MovieConfiguration with _$MovieConfiguration {
  const factory MovieConfiguration({
    @JsonKey(name: 'images')
    required MovieConfigurationImages images,
    @JsonKey(name: 'change_keys')
    required List<String> changeKeys,
  }) = _MovieConfiguration;

  factory MovieConfiguration.fromJson(Map<String, dynamic> json) =>
_$MovieConfigurationFromJson(json);
}

@freezed
class MovieConfigurationImages with _$MovieConfigurationImages {
  const factory MovieConfigurationImages({
    @JsonKey(name: 'base_url')
    required String baseUrl,
    @JsonKey(name: 'secure_base_url')
    required String secureBaseUrl,
    @JsonKey(name: 'backdrop_sizes')
```

```
    required List<String> backdropSizes,
    @JsonKey(name: 'logo_sizes')
    required List<String> logoSizes,
    @JsonKey(name: 'poster_sizes')
    required List<String> posterSizes,
    @JsonKey(name: 'profile_sizes')
    required List<String> profileSizes,
    @JsonKey(name: 'still_sizes')
    required List<String> stillSizes,
  }) = _MovieConfigurationImages;

  factory MovieConfigurationImages.fromJson(Map<String, dynamic>
json) => _$MovieConfigurationImagesFromJson(json);
}
```

This holds all the information on the movie images.

3.  Create a new file in the **data/models** folder called **models.dart** to hold the list of all the models for the UI. Add all of the models:

```
export 'genre.dart';
export 'movie_response.dart';
export 'movie_results.dart';
export 'movie_details.dart';
export 'movie_credits.dart';
export 'movie_videos.dart';
export 'movie_configuration.dart';
```

This is useful when you need several model imports. By importing this file, you will get all models.

# Images

Now that we have a configuration class, we can update our utility methods for getting the image URL. Open **utils.dart** and replace **getImageUrl** with the following:

```
String imageUrl(String baseUrl, String size, String file) =>
'$baseUrl$size$file';

String? getSizedImageUrl(ImageSize size, MovieConfiguration configuration,
String? file) {
  if (file == null) {
    return null;
  }
  switch (size) {
```

```
    case ImageSize.small:
       return imageUrl(configuration.images.baseUrl, configuration.images.
posterSizes[1], file);
    case ImageSize.large:
       return imageUrl(configuration.images.baseUrl, configuration.images.
posterSizes[5], file);
  }
}
String? getMovieDetailsImagePath(
    MovieDetails details, MovieConfiguration configuration) {
  return getSizedImageUrl(ImageSize.large, configuration, details.
backdropPath);
}
```

This uses the **MovieConfiguration** class to build the URL. The **getMovieDetailsImagePath** method will return a larger image using the **backdropPath** URL.

# Database models

Now, we can start creating database models of genres and favorites. Genres will just be a list of supported genres from TMDB. Favorites will be what the user selects as a movie favorite and will be stored so that when they restart the app, all of their favorites are listed. Now, start creating the database models:

1. In the **data** folder, create a new folder named **database**.

2. In the **database** folder, create a new folder named **models**.

3. In the **models** folder, create a new file named **genre.dart**.

4. Add the following:

```
import 'package:freezed_annotation/freezed_annotation.dart';

part 'genre.freezed.dart';

part 'genre.g.dart';

@freezed
class DBMovieGenre with _$DBMovieGenre {
  const factory DBMovieGenre({
    required int id,
    required int remoteId,
    required String name,
  }) = _DBMovieGenre;

  // Add this private constructor
```

```
    const DBMovieGenre._();

    factory DBMovieGenre.fromJson(Map<String, dynamic> json) =>
_$DBMovieGenreFromJson(json);

}
```

5. Create a file named **favorite.dart** and add:

```
import 'package:freezed_annotation/freezed_annotation.dart';

part 'favorite.freezed.dart';

part 'favorite.g.dart';

@freezed
class DBFavorite with _$DBFavorite {
  const factory DBFavorite({
    required int id,
    required int movieId,
    required String backdropPath,
    required String posterPath,
    required bool favorite,
    required double popularity,
    required DateTime releaseDate,
    required String title,
    required String overview,
  }) = _DBFavorite;

  // Add this private constructor
  const DBFavorite._();

  factory DBFavorite.fromJson(Map<String, dynamic> json) =>
_$DBFavoriteFromJson(json);
}
```

Note that **DBFavorite** is more like **MovieDetails** than the **Favorite** class. This is because we want to save all the details about the movie without making another network call.

6. Next, create the file **configuration.dart**. This file will hold the movie configuration information and has image sizing values:

```
import 'package:freezed_annotation/freezed_annotation.dart';

part 'configuration.freezed.dart';
part 'configuration.g.dart';

@freezed
```

```dart
class DBConfiguration with _$DBConfiguration {
  const factory DBConfiguration({
    required int id,
    required DBConfigurationImages images,
    required List<String> changeKeys,
  }) = _DBConfiguration;
  // Add this private constructor
  const DBConfiguration._();
  factory DBConfiguration.fromJson(Map<String, dynamic> json) =>
_$DBConfigurationFromJson(json);

}

@freezed
class DBConfigurationImages with _$DBConfigurationImages {
  const factory DBConfigurationImages({
    required String baseUrl,
    required String secureBaseUrl,
    required List<String> backdropSizes,
    required List<String> logoSizes,
    required List<String> posterSizes,
    required List<String> profileSizes,
    required List<String> stillSizes,
  }) = _DBConfigurationImages;
  const DBConfigurationImages._();
  factory DBConfigurationImages.fromJson(Map<String, dynamic> json)
=> _$DBConfigurationImagesFromJson(json);
}
```

7. Next, create the file **database_models.dart**. This is called a barrel file and holds all of the model files:

```dart
export 'configuration.dart';
export 'genre.dart';
export 'favorite.dart';
```

8. Then, type **dart run build_runner build**.

9. Now, add the **drift** plugins. In **pubspec.yaml** add the following:

```yaml
drift: ^2.20.2
drift_flutter: ^0.2.0
sqlite3_flutter_libs: ^0.5.24
path_provider: ^2.1.4
path: ^1.9.0
```

10. In the **dev_dependencies** section, add:

```
drift_dev: ^2.20.3
```

11. Then, add the following to resolve some dependency conflicts:

```
dependency_overrides:
  web: ^1.0.0
```

12. In the **database** folder, create a new file named **database_interface.dart.** Add the following:

```
import 'package:movies/data/database/models/database_models.dart';

abstract class IDatabase {
  Future deleteDatabase();

  Future<List<DBMovieGenre>> getGenres();

  Future saveGenres(List<DBMovieGenre> genres);

  Future<DBConfiguration?> getMovieConfiguration();

  Future<DBConfiguration?> getMovieConfigurationById(int id);

  Future saveMovieConfiguration(DBConfiguration configuration);

  Future saveFavorite(DBFavorite favorite);

  Future<bool> removeFavorite(int id);

  Future<List<DBFavorite>> getFavorites();

  Stream<List<DBFavorite>> streamFavorites();
}
```

This will be the interface for all databases.

13. To create the drift database, create a new folder named **drift** in the **database** folder.

14. Create the file **movie_database.dart** in the **drift** folder. Add:

```
import 'package:drift/drift.dart';
import 'package:drift_flutter/drift_flutter.dart';

part 'movie_database.g.dart';

class DriftConfigurationImages extends Table {
  // TODO Add fields
}

class DriftFavorite extends Table {
  // TODO Add fields
}
```

```
class DriftGenre extends Table {
  // TODO Add fields
}

@DriftDatabase(
  tables: [DriftFavorite, DriftConfigurationImages, DriftGenre],
)
class MovieDatabase extends _$MovieDatabase {
  MovieDatabase() : super(driftDatabase(name: 'Movies'));

  @override
  int get schemaVersion => 1;
}
```

This defines tables for movie image configuration, favorites, and genres. The **MovieDatabase** class is pretty simple. Just pass in the name of the movie file and annotate the class with the **@DriftDatabase** annotation, which has all three tables.

15. Next, add the **DriftConfigurationImages** fields:

```
IntColumn get id => integer().autoIncrement()();

TextColumn get baseUrl => text()();

TextColumn get secureBaseUrl => text()();

TextColumn get backdropSizes => text()();

TextColumn get logoSizes => text()();

TextColumn get posterSizes => text()();

TextColumn get profileSizes => text()();

TextColumn get stillSizes => text()();
```

This defines an id field as well as URLs and size strings.

16. Next, add the **DriftFavorite** fields:

```
IntColumn get id => integer().autoIncrement()();

IntColumn get movieId => integer()();

TextColumn get backdropPath => text()();

TextColumn get posterPath => text()();

BoolColumn get favorite => boolean()();

RealColumn get popularity => real()();

DateTimeColumn get releaseDate => dateTime()();
```

```
    TextColumn get title => text()();

    TextColumn get overview => text()();
```

17. Next, add the **DriftGenre** fields:

```
    IntColumn get id => integer().autoIncrement()();

    IntColumn get remoteId => integer()();

    TextColumn get name => text()();
```

18. Create the file **drift_database.dart** in the **drift** folder. This file will do the work of retrieving and saving database information. Add the following code:

```
import 'package:drift/drift.dart';
import 'package:movies/data/database/models/database_interface.
dart';
import 'package:movies/data/database/models/database_models.dart';
import 'package:movies/data/database/drift/movie_database.dart';

class DriftDatabase implements IDatabase {
  final MovieDatabase movieDatabase = MovieDatabase();

  DriftDatabase();

  @override
  Future deleteDatabase() async {}

  @override
  Future<List<DBFavorite>> getFavorites() async {
    // TODO Add getFavorites
  }

  @override
  Future<List<DBMovieGenre>> getGenres() async {
    // TODO Add getGenres
  }

  @override
  Future<DBConfiguration?> getMovieConfiguration() async {
    // TODO Add getMovieConfiguration
  }

  @override
  Future<DBConfiguration?> getMovieConfigurationById(int id) async {
    return getMovieConfiguration();
  }
```

```
    @override
    Future<bool> removeFavorite(int id) async {
      // TODO Add removeFavorite
    }

    @override
    Future saveFavorite(DBFavorite favorite) async {
      // TODO Add saveFavorite
    }

    @override
    Future saveGenres(List<DBMovieGenre> genres) async {
      // TODO Add saveGenres
    }

    @override
    Future saveMovieConfiguration(DBConfiguration configuration) async {
      // TODO Add saveMovieConfiguration
    }

    @override
    Stream<List<DBFavorite>> streamFavorites() {
      // TODO Add streamFavorites
    }
  }
```

19. Now, add the **getFavorites** code:

```
// 1
    final favorites = await movieDatabase.managers.driftFavorite.
get();
    final dbFavorites = <DBFavorite>[];
    for (final favorite in favorites) {
// 2
      dbFavorites.add(DBFavorite(
          id: favorite.id,
          movieId: favorite.movieId,
          backdropPath: favorite.backdropPath,
          posterPath: favorite.posterPath,
          favorite: favorite.favorite,
          popularity: favorite.popularity,
          releaseDate: favorite.releaseDate,
          title: favorite.title,
          overview: favorite.overview));
    }
    return dbFavorites;
```

    a.  Drift creates a managers field that has a driftXXXX getter for each table.

    b.  For each favorite, add a database favorite to the array.

20.  Add the **getGenres** code:

```
final genres = await movieDatabase.managers.driftGenre.get();
final dbGenres = <DBMovieGenre>[];
for (final genre in genres) {
  dbGenres.add(DBMovieGenre(
    id: genre.id,
    remoteId: genre.remoteId,
    name: genre.name,
  ));
}
return dbGenres;
```

This is similar to favorites but with genres.

21.  Add the **getMovieConfiguration** code:

```
final images = await movieDatabase.managers.driftConfigurationImages.
get();
final dbImages = <DBConfigurationImages>[];
for (final genre in images) {
  dbImages.add(DBConfigurationImages(
    baseUrl: genre.baseUrl,
    secureBaseUrl: genre.secureBaseUrl,
    backdropSizes: genre.backdropSizes.split(','),
    logoSizes: genre.logoSizes.split(','),
    posterSizes: genre.posterSizes.split(','),
    profileSizes: genre.profileSizes.split(','),
    stillSizes: genre.stillSizes.split(','),
  ));
}
if (dbImages.isEmpty) {
  return null;
}
// Don't care about changeKeys
return DBConfiguration(id: 1, images: dbImages[0], changeKeys:
[]);
```

This creates an array of image configurations.

22.  Add the **removeFavorite** code:

```
return await movieDatabase.driftFavorite
```

```
        .deleteWhere((table) => table.id.equals(id)) !=
        -1;
```

This will delete a favorite that has the passed in ID.

23. Add the **saveFavorite** code:

```
movieDatabase.managers.driftFavorite.create((x) =>
    DriftFavoriteData(
        id: favorite.id,
        movieId: favorite.movieId,
        backdropPath: favorite.backdropPath,
        posterPath: favorite.posterPath,
        favorite: favorite.favorite,
        popularity: favorite.popularity,
        releaseDate: favorite.releaseDate,
        title: favorite.title,
        overview: favorite.overview,
    ));
```

This uses the create method to create a new favorite row in the database.

24. Add the **saveGenre** code:

```
for (final genre in genres) {
  movieDatabase.managers.driftGenre.create((x) =>
      DriftGenreData(
            id: genre.id, remoteId: genre.remoteId, name: genre.
name));
    }
```

This will go through the list and create new genre entries. This will happen only once.

25. Add the **saveMovieConfguration** code:

```
movieDatabase.managers.driftConfigurationImages
    .create((x) =>
    DriftConfigurationImagesCompanion.insert(
      baseUrl: configuration.images.baseUrl,
      secureBaseUrl: configuration.images.secureBaseUrl,
      backdropSizes: configuration.images.backdropSizes.join(','),
      logoSizes: configuration.images.logoSizes.join(','),
      posterSizes: configuration.images.posterSizes.join(','),
      profileSizes: configuration.images.profileSizes.join(','),
      stillSizes: configuration.images.stillSizes.join(','),
    ));
```

This will create a movie image configuration row.

26. Add the **streamFavorites** code:

```
    return movieDatabase.managers.driftFavorite.watch().
map((dbFavorites) {
        final favorites = <DBFavorite>[];
        for (final favorite in dbFavorites) {
          favorites.add(DBFavorite(id: favorite.id,
              movieId: favorite.movieId,
              backdropPath: favorite.backdropPath,
              posterPath: favorite.posterPath,
              favorite: favorite.favorite,
              popularity: favorite.popularity,
              releaseDate: favorite.releaseDate,
              title: favorite.title,
              overview: favorite.overview));
      }
      return favorites;
    });
```

Drift supports streams. Using the watch method returns a stream, and then we follow that with a map, which will convert the returned type into one we can work with.

# Movie view model

Now that you have the repository done, you need to update the **MovieViewModel** to use it. Open **movie_viewmodel.dart**. Follow these steps:

1. After the **movieAPIService** field, add the following:

   ```
   final IDatabase database;
   ```

2. Add a movie configuration field:

   ```
   MovieConfiguration? movieConfiguration;
   ```

3. Remove the following:

   ```
   Stream<List<Favorite>>? favoriteStream;

   List<Favorite>? favoriteList;
   ```

4. Change the constructor to:

   ```
       MovieViewModel({required  this.movieAPIService,  required  this.
   database});
   ```

5. Change **setupConfiguration** to:

```
    Future setupConfiguration() async {
    final response = await movieAPIService.getMovieConfiguration();
    if (response.statusCode == 200) {
      movieConfiguration = MovieConfiguration.fromJson(response.data);
    } else {
      logError(
          'Failed to load genres with error ${response.statusCode} and
message ${response.statusMessage}');
    }
  }
```

6. Add the following method:

```
    String? getImageUrl(ImageSize size, String? file) {
    if (file == null || movieConfiguration == null) {
        logMessage('movieConfiguration is null for getImageUrl file:
$file');
      return null;
    }
    return getSizedImageUrl(size, movieConfiguration!, file);
  }
```

7. Remove **streamFavorites** and **updateFavorite** and replace it with:

```
    Future saveFavorite(MovieDetails movieDetails) async {
    database.saveFavorite(DBFavorite(
        id: movieDetails.id,
        movieId: movieDetails.id,
        backdropPath: movieDetails.backdropPath,
        posterPath: movieDetails.posterPath,
        favorite: true,
        popularity: movieDetails.popularity,
        releaseDate: movieDetails.releaseDate,
        title: movieDetails.title,
        overview: movieDetails.overview));
  }

  Future<bool> removeFavorite(int id) async {
    return database.removeFavorite(id);
  }

  Future<List<DBFavorite>> getFavorites() async {
    return database.getFavorites();
  }

  Stream<List<DBFavorite>> streamFavorites() {
```

```
      return database.streamFavorites();
   }
```

8. Open up **providers.dart** to add new providers and update the **viewmodel** provider. Add the following:

```
@Riverpod(keepAlive: true)
MovieAPIService movieAPIService(MovieAPIServiceRef ref) =>
MovieAPIService();
```

9. Then change **movieViewModel** to:

```
   final database = await ref.read(driftDatabaseProvider.future);
    final model = MovieViewModel(database: database, movieAPIService:
ref.read(movieAPIServiceProvider));
   await model.setup();
   return model;
```

10. At the end of the file add:

```
@Riverpod(keepAlive: true)
Future<IDatabase> driftDatabase(DriftDatabaseRef ref) {
   return Future.value(DriftDatabase());
}
```

This adds a provider for the drift database.

11. Then type **dart run build_runner build**.

12. Open **favorite_screen.dart**.

13. Change **Favorite** to **DBFavorite** everywhere in the file.

14. In the **onFavoritesTap** call, change the **setState** code with the following:

```
removeFavorite(favorite);
```

15. Change the **removeFavorite** method to:

```
      await movieViewModel.removeFavorite(favorite.id);
      setState(() {});
```

16. In **vert_favorite_list.dart** change **Favorite** to **DBFavorite**.

17. In **favorite_row.dart** change **Favorite** to **DBFavorite**.

18. Change the **imageUrl** field to:

```
final imageUrl = movieViewModel.getImageUrl(ImageSize.small,
favorite.posterPath);
```

19. Since **imageUrl** will be null if there is no value, remove the **if  (imageUrl. isNotEmpty) check** and the **else** block of code.

20. Change the **CachedNetworkImage** call to:

```
            child: imageUrl != null ? CachedNetworkImage(
              imageUrl: imageUrl,
              alignment: Alignment.topCenter,
              fit: BoxFit.cover,
              height: 140,
              width: 100,
            ): emptyWidget,
```

21. Change the Title string to **favorite.title**.

22. Change the '1972' text to **yearFormat.format(favorite.releaseDate)**.

23. In **utils.dart,** change the **OnFavoriteResultsTap** to use a DBFavorite.

24. Change all calls of **getImageUrl** to call the movieViewModel's **getImageUrl** in all files. (do a find and replace).

# Cleanup

There are a few files that need to be cleaned up due to all of the changes. Start with **home_ screen_image.dart**:

1.  Change the **CachedNetworkImage** call to:

```
            child: imageUrl != null
                ? CachedNetworkImage(
                    imageUrl: imageUrl,
                    alignment: Alignment.topCenter,
                    fit: BoxFit.fitHeight,
                    height: 374,
                    width: screenWidth,
                  )
                : emptyWidget,
```

2.  In **horiz_movies.dart** change the extended class from **StatelessWidget** to **ConsumerWidget** to allow us to get the movie view model.

3.  Change the build method to:

```
      Widget build(BuildContext context, WidgetRef ref) {
```

4.  Then add and wrap the **SizedBox** with:

```
            final movieAsync = ref.watch(movieViewModelProvider);
            return movieAsync.when(
              error: (e, st) => Text(e.toString()),
              loading: () => Container(),
```

```
                data: (viewModel) {
```

5.  Change the **imageUrl** and **MovieWidget** to:

```
                final imageUrl =
                    viewModel.getImageUrl(ImageSize.small,
        movies[index].posterPath);
                return imageUrl != null ? MovieWidget(
                  movieId: movies[index].id,
                  movieUrl: imageUrl,
                  onMovieTap: onMovieTap,
                  movieType: movieType,
                ) : emptyWidget;
```

6.  In **detail_image.dart** add a **movieConfiguration** field and change the constructor to:

```
    final MovieConfiguration movieConfiguration;
    const DetailImage(
        {super.key, required this.details, required this.
    movieConfiguration});
```

7.  Change the **imageUrl** definition to:

```
    final imageUrl = getMovieDetailsImagePath(widget.details, widget.
    movieConfiguration);
```

    This method is a bit different as it uses the **backdropPath** and a large image.

8.  Change the **CachedNetworkImage** call to:

```
                child: imageUrl != null ? CachedNetworkImage(
                  imageUrl: imageUrl,
                  alignment: Alignment.topCenter,
                  fit: BoxFit.fitWidth,
                  height: 200,
                  width: screenWidth,
                ) : emptyWidget,
```

9.  In **movie_detail.dart**, add the following after the **movieVideos** field definition:

```
    List<DBFavorite> favorites = [];
    int currentFavoriteId = -1;
```

10. After setting the **movieViewModel** in the **data: (viewModel)**, add the following:

```
    getFavorites();
```

11. Add the following two methods:

```
    Future getFavorites() async {
      favorites = await movieViewModel.getFavorites();
```

```
        favoriteNotifier.value = isMovieFavorite(widget.movieId);
    }

    bool isMovieFavorite(int id) {
      return favorites.firstWhereOrNull((favorite) => favorite.movieId
== id) != null;
    }
```

12. Import the **collection.dart** package (for **firstWhereOrNull**).

13. Change the call to **DetailImage** to:

```
        DetailImage(
          details: movieDetails,
          movieConfiguration:
          movieViewModel.movieConfiguration!,
        ),
```

14. Change the **onFavoriteSelected** callback to:

```
onFavoriteSelected: () async {
    if (favoriteNotifier.value) {
      if (currentFavoriteId != -1) {
        movieViewModel
              .removeFavorite(currentFavoriteId);
      }
        favoriteNotifier.value = false;
    } else {
        currentFavoriteId = movieDetails.id;
        await movieViewModel
              .saveFavorite(movieDetails);
        favoriteNotifier.value = true;
    }
},
```

15. Change the call to **HorizontalCast** to:

```
    HorizontalCast(movieViewModel: movieViewModel, castList: credits?.
cast ?? []),
```

16. Open **horiz_cast.dart**, add the movie view model, and change the constructor:

```
final MovieViewModel movieViewModel;

const HorizontalCast({required this.movieViewModel, required this.
castList, super.key});
```

17. Change the **CastImage** call to:

```
        var imageUrl = movieViewModel.getImageUrl(ImageSize.small,
```

```
castList[index].profilePath);

        return imageUrl != null ? CastImage(imageUrl: imageUrl,
name: castList[index].name): emptyWidget;
```

18. Open **movie_row.dart** and remove the check for **imageUrl** being empty.

19. Change the **CachedNetworkImage** call to:

```
                child: imageUrl != null
                    ? CachedNetworkImage(
                        imageUrl: imageUrl,
                        alignment: Alignment.topCenter,
                        fit: BoxFit.cover,
                        height: 142,
                        width: 100,
                      )
                    : emptyWidget,
```

Since the app has had multiple plugins added, you will need to stop and restart it. Rerun the app and test the added features:

• Try selecting multiple genres on the Genre screen. Stop/restart the app to see if they are still there.

• In a Movie detail screen, click the favorite button and then go to the favorites page to see if it is there.

• Click on the favorite button in the favorites screen to make sure it is removed.

• Go back to the detail screen of a favorite movie and ensure the favorite button is red.

# Conclusion

In this chapter, you learned all about SharedPreferences and how you can save key/value data. You saved selected genre information. You could also have saved information like whether the user chose a light/dark theme or any other information that can be contained as a basic dart type. You then explored different databases and used the drift database to save genre, movie configuration, and favorite information. This will provide cached genre and movie configuration and allow the user to save their favorite movies.

In the next chapter, you will learn how to modify your app to work on the web and the desktop. Two great platforms that expand the reach of your apps. You will learn how to handle menus for desktop apps as well as adjust your UI to handle larger screens. You will also learn how to deploy web apps using Firebase hosting. You will then be able to create desktop apps for macOS and Windows.

# CHAPTER 13

# Web and Desktop

## Introduction

In this chapter, you will learn how to run Flutter apps on desktop platforms like macOS, Windows, and Linux, as well as on the web. You will create menus for desktop apps that allow the app to perform more like native apps. Learn about some of the issues when running on the web and learn how to make your UIs more adaptive to the width of larger screens. Learn how to use navigation rails instead of the bottom navigation on the desktop and web. Finally, you will host your web app on Firebase Hosting so that others can see it.

## Structure

The chapter covers the following topics:

- Other platforms
- MacOS
- Menus
- AdaptiveScaffold
- Windows
- Web
- Firebase Hosting

# Objectives

By the end of this chapter, you will know how to create desktop apps for Mac and Windows, as well as menus. You will know how to create an adaptive UI that can expand and change based on the size of the screen. You will have created a web app that solves database issues, allowing your database to run on the web.

# MacOS

One of the great benefits of Flutter is that it can run not only on mobile devices but also on the desktop and web. Most of the time, there are not many changes needed to get the app to work on these platforms. Since these platforms have different forms and inputs, they will have different needs. The most obvious is the size difference. The user usually has more room to display information on the desktop and the web. To account for those differences, you may want to show different layouts. If you are familiar with *Gmail*, you will notice that on the web, there is a list of labels on the left, and you can split your screen into email lists and content. To use the same code, you would break your UI into different components and display them in different holders, depending on the platform. For example, you could have a list of emails as one component that would show up as one screen on a phone but just a part of a larger screen on the desktop or web. You also have menus on desktop platforms that allow you to easily access different parts of the app. Usually, there will be a file menu with all of the actions you can do to files and an edit menu for cut, copy, paste, and so on. You would then have app-specific menus, like accessing search.

If you are using a Mac or have seen one used, you know that each app has a window with three colored icons in the top left of the window that allows a user to close, minimize, and expand that window. Mac apps also have a menu system that is built into the screen's top row. This usually has the System Apple menu, a menu with the app's name, and any app-specific menu. Usually, Mac apps are developed in Xcode, and you can edit the menus there. To fully understand how this works, open up Xcode and navigate to your app's **macOS** folder.

1.  Choose File | **Open**:

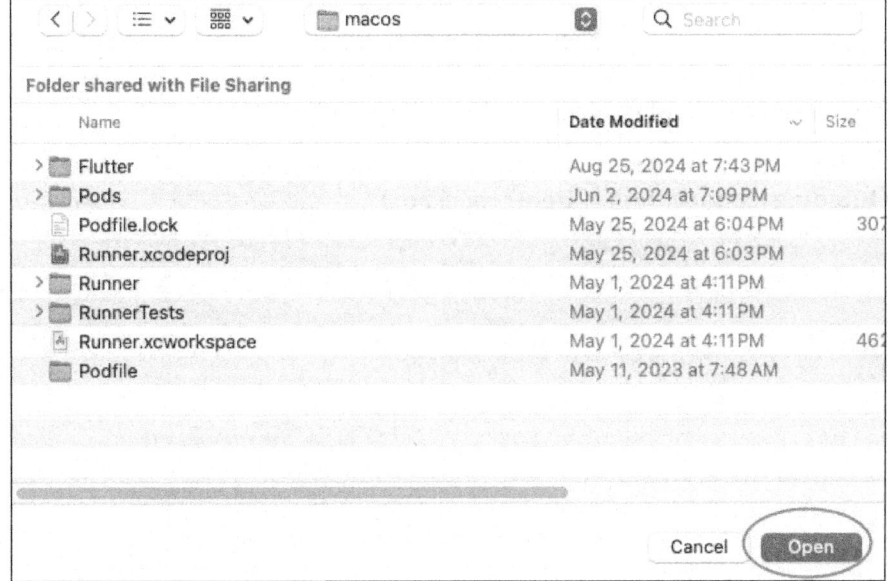

**Figure 13.1**: *macOS folder*

Click the **Open** button. This will open the correct file for the project. If you click on the **Runner** folder on the left, you should see the following:

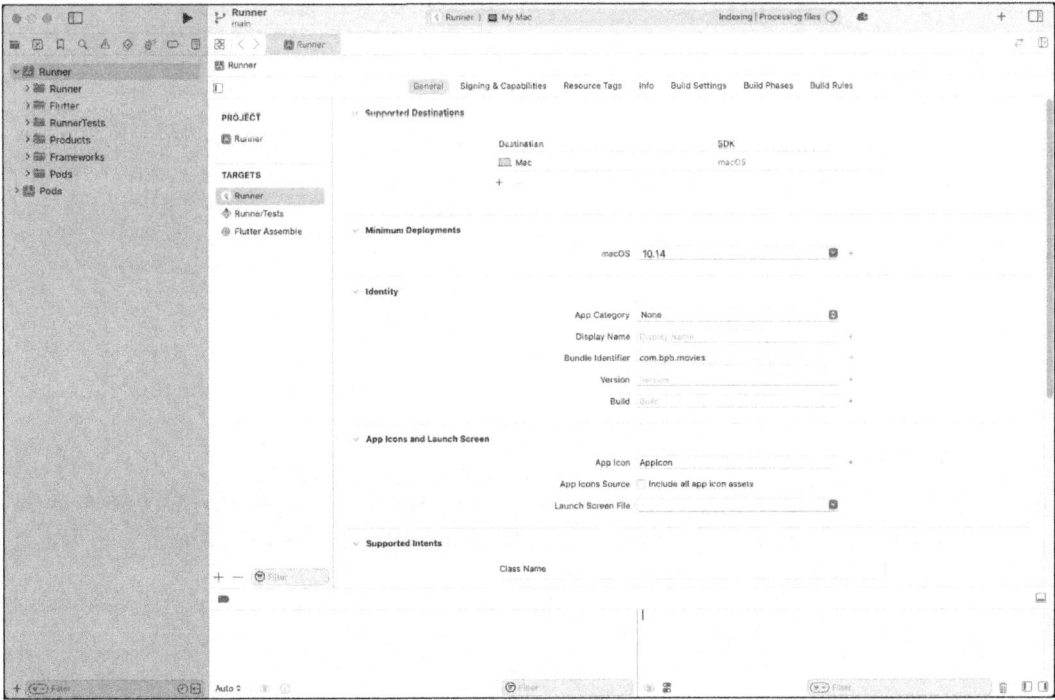

**Figure 13.2**: *Runner general screen*

This is the **General** screen and has the targeted **macOS** version, **App Category**, **Display Name**, and **Bundle Identifier**. Some of these values have already been added when the project was created but you can change them here. For example, you can add a **Display Name** and version numbers.

2. Go back to the **Runner** screen and click on **Signing & Capabilities**. Select the **Outgoing Connections (Client)** checkbox:

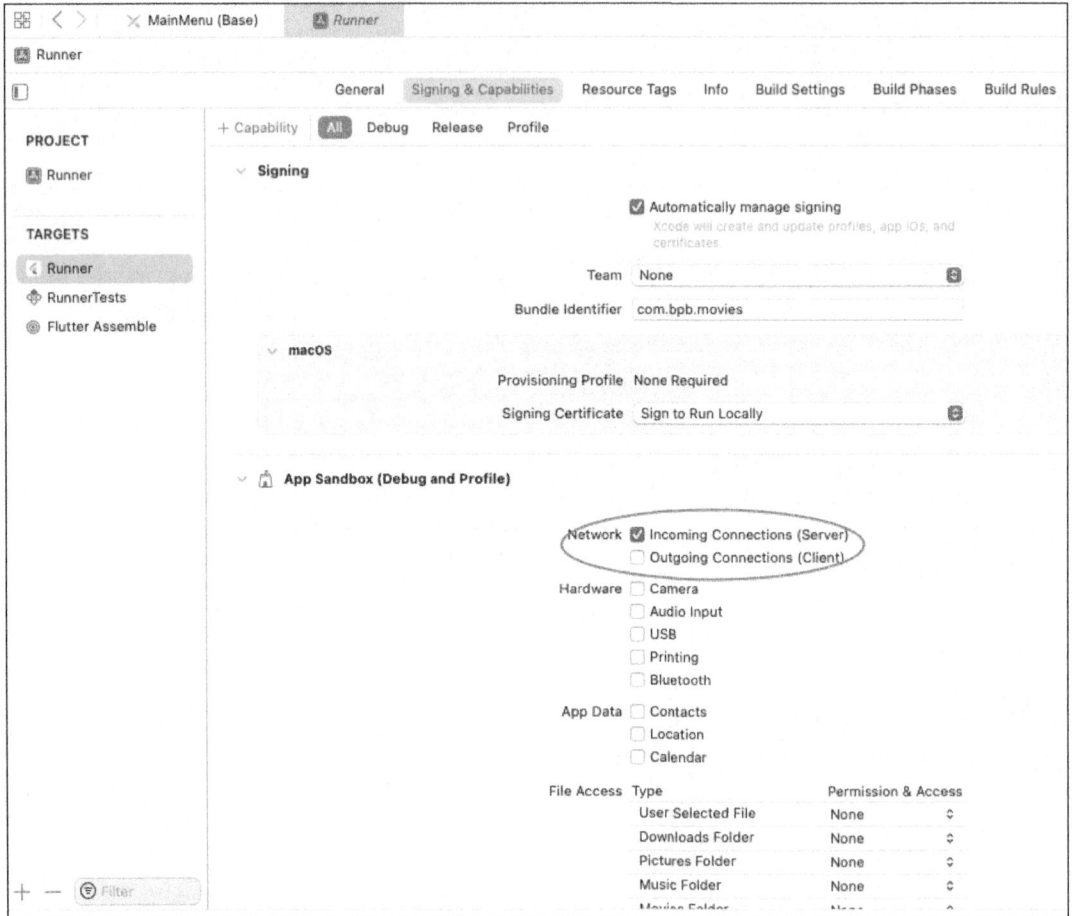

*Figure 13.3*: *Connections*

3. In Android Studio, change the device from your current phone to macOS (desktop) and run the app. You should see just the **movies** menu, as follows:

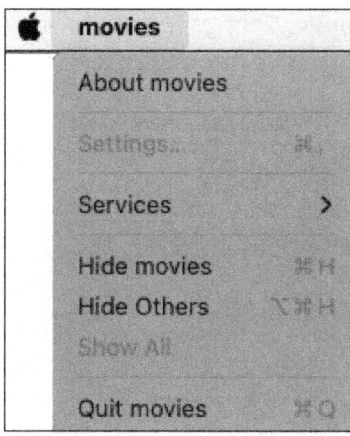

*Figure 13.4: Movie menu*

4. To fix the lowercase movie name, return the Xcode and enter a **Display Name**:

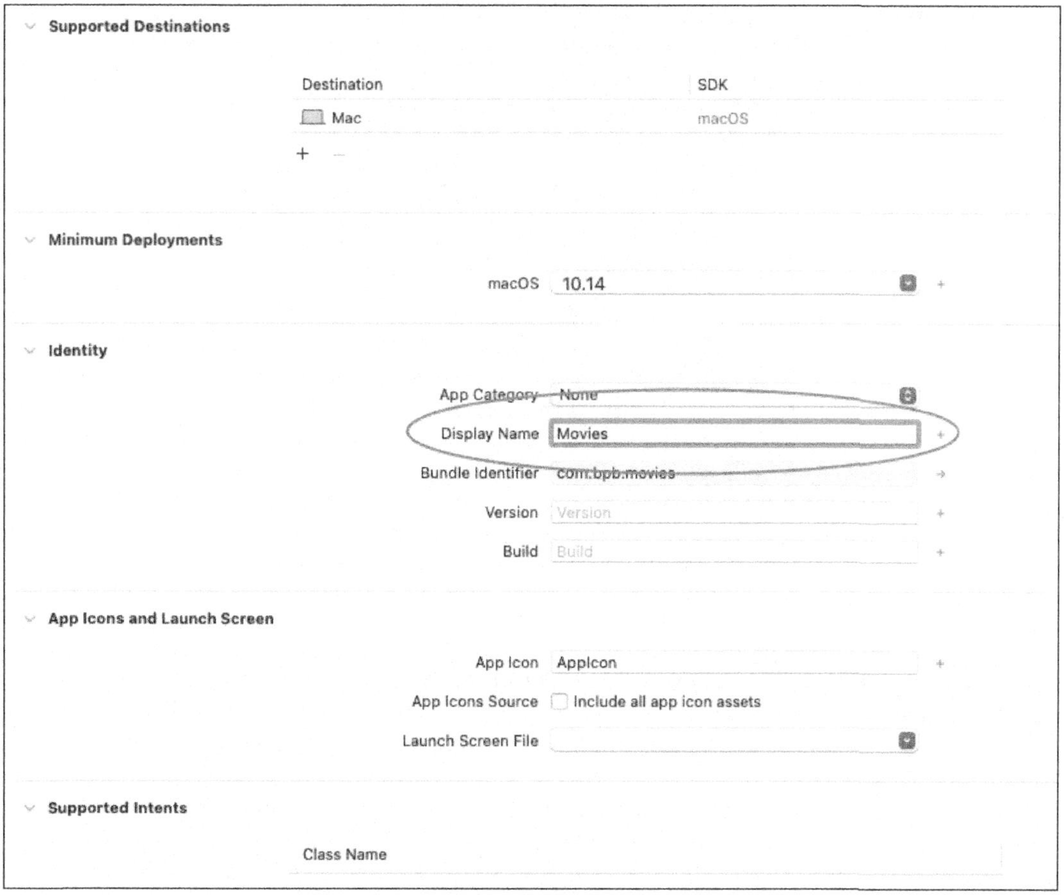

| Supported Destinations | | |
| --- | --- | --- |
| | Destination | SDK |
| | Mac | macOS |
| | + − | |

| Minimum Deployments | |
| --- | --- |
| macOS | 10.14 |

| Identity | |
| --- | --- |
| App Category | None |
| Display Name | Movies |
| Bundle Identifier | com.bpb.movies |
| Version | Version |
| Build | Build |

| App Icons and Launch Screen | |
| --- | --- |
| App Icon | AppIcon |
| App Icons Source | ☐ Include all app icon assets |
| Launch Screen File | |

Supported Intents

Class Name

*Figure 13.5: Display name*

5.  Then open **Runner/Runner/Configs/AppInfo**. Change **movies** to **Movies**:

```
 1  // Application-level settings for the Runner target.
 2  //
 3  // This may be replaced with something auto-generated from metadata (e.g., pubspec.yaml) in the
 4  // future. If not, the values below would default to using the project name when this becomes a
 5  // 'flutter create' template.
 6
 7  // The application's name. By default this is also the title of the Flutter window.
 8  PRODUCT_NAME = movies
 9
10  // The application's bundle identifier
11  PRODUCT_BUNDLE_IDENTIFIER = com.bpb.movies
12
13  // The copyright displayed in application information
14  PRODUCT_COPYRIGHT = Copyright © 2024 com.bpb. All rights reserved.
15
```

*Figure 13.6: AppInfo*

Stop and restart the app. You may encounter the following dialog. Select **Open Anyway**:

*Figure 13.7: Debug running*

This should happen just during development. Your app should work and look as follows:

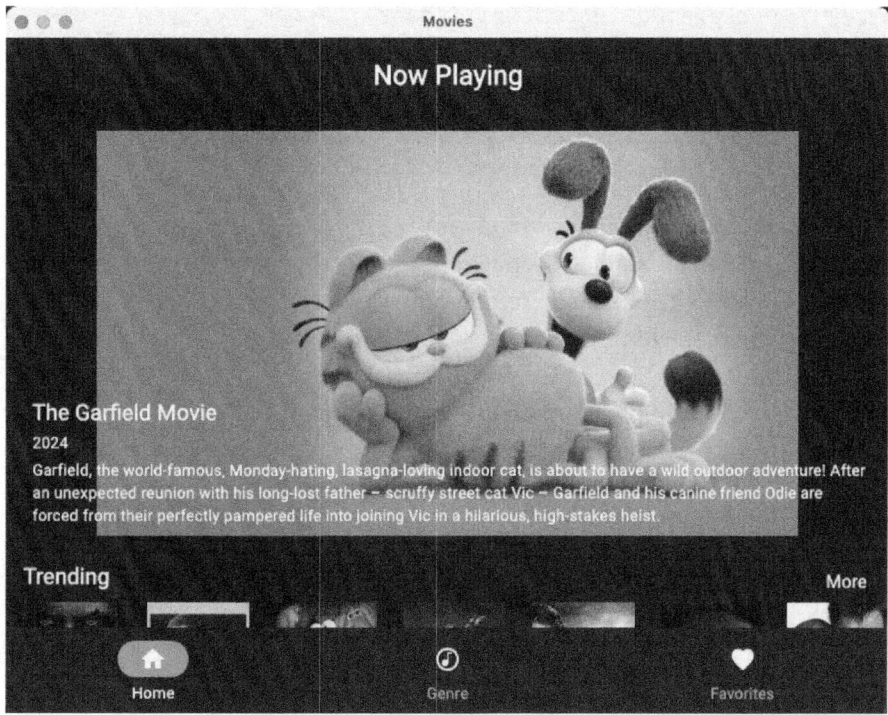

*Figure 13.8: macOS app*

# Menus

Menus are now built into Flutter but do not work on all platforms yet. The **PlatformMenu** and the **PlatformMenuItem** are used to define menu items. These classes define a label and, in the case of **PlatformMenu**, a list of menus of type **PlatformMenuItem**. The **PlatformMenuItem** has an **onSelected** parameter that is used to handle the user selecting the menu. You can also provide a shortcut or keyboard command. To create your own set of menus you will use Flutter code to create the menus and add them before the **MaterialApp** call. This will not affect mobile devices. One of the problems with the menu system is that it sits above all of the screens, and a way to communicate the selection of a menu item to the rest of the app is needed. There are several ways to handle this. We will use the **EventBus** package. This is a package that allows classes to subscribe or listen to events. Any class can send events.

1. Add the **EventBus** package to **pubspec.yaml**:

   ```
   event_bus: ^2.0.0
   ```

2. Do a Pub get.

3. In the **ui** folder, create the file **menus.dart**. We will start by adding a few event classes. Add:

```
import 'package:flutter/material.dart';
import 'package:flutter/services.dart';
import 'package:movies/providers.dart';
import 'package:flutter_riverpod/flutter_riverpod.dart';

sealed class MenuEvent {}
class QuitEvent extends MenuEvent {}
class HomeEvent extends MenuEvent {}
class GenreEvent extends MenuEvent {}
class FavoritesEvent extends MenuEvent {}
class SearchEvent extends MenuEvent {}
class SearchMovieEvent extends MenuEvent {
  final String searchText;

  SearchMovieEvent(this.searchText);
}
```

This defines a top level **MenuEvent** class that all the other classes extend. Most of these do not have any information attached to them, except for the **SearchMovieEvent**, which has a **searchText** string used for a search.

4.  Next, create the **MenuManager** class:

```
class MenuManager {
  final ProviderRef ref;

  MenuManager(this.ref);

  List<PlatformMenu> createMenus() {
    return [
      createMovieMenu(),
      createOptionsMenu(),
    ];
  }
}
```

This class just takes a **Riverpod ProviderRef** so that it can access other providers. The main **createMenus** method will return a list of menus.

5.  Next, add the **createMovieMenu** method at the end of the class:

```
PlatformMenu createMovieMenu() {
  return PlatformMenu(label: 'Movies', menus: [
    PlatformMenuItem(
        label: 'Quit',
        onSelected: () => ref.read(eventBusProvider).
fire(QuitEvent()),
```

```
         shortcut: const SingleActivator(LogicalKeyboardKey.keyQ,
meta: true)),
      ]);
   }
```

This returns a **PlatformMenu** with a label and just a **Quit** menu item. This will fire a **Quit** event. We will create the **eventBusProvider** later. Notice the **SingleActivator**. This is used to allow the user to use the keyboard for keyboard commands. In this case, *Command+Q* is to quit the app. On Windows, this will be *Ctrl+Q*.

6. Next, create an options menu:

```
   PlatformMenu createOptionsMenu() {
      return PlatformMenu(label: 'Options', menus: [
         PlatformMenuItem(
            label: 'Home',
            onSelected: () => ref.read(eventBusProvider).
fire(HomeEvent()),
            shortcut: const SingleActivator(LogicalKeyboardKey.keyH,
meta: true)),
         PlatformMenuItem(
            label: 'Genre',
            onSelected: () => ref.read(eventBusProvider).
fire(GenreEvent()),
            shortcut: const SingleActivator(LogicalKeyboardKey.keyG,
meta: true)),
         PlatformMenuItem(
            label: 'Favorites',
            onSelected: () => ref.read(eventBusProvider).
fire(FavoritesEvent()),
            shortcut: const SingleActivator(LogicalKeyboardKey.keyF,
meta: true)),
         PlatformMenuItem(
            label: 'Search',
            onSelected: () => ref.read(eventBusProvider).
fire(SearchEvent()),
            shortcut: const SingleActivator(LogicalKeyboardKey.keyS,
meta: true)),
      ]);
   }
```

   a. This creates four menus:

      • **Home**: Go to the home page

- **Genre**: Go to the genre page

- **Favorites**: Go to the favorites page

- **Search**: Bring up the search dialog

7. Open up **providers.dart**. Add:

```
final searchTextProvider = StateProvider<String>((ref) {
  return '';
});
final currentIndexProvider = StateProvider<int>((ref) {
  return 0;
});


@Riverpod(keepAlive: true)
MenuManager menuManager(MenuManagerRef ref) => MenuManager(ref);

@Riverpod(keepAlive: true)
EventBus eventBus(EventBusRef ref) => EventBus();
```

The first provider just stores the current search string. The second is to keep track of the current index and the third is for the menu manager and the fourth is for the **EventBus**.

8. In the terminal, type:

```
dart run build_runner build.
```

9. Open **main.dart**. In the **build** method, wrap the **MaterialApp** so that the build method now looks like:

```
final router = ref.watch(appRouterProvider);
final menuManager = ref.watch(menuManagerProvider);
return PlatformMenuBar(
  menus: menuManager.createMenus(),
  child: MaterialApp.router(
    routerConfig: router.config(),
    title: 'Movies',
    debugShowCheckedModeBanner: false,
    theme: createTheme(),
  ),
);
```

This wraps **MaterialApp** with a **PlatformMenuBar** and calls our **createMenus** method. Stop and restart your Mac app. Your menus should look like the following:

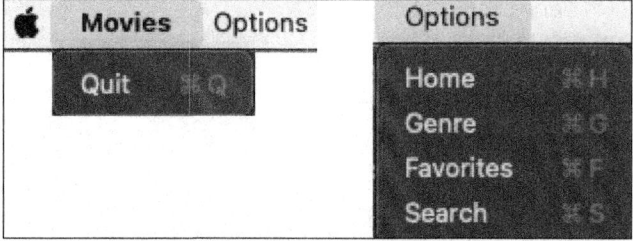

**Figure 13.9**: *macOS menus*

# Platforms

One question you may have is, *How do I tell which platform I am on?* Flutter has a **Platform** class that answers these questions. This is found in the **dart:io** package. The steps are as follows:

1. Open **utils.dart**.

2. Add the following:

```
import 'dart:io';

import 'package:flutter/foundation.dart';

bool isWeb() {
  return kIsWeb;
}

bool isDesktop() {
  if (kIsWeb) {
    return false;
  }
  return Platform.isWindows || Platform.isLinux || Platform.isMacOS;
}

bool isMobile() {
  if (kIsWeb) {
    return false;
  }
  return Platform.isIOS || Platform.isAndroid;
}

bool isMac() {
  if (kIsWeb) {
    return false;
  }
```

```
      return Platform.isMacOS;
}

bool isWindows() {
  if (kIsWeb) {
    return false;
  }
  return Platform.isWindows;
}
```

The **kIsWeb** constant is from Flutter and is how you tell if you are running a web app. For desktop, we check the different desktop platforms. For mobile, we check for iOS and Android. If you need to check for Mac or Windows specifically, use the last two methods.

# DesktopWindow

One noticeable difference between mobile and desktop is the use of a free floating window to hold your app's content. These windows can be resized quite a bit. At some point, when making the window smaller, your app becomes unusable. To prevent that, there is a package called **DesktopWindow**. This package only has a few methods, but they are very helpful. Here are a few of these methods:

- setWindowSize
- setMinWindowSize
- setMaxWindowSize
- setFullScreen

We will be using the **setWindowSize** and **setMinWindowSize** methods. The steps are as follows:

1. Add the **DesktopWindow** package to **pubspec.yaml**:

   ```
   desktop_window: ^0.4.0
   ```

2. Do a Pub get.

3. Open **main.dart**. Add the following before the **runApp** call:

   ```
   if (isDesktop()) {
     await DesktopWindow.setWindowSize(const Size(700, 600));

     await DesktopWindow.setMinWindowSize(const Size(700, 600));
   }
   ```

   Stop and run the app, and you will see that you cannot make your window size smaller than 700x600. You will see some errors related to SQLite. To fix these, update the drift libraries to newer versions.

4. In **pubspec.yaml** change:

   ```
   drift: ^2.20.2
   ```

   And in **dev_dependencies**:

   ```
   drift_dev: ^2.20.3
   ```

# AdaptiveScaffold

As we mentioned, desktop windows can be resized. It would be nice if we could change the layout when the screen changes sizes. If you had an email app, you could show just the list of emails when the screen is small but show the list and the contents of the email when the screen gets bigger. Enter the Flutter Adaptive Scaffold package. This package adapts to a variety of screens and has presets for different screen sizes. This package divides the screen as follows:

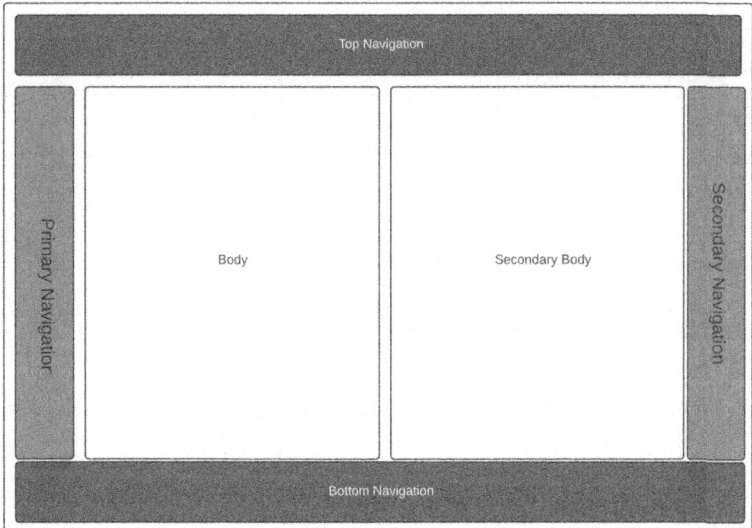

*Figure 13.10*: *Screen layout*

Currently, the movie app just has body and bottom navigation elements. One nice feature of desktop apps is the use of a navigation rail. This is a smaller navigation item that can be placed on the left or right. We still want to use a **BottomNavigationBar** on a small mobile device but use a **NavigationRail** on larger devices. The body is the primary screen that takes up the space left by the navigational elements. The **secondaryBody** acts as an option to split the space between two panes for purposes such as having a detailed view. To make this change, we will update the **main_screen.dart** file. This will be almost a complete rewrite. The steps are as follows:

1. Open **pubspec.yaml**. Add:

   ```
   flutter_adaptive_scaffold: ^0.3.1
   ```

2. Do a Pub get.

3. Open the **main_screen.dart** file.

4. Replace the code with:

```
class MainScreen extends ConsumerStatefulWidget {
  const MainScreen({super.key});

  @override
  ConsumerState<MainScreen> createState() => _MainScreenState();
}

class _MainScreenState extends ConsumerState<MainScreen> {
  int currentIndex = 0;
  List<Widget> tabScreens = [];
  // TODO add other methods
}
```

5. Add the **initState** method:

```
  @override
  void initState() {
    super.initState();
// 1
    tabScreens.add(const HomeScreen());
    tabScreens.add(const GenreScreen());
    tabScreens.add(const FavoriteScreen());
// 2
    ref.read(eventBusProvider).on<MenuEvent>().listen(((event) {
      switch (event) {
        case HomeEvent():
          setState(() {
            currentIndex = 0;
            ref.read(currentIndexProvider.notifier).state =
currentIndex;
          });
        case GenreEvent():
          setState(() {
            currentIndex = 1;
            ref.read(currentIndexProvider.notifier).state =
currentIndex;
          });
        case FavoritesEvent():
          setState(() {
            currentIndex = 2;
```

```
                    ref.read(currentIndexProvider.notifier).state =
currentIndex;
            });
          case QuitEvent():
            SystemNavigator.pop();
          case SearchEvent():
// 3
            showDialog(
                context: context, builder: (context) => const
SearchDialog());

          case SearchMovieEvent():
// 4
            ref.read(searchTextProvider.notifier).state = event.
searchText;
            currentIndex = 1;
            ref.read(currentIndexProvider.notifier).state =
currentIndex;
        }
      });
  }
```

a. Here we have the following:

1. Add screens to a list to avoid re-creating the screens each time.

2. Listen for event bus events.

3. Set the current index.

4. Set the current index in the provider.

5. Show the search dialog. (**SearchDialog** not written yet)

6. Set the search text for the **SearchMovieEvent**.

# AdaptiveLayout

Next, we will be adding the **AdaptiveLayout**:

1. Open the **main_screen.dart** file.

2. Add the **build** method:
```
   @override
   Widget build(BuildContext context) {
// 1
     currentIndex = ref.watch(currentIndexProvider);
// 2
```

```
        return AdaptiveLayout(
// 3
    primaryNavigation: SlotLayout(
      config: <Breakpoint, SlotLayoutConfig>{
        Breakpoints.mediumAndUp: SlotLayout.from(
            key: const Key('PrimaryNavigation'),
            builder: (_) {
// 4
                return AdaptiveScaffold.standardNavigationRail(
                  padding: const EdgeInsets.all(0),
                  destinations: const [
                    NavigationRailDestination(
                      icon: Icon(Icons.home),
                      label: Text('Home'),
                    ),
                    NavigationRailDestination(
                      icon: Icon(Symbols.genres),
                      label: Text('Genre'),
                    ),
                    NavigationRailDestination(
                      icon: Icon(Icons.favorite),
                      label: Text('Favorites'),
                    ),
                  ],
                  onDestinationSelected: (int index) {
                    setState(() {
                      currentIndex = index;
                      ref.read(currentIndexProvider.notifier).state =
currentIndex;
                    });
                  },
                  selectedIndex: currentIndex,
                  backgroundColor: Colors.black,
                );
            })
        },
    ),
// 5
    body: SlotLayout(config: <Breakpoint, SlotLayoutConfig?>{
      Breakpoints.standard: SlotLayout.from(
          key: const Key('body'),
          builder: (_) {
```

```
                    return Scaffold(
                      body: tabScreens[currentIndex],
                    );
                }),
            }),
// 6
        bottomNavigation: SlotLayout(
          config: <Breakpoint, SlotLayoutConfig?>{
            Breakpoints.small: SlotLayout.from(
              key: const Key('bottomNavigation'),
              builder: (_) => SizedBox(
                height: 80,
                child: BottomNavigationBar(
                  currentIndex: currentIndex,
                  onTap: (index) {
                    setState(() {
                      currentIndex = index;
                      ref.read(currentIndexProvider.notifier).state =
currentIndex;
                    });
                  },
                  items: const <BottomNavigationBarItem>[
                    BottomNavigationBarItem(
                      icon: Icon(Icons.home),
                      label: 'Home',
                    ),
                    BottomNavigationBarItem(
                      icon: Icon(Symbols.genres),
                      label: 'Genre',
                    ),
                    BottomNavigationBarItem(
                      icon: Icon(Icons.favorite),
                      label: 'Favorites',
                    ),
                  ],
                ),
              ),
            ),
          },
        ),
      );
  }
```

Here, we use the **AdaptiveLayout** and set three items:

- **primaryNavigation**: This will be a navigation rails for medium and higher screens.
- **Body**: This will be our screens.
- **bottomNavigation**: This will be a bottom navigation bar on small screens.

Here is a description of the code:

1. Get the current index.
2. Use the AdaptiveLayout for the top level widget.
3. For the primary navigation, use a SlotLayout for medium size layouts.
4. Create a navigation rail on the left side.
5. For the body, use the tab screens.
6. For the bottom, use a BottomNavigationBar for a small display.

# Search dialog

Now that we have the event for searching, we need to create a search dialog. Flutter has a system method called **showDialog** that displays a modal dialog with the given content. The steps are as follows:

1. In the **genres** folder, create the new file **search_dialog.dart**.

2. Add the following:

```
import 'package:auto_route/auto_route.dart';
import 'package:flutter/material.dart';
import 'package:flutter_riverpod/flutter_riverpod.dart';
import 'package:movies/providers.dart';
import 'package:movies/ui/menus.dart';
import 'package:movies/utils/utils.dart';

class SearchDialog extends ConsumerStatefulWidget {
  const SearchDialog({super.key});

  @override
  ConsumerState<SearchDialog> createState() => _SearchDialogState();
}

class _SearchDialogState extends ConsumerState<SearchDialog> {
  TextEditingController searchTextController =
TextEditingController();

  @override
```

```
  void dispose() {
    searchTextController.dispose();
    super.dispose();
  }

  @override
  Widget build(BuildContext context) {
  // TODO Add AlertDialog
  }
}
```

This creates a widget with a text controller for the search value.

3. Add the code for the dialog:
```
    final query = MediaQuery.of(context);
    final width = query.size.width * 0.7;
    const height = 300.0;
    return AlertDialog(
      contentPadding: const EdgeInsets.fromLTRB(24.0, 0.0, 0.0,
24.0),
      shape: RoundedRectangleBorder(borderRadius: BorderRadius.
circular(10.0)),
      content: SizedBox(
        width: width,
        height: height,
        child: SingleChildScrollView(
          child: SizedBox(
            width: width,
            height: height,
            child: Column(
              crossAxisAlignment: CrossAxisAlignment.center,
              children: [
                Expanded(
                  child: TextField(
                    cursorColor: Colors.black,
                    decoration: const InputDecoration(
                      border: InputBorder.none,
                      hintText: 'Search Movies',
                      // hintStyle: TextStyle(color: Colors.black),
                    ),
                    autofocus: true,
                    style: const TextStyle(color: Colors.black),
```

```
                        textInputAction: TextInputAction.done,
                        onSubmitted: (value) {
                          ref.read(eventBusProvider).
fire(SearchMovieEvent(value));
                          context.router.maybePop();
                        },
                        controller: searchTextController,
                      ),
                    ),
                    Row(
                      mainAxisAlignment: MainAxisAlignment.center,
                      children: [
                        ElevatedButton(
                            onPressed: () => context.router.maybePop(),
                            child: const Text('Cancel')),
                        addHorizontalSpace(8),
                        ElevatedButton(
                            onPressed: () {
                              ref.read(eventBusProvider).fire(
                                  SearchMovieEvent(searchTextController.
text));
                              context.router.maybePop();
                            },
                            child: const Text('Search'))
                      ],
                    )
                  ],
                ),
              ),
            ),
          ),
        );
```

This is just a **TextField** and two buttons: one to cancel and one to send a search event. To implement this event we need to make some changes to the **GenreScreen**.

4. Open **genre_screen.dart**.

5. Remove the **currentSearchString** field.

6. Add a new field:

```
final searchTextNotifier = ValueNotifier<String>('');
```

7. In the **buildScreen** method add the following before the return.

```
final searchText = ref.watch(searchTextProvider);
if (searchText != searchTextNotifier.value) {
  searchTextNotifier.value = searchText;
  currentMovieResponse = null;
  expandedNotifier.value = false;
  search();
}
```

8. Change the call to **GenreSearchRow** to:

```
ValueListenableBuilder<String>(
    valueListenable: searchTextNotifier,
    builder: (BuildContext context, String value, Widget?
child) {
        return GenreSearchRow(searchTextNotifier.value,
(searchString) {
            searchTextNotifier.value = searchString;
            currentMovieResponse = null;
            FocusScope.of(context).unfocus();
            expandedNotifier.value = false;
            search();
        });
    },
),
```

9. Change all instances of **currentSearchString** to **searchTextNotifier.value**.

Next, we need to change **GenreSearchRow**. The steps are as follows:

1. Open **genre_search_row.dart**.

2. Add a new field and change the constructor:

```
final String searchText;
final OnSearch onSearch;

const GenreSearchRow(this.searchText, this.onSearch, {super.key});
```

3. Change the **movieTextController** to:

```
late TextEditingController movieTextController =
TextEditingController(text: widget.searchText);
```

4. Remove the **initState** method as it is not needed any more.

5. At the beginning of the **build** method, add:

```
movieTextController.text = widget.searchText;
```

Do a hot restart and try selecting the search menu. It should bring up the search dialog and take you to the genre screen with search results. Try the other menu items and make sure they take you to the given screen.

You should see the navigation rails on the left, as shown in the following figure:

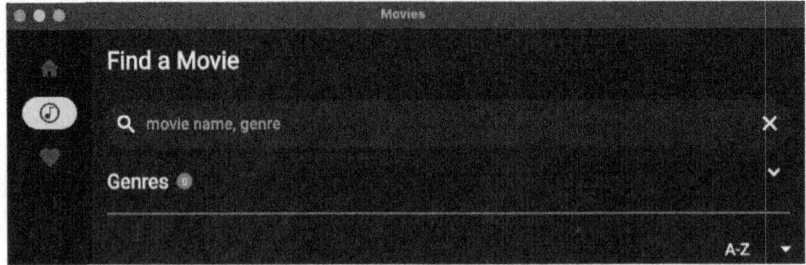

*Figure 13.11*: Navigation rails

# Windows

In addition to the Mac, Flutter runs on Windows. Very little needs to be done to get it to work. However, the one area that still needs work is the menus. On Windows, menus are in the window itself. This window is part of the Windows operating system and not Flutter. Currently, the `PlatformMenuBar` only works on Mac. To create menus on Windows, we need a plugin that helps. There are a lot of packages that put a menu inside of the Flutter canvas but not in the window. We will use an older `menubar` plugin that will help until `PlatformMenuBar` works on Windows.

On Windows, running the app should look as follows:

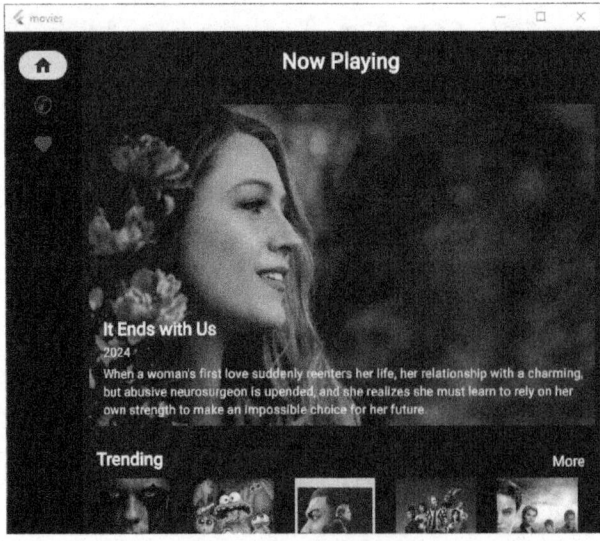

*Figure 13.12*: Windows version

To add the menu package, do the following:

1. Add the **menubar** package to **pubspec.yaml**:

```
menubar:
  git:
    url: https://github.com/google/flutter-desktop-embedding
    path: plugins/menubar
    ref: 12decbe0f592e14e03223f6f2c0c7e0e2dbd70a1
```

This uses a different way to bring in a plugin. This uses git, specifying a URL, path, and a commit reference.

2. Do a Pub get.

3. Open **menus.dart**. Add:

```
void createWindowsMenus() {
  setApplicationMenu([
    createWindowsMovieMenu(),
    createWindowsOptionsMenu(),
  ]);
}

NativeSubmenu createWindowsMovieMenu() {
  return NativeSubmenu(label: 'Movies', children: [
    NativeMenuItem(
        label: 'Quit',
        onSelected: () => ref.read(eventBusProvider).
fire(QuitEvent()),
        shortcut: LogicalKeySet(
            LogicalKeyboardKey.control, LogicalKeyboardKey.keyQ)),
  ]);
}

NativeSubmenu createWindowsOptionsMenu() {
  return NativeSubmenu(label: 'Options', children: [
    NativeMenuItem(
        label: 'Home',
        onSelected: () => ref.read(eventBusProvider).
fire(HomeEvent()),
        shortcut: LogicalKeySet(
            LogicalKeyboardKey.control, LogicalKeyboardKey.keyH)),
    NativeMenuItem(
        label: 'Genre',
```

```
            onSelected: () => ref.read(eventBusProvider).
fire(GenreEvent()),
            shortcut: LogicalKeySet(
                LogicalKeyboardKey.control, LogicalKeyboardKey.keyG)),
        NativeMenuItem(
            label: 'Favorites',
            onSelected: () => ref.read(eventBusProvider).
fire(FavoritesEvent()),
            shortcut: LogicalKeySet(
                LogicalKeyboardKey.control, LogicalKeyboardKey.keyF)),
        NativeMenuItem(
            label: 'Search',
            onSelected: () => ref.read(eventBusProvider).
fire(SearchEvent()),
            shortcut: LogicalKeySet(
                LogicalKeyboardKey.control, LogicalKeyboardKey.keyS)),
    ]);
  }
```

This uses the **menubar** package to create menus.

4.  Open **main.dart**. Replace the code in **_MainAppState** with:

```
var initialized = false;

  @override
  Widget build(BuildContext context) {
// 1
    WidgetsBinding.instance.addPostFrameCallback((_) {
      if (initialized) {
        return;
      }
// 2
      if (isWindows()) {
        final menuManager = ref.read(menuManagerProvider);
        menuManager.createWindowsMenus();
      }
      initialized = true;
    });
    final router = ref.watch(appRouterProvider);
    final menuManager = ref.watch(menuManagerProvider);
    if (isMac()) {
// 3
```

```
        return PlatformMenuBar(
          menus: menuManager.createMenus(),
          child: MaterialApp.router(
            routerConfig: router.config(),
            title: 'Movies',
            debugShowCheckedModeBanner: false,
            theme: createTheme(),
          ),
        );
      } else {
  // 4
        return MaterialApp.router(
          routerConfig: router.config(),
          title: 'Movies',
          debugShowCheckedModeBanner: false,
          theme: createTheme(),
        );
      }
    }
```

This code will add a **PostFrameCallback** that will be called when the **build** method finishes drawing. The steps are as follows:

1. Add a callback to be called when UI finishes drawing.

2. If we are on Windows, create the menus (only once).

3. If we are on a Mac, use the **PlatformMenuBar** class for menus.

4. Otherwise just use a **MaterialApp**.

On Windows, run the app. You should see two menus, namely, the **Movies** and **Option** menus (*Figure 13.13*). If you are a regular Windows user, you will notice that this is not exactly what Windows apps look like but is closer than other plugins. Until **PlatformMenuBar** works with Windows, there will have to be work arounds:

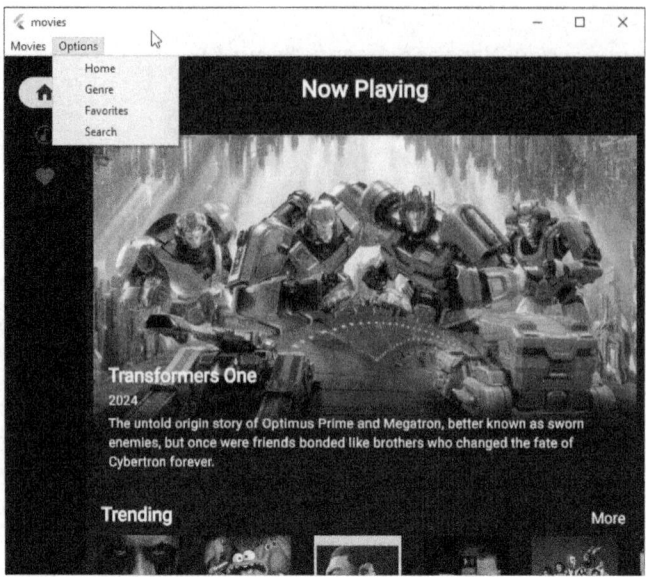

*Figure 13.13: Windows menus*

# Web

The web version of Flutter is unique from other platforms. It compiles and renders in three different running ways:

- **HTML**: Uses HTML elements and CSS to render the UI. This has been deprecated.

- **CanvasKit**: Uses the Skia graphics engine. It is slower to load but renders fast.

- **WebAssembly**: It compiles to a binary format that the web can understand.

To get our app to run on the web, we must make several changes, mostly related to the database. Since Flutter updates quite frequently and our **web** folder is now pretty old, it is time to recreate the folder. Since we have not added any of our files to this folder, it is okay to delete them. Follow these steps:

1.  Delete the **web** folder.

2.  From the terminal type:

    ```
    flutter create --platforms web .
    flutter config --enable-web
    ```

3.  Delete the newly created **widget_test.dart** in the test folder. This should create an updated **index.html** file. If the **web** folder was created with an earlier version of generated code, or you have problems running on the web, this is a good way to fix issues. However, if you have made any custom changes, you must back up the folder first and then copy your changes. As we are using the drift package, we will

need a special file: **sqlite3.wasm**. You can find this file in the project resources for this chapter.

4.  Copy **sqlite3.wasm** and **drift_worker.js** to the web folder.

5.  In the **data/database/drift** folder, create a new file named **connection.dart**. Add the following:

```
// We use a conditional export to expose the right connection factory depending
// on the platform.
export 'unsupported.dart'
if (dart.library.js) 'web.dart'
if (dart.library.ffi) 'native.dart';
```

6.  Create a new file named **native.dart**. Add:

```
import 'dart:io';

import 'package:drift/drift.dart';
import 'package:drift/native.dart';
import 'package:path_provider/path_provider.dart';
import 'package:path/path.dart' as p;

DatabaseConnection connect() {
  return DatabaseConnection.delayed(Future(() async {
    final dbFolder = await getApplicationDocumentsDirectory();
    final file = File(p.join(dbFolder.path, 'movies.sqlite'));
    return NativeDatabase.createBackgroundConnection(file);
  }));
}
```

This will get the application directory and create a file named **movies.sqlite** and then create a **DatabaseConnection**.

7.  Create a new file **unsupported.dart**. Add:

```
import 'package:drift/drift.dart';

Never _unsupported() {
  throw UnsupportedError(
      'No suitable database implementation was found on this platform.');
}

// Depending on the platform the app is compiled to, the following stubs will
// be replaced with the methods in native.dart or web.dart
```

```
DatabaseConnection connect() {
  _unsupported();
}

Future<void> validateDatabaseSchema(GeneratedDatabase database)
async {
  _unsupported();
}
```

This is used when there is an unsupported version of Flutter.

8.  Create a new file **web.dart**. Add the following:

```
import 'package:drift/drift.dart';
import 'package:drift/wasm.dart';
import 'package:flutter/foundation.dart';

DatabaseConnection connect() {
    return DatabaseConnection.delayed(
      Future.sync(() async {
        final db = await WasmDatabase.open(
          databaseName: 'movies',
          sqlite3Uri: Uri.parse('/sqlite3.wasm'),
          driftWorkerUri: Uri.parse('/drift_worker.js'),
        );

        if (db.missingFeatures.isNotEmpty) {
          debugPrint('Using ${db.chosenImplementation} due to
unsupported '
              'browser features: ${db.missingFeatures}');
        }

        return db.resolvedExecutor;
      }),
    );
}
```

This will use the **sqlite3.wasm** and **drift_worker.js** file to create a **database** file on the web.

9.  Open **movie_database.dart** and add the following import:

```
import 'package:movies/data/database/drift/connection.dart' as impl;
```

10.  Change the constructor to:

```
MovieDatabase() : super(impl.connect());
```

Unfortunately, the **dotenv** package does not work on the web, and the web cannot load files with a dot in the file name, so we need to copy this file and then read it from the **assets** folder. The steps are as follows:

1.  Copy the **.env** file to **dotenv**.

2.  Add the following after the **.env** in the **pubspec.yaml** file:

    ```
    - dotenv
    ```

3.  Update **movie_api_service.dart**.

    a.  Change the definition of the **apiKey** to:

    ```
    late String apiKey;
    ```

    b.  Change the constructor and add another method:

    ```
    MovieAPIService();

    Future init() async {
      if (!isWeb()) {
        apiKey = dotenv.env['TMDB_KEY']!;
        configureDio();
      } else {
        await webLoad();
      }
    }

    Future webLoad() async {
      try {
        final dotEnvString = await rootBundle.
    loadString('dotenv');
          if (dotEnvString.contains('TMDB_KEY')) {
            final parts = dotEnvString.split('=');
            if (parts.length == 2) {
              apiKey = parts[1];
              if (apiKey.contains("'")) {
                apiKey = apiKey.replaceAll("'", "");
              }
            }
          } else {
            apiKey = dotEnvString;
          }
      } catch (e) {
        print(e);
    ```

```
    }
    configureDio();
  }
```

This will load the **dotenv** file and get the API key. Then, we will call the **configureDio** method.

4. Update **utils.dart**. Change the **getSizedImageUrl** method to use the secure base URL, as websites do not like the http non-secured links.

```
String? getSizedImageUrl(ImageSize size, MovieConfiguration
configuration, String? file) {
  if (file == null) {
    return null;
  }
  switch (size) {
    case ImageSize.small:
      return imageUrl(configuration.images.secureBaseUrl,
configuration.images.posterSizes[1], file);
    case ImageSize.large:
      return imageUrl(configuration.images.secureBaseUrl,
configuration.images.posterSizes[5], file);
  }
}
```

5. Change **main.dart** to not load the **.env** file if on the web:

```
if (!isWeb()) {
  await dotenv.load(fileName: '.env');
}
```

6. Open **providers.dart** and replace the **movieAPIService** and **movieViewModel** with:

```
@Riverpod(keepAlive: true)
Future<MovieAPIService> movieAPIService(MovieAPIServiceRef ref)
async {
  final service = MovieAPIService();
  await service.init();
  return service;
}
@Riverpod(keepAlive: true)
Future<MovieViewModel> movieViewModel(MovieViewModelRef ref) async {
  final database = await ref.read(driftDatabaseProvider.future);
  final service = await ref.read(movieAPIServiceProvider.future);
```

```
    final model = MovieViewModel(database: database, movieAPIService:
service);
    await model.setup();
    return model;
}
```

7.  In the terminal, type the following:

    ```
    dart run build_runner build.
    ```

Run the app on the web. Try different pages and notice any problems. One issue you may encounter is problems loading images. Since all these images are from the internet, some websites do not allow you to use them on a web page. This is called **cross-origin resource sharing** (**CORS**). This is a security mechanism implemented in browsers to prevent web pages from accessing resources from other domains. Some sites like *TMDB* allow you to use their images freely while others like *YouTube* make you use their APIs instead. To fix this, we will change the **Trailer** class. The steps are as follows:

1.  Open **trailers.dart**.

2.  Change the **CachedNetworkImage** call to:

    ```
    CachedNetworkImage(
        imageUrl: youtubeImageFromId(movieVideo.key),
        alignment: Alignment.topLeft,
        fit: BoxFit.fitHeight,
        height: 98,
        errorWidget: (_,__,___) => const Placeholder(),
    ),
    ```

This will show a placeholder widget when there is an error. Seeing the Favorites screen on the web shows an overflow problem. To fix that, do the following:

1.  Open **widgets/favorite_row.dart**.

2.  Remove the **textWidth** variable.

3.  Wrap the **Stack** widget with an **Expanded** widget.

4.  Remove the **SizedBox** widget surrounding the **AutoSizeText**.

This should make the favorite row fit better.

# Firebase Hosting

When you build a web project, you need a place to host your web page. There are many ways to do this, but Firebase Hosting is an easy way to host your site. This will require some configuration and setup of Firebase. We will also need to change some of our Dart code to handle web issues. To start, you will need to set up Firebase:

1. Go **to https://console.firebase.google.com/** and sign up or log in if you already have an account.

2. Create a new project.

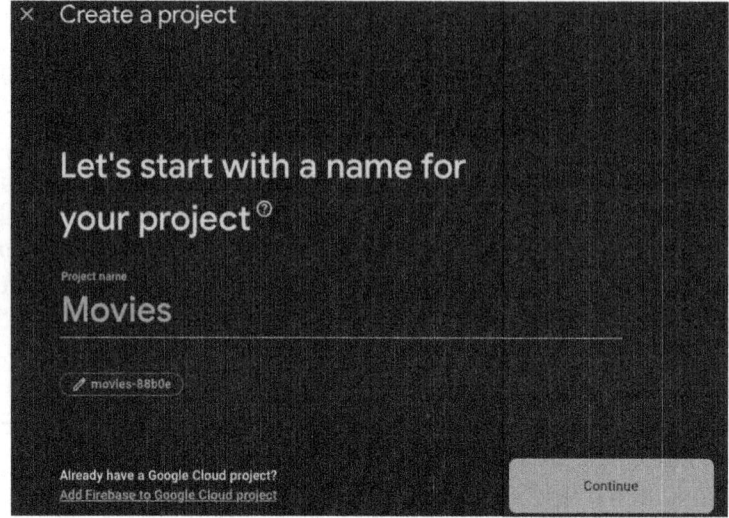

*Figure 13.14*: *New project*

3. Type a name for the project and press **Continue**, as shown in *Figure 13.15*:

*Figure 13.15*: *Analytics*

4.  Disable analytics (unless you want it) and press **Create project**, as done in *Figure 13.16*. You will see the following screen while Firebase creates your project:

*Figure 13.16: Loading*

5.  When finished, press **Continue**. The screen is as follows:

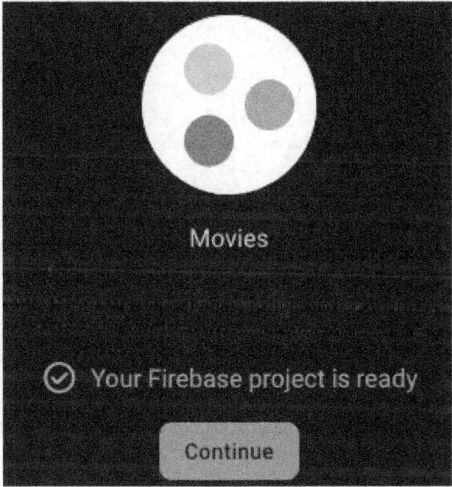

*Figure 13.17: Project finished*

6.  Add a new web app. You should see a set of icons for the different types of projects you can create. Click on the </> icon:

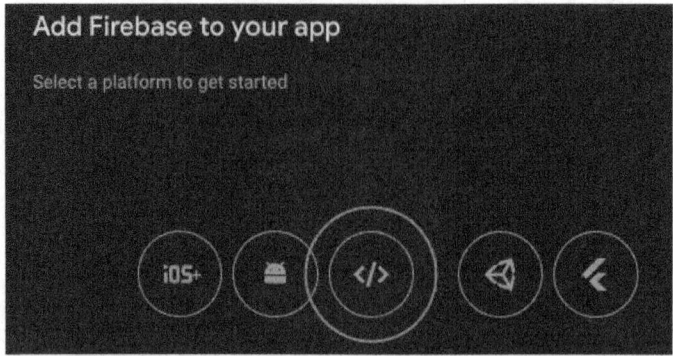

*Figure 13.18: Add web app*

7.  In the following screen, give your app a name, click the checkbox for **Firebase Hosting** and then click on **Register app**:

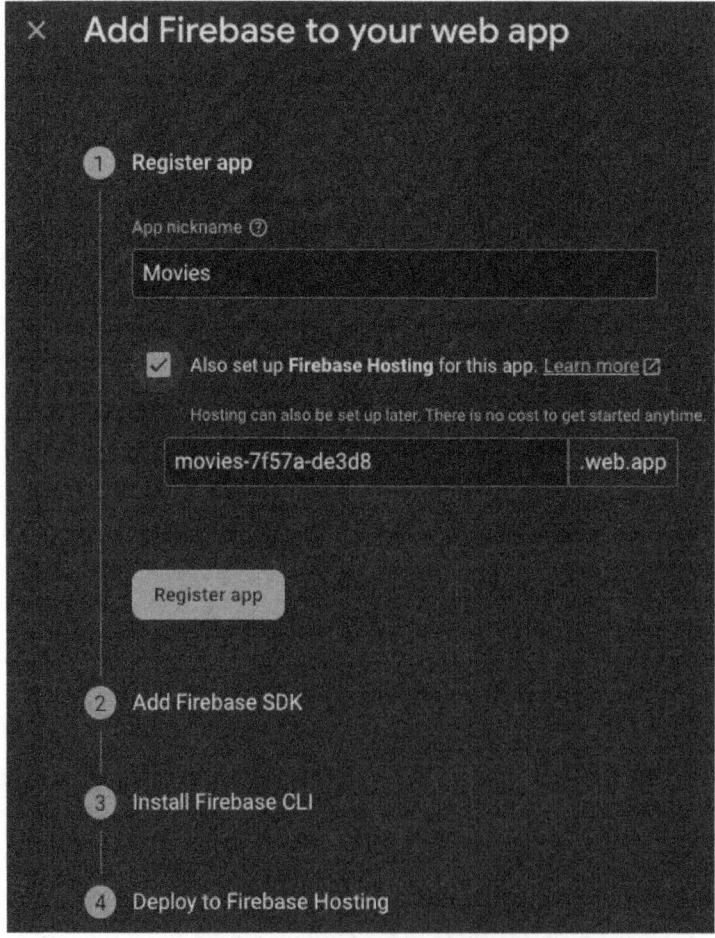

*Figure 13.19: Adding Firebase to web app*

8.  Deploy to Firebase Hosting page:

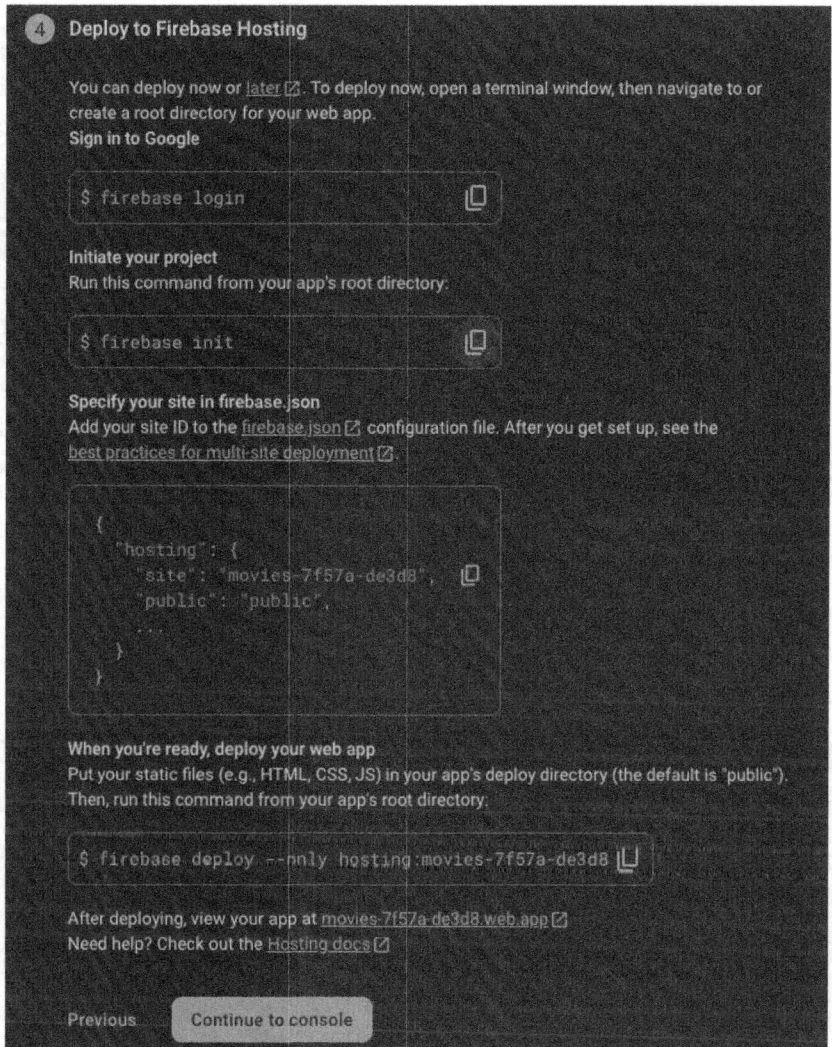

*Figure 13.20*: *Deploy setup*

9.  Install the Firebase tools:

```
npm install -g firebase-tools
```

10. Login to Firebase:

```
firebase login
```

11. Initialize Hosting:

```
firebase init
```

You should see the following output:

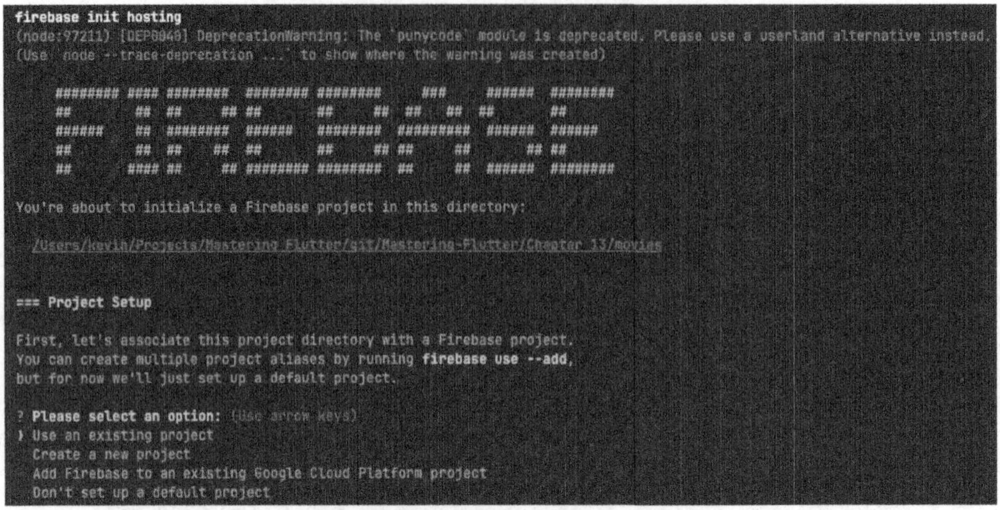

*Figure 13.21*: *Firebase initialization*

Choose the **Use an existing project** option if you have one already created or **Create a new Project** if not.

12. Choose hosting. You will see the following output:

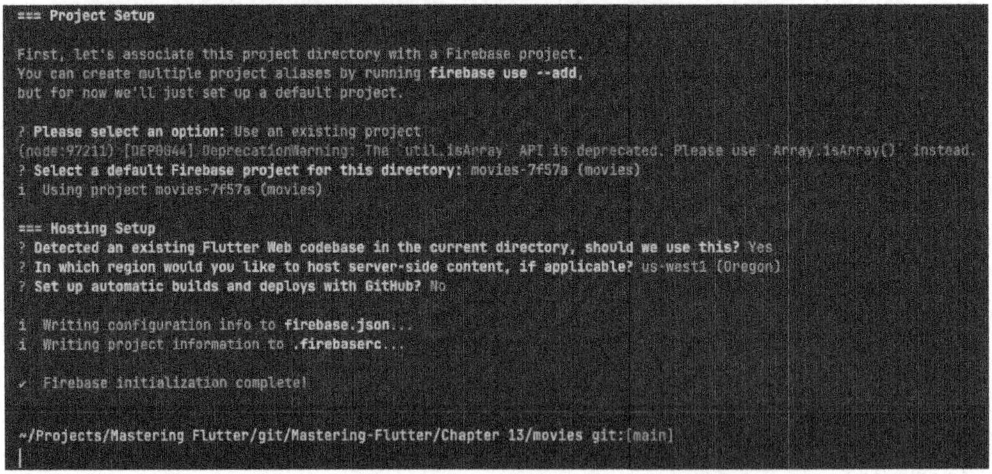

*Figure 13.22*: *Setup*

13. Open **firebase.json** and add your site below the **hosting** section:

```
"site": "<your site name>",
```

14. Deploy the project using the following command:

```
Firebase deploy
```

You will see the following output:

*Figure 13.23*: *Deploying*

15. Click on the **Hosting URL** link to see the page:

*Figure 13.24*: *Website*

# Conclusion

In this chapter, you have learned how to create apps for the Mac, Windows, and the web. You know how to create menus for desktop platforms, and you have created an adaptive layout that can be adapted to many different form factors. You have also created a dialog for doing searches. You took the leap onto the web and learned about many of the issues with developing websites. You were able to host the site on Firebase, which will allow others to view the work you have done.

In the next chapter, you will learn all about user input and gestures. This will be helpful for apps that require field entry and note taking, as well as handling different types of gestures, like tapping, long pressing, and more.

## Join our book's Discord space

Join the book's Discord Workspace for Latest updates, Offers, Tech happenings around the world, New Release and Sessions with the Authors:

**https://discord.bpbonline.com**

# CHAPTER 14

# Handling User Input and Gestures

## Introduction

In this chapter, you will learn how to handle user input. There are many ways to capture a user's input, from buttons to text fields. Buttons are the most common input method and provide a variety of styling options to indicate different states. You will learn about the all-important `GestureDetector` widget for handling taps and other gestures. Ink widgets are a great way to provide splash feedback for a user pressing your widgets. You will learn about repositories and how to separate your code to make it easier to switch components. And finally, you will implement infinite scrolling and paging API calls to show a complete list of movies.

## Structure

The chapter covers the following topics:

- User input and event handling
- GestureDetector
- Focus management
- Text
- Ink widgets
- KeyboardListener

- Repositories
- Movie listing

# Objectives

By the end of this chapter, you will know how to handle events from several different input types and how to handle focus management. You will learn how to handle gestures such as taps, long presses, and keyboard entries for specific widgets. You will learn about Ink widgets, part of Google's Material Design. You will learn how to create a repository and separate database and network API calls. You will also learn how to create an infinite scrolling list of movies.

# User input and event handling

User input and event handling are important for building interactive and responsive Flutter applications. They allow your app to react to user actions, such as taps, gestures, keyboard input, and more. As you have seen in the movie app, the user will tap on a movie to go to the detail page. If they are on a desktop machine, they will usually click with a mouse, and if they are on a tablet, they can use a stylus. For desktop apps, using the keyboard and keyboard shortcuts makes your app more useable for power users, while touch is the most common input source on mobile devices. Flutter provides the **GestureDetector** widget to detect various touch gestures like taps, drags, scaling, and more. **GestureDectector** also handles mouse clicks on desktop and web apps. For text input, Flutter's **TextField** and **TextFormField** widgets handle text input, while **FocusNode** and **FocusScope** manage keyboard focus and navigation. You can also use **RawKeyboardListener** for lower-level keyboard event handling. Flutter can also handle input from game controllers, accessibility devices, and other platform-specific input mechanisms.

For the desktop, changing the cursor when in different areas of the app helps the user know what to do in that area. For example, when moving the mouse over a text field, you can change the cursor to a text input cursor as follows:

```
MouseRegion(
        cursor: SystemMouseCursors.text,
        child: TextField(),
)
```

Callback functions are the core of event handling in Flutter. These functions are triggered when specific events occur, such as a button tap, text field change, or gesture detection.

# GestureDetector

The **GestureDetector** widget in Flutter is the main widget for capturing and responding to user interactions with your app. It is a powerful tool that allows you to detect a wide range of gestures, from simple taps to complex multi-touch gestures like pinch-to-zoom. **GestureDetector** itself does not have a visual representation. It acts as an invisible wrapper around its child widget, capturing user interactions on that child. It listens for pointer events (touches, mouse clicks, etc.) on its child and attempts to recognize specific gestures for the provided callbacks. You provide callback functions to the **GestureDetector** for the gestures you want to detect. These callbacks are triggered when the corresponding gesture is recognized. There are many different methods **GestureDetector** handles:

- onTap
- onDoubleTap
- onLongPress
- onPanUpdate
- onScaleUpdate

These are just a few of the provided methods. There are other methods for secondary and tertiary taps. If you want to handle panning or scaling an image, use the following methods:

- onPanDown
- onPanStart
- onPanUpdate
- onPanEnd
- onPanCancel

Similar methods exist for scaling. For dragging, there are several callbacks to use:

- onVerticalDragDown
- onVerticalDragStart
- onVerticalDragUpdate
- onVerticalDragEnd
- onVerticalDragCancel

There are callbacks for Horizontal drags as well. You have seen instances of **GestureDetector** in classes like **FavoriteRow**:

```
GestureDetector(
    onTap: () => onMovieTap(favorite.movieId)
```

You will mostly just use the **onTap** method, but the other methods exist for more complex interactions.

# Focus management

The **FocusManager** class plays a central role in managing focus within your application. It acts as a singleton service that provides access to the focus tree and offers methods for controlling focus behavior. The **FocusManager** maintains the focus tree, tracks the primary focus, and sends key events to the primary focus. It also maintains the **rootScope**, which is the top-level scope for focus nodes. You can get an instance of the **FocusManager** with:

**FocusManager focusManager = FocusManager.instance;**

There are only a few methods you can use with the **FocusManager**:

- **addEarlyKeyEventHandler**: Handle key events before widgets
- **addLateKeyEventHandler**: Handle key events if not handled by other widgets

You will not usually use the **FocusManager** as the **FocusNode** class is used with widgets. Flutter's focus management system is key to controlling which widget receives input from the keyboard or other input devices. It ensures a smooth and intuitive user experience, especially when dealing with forms, text fields, and interactive elements. On a mobile device, the keyboard's next arrow will go to the next focusable widget, while on the desktop or web, the tab key will move to the next widget.

**FocusNode** is a fundamental class for managing focus in Flutter. Each widget that wants to receive focus needs to be associated with a **FocusNode**. You will create one focus node for each **TextField**. **FocusNodes** form a hierarchical tree structure that mirrors the widget tree. This tree helps determine the flow of focus between widgets. Setting the autofocus property to true on a **TextField** automatically gives it focus when it is first built. The easiest way to programmatically request focus for a widget is to use **focusNode. requestForcus()** for the focus node associated with that widget. You can attach a listener to a **FocusNode** to be notified when its focus state changes by calling **addListener()**. This allows you to perform actions or update the UI based on focus events. Here is a sample code that detects when the focus is lost and sets the editing flag to false:

```
textFocusNode.addListener(() {
  if (!textFocusNode.hasFocus && widget.editing) {
    setState(() {
      widget.editing = false;
    });
  }
});
```

**FocusNode methods**:

- **hasFocus**: Indicates whether the **FocusNode** currently has focus.
- **requestFocus()**: Requests focus on the associated widget.
- **unfocus()**: Removes focus from the associated widget.
- **addListener()**: Allows you to listen for focus changes on the **FocusNode**.

A **FocusScope** defines a subtree in the focus tree. It allows you to manage focus within that subtree, such as moving focus to the next or previous widget within the scope.

Each **FocusScope** is associated with a **FocusScopeNode**, which is a special type of **FocusNode** that manages the focus within its scope. You will typically only need these if you use a **FocusScope**.

**FocusScopeNode methods**:

- **requestFocus()**: Requests focus for a specific **FocusScopeNode** within the scope.
- **nextFocus()**: Moves focus to the next focusable widget in the scope.
- **previousFocus()**: Moves focus to the previous focusable widget in the scope.
- **unfocus()**: Removes focus from any focused widget within the scope.

If you need to have a grouped set of widgets with their own specialized traversal policy, you will use a **FocusTraversalGroup**. This widget has a **FocusTraversalPolicy** to determine how focusable widgets are traversed. This is more complex than you really need, but if you have a large screen with a lot of form widgets and you need to have different traversal policies for each, this will be the widget you need. There are some predefined policies like **WidgetOrderTraversalPolicy** (which is just the order in which the widgets were created) or **ReadingOrderTraversalPolicy** (which is the natural ready order). You can use **OrderedTraversalPolicy** to specify a specific order.

# Text

**TextField** widgets in Flutter are the primary way to capture text input from users. They are versatile and offer a range of features for creating various input experiences, from simple single line entries to complex multi-line text editors. Here is a closer look at how they work and contribute to event handling. The **TextField** widget offers callbacks like **onChanged** (for text changes), **onSubmitted** (for text submission), and **onEditingComplete** (for editing completion). You can set a **FocusNode** on a **TextField** by setting the **focusNode** field with an instance of a **FocusNode**. You can make a **TextField** multi-line by using these fields:

```
keyboardType: TextInputType.multiline,
maxLines: null,
```

To listen for text changes, use a statement like:

```
onChanged: (String text) => _phone = text,
```

For a final submitted text value, use:

```
onSubmitted: (value) {},
```

To change the keyboard type for different fields, use the **keyboardType** parameter. This can be:

- `TextInputType.text`
- `TextInputType.decimal`

- TextInputType.number
- TextInputType.phone
- TextInputType.datetime
- TextInputType.emailAddress
- TextInputType.url
- TextInputType.visiblePassword
- TextInputType.name
- TextInputType.streetAddress

To set the action button on the keyboard, use the **textInputAction** field. These can be:

- TextInputAction.done
- TextInputAction.go
- TextInputAction.search
- TextInputAction.send
- TextInputAction.previous
- TextInputAction.continueAction (iOS – Return key)
- TextInputAction.join (iOS – Return Key Join)
- TextInputAction.route (iOS – route)
- TextInputAction.newline – carriage return
- TextInputAction.emergencyCall

For passwords, you need to set the **obsureText** field to **true**. Here is a sample showing a **TextField** with a few fields set:

```
TextField(
           autofocus: true,
           focusNode: textFocusNode,
           textInputAction: TextInputAction.done,
           onSubmitted: (value) {
             // Handle text value
           },
           controller: searchTextController,
       ),
```

# Ink widgets

Ink widgets are part of Material Design's widgets. This is made up of widgets like:

- Ink
- InkWell

- InkResponse

**Ink** will draw a color or decoration under the child, while the **InkWell** will draw on top of an **Ink** widget. The **InkWell** widget provides material style visual feedback (like ripple effects) when a user interacts with certain areas of the UI. It handles taps and clicks, making them ideal for buttons and clickable UI elements. **InkWell** is an ink splash effect that makes your UI feel responsive. It is a great way to provide visual feedback to users when they interact with tappable elements. You can change the splash color and the radius of the splash, as well as a few more fields, to customize the look of the splash. **InkWell** relies on the **GestureDectector** to handle taps. It handles all types of taps and hovers (entering and exiting the area) with the **onHover** callback, mouse cursors for desktop and web, and can use different colors for different states. **InkWell** requires a Material ancestor. This can be the **MaterialApp** at the root of your UI, or it can be wrapped in a Material widget. Be careful when using containers with colors, as this will cause the ripple effect not to work. Here is an example of an **InkWell** inside of an **Ink** widget. This shows a green square that, when tapped has a blue ripple effect:

```
Ink(
  color: Colors.green,
  width: double.infinity,
  height: 300,
  child: InkWell(
      splashColor: Colors.blue,
      onTap: () {},
      child: const Center(child: Text('Tap Me'))),
),
```

# InkResponse

**InkWells** are designed for rectangular areas, while **InkResponses** can be of any shape. You can use the **splashFactory** field to define an **InteractiveInkFeatureFactory** instance. You can use existing factories such as **InkRipple.splashFactory** and **InkSplash.splashFactory** or create your own. This class has most of the same fields as an **InkWell** but is more customizable. **InkResponses** can clip splashes that extend outside of its bounds. To set the shape used to highlight when pressed or focused, use the **highlightShape** field. You can change borders and many different colors:

- Focus
- Hover
- Highlight
- Overlay
- Splash

# KeyboardListener

**KeyboardListener** is a widget in Flutter that allows you to listen to and respond to raw keyboard events in your application. It gives you lower-level access to keyboard input, enabling you to build custom interactions or handle scenarios where the standard focus-based input handling might not be sufficient. The **onKeyEvent** field is the primary callback function that is triggered whenever a key event occurs. It receives a **KeyEvent** object as an argument, which contains information about the key that was pressed or released. This event contains the **physicalKey**, which represents the physical key that was pressed or released (e.g., **PhysicalKeyboardKey.keyA**, **PhysicalKeyboardKey.arrowUp**). The **logicalKey** represents the logical key, which considers modifiers like *Shift* or *Alt* (e.g., **LogicalKeyboardKey.keyA**, **LogicalKeyboardKey.shiftLeft**). The character is the Unicode character string that would be produced by the key press (if applicable). Note that the character field is not available on key up events. The event you get will either be a **KeyUpEvent** or a **KeyDownEvent,** indicating what type of event it is. Here is an example of a **KeyboardListener** wrapping a **TextField** that will handle the enter or escape keys:

```
KeyboardListener(
        focusNode: textFocusNode,
        onKeyEvent: (event) {
          if (event.runtimeType == KeyDownEvent &&
             ((event.logicalKey == LogicalKeyboardKey.enter) ||
                (event.logicalKey == LogicalKeyboardKey.escape))) {
            setState(() {
              // Do something when these events happen
            });
          }
        },
        child: TextField()
)
```

You also saw the **SingleActivator** class used in your menus. This is a shortcut that uses the **LogicalKeyboardKey**.

# Repositories

Notice that we now have several different types of models. We have models that the UI uses and models that the database uses. This is because database models may have different fields (like IDs) that the UI does not need. Your UI may only show a small portion of the data downloaded. To solve this problem, you need to convert database models to UI models and the reverse. To do this, create a set of methods to convert from one model type to another:

1. Create a new file called **model_converter.dart** in the **database** folder.

2. Add the methods for converting genres:

```
import 'package:movies/data/database/models/database_models.dart';
import 'package:movies/data/models/models.dart';

List<Genre> databaseGenreToGenre(List<DBMovieGenre> databaseGenres)
{
  return databaseGenres
      .map((databaseGenre) =>
          Genre(id: databaseGenre.remoteId, name: databaseGenre.
name))
      .toList();
}
List<DBMovieGenre> movieGenreToDatabaseGenre(List<Genre> genres) {
  return genres
      .map((genre) =>
      DBMovieGenre(id: genre.id, remoteId: genre.id, name: genre.
name))
      .toList();
}
```

The first method takes a list of database genres and converts them to a list of genres and the second converts genres to database genres.

3. Add the movie configuration methods:

```
MovieConfiguration? databaseMovieConfigurationToMovieConfiguration(
    DBConfiguration? databaseMovieConfiguration) {
  if (databaseMovieConfiguration == null) {
    return null;
  }
  return MovieConfiguration(
    images: databaseImagesToImages(databaseMovieConfiguration.
images),
    changeKeys: databaseMovieConfiguration.changeKeys,
  );
}
DBConfiguration? movieConfigurationToDbConfiguration(
    MovieConfiguration movieConfiguration) {
  final dbConfiguration = DBConfiguration(id: 1, images:
imagesToDbImages(movieConfiguration.images),
      changeKeys: [...movieConfiguration.changeKeys]);
  return dbConfiguration;
}
```

4. Add the configuration image methods:

```
MovieConfigurationImages databaseImagesToImages(DBConfigurationImages
databaseImages) {
  return MovieConfigurationImages(
    baseUrl: databaseImages.baseUrl,
    secureBaseUrl: databaseImages.secureBaseUrl,
    backdropSizes: databaseImages.backdropSizes,
    logoSizes: databaseImages.logoSizes,
    posterSizes: databaseImages.posterSizes,
    profileSizes: databaseImages.profileSizes,
    stillSizes: databaseImages.stillSizes,
  );
}

DBConfigurationImages imagesToDbImages(MovieConfigurationImages
images) {
  final dbImages = DBConfigurationImages(
    baseUrl: images.baseUrl,
    secureBaseUrl: images.secureBaseUrl,
    backdropSizes: [...images.backdropSizes],
    logoSizes: [...images.logoSizes],
    posterSizes: [...images.posterSizes],
    profileSizes: [...images.profileSizes],
    stillSizes: [...images.stillSizes],
  );
  return dbImages;
}
```

# Sources

Interfaces are a great way to define a set of methods but have different implementations. To do this, we will create a **MovieSource** interface that will define the methods required for implementing a class of type **MovieSource**. This class will be abstract so that it cannot be created by itself.

1. In the **data** folder, create a new folder named **sources**.

2. Create a new file named **movie_source.dart**.

3. Add the following interface:

```
import 'package:movies/data/database/models/favorite.dart';
import 'package:movies/data/models/models.dart';
```

```
abstract class MovieSource {
  Future<List<Genre>> getGenres();

  Future<MovieResponse?> getTrending(int page);

  Future<MovieResponse?> getNowPlaying(int page);

  Future<MovieResponse?> getTopRated(int page);

  Future<MovieResponse?> getPopular(int page);

  Future<MovieResponse?> searchMovies(String query, int page);

  Future<MovieResponse?> searchMoviesByGenre(String genre, int
page);

  Future<MovieDetails?> getMovieDetails(int movieId);

  Future<MovieVideos?> getMovieVideos(int movieId);

  Future<MovieConfiguration?> getMovieConfiguration();

  Future<MovieCredits?> getMovieCredits(int movieId);

  Future saveFavorite(MovieDetails movieDetails);

  Future<bool> removeFavorite(int id);

  Future<List<DBFavorite>> getFavorites();

  Stream<List<DBFavorite>> streamFavorites();

}
```

This defines some of the methods that we have already used. We will now create two sources: one for the database and one for the network API.

4. Create a new file named **network_movie_source.dart**. Add:

```
import 'package:lumberdash/lumberdash.dart';
import 'package:movies/data/database/models/favorite.dart';
import 'package:movies/data/models/models.dart';
import 'package:movies/network/movie_api_service.dart';
import 'package:movies/data/sources/movie_source.dart';

class NetworkMovieSource implements MovieSource {
  final MovieAPIService _movieAPIService;

  NetworkMovieSource(this._movieAPIService);
  // TODO implement methods
}
```

5. Add the **getGenres** method:

```
@override
Future<List<Genre>> getGenres() async {
```

```
final response = await _movieAPIService.getGenres();
if (response.statusCode == 200) {
  return Genres.fromJson(response.data).genres;
} else {
  logError('Failed to load genres with error ${response.
statusCode} and message ${response.statusMessage}');
  return [];
}
}
```

This uses the movie service to get the genre list, convert the data from JSON and return the result.

6. Add the getTrending method:

```
@override
Future<MovieResponse?> getTrending([int page = 1]) async {
  final response = await _movieAPIService.getTrending(page);
  if (response.statusCode == 200) {
    return MovieResponse.fromJson(response.data);
  } else {
    logError('Failed to load trending movies with error
${response.statusCode} and message ${response.statusMessage}');
    return null;
  }
}
```

7. Add the **getNowPlaying** method:

```
@override
Future<MovieResponse?> getNowPlaying([int page = 1]) async {
  final response = await _movieAPIService.getNowPlaying(page);
  if (response.statusCode == 200) {
    return MovieResponse.fromJson(response.data);
  } else {
    logError('Failed to load now playing movies with error
${response.statusCode} and message ${response.statusMessage}');
    return null;
  }
}
```

8. Add the **getTopRated** method:

```
@override
Future<MovieResponse?> getTopRated([int page = 1]) async {
```

```
      final response = await _movieAPIService.getTopRated(page);
      if (response.statusCode == 200) {
        return MovieResponse.fromJson(response.data);
      } else {
        logError('Failed to load top rated movies with error
  ${response.statusCode} and message ${response.statusMessage}');
        return null;
      }
    }
```

9. Add the **getPopular** method:

```
    @override
    Future<MovieResponse?> getPopular([int page = 1]) async {
      final response = await _movieAPIService.getPopular(page);
      if (response.statusCode == 200) {
        return MovieResponse.fromJson(response.data);
      } else {
        logError('Failed to load popular movies with error ${response.
  statusCode} and message ${response.statusMessage}');
        return null;
      }
    }
```

10. Add the **getMovieConfiguration** method:

```
    @override
    Future<MovieConfiguration?> getMovieConfiguration() async {
      final response = await _movieAPIService.getMovieConfiguration();
      if (response.statusCode == 200) {
        return MovieConfiguration.fromJson(response.data);
      } else {
        logError('Failed to load movie configuration with error
  ${response.statusCode} and message ${response.statusMessage}');
        return null;
      }
    }
```

11. Add the **getMovieCredits** method:

```
    @override
    Future<MovieCredits?> getMovieCredits(int movieId) async {
      final response = await _movieAPIService.getMovieCredits(movieId);
      if (response.statusCode == 200) {
```

```
      return MovieCredits.fromJson(response.data);
    } else {
      logError('Failed to load movie credits with error ${response.
  statusCode} and message ${response.statusMessage}');
      return null;
    }
  }
```

12. Add the **getMovieDetails** method:

```
  @override
  Future<MovieDetails?> getMovieDetails(int movieId) async {
    final response = await _movieAPIService.getMovieDetails(movieId);
    if (response.statusCode == 200) {
      try {
        return MovieDetails.fromJson(response.data);
      } catch (e) {
        logError('Failed to parse movie details with error $e');
        return null;
      }
    } else {
      logError('Failed to load movie details with error ${response.
  statusCode} and message ${response.statusMessage}');
      return null;
    }
  }
```

13. Add the **getMovieVideos** method:

```
  @override
  Future<MovieVideos?> getMovieVideos(int movieId) async {
    final response = await _movieAPIService.getMovieVideos(movieId);
    if (response.statusCode == 200) {
      return MovieVideos.fromJson(response.data);
    } else {
      logError('Failed to load movie details with error ${response.
  statusCode} and message ${response.statusMessage}');
      return null;
    }
  }
```

14. Add the **searchMovies** method:

```
  @override
```

```
    Future<MovieResponse?> searchMovies(String query, [int page = 1])
async {
        final response = await _movieAPIService.searchMovies(query,
page);
        if (response.statusCode == 200) {
            return MovieResponse.fromJson(response.data);
        } else {
            logError('searchMovies failed movies with error ${response.
statusCode} and message ${response.statusMessage}');
            return null;
        }
    }
```

15. Add the **searchMoviesByGenre** method:

```
    @override
    Future<MovieResponse?> searchMoviesByGenre(String genre, [int page
= 1]) async {
        final response = await _movieAPIService.searchMoviesByGenre(genre,
page);
        if (response.statusCode == 200) {
            return MovieResponse.fromJson(response.data);
        } else {
            logError('searchMoviesByGenre failed with error ${response.
statusCode} and message ${response.statusMessage}');
            return null;
        }
    }
```

16. Add the **saveFavorite** method:

```
    @override
    Future<int> saveFavorite(MovieDetails movieDetails) async {
        return 0;
    }
```

This method is not used for the network API so it just returns 0.

17. Add the **removeFavorite** method:

```
    @override
    Future<bool> removeFavorite(int id) async {
        return false;
    }
```

This is not used as well.

18. Add the **getFavorites** method:

```
@override
Future<List<DBFavorite>> getFavorites() async {
  return <DBFavorite>[];
}
```

This is not used.

19. Add the **streamFavorites** method:

```
@override
Stream<List<DBFavorite>> streamFavorites() {
  return Stream.value(<DBFavorite>[]);
}
```

Now that you have the network source, you can create a database source. This will contain only the methods needed to access the database.

Create a new file in the **sources** directory named **database_source.dart**. Add the following:

```
import 'package:movies/data/models/models.dart';

import 'package:movies/data/database/drift/database_interface.dart';
import 'package:movies/data/database/model_converter.dart';

class DatabaseSource {
  final IDatabase? _database;

  DatabaseSource(this._database);

  Future<List<Genre>> getGenres() async {
    final genres = <Genre>[];
    if (_database == null) {
      return genres;
    }
    final networkGenres = await _database.getGenres();
    genres.addAll(databaseGenreToGenre(networkGenres));
    return genres;
  }

  Future<MovieConfiguration?> movieConfiguration() async {
    if (_database == null) {
      return null;
    }
    return databaseMovieConfigurationToMovieConfiguration(
```

```
      await _database.getMovieConfiguration());
  }
}
```

This is pretty simple, as we only save genres and the configuration to the database.

# Repository

Just as we have abstracted out the different sources, we want to separate out calling the database and the network. To do that, we want to create a repository class that will call either the database or the network APIs, depending on the call. This class will implement the **MovieSource** interface. Next, create the **MovieRepository** class:

1.  In the **data** folder, create a new folder named **repository**.

2.  Create a new file named **movie_repository.dart**. Add the following:

    ```dart
    import 'package:lumberdash/lumberdash.dart';
    import 'package:movies/data/database/models/favorite.dart';

    import 'package:movies/data/database/drift/database_interface.dart';
    import 'package:movies/data/database/model_converter.dart';
    import 'package:movies/data/models/models.dart';
    import 'package:movies/data/sources/movie_source.dart';

    class MovieRepository implements MovieSource {
      final MovieSource _movieSource;
      final IDatabase? _database;

      MovieRepository(this._movieSource, this._database);
    }
    ```

    This takes in both the movie source and the database interface. Note that by using the database interface, we can test this repository. (See *Chapter 18, Testing and Performance*)

3.  Add the **getGenres** method:

    ```dart
    @override
    Future<List<Genre>> getGenres() async {
      try {
        final dbMovieGenres = await _database?.getGenres();
        if (dbMovieGenres?.isEmpty == true) {
          final genres = await _movieSource.getGenres();
          await _database?.saveGenres(movieGenreToDatabaseGenre(genres));
          return genres;
    ```

```
    }
    if (_database == null) {
      return [];
    }
    return databaseGenreToGenre(dbMovieGenres!);
  } catch (e) {
    logMessage('getGenres: ${e.toString()}');
    logError(e);
    return [];
  }
}
```

This uses the database interface to get the genre list. If this does not exist, we call the network movie source to get the list of genres and then save the genres to the database. This should only happen once, as subsequent calls will just retrieve the data from the database and save a call to the network.

4. Add the **getTrending** method:

```
@override
Future<MovieResponse?> getTrending(int page) async {
  try {
    return _movieSource.getTrending(page);
  } catch (e) {
    logMessage('getTrending: ${e.toString()}');
    logError(e);
  }
  return null;
}
```

5. Add the **getNowPlaying** method:

```
@override
Future<MovieResponse?> getNowPlaying(int page) async {
  try {
    return _movieSource.getNowPlaying(page);
  } catch (e) {
    logMessage('getNowPlaying: ${e.toString()}');
    logError(e);
  }
  return null;
}
```

6. Add the **getTopRated** method:

```
@override
Future<MovieResponse?> getTopRated(int page) async {
  try {
    return _movieSource.getTopRated(page);
  } catch (e) {
    logMessage('getTopRated: ${e.toString()}');
    logError(e);
  }
  return null;
}
```

7. Add the **getPopular** method:

```
@override
Future<MovieResponse?> getPopular(int page) async {
  try {
    return _movieSource.getPopular(page);
  } catch (e) {
    logMessage('getPopular: ${e.toString()}');
    logError(e);
  }
  return null;
}
```

8. Add the **getMovieConfiguration** method:

```
@override
Future<MovieConfiguration?> getMovieConfiguration() async {
  try {
    final dbMovieConfiguration = await _database?.
getMovieConfiguration();
    if (dbMovieConfiguration == null) {
      final movieConfiguration = await _movieSource.
getMovieConfiguration();
      if (movieConfiguration == null) {
        return null;
      }
      final dbConfiguration =
          movieConfigurationToDbConfiguration(movieConfiguration);
      await _database?.saveMovieConfiguration(dbConfiguration!);
      return movieConfiguration;
    }
```

```
      return databaseMovieConfigurationToMovieConfiguration(
          dbMovieConfiguration);
    } catch (e) {
      logMessage('getMovieConfiguration: ${e.toString()}');
      logError(e);
    }
    return null;
  }
```

This will first check the database for the configuration information. If it has not been stored, retrieve it using the movie source and save it to the database.

9. Add the **getMovieCredits** method:

```
  @override
  Future<MovieCredits?> getMovieCredits(int movieId) async {
    try {
      return _movieSource.getMovieCredits(movieId);
    } catch (e) {
      logMessage('getMovieCredits: ${e.toString()}');
      logError(e);
    }
    return null;
  }
```

10. Add the **getMovieDetails** method:

```
  @override
  Future<MovieDetails?> getMovieDetails(int movieId) async {
    try {
      return _movieSource.getMovieDetails(movieId);
    } catch (e) {
      logMessage('getMovieDetails: ${e.toString()}');
      logError(e);
    }
    return null;
  }
```

11. Add the **getMovieVideos** method:

```
  @override
  Future<MovieVideos?> getMovieVideos(int movieId) async {
    try {
      return _movieSource.getMovieVideos(movieId);
```

```
    } catch (e) {
      logMessage('getMovieVideos: ${e.toString()}');
      logError(e);
    }
    return null;
  }
```

12. Add the **searchMovies** method:

```
  @override
  Future<MovieResponse?> searchMovies(String query, int page) async
{
    try {
      return _movieSource.searchMovies(query, page);
    } catch (e) {
      logMessage('searchMovies: ${e.toString()}');
      logError(e);
    }
    return null;
  }
```

13. Add the **searchMoviesByGenre** method:

```
  @override
  Future<MovieResponse?> searchMoviesByGenre(String genre, int page)
async {
    try {
      return _movieSource.searchMoviesByGenre(genre, page);
    } catch (e) {
      logMessage('searchMoviesByGenre: ${e.toString()}');
      logError(e);
    }
    return null;
  }
```

Use the movie source to search for movies by genre.

14. Add the **saveFavorite** method:

```
  @override
  Future saveFavorite(MovieDetails movieDetails) async {
    if (_database == null) {
      return;
    }
```

```
   try {
     final favorite = DBFavorite(
         id: movieDetails.id,
         movieId: movieDetails.id,
         backdropPath: movieDetails.backdropPath,
         posterPath: movieDetails.posterPath,
         favorite: true,
         popularity: movieDetails.popularity,
         releaseDate: movieDetails.releaseDate,
         title: movieDetails.title,
         overview: movieDetails.overview);
     _database.saveFavorite(favorite);
   } catch (e) {
     logMessage('saveFavorite: ${e.toString()}');
     logError(e);
   }
 }
```

This method saves a favorite to the database.

15. Add the **removeFavorite** method:

```
@override
Future<bool> removeFavorite(int id) async {
  if (_database == null) {
    return false;
  }
  try {
    return _database.removeFavorite(id);
  } catch (e) {
    logMessage('removeFavorite: ${e.toString()}');
    logError(e);
  }
  return false;
}
```

This will remove a favorite from the database.

16. Add the **getFavorites** method:

```
@override
Future<List<DBFavorite>> getFavorites() async {
  if (_database == null) {
```

```
      return [];
    }
    try {
      return _database.getFavorites();
    } catch (e) {
      logMessage('getFavorites: ${e.toString()}');
      logError(e);
    }
    return [];
  }
```

This will get the list of favorites saved to the database.

17. Add the **streamFavorites** method:

```
@override
Stream<List<DBFavorite>> streamFavorites() {
    if (_database == null) {
      return Stream.value(<DBFavorite>[]);
    }
    return _database.streamFavorites();
}
```

This will stream favorites from the database so that when the database is updated, the UI will also update.

# MovieViewModel

Now that you have the repository done, you need to update the **MovieViewModel** to use it. Open **movie_viewmodel.dart** and change all methods to use the new repository:

1. Instead of directly using the API service, change:

    ```
    final MovieAPIService movieAPIService;
    ```

   To:

    ```
    final MovieSource _movieRepository;
    ```

   Remove:

    ```
    final IDatabase database;
    ```

   Change the constructor to:

    ```
    MovieViewModel(this._movieRepository);
    ```

2. Change **setupConfiguration** to:

    ```
    Future setupConfiguration() async {
    ```

```
    final configuration = await _movieRepository.getMovieConfiguration();
    if (configuration != null) {
      movieConfiguration = configuration;
    }
  }
```

3. Change **setupGenres** to:

```
Future setupGenres() async {
  movieGenres = await _movieRepository.getGenres();
}
```

4. Remove **streamFavorites**. Replace the following methods:

```
Future saveFavorite(MovieDetails movieDetails) async {
  _movieRepository.saveFavorite(movieDetails);
}

Future<bool> removeFavorite(int id) async {
  return _movieRepository.removeFavorite(id);
}

Future<List<DBFavorite>> getFavorites() async {
  return _movieRepository.getFavorites();
}

Stream<List<DBFavorite>> streamFavorites() {
  return _movieRepository.streamFavorites();
}
```

5. Replace the **getXXXMovies** calls with:

```
Future<MovieResponse?> getTrendingMovies(int page) async {
  final response = await _movieRepository.getTrending(page);
  if (response != null) {
    trendingMovies = response.results;
  }
  return response;
}

Future<MovieResponse?> getPopular(int page) async {
  final response = await _movieRepository.getPopular(page);
  if (response != null) {
    popularMovies = response.results;
  }
  return response;
```

```
    }

    Future<MovieResponse?> getTopRated(int page) async {
      final response = await _movieRepository.getTopRated(page);
      if (response != null) {
        topRatedMovies = response.results;
      }
      return response;
    }

    Future<MovieResponse?> getNowPlaying(int page) async {
      final response = await _movieRepository.getNowPlaying(page);
      if (response != null) {
        nowPlayingMovies = response.results;
      }
      return response;
    }
```

6. Replace the rest of the methods with:

```
    Future<MovieDetails?> getMovieDetails(int movieId) async {
      return _movieRepository.getMovieDetails(movieId);
    }
     Future<MovieVideos?> getMovieVideos(int movieId) async {
      return _movieRepository.getMovieVideos(movieId);
    }

    Future<MovieCredits?> getMovieCredits(int movieId) async {
      return _movieRepository.getMovieCredits(movieId);
    }

   /// genres is a pipe delimited string
    Future<MovieResponse?> searchMoviesByGenre(String genres, int
  page) async {
      final response = await _movieRepository.
  searchMoviesByGenre(genres, page);
      if (response != null) {
        nowPlayingMovies = response.results;
      }
      return response;
    }

    Future<MovieResponse?> searchMovies(String searchText, int page)
```

```
async {
    final response = await _movieRepository.searchMovies(searchText,
page);
    if (response != null) {
      nowPlayingMovies = response.results;
    }
    return response;
  }
```

7. Open up **providers.dart** to add new providers and update the **viewmodel** provider.

8. After **movieAPIService**, add:

```
@Riverpod(keepAlive: true)
Future<MovieSource> networkMovieSource(NetworkMovieSourceRef ref)
async {
  final service = await ref.read(movieAPIServiceProvider.future);
  return NetworkMovieSource(service);
}

@Riverpod(keepAlive: true)
Future<MovieSource> movieRepository(MovieRepositoryRef ref) async {
  final databaseFuture = ref.watch(driftDatabaseProvider.future);
  final serviceFuture = ref.watch(networkMovieSourceProvider.future);
  return MovieRepository(
      await serviceFuture, await databaseFuture);
}
```

9. Then change **movieViewModel** to:

```
final repositoryFuture = ref.watch(movieRepositoryProvider.future);
final model = MovieViewModel(await repositoryFuture);
await model.setup();
return model;
```

10. Make sure you have all of the required imports.

11. Then type:

```
dart run build_runner build.
```

# Movie listing

One area that we have not finished is the More link on the home page. We want to bring up a new screen that shows the full list of trending, now playing, popular, or top-rated movies. It would also be nice if the listing would only load one page at a time so that we have an infinite (or at least how many movies exist) list of movies. We will use a package that will help in managing the pages and scrolling. Open up **home_screen.dart,** and you can see that the **onMoreClicked** method is empty. Start by creating the movie listing page:

1. Create a new folder in **ui/screens** named **movie_listing**.

2. Create a new file named **movie_listing.dart**.

3. Add the **MovieListing** class:

```dart
import 'package:auto_route/auto_route.dart';
import 'package:flutter/material.dart';
import 'package:flutter_riverpod/flutter_riverpod.dart';
import 'package:infinite_scroll_pagination/infinite_scroll_pagination.dart';

import 'package:movies/data/models/models.dart';
import 'package:movies/providers.dart';
import 'package:movies/router/app_routes.dart';
import 'package:movies/ui/widgets/movie_widget.dart';
import 'package:movies/ui/theme/theme.dart';
import 'package:movies/ui/widgets/movie_row.dart';
import 'package:movies/ui/widgets/not_ready.dart';
import 'package:movies/ui/movie_viewmodel.dart';

const pageCount = 20;
const movieRowHeight = 140;

@RoutePage(name: 'MovieListingRoute')
class MovieListing extends ConsumerStatefulWidget {
  final MovieType movieType;

  const MovieListing(this.movieType, {super.key});

  @override
  ConsumerState<MovieListing> createState() => _MovieListingState();
}

class _MovieListingState extends ConsumerState<MovieListing> {
}
```

4. Add the needed fields:

```dart
late MovieViewModel movieViewModel;

bool loading = false;
```

```
int totalPagesAvailable = 0;
int totalMoviesAvailable = 0;
int currentPage = 1;
MovieResponse? currentMovieResponse;
final PagingController<int, MovieResults> _pagingController =
    PagingController(firstPageKey: 0);
```

We will use the view model to get the movies. The other variables are for keeping track of how many pages and movies are available. Also, we need to keep track of the last page we loaded. The paging controller is from the **infinite_scroll_pagination** package. This is a great package for helping load and keep track of what we have downloaded.

5.  Add the **initState** method:

```
@override
void initState() {
  super.initState();
  _pagingController.addPageRequestListener((pageKey) {
    loadMovies();
  });
}
```

This will add a listener to the controller that will call our **loadMovies** method.

6.  Add the build method:

```
@override
Widget build(BuildContext context) {
  final movieViewModelAsync = ref.watch(movieViewModelProvider);
  return movieViewModelAsync.when(
    error: (e, st) => Text(e.toString()),
    loading: () => const NotReady(),
    data: (viewModel) {
      movieViewModel = viewModel;
      return buildScreen();
    },
  );
}
```

This method just waits for the view model to load and then calls **buildScreen**.

7.  Add the **buildScreen** method:

```
Widget buildScreen() {
  return SafeArea(
```

```
// 1
     child: FutureBuilder(
       future: loadMovies(),
       builder: (context, snapshot) {
         if (snapshot.connectionState != ConnectionState.done) {
           return const Center(child: CircularProgressIndicator());
         }
         return Scaffold(
           appBar: AppBar(
             backgroundColor: screenBackground,
             leading: BackButton(
               color: Colors.white,
               onPressed: () {
                 context.router.maybePopTop();
               },
             ),
             centerTitle: false,
             title: Text('Back', style: Theme.of(context).
textTheme.headlineMedium),
           ),
           body: Container(
             color: screenBackground,
             child: Column(
               mainAxisSize: MainAxisSize.min,
               mainAxisAlignment: MainAxisAlignment.start,
               crossAxisAlignment: CrossAxisAlignment.start,
               children: [
                 Padding(
                   padding: const EdgeInsets.fromLTRB(16, 16.0,
0.0, 24.0),
                   child: Text(getTitle(), style: Theme.
of(context).textTheme.titleLarge),
                 ),
                 const Divider(),
                 Expanded(
// 2
                   child: PagedListView<int, MovieResults>(
                     pagingController: _pagingController,
                     builderDelegate:
PagedChildBuilderDelegate<MovieResults>(
```

```
// 3
                              itemBuilder: (context, item, index) =>
MovieRow(
                         movie: item,
                         movieViewModel: movieViewModel,
                         onMovieTap: (movie) {
                           context.router
                               .push(MovieDetailRoute(movieId:
item.id));
                         },
                       ),
                     ),
                   ),
                 ),
               ],
             ),
           ),
         );
       },
     ),
   );
 }
```

This has some of the basic elements of the screen and then uses a **PagedListView** with our paging controller and a movie row being returned:

   a.   Use a **FutureBuilder** to load the current page of movies.

   b.   The **PagedListView** is from the **infinite_scroll_pagination** package.

   c.   The **itemBuilder** just returns a **MovieRow**.

8.   Add the **getTitle** and **onMovieTap** methods:

```
String getTitle() {
  switch (widget.movieType) {
    case MovieType.trending:
      return 'Trending';
    case MovieType.popular:
      return 'Popular';
    case MovieType.topRated:
      return 'Top Rated';
    case MovieType.nowPlaying:
      return 'Now Playing';
```

```
      }
    }
    void onMovieTap(int movieId) {
      context.router.push(MovieDetailRoute(movieId: movieId));
    }
```

9.  Add the **loadMovies** method:

```
    Future loadMovies() async {
      if (loading) {
        return;
      }
      loading = true;
      if (totalPagesAvailable == 0) {
        currentPage = 1;
      }
// 1
      switch (widget.movieType) {
        case MovieType.trending:
          currentMovieResponse =
              await movieViewModel.getTrendingMovies(currentPage);
        case MovieType.popular:
          currentMovieResponse = await movieViewModel.
getPopular(currentPage);
        case MovieType.topRated:
          currentMovieResponse = await movieViewModel.
getTopRated(currentPage);
        case MovieType.nowPlaying:
          currentMovieResponse = await movieViewModel.
getNowPlaying(currentPage);
      }
      if (currentMovieResponse != null) {
// 2
        totalPagesAvailable = currentMovieResponse!.totalPages;
        totalMoviesAvailable = currentMovieResponse!.totalResults;
        currentPage++;
// 3
        final isLastPage =
            (_pagingController.itemList?.length ?? 0 + pageCount) >=
                totalMoviesAvailable;
// 4
```

```
        if (isLastPage) {
            _pagingController.appendLastPage(currentMovieResponse!.
results);
        } else {
// 5
            _pagingController.appendPage(
                currentMovieResponse!.results, currentPage);
        }
    }
    loading = false;
  }
```

This method does the following:

    a.  Call the proper method from the view model based on the movie type.

    b.  Gets the total pages and total results.

    c.  Check if we are on the last page.

    d.  If we are on the last page, append it to the end of the list.

    e.  Otherwise, append the page of results.

10.  In the terminal, type:

```
dart run build_runner build.
```

Now, we need to update the **HomeScreen** class to call this class.

11.  Open **home_screen.dart**.

12.  Change the **SingleChildScrollView** to a **CustomScrollView**:

```
        return CustomScrollView(slivers: [
          SliverFillRemaining(
            hasScrollBody: false,
```

13.  Fix the ending parenthesis.

14.  Change the call to **HomeScreenImage**:

```
                HomeScreenImage(
                  movieViewModel: movieViewModel,
                  onMovieTap: onMovieTap,
                ),
```

15.  In the first TitleRow's **onMoreClicked** add:

```
                context.router.push(
```

```
                          MovieListingRoute(movieType: MovieType.
trending));
```

16. Add the other routes. For **popular**:

```
                     context.router.push(
                          MovieListingRoute(movieType: MovieType.
popular));
```

17. Top rated:

```
                     context.router.push(
                          MovieListingRoute(movieType: MovieType.
topRated));
```

18. Open **app_routes.dart** and add the movie listing route at the end:

```
CustomRoute(
  page: MovieListingRoute.page,
  maintainState: false,
  transitionsBuilder: TransitionsBuilders.fadeIn,
  durationInMilliseconds: 500,
),
```

Do a hot restart and click on the More link. You should see something as follows:

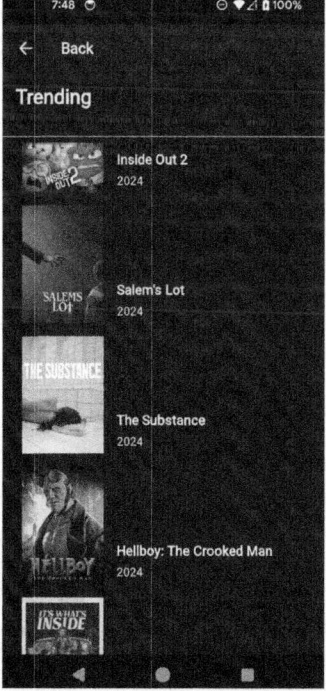

***Figure 14.1:*** *Movie listing page*

Try scrolling and make sure you can see multiple pages of movies. Depending on your internet connection, it should be pretty smooth.

# Conclusion

In this chapter, you learned how to handle user input. There are many ways to capture a user's input, from buttons to text fields. The most important widget to remember is the **GestureDetector**. This makes any widget clickable. Focus management is an important area to understand and is key to making it easier to traverse your app. You also learned about repositories and how to separate your code to make it easier to switch components. Finally, you implemented infinite scrolling and paging API calls.

In the next chapter, you will learn all about Firebase, including its NoSQL database, authentication, and cloud messaging. This is an easy-to-setup and use server. You will learn how to set up Firebase, install the Firebase packages, and implement Firebase database calls.

## Join our book's Discord space

Join the book's Discord Workspace for Latest updates, Offers, Tech happenings around the world, New Release and Sessions with the Authors:

**https://discord.bpbonline.com**

# Chapter 15
# Firebase

## Introduction

In this chapter, you will learn about many of the services that Firebase provides. You will learn how to sign up for Firebase and create a Cloud Firestore database. You will also learn how to retrieve and save data in Firestore. There are many services that Firebase provides, and you will learn about a few of the most important ones. Now that your movie app is taking shape and getting ready for release, you will learn how to track crashes in your app with Crashlytics. You will switch your database from Drift to Firebase with just a change to a Riverpod provider.

## Structure

The chapter covers the following topics:

- Introduction to Firebase
- Authentication
- Cloud Firestore
- Collections
- Reading and writing data

- Crashlytics
- Other services

# Objectives

By the end of this chapter, you will have learned about several Firebase services. You will be able to investigate the services that we do not cover in detail in this chapter. You will learn how to set up Firebase and *Cloud Firestore* and you will learn about *Collections* and documents that make up the database. Finally, you will have learned how to set up *Crashlytics* to start tracking crashes in the movie app.

# Introduction to Firebase

Firebase is a set of online services that *Google* bought in 2014 and has been adding to ever since. Their first product was the Firebase Realtime Database, which synchronizes data between iOS, Android, and web devices. They then launched Firebase Hosting and Authentication. This positioned the company as a mobile backend service. In 2016, they launched Firebase Analytics, and then in 2017, they acquired Crashlytics. In the same year, they launched Cloud Firestore, a real-time document database. Cloud Firestore is more powerful than Realtime Database and can handle larger datasets. Many developers use Firebase to save data, handle notifications to mobile devices, handle crashes, distribute apps, and remotely configure their devices. Firebase is easy to set up and start using. Crashlytics has been a staple for dealing with crashes. It is a great tool to monitor any crashes your users are encountering, and plan fixes around them. It will show how many users are experiencing each crash and the stack trace for each one so you can figure out what is causing the crash. Google is also advertising its generative AI ability with Firebase. There are more features than can be described in this chapter. It is recommended to go to **https://firebase.google.com/** to read more. In this chapter, we will be working with the Cloud Firestore database and replacing drift with Firestore.

> **Note: Google also provides Firestore Cloud SQL, which is a relational database.**

# Setting up Firebase

In *Chapter 13, Web and Desktop*, you worked with Firebase to host your app as a web page. If you want to create a new project with Firebase, perform the following:

1. Go to **https://console.firebase.google.com/** and log in.

2. Create a new Firebase project:

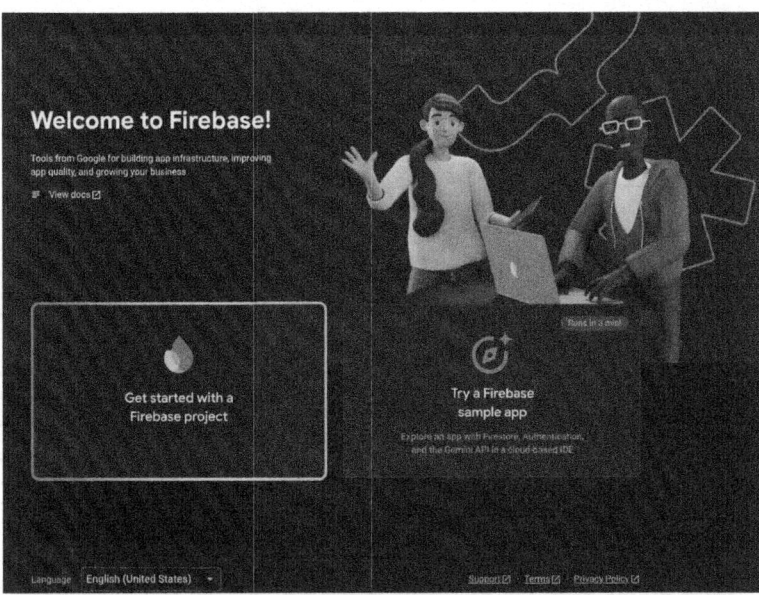

*Figure 15.1*: *New project*

3. **Create a project:**

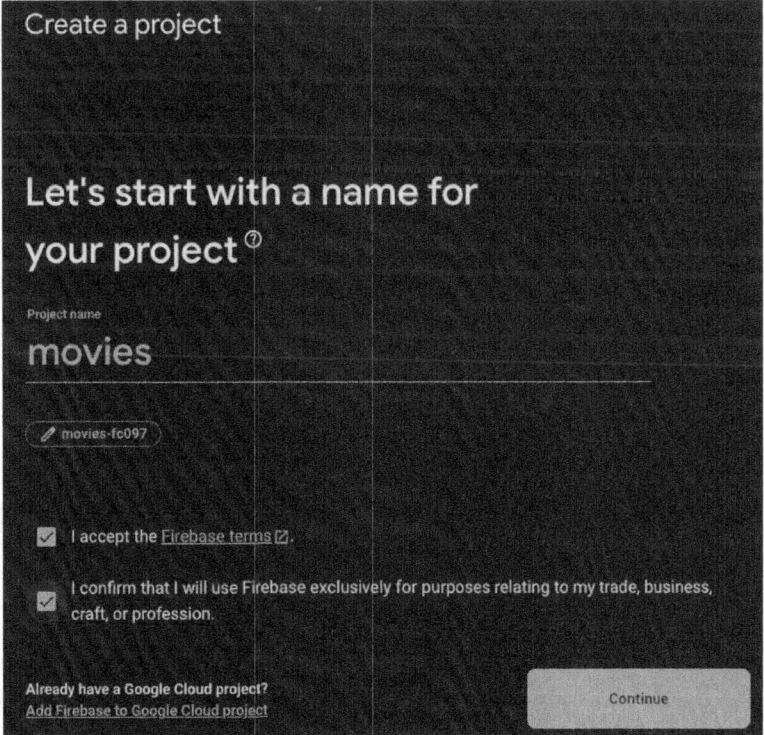

*Figure 15.2*: *Name project*

4.  Enable/disable analytics:

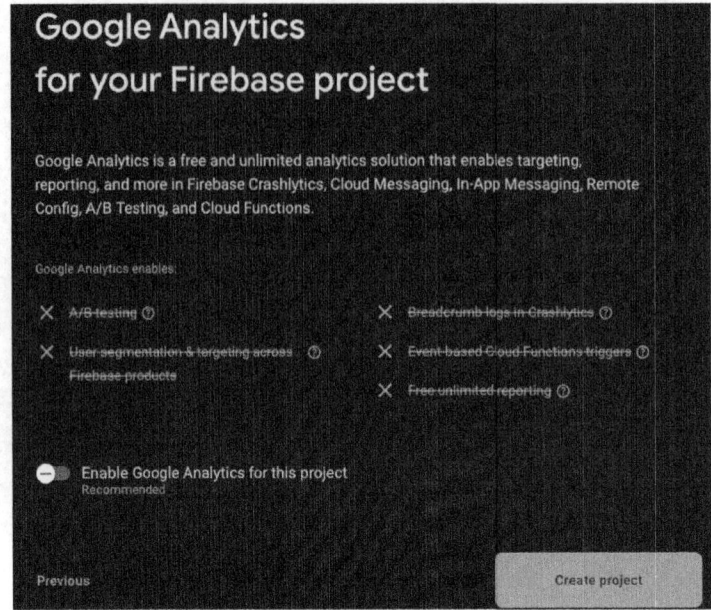

*Figure 15.3: Analytics*

5.  Press **Create project**:

*Figure 15.4: Preparing*

6.  Press **Continue**:

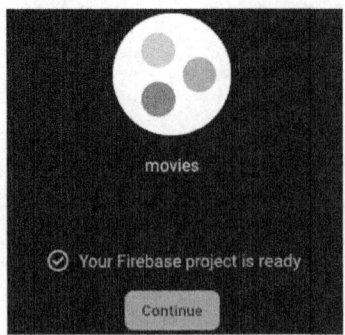

*Figure 15.5: Project created*

7.  The project has been created:

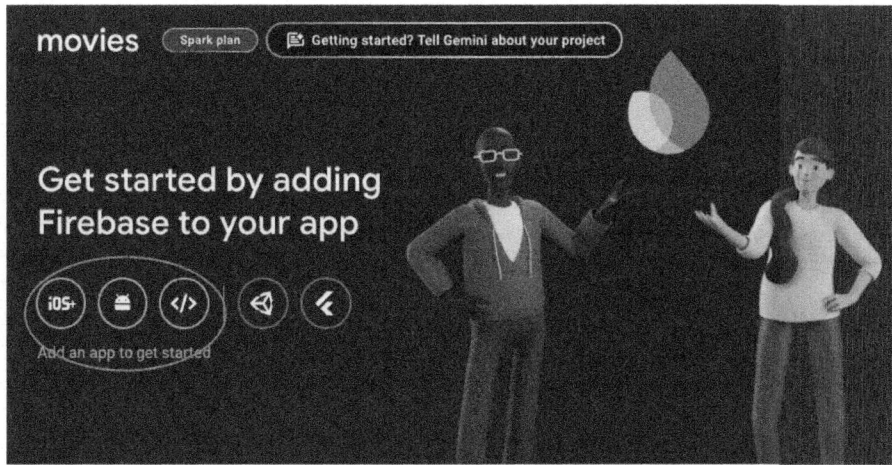

*Figure 15.6*: *Add apps*

Firebase has some command line tools that make it easy to add Firebase to your app. You can find a full description here: **https://firebase.google.com/docs/flutter/ setup?platform=android.** The first step is to install the Firebase CLI tool:

1.  Go to **https://firebase.google.com/docs/cli - setup_update_cli.**

2.  Follow the procedures for your OS.

3.  For macOS, type the following in a terminal:

    ```
    curl -sL https://firebase.tools | bash
    ```

4.  To login to Firebase, in a terminal type:

    ```
    firebase login
    ```

5.  Install Firebase Dart tool:

    ```
    dart pub global activate flutterfire_cli
    ```

6.  Configure Firebase, adding all platforms:

    ```
    flutterfire configure
    ```

```
~/Projects/Mastering Flutter/git/Mastering-Flutter/Chapter 15/movies git:[main]
flutterfire configure
✓ You have an existing `firebase.json` file and possibly already configured your project for Firebase. Would you prefer to reuse the values in your existing `firebase.json` file to configure your project?  no
i Found 13 Firebase projects. Selecting project movies-7f57a.
✓ Which platforms should your configuration support (use arrow keys & space to select)?  android, ios, macos, web, windows
i Firebase android app com.bpb.movies registered.
i Firebase ios app com.bpb.movies registered.
i Firebase macos app com.bpb.movies registered.
i Firebase web app movies (web) registered.
i Firebase windows app movies (windows) is not registered on Firebase project movies-7f57a.
i Registered a new Firebase windows app on Firebase project movies-7f57a.

Firebase configuration file lib/firebase_options.dart generated successfully with the following Firebase apps:

Platform  Firebase App Id
web       1:758270443672:web:e04470f3d8e5021480b0ed
android   1:758270443672:android:37aa2ad3cce4bfee88b69ed
ios       1:758270443672:ios:aca964a899bb37b68b69ed
macos     1:758270443672:ios:aca964a899bb37b68b69ed
windows   1:758270443672:web:39a4ce15eee1e0789e0ed
```

*Figure 15.7*: *flutterfire configure*

7. In your project's folder, add the Firebase packages:

```
flutter pub add firebase_core
flutter pub add cloud_firestore
flutter pub add firebase_auth
flutter pub add google_sign_in
```

This adds the core Firebase library, Firestore, Firebase Auth, and Google sign in.

8. For iOS, you may need to go into the iOS directory and type:

```
pod install
```

This will update the iOS libraries. You may also get some errors that will require you to open the project in Xcode to update the target configuration.

9. Inside of **main.dart**, add the following imports:

```
import 'package:firebase_core/firebase_core.dart';

import 'firebase_options.dart';
```

10. Add the following after **putLumberdashToWork**:

```
await Firebase.initializeApp(
  options: DefaultFirebaseOptions.currentPlatform,
);
```

Stop and re-run your app to make sure everything still works.

# Authentication

Firebase provides authentication. If you have an app that requires different data for different users, you will want a way to create user accounts, allow the user to sign in, and retrieve data just for that user. While the movie app uses the same data for each user and does not require a login, we will create a sample function for signing in with the Google sign-in package. The steps are as follows:

1. In the **data/database** folder, create a new folder named **firebase**.

2. Create a new file: **firebase_auth.dart**.

3. Add the following:

```
import 'package:firebase_auth/firebase_auth.dart';
import 'package:google_sign_in/google_sign_in.dart';

Future<UserCredential> signInWithGoogle() async {
  // Trigger the authentication flow
  final googleUser = await GoogleSignIn().signIn();

  // Obtain the auth details from the request
  final googleAuth = await googleUser?.authentication;
```

```
  // Create a new credential
  final credential = GoogleAuthProvider.credential(
    accessToken: googleAuth?.accessToken,
    idToken: googleAuth?.idToken,
  );

  // Once signed in, return the UserCredential
  return FirebaseAuth.instance.signInWithCredential(credential);
}
```

This function starts the process of launching a sign-in screen for Google accounts. Once the user signs in, you will get a Google user. For a real app, you would need to do some error handling and check that a user was returned. We then use the return authentication to get a credential and sign in with that credential. You would want to save the user credential to get a **User** class. This **User** class has a display name, email, and user ID.

4.  Open **firebase_options.dart** in the **lib** folder.

5.  For iOS, copy the **iosClientId** value.

6.  For iOS, open the **info.plist** file in the **ios/Runner** directory.

7.  Find the following:

```
<key>CFBundleURLSchemes</key>
<array>
```

8.  Add:

```
<string><reverse the copied iosClientID></string>
```

For example, the client id is:

**750270443672-6euf75e6k3vi979qqrop37fq78omk3jt.apps.googleusercontent.com**

My string is:

**<string>com.googleusercontent.apps.750270443672-6euf75e6k3vi979qqrop37fq78omk3jt</string>**

9.  Find a place to put a call to the sign in. To test, put it in the call for the rate button as it does not have any functionality at this point (and this is just for testing):

```
            icon: IconButton(
              onPressed: () {
                signInWithGoogle();
              },
```

10. Run your app on iOS and test sign in. It should take you to a Google sign in.

# Cloud Firestore

Cloud Firestore is Google's newest NoSQL document database. NoSQL is a non-relational database that does not rely on tables. There is nothing in the database that defines how the data should be stored. Data is stored first in collections and then in documents and usually contain JSON data. These documents have unique IDs. You can nest documents as far as you want but that can complicate data retrieval and storage. NoSQL can be useful for large data sets, real-time applications (like chat, games, etc.), or other types.

Realtime Database was the first version, and while they are both NoSQL databases, they have a few differences:

- **Realtime database**:
    - Stores data as a single JSON tree.
    - Queries retrieve the entire subtree.
    - Optimized for real-time synchronization and low latency.
    - Optimized for smaller datasets.

- **Cloud Firestore**:
    - Stores data in documents, organized into collections
    - More powerful and flexible queries.
    - Better for larger datasets.

Both provide offline support with local caching and use a rule-based system to secure data. Realtime charges are based on bandwidth and storage, while Firestore charges are based mostly on read/write operations and less on bandwidth and storage.

To get an instance of Firestore, you would call:

```
final firebase = FirebaseFirestore.instance;
```

To initialize Firebase, you would use:

```
FirebaseApp firebaseApp = await Firebase.initializeApp(
  options: DefaultFirebaseOptions.currentPlatform,
);
```

# Collections

For Firestore, collections are containers for documents. The way this works is you would create a collection with a given name. You can do this both from the console or from code. For example, the movie app will have a collection named Favorites. This will store all the favorites that a user would make. You can then have documents inside of that collection. How you store those documents is crucial to how easy it is to retrieve them. If you just add a document without an ID, Firestore will assign a unique ID for you. This might look something like 4Kc59lp62s74BGJtAxlE. Inside of that document is the JSON data for that favorite. For our app, we will be storing favorites with no user-identifying information. If you want the app to be useable by multiple users, you would either embed a user ID in the record or have a sub-collection for that user. Designing the layout of your collections is important for loading and saving data speed. Storing your data in a deep layout will make retrieval quicker but make your code more complex while making your collection structure shallow would require you to load more data than you would probably need. You can also nest collections. For example, you can have a collection that then has a list of documents that are user IDs; those can then have sub-collections with documents. This will make your code more complex, so you must decide how you want to structure your data. It is recommended to do tests with different collection layouts to see the performance difference and what it would take to implement. One important thing to note about NoSQL databases is that you do not have JOIN operations that you would have in a typical SQL database. This means you cannot query multiple tables with linked fields at once. This means you will probably have to duplicate information in different documents and keep that information synced. This is not trivial and should be considered when deciding on using a NoSQL database.

To create a collection in code, you would call:

```
final favoritesCollection = FirebaseFirestore.instance.
collection('favorites');
```

This gets an instance of Firebase Firestore and creates a collection object with the name favorites.

# Reading and writing data

To read data, you would use the collections **get** method. This returns to a **QuerySnapshot** class. From this class, you can get a list of documents and create classes from each document's data. For example, to get a list of favorites:

```
final favorites = <DBFavorite>[];
final querySnapshot = await favoritesCollection.get();
for (final doc in querySnapshot.docs) {
  var favorite = DBFavorite.fromJson(doc.data());
  favorite = favorite.copyWith(id: int.tryParse(doc.id) ?? 0);
  favorites.add(favorite);
}
```

This waits for the collection's get call to finish and then iterates through each doc to get a new favorite. Writing data is even easier:

```
final ref = await favoritesCollection.add(favorite.toJson());
return Future.value(ref.id);
```

This just adds the JSON to the collection. The result is a **DocumentReference**, which has an ID and a few methods for dealing with the document.

To remove a favorite, you would need to get the specific favorite document and then delete it. This is a bit tricky. This is an example of searching for a favorite with a given ID:

```
final ref = await favoritesCollection.where('id', isEqualTo: id).get();
if (ref.docs.isNotEmpty) {
  ref.docs[0].reference.delete();
}
```

Here, we search the collection for a document with the given ID and then get it. If it exists, we get the first document and delete it. A where statement can return multiple documents, but in our case, we are searching for a unique ID.

# Firebase database

To create our Firebase database class, perform the following:

1.  Create a new file named **firebase_database.dart** in the **firebase** directory.

2.  Add the class definition:

```
import 'package:cloud_firestore/cloud_firestore.dart';
import 'package:firebase_core/firebase_core.dart';
import 'package:movies/data/database/drift/database_interface.dart';
import 'package:movies/data/database/models/configuration.dart';
import 'package:movies/data/database/models/favorite.dart';
import 'package:movies/data/database/models/genre.dart';

import 'package:movies/firebase_options.dart';

const favorites = 'favorites';
const genres = 'genres';
const configuration = 'configuration';
const images = 'images';

class FirebaseDatabase implements IDatabase {
}
```

Besides the imports, we define some constants for our collection names.

3.  Add the variables:

```
static late FirebaseApp firebaseApp;
final firebase = FirebaseFirestore.instance;
final favoritesCollection = FirebaseFirestore.instance.
collection(favorites);
```

```
  final genresCollection = FirebaseFirestore.instance.
collection(genres);
    final configurationCollection =
        FirebaseFirestore.instance.collection(configuration);
    final imagesCollection = FirebaseFirestore.instance.
collection(images);
```

This gets an instance of the **FirebaseFirestore** class and creates collection references.

4.  Initialize Firestore:

```
    static Future initialize() async {
      firebaseApp = await Firebase.initializeApp(
        options: DefaultFirebaseOptions.currentPlatform,
      );
    }
```

This needs to be called before Firestore can be used and will be initialized in the Riverpod providers file.

5.  Override the **deleteDatabase** method. This will not do anything:

```
    @override
    Future deleteDatabase() {
      return Future.value(null);
    }
```

You would normally not want to delete a server database from the code. If you need to delete the database, you can go to the Firebase console.

6.  Get the list of favorites:

```
    @override
    Future<List<DBFavorite>> getFavorites() async {
      final favorites = <DBFavorite>[];
      final querySnapshot = await favoritesCollection.get();
      for (final doc in querySnapshot.docs) {
        var favorite = DBFavorite.fromJson(doc.data());
        favorite = favorite.copyWith(id: int.tryParse(doc.id) ?? 0);
        favorites.add(favorite);
      }
      return favorites;
    }
```

This is just like the sample above.

7.  Stream Favorites:

```
@override
Stream<List<DBFavorite>> streamFavorites() {
  return favoritesCollection
      .snapshots()
      .map((snapShot) => snapShot.docs
          .map((doc) => DBFavorite.fromJson(doc.data()))
          .toList())
      .asBroadcastStream();
}
```

Firestore can also stream collections. The **snapshots** call returns a stream of **QuerySnapshots** that we map to our favorite class.

8. Remove a favorite:

```
@override
Future<bool> removeFavorite(int id) async {
  final ref = await favoritesCollection.where('id', isEqualTo: id).get();
  if (ref.docs.isNotEmpty) {
    ref.docs[0].reference.delete();
  }
  return Future.value(true);
}
```

Just like the example we gave above.

9. Save a favorite:

```
@override
Future saveFavorite(DBFavorite favorite) async {
  final ref = await favoritesCollection.add(favorite.toJson());
  return Future.value(ref.id);
}
```

10. Get all genres:

```
@override
Future<List<DBMovieGenre>> getGenres() async {
  final genres = <DBMovieGenre>[];
  final querySnapshot = await genresCollection.get();
  for (final doc in querySnapshot.docs) {
    var genre = DBMovieGenre.fromJson(doc.data());
    genre = genre.copyWith(id: int.tryParse(doc.id) ?? 0);
    genres.add(genre);
  }
```

```
      return genres;
    }
```

11.  Save a list of genres:

```
    @override
    Future saveGenres(List<DBMovieGenre> genres) {
      for (final genre in genres) {
        genresCollection.add(genre.toJson());
      }
      return Future.value(null);
    }
```

12.  Get the Movie configuration:

```
    @override
    Future<DBConfiguration?> getMovieConfiguration() async {
      final querySnapshot = await configurationCollection.get();
      for (final doc in querySnapshot.docs) {
        var configuration = DBConfiguration.fromJson(doc.data());
        configuration = configuration.copyWith(id: int.tryParse(doc.id)
  ?? 0);
        final imagesSnapshot = await imagesCollection.get();
        if (imagesSnapshot.docs.isNotEmpty) {
          final images =
              DBConfigurationImages.fromJson(imagesSnapshot.docs[0].
  data());
          configuration = configuration.copyWith(images: images);
        }
        return configuration;
      }
      return Future.value(null);
    }
```

13.  Get a movie configuration by ID:

```
    @override
    Future<DBConfiguration?> getMovieConfigurationById(int id) async {
        final docRef = await configurationCollection.doc(id.toString()).
  get();
      final data = docRef.data();
      if (data != null) {
        return DBConfiguration.fromJson(data);
      }
```

```
    return null;
  }
```

14. Save a movie configuration:

```
@override
Future saveMovieConfiguration(DBConfiguration configuration) {
  final configJson = configuration.toJson();
  print(configJson);
  configurationCollection.add(configJson);
  return Future.value(null);
}
```

# Firebase provider

For this chapter, we are going to switch from using the drift database to Firebase. To do that we will create a new provider for Firebase and use that in place of drift. Since they both implement the **IDatabase** interface, we can swap them. Next, add the Firebase provider to the providers file:

1. Open up **providers.dart**.

2. Add the Firebase provider:

```
@Riverpod(keepAlive: true)
IDatabase firebase(FirebaseRef ref) => FirebaseDatabase();
```

3. Add a database provider that we can use to switch between the two databases:

```
@Riverpod(keepAlive: true)
Future<IDatabase> database(DatabaseRef ref) {
  // Change this to what we want to use
  return Future.value(ref.watch(firebaseProvider));
}
```

4. Modify the **movieViewModel** to:

```
@Riverpod(keepAlive: true)
Future<MovieSource> movieRepository(MovieRepositoryRef ref) async {
  final database = await ref.watch(databaseProvider.future);
  final serviceFuture = ref.watch(networkMovieSourceProvider.future);
  return MovieRepository(
      await serviceFuture, database);
}
```

With the addition of Firebase, we will need to make a few changes. Firebase requires a minimum Android SDK value of 23.

5. Open **android/app/build.gradle.**

6. Change the **minSdkVersion** to:

   ```
   minSdkVersion 23
   ```

   Finally, we need to use a special file for improving our JSON serialization.

7. In the root folder, create a new file named **build.yaml.**

8. Add:

   ```yaml
   targets:
     $default:
       builders:
         json_serializable|json_serializable:
           options:
             explicit_to_json: true
             include_if_null: false
   ```

   This will fix the problem of the **DBConfiguration** images not fully being serialized.

9. In the terminal, run the following:

   ```
   dart run build_runner build
   ```

   Stop and restart your app to make sure everything works. Try saving some favorites and check your Firebase console. You should see something like this:

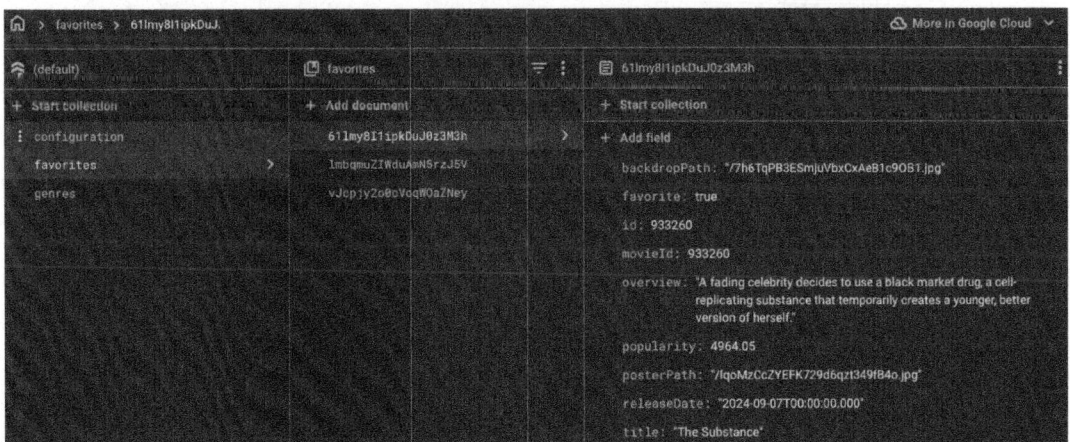

*Figure 15.8: Favorites*

This shows the configuration, favorites, and genre collections. The favorites collection is selected and there are three documents. Each document has a favorite JSON.

# Crashlytics

Crashlytics is Firebase's real-time crash and error reporting system. This is a great way to keep track of how your app is doing and fix crashes before they get out of control. Crashlytics has a dashboard where you can view all of your crashes and stack traces. To add Crashlytics to the movie app, follow these steps:

1. Add Crashlytics. In a terminal type:

   ```
   flutter pub add firebase_crashlytics
   ```

2. Configure Crashlytics:

   ```
   flutterfire configure
   ```

3. In **main.dart** add the following after **Firebase.initializeApp**:

   ```
   FlutterError.onError = (errorDetails) {
     FirebaseCrashlytics.instance.
   recordFlutterFatalError(errorDetails);
   };
   // Pass all uncaught asynchronous errors that aren't handled by
   the Flutter framework to Crashlytics
   PlatformDispatcher.instance.onError = (error, stack) {
     FirebaseCrashlytics.instance.recordError(error, stack, fatal:
   true);
     return true;
   };
   ```

   This will catch both regular and asynchronous errors. To finish the setup, you will need to cause a crash. Let us reuse the Rate icon we used.

4. Change the **onPressed** for the rate icon in **button_row.dart** to:

   ```
   throw Exception();
   ```

5. Run the app and click on the Rate button.

6. Go to the Crashlytics tab in the Firebase console. You should see the following:

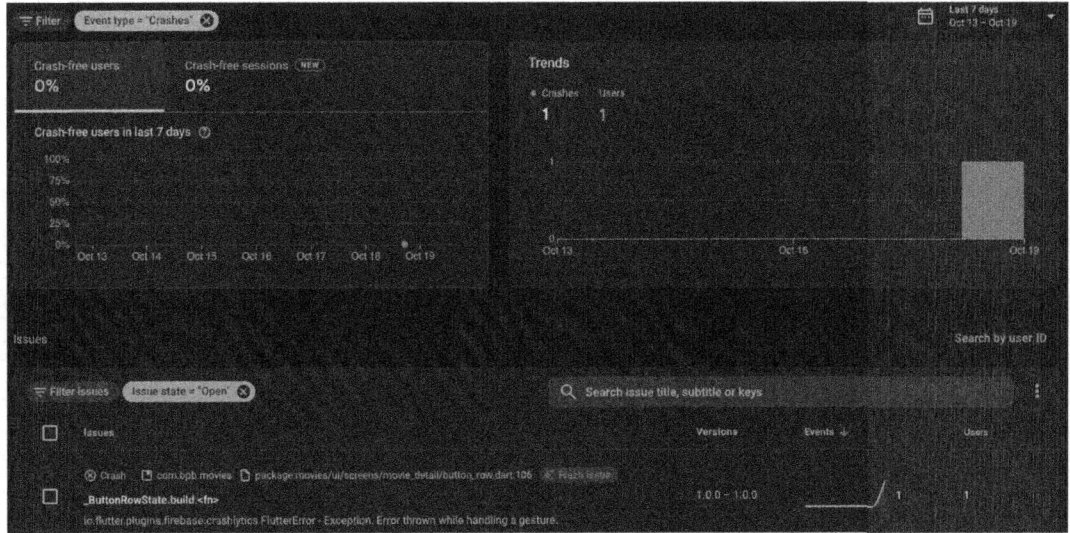

*Figure 15.9*: Crashlytics

**Note: iOS may have issues running. You may have to delete the Crashlytics build script in Xcode in the Build Phases section.**

# Other services

Firebase has more services than we can cover in this chapter. Some of the notable services include:

- **Cloud messaging**: Provides a connection from your server to all devices to send notifications.

- **Remote config**: Allows you to dynamically personalize an app and provide experiments. You set up variables that your app checks for. You can provide different UIs or features based on those settings.

- **App distribution**: Used for managing pre-release versions of your apps to testers.

- **App hosting**: Used to host web apps. Can be used for Flutter web apps.

- **A/B testing**: Used for experiments. Allows you to analyze results.

- **Analytics**: A way to analyze events from your app.

- **Test lab**: A cloud-based app testing service run on real devices.

- **Performance monitoring**: Measure network requests, screen rendering, and other performance-related tasks.

- **Generative AI integration**: Integrate with Google's Gemini and other AI technologies.

All of this adds up to a powerful set of tools that will help you in your journey to developing your application.

# Conclusion

In this chapter, you learned about a lot of the services that Firebase provides. Many of these services are free or free for a certain amount of usage. You learned how to set up Firebase and, specifically, Firebase Cloud Firestore. You know how to retrieve and save data in Firestore as well as how this information is stored: collections and documents. You can also keep track of any crashes, thanks to Crashlytics.

In the next chapter, you will learn more about packages and how to create your own. Packages form the backbone of many apps, and having the ability to break your app up into multiple packages will make your build faster and allow it to be worked on by multiple teams.

## Join our book's Discord space

Join the book's Discord Workspace for Latest updates, Offers, Tech happenings around the world, New Release and Sessions with the Authors:

**https://discord.bpbonline.com**

# CHAPTER 16
# Packages

## Introduction

In this chapter, you will learn all about packages and how to create one. You will also learn how to fix any errors that come with refactoring a project with a package. Share your projects with the Flutter community by publishing your very own package. You will also learn about the importance of being a verified publisher. These skills will help you reuse your code for other projects as well as sharing with others. While you will use other packages, there is great satisfaction in helping others with the knowledge you have learned by writing packages that can be shared with others.

## Structure

The chapter covers the following topics:

- Introduction to packages
- Creating a package
- Refactoring code to package
- Publishing a package

# Objectives

By the end of this chapter, you will have learned all about packages and how to create a new one. You will learn how to register to become a verified publisher and how to publish a package. You will have a good understanding of what a package is and some of the benefits of using your own package.

# Introduction to packages

Packages are collections of Dart code put into their own project. Think of it as a mini-Flutter project. The project does not have to be Flutter related but can be just Dart code. Packages can also include assets and will have a **pubspec.yaml** file, just like a Flutter project. This **pubspec.yaml** does the same thing as in a Flutter project. The difference between a package and a plugin is that a package does not contain native code, just Dart. The most common place to store packages is at Google's **pub.dev** site. While you can publish to other sites, most people expect packages to be at **pub.dev**. Each package on the site has a score that developers can use to judge the quality of the package. People can like a package, but **pub.dev** also auto-generates a popularity value (measured as the number of apps that depend on this package over the last 60 days) and pub points, which are a combination of:

- Following Dart file conventions, up to 30 points.

- Provides documentation, up to 20 points.

- Platform support (how many platforms), up to 20 points.

- Pass static analysis, up to 50 points. Errors will count against.

- Up-to-date dependencies, up to 20 points.

To add a *local* package to your project (and not one from **pub.dev**), you would give the package a name and a path. For example:

```
my_package:
  path: ../my_package
```

Remember that when we added the **menubar** package, we used **git** settings. Those were as follows:

```
menubar:
  git:
    url: https://github.com/google/flutter-desktop-embedding
    path: plugins/menubar
    ref: 12decbe0f592e14e03223f6f2c0c7e0e2dbd70a1
```

Here, the URL is the path to GitHub, the path is the sub-project, and the ref is the git commit hash. As you can see, there are several ways to import a package. We will use the local package method for our new package.

# Creating a package

We are going to create our own package by moving all of the database and networking code to its own package. This will isolate the code so that other team members can work on just that portion of the project to improve or make changes to it. You could also create a package if you felt your code would be useful to others. For example, I created a package to make it easier to use the **Supabase Postgres** database. Initially, I had it as part of one project and then realized that I needed that same code for other projects. By creating it in its own package, and eventually publishing it, I was able to make changes in one place, and all projects would get those updates. Of course, updating a package requires updating the version number in the **pubspec.yaml** file.

To create a project, you can use your IDE or create one from the command line. To create a new package from the command line, you would use the **flutter create** command as follows:

```
flutter create --template=package  --org=<org> --project-name=<project name>
<directory name>
```

# Movie data project

To create our package, do the following:

1.  Go to the Terminal app.

2.  Go to the directory above your current directory.

3.  Type the following:

```
flutter create --template=package  --org=com.bpb.movies --project-
name=movie_data movie_data
```

This will create a new folder named **movie_data** with a new package. If you look at the generated files, they look pretty similar. The packages have:

*   A **lib** directory for source files.

*   A **test** directory for test files.

*   A **pubspec.yaml** file for other packages.

What it does not have are the platform directories:

*   **android**
*   **ios**
*   **windows**
*   **macos**
*   **linux**
*   **web**

One of the files created from this process is the **README.md** file. This is an important file that is shown as the main page when you publish your package. The other two files that are generated for you are:

- **ChangeLog.md**: Lists changes for each version.
- **LICENSE file**: What type of license this project is under.

# Example app

In addition to the package documentation in the README file, it is really helpful to create an example project. This example project will be inside of the package at the root level. This will be an application, and when created, it will have the typical counter app. It is recommended to replace this with a sample app that demonstrates how to use your package. In our case, you might have different screens that make calls into the movie API or database calls so that the user can see how your code is called.

To create the example app, go to the terminal and perform the following:

1. Create the example directory.
   ```
   mkdir example
   ```
2. Go into the example directory.
   ```
   cd example
   ```
3. Create a new project.
   ```
   Flutter create .
   ```

Take a look at the generated project. It looks like a normal Flutter app and has the **android**, **ios**, **linux**, **macos**, **web**, and **windows** directories. Inside the **lib** folder is one **main.dart** file. You can delete all the code here and create or own and even create other files. Sometimes, copying files from your main project will help create this sample app.

# Refactoring code to package

What we want to do is move all of the files in the data and network folders to these new packages. The steps are as follows:

1. Open the **movie_data** project.
2. Inside of the **lib** directory create a new **src** directory.

> Note that packages use a **src** directory instead of being directly inside of the **lib** directory. These files are hidden unless you export them via the **movie_data.dart** file.

3. From the Finder, File Explorer, or other file system app, move the **data** and **network** directories to the **src** directory in the new package. (You can do this in some IDEs, but it might be harder)

4. Move the following packages from the movies project's **pubspec.yaml** to the **movie_data** project's **pubspec.yaml** file:

```
json_annotation: ^4.8.1
freezed_annotation: ^2.4.1
dio: ^5.4.3+1
drift: ^2.20.2
drift_flutter: ^0.2.0
sqlite3_flutter_libs: ^0.5.24
cloud_firestore: ^5.4.4
firebase_auth: ^5.3.1
google_sign_in: ^6.2.1
```

Add the following dependencies:

```
intl: ^0.18.1
lumberdash: ^3.0.0
firebase_core: ^3.6.0
```

Move the following **dev_dependencies**:

```
json_serializable: ^6.7.1
freezed: ^2.4.7
drift_dev: ^2.20.3
```

Add these **dev_dependencies**:

```
build_runner: ^2.4.8
```

5. Do a global replace in **movie_data** to replace **'package:movies'** to **'package:movie_data/src'**. Most IDE's have a global find and replace function.

6. Delete the **test/movie_data_test.dart** file.

7. Move the file **database_interface.dart** in the **data/database/drift** folder to the **database** folder.

8. Fix any incorrect imports to **database_interface**.

9. Open **firebase_database.dart**. We need to make a few changes.

10. Remove the **firebase_options.dart** import.

11. Add a new field below **imagesCollection**, add a constructor, and change the initialize method.

```
final FirebaseOptions options;

FirebaseDatabase(this.options);
```

12. Remove the **initialize** method.

13. Open **movie_api_service.dart**.

14. Remove the two imports that do not exist.

15. Change the constructor and **init** method to:

```
MovieAPIService(this.apiKey);

Future init() async {
  configureDio();
}
```

16. Remove the **webload** method.

    Notice the **movie_data.dart** file. This is the entry point for projects using your package.

17. Open **movie_data.dart**. This is the barrel file for the package (a barrel file is simply a list of dart files you export).

18. Remove the generated calculator method.

19. Add the following exports so that users of the package will see the files:

```
library movie_data;

export 'src/data/models/models.dart';
export 'src/data/database/models/database_models.dart';
export 'src/data/database/firebase/firebase_database.dart';
export 'src/data/database/firebase/firebase_auth.dart';
export 'src/data/database/drift/drift_database.dart';
export 'src/data/repository/movie_repository.dart';
export 'src/data/sources/database_source.dart';
export 'src/data/sources/movie_source.dart';
export 'src/data/sources/network_movie_source.dart';
export 'src/network/movie_api_service.dart';
export 'src/data/database/database_interface.dart';
```

    The model files have all of the models in them.

20. Open **src/data/models/models.dart**.

21. Add a missing export:

    **export 'genre_state.dart';**

22. Copy the **build.yaml** file over.

23. In the terminal, type:

    **dart run build_runner build.**

    To make sure the build system works probably.

# Movies project

Now, we need to update the main project.

1. Open **pubspec.yaml**.

2. Remove the following packages, if you have not already.

```
json_annotation: ^4.8.1
freezed_annotation: ^2.4.1
dio: ^5.4.3+1
drift: ^2.20.2
drift_flutter: ^0.2.0
sqlite3_flutter_libs: ^0.5.24
cloud_firestore: ^5.4.4
firebase_auth: ^5.3.1
google_sign_in: ^6.2.1

dev_dependencies:
  drift_dev: ^2.20.3
    json_serializable: ^6.7.1
    freezed: ^2.4.7
```

3. Add the **movies_data** package:

```
movie_data:
    path: ../movie_data
```

4. Do a Pub Get.

5. Find all files with the old imports and places with errors and replace them with:

```
import 'package:movie_data/movie_data.dart';
```

6. Open **providers.dart** and remove the incorrect imports.

7. Change the **movieAPIService** call to (and add needed imports):

```
@Riverpod(keepAlive: true)
Future<MovieAPIService> movieAPIService(MovieAPIServiceRef ref)
async {
  String apiKey;
  if (!isWeb()) {
    apiKey = dotenv.env['TMDB_KEY']!;
  } else {
    apiKey = await webLoad();
  }
  final service = MovieAPIService(apiKey);
  await service.init();
```

```
      return service;
  }

  Future<String> webLoad() async {
    String apiKey = '';
    try {
      final dotEnvString = await rootBundle.loadString('dotenv');
      if (dotEnvString.contains('TMDB_KEY')) {
        final parts = dotEnvString.split('=');
        if (parts.length == 2) {
          apiKey = parts[1];
          if (apiKey.contains("'")) {
            apiKey = apiKey.replaceAll("'", "");
          }
        }
      } else {
        apiKey = dotEnvString;
      }
    } catch (e) {
      print(e);
    }
    return apiKey;
  }
```

8. Change the database, and Firebase calls to:

```
@Riverpod(keepAlive: true)
Future<IDatabase> database(DatabaseRef ref) {
  // Change this to what we want to use
  final firebaseFuture = ref.watch(firebaseProvider.future);
  return firebaseFuture;
}

@Riverpod(keepAlive: true)
Future<IDatabase> firebase(FirebaseRef ref) async {
  return FirebaseDatabase(DefaultFirebaseOptions.currentPlatform);
}
```

9. In the terminal, type:

   **dart run build_runner build.**

10. To fix a few problems with iOS overflow and the top system, open **ui/theme/ theme.dart**. Add the following to the **ThemeData**:

```
    scaffoldBackgroundColor: Colors.black,
```

11. In `main_screen.dart`, remove the `SizedBox` around the `BottomNavigationBar`.

Try running the app now to make sure that it works. Test both Android and iOS platforms.

# Publishing a package

If you would like to share your package with others, then **pub.dev** is the place where other developers can find it. **pub.dev** has the ability to easily search for packages that are sorted by relevance and popularity. To get popular, you need to have good documentation and make your package easy to use. To publish a package, there are a few things that are required for a package. The most important file is the **pubspec.yaml**. This will describe the package. In order for the user on **pub.dev** to know what your package is all about; they would read what you put into the Readme.md file. This is a markdown file and should be formatted using the markdown language. One site for documentation on markdown is **https://www.markdownguide.org/**. Without a good Readme, users will not know why to use your package. So, it is critical that you describe your package, what it does, how to use it, and maybe even why they should use it. To know what you have done for each version, you will update the `Changelog.md` file describing what you have done in each version. Finally, you need a license that lets the user know how they can use your package.

## pubspec.yaml

You already know about this file, but it is also used by the publishing tool, so certain fields need to be filled out. Make sure you fill out:

- **name**: Name of the package.
- **description**: A small description of the package.
- **version**: The current version of the package.
- **repository**: URL to your repo, usually a GitHub site. (Optional)
- **homepage**: URL to a homepage for the package. It can also be the GitHub site. (Optional)

## Readme.md

This is your place to describe your package and explain how to use it. Here is a quick set of markdown characters:

- Use the `'#'` characters for different header levels. One # is a top level, ## is the second level, etc.
- Use the triple backtick character for the code. For example:

```dart
Final configuration = Configuration();
```

- Use the `'**'` character to surround the text to make it bold.

Use a markdown app to view the results before publishing. If you can add graphics, it would be even better, as that will catch the eyes of readers. If you are building a widget, show what the widget looks like in its different variations.

## Changelog.md

This file is for commenting on the changes you make for each version. Make sure you update this file every time you publish a new version. The first version goes at the bottom, and the newer versions go above that. Here is an example:

```
## 1.0.1
* Add Movie Theme

## 1.0.0-dev.1
* First release.
```

Make sure you keep the version in the **pubspec.yaml** synced with the **Changelog** file.

## License file

To publish a package, you will need a license file. The recommended license is the BSD 3-clause file. **https://opensource.org/license/BSD-3-Clause**. If you need any other type of license, you can find them online. Just put it in the LICENSE file.

# Requirements

There are a few other requirements:

- The package size should be less than 100 MB after compression. You can split it into multiple packages if needed.

- Included packages should be from **pub.dev**.

- You will need a Google account to manage permissions.

## Verified publisher

Being a verified publisher means that you have your own domain that can be verified by Google. You can publish your package as an unverified publisher, but it is not recommended. You will have a higher rating, and people will trust your package more if you are a verified publisher. It takes a bit of time, but it is worth it. To become a verified publisher, do the following:

- Go to **pub.dev**.

- Log in with your Google account:

Sign in
Help

*Figure 16.1: Pub.dev sign-in*

- Select **Create publisher**:

My pub.dev
Publishers
Packages
Likes
Activity log
Create publisher

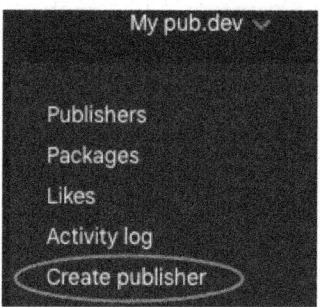

*Figure 16.2: Create publisher*

- Follow the instructions on the next page:

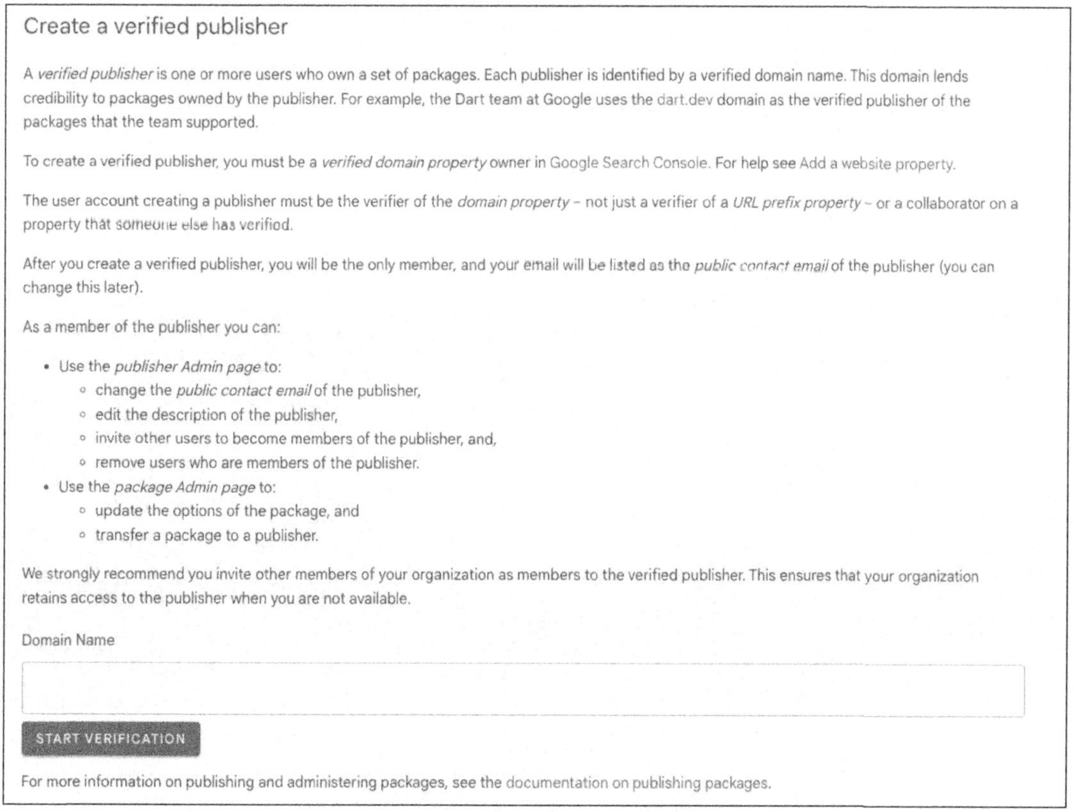

Create a verified publisher
A verified publisher is one or more users who own a set of packages. Each publisher is identified by a verified domain name. This domain lends credibility to packages owned by the publisher. For example, the Dart team at Google uses the dart.dev domain as the verified publisher of the packages that the team supported.
To create a verified publisher, you must be a verified domain property owner in Google Search Console. For help see Add a website property.
The user account creating a publisher must be the verifier of the domain property – not just a verifier of a URL prefix property – or a collaborator on a property that someone else has verified.
After you create a verified publisher, you will be the only member, and your email will be listed as the public contact email of the publisher (you can change this later).
As a member of the publisher you can:
Use the publisher Admin page to:
change the public contact email of the publisher,
edit the description of the publisher,
invite other users to become members of the publisher, and,
remove users who are members of the publisher.
Use the package Admin page to:
update the options of the package, and
transfer a package to a publisher.
We strongly recommend you invite other members of your organization as members to the verified publisher. This ensures that your organization retains access to the publisher when you are not available.
Domain Name
START VERIFICATION
For more information on publishing and administering packages, see the documentation on publishing packages.

*Figure 16.3: Start verification*

It takes quite a bit of work after this, as you will have to have access to your domain settings by setting some DNS-CNAME records. Google will then verify these settings, and after some time, you will become verified.

# Publishing

To publish, you will use the dart command-line tool. You can find more information at **https://dart.dev/tools/pub/cmd/pub-lish** and **https://dart.dev/tools/pub/publishing**. The command for publishing is:

```
dart pub publish
```

This has an additional optional parameter of **–dry-run**. This allows you to test your publishing before it actually sends it to **pub.dev**. Once you have everything ready: from the readme, changelog, license file, and **pubspec.yaml**, you can try to publish.

Note: It is critical that you have this in a Git repo as the publish command uses git to list files.

> **Note: Some readers may find some of the topics discussed to be overly elementary. However, we hope that while you read, you will learn some new and useful ideas. The intention is for all readers to be familiar with these foundations and be able to utilize Wireshark to its full potential.**

To do a dry run for publishing the package, apply the following:

1. In the terminal type:

   ```
   dart pub publish –dry-run
   ```

   Trying a **dry-run** in our package produces:

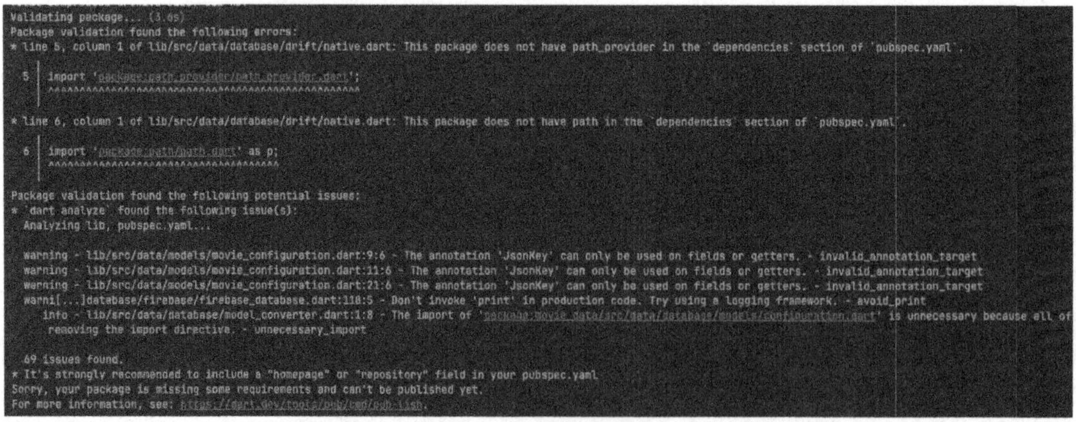

*Figure 16.4: Publish dry run*

As you can see, we have a few errors we need to fix. This tells us that we are missing the **path_provider** and the path package as it is needed for the drift package.

2.  Add the two missing packages to **pubspec.yaml**:

    ```
    path_provider: ^2.1.5
    path: ^1.9.0
    ```

3.  From the command line type:

    ```
    dart pub publish --dry-run
    ```

    Look through the errors to see if you can fix any issues before you publish. Also, note that having your package in a path that has spaces in the name could cause issues as well. If you have files that you do not want to be published, create a **.pubignore** file and add those files to that file. The output from the **publish** command looks like:

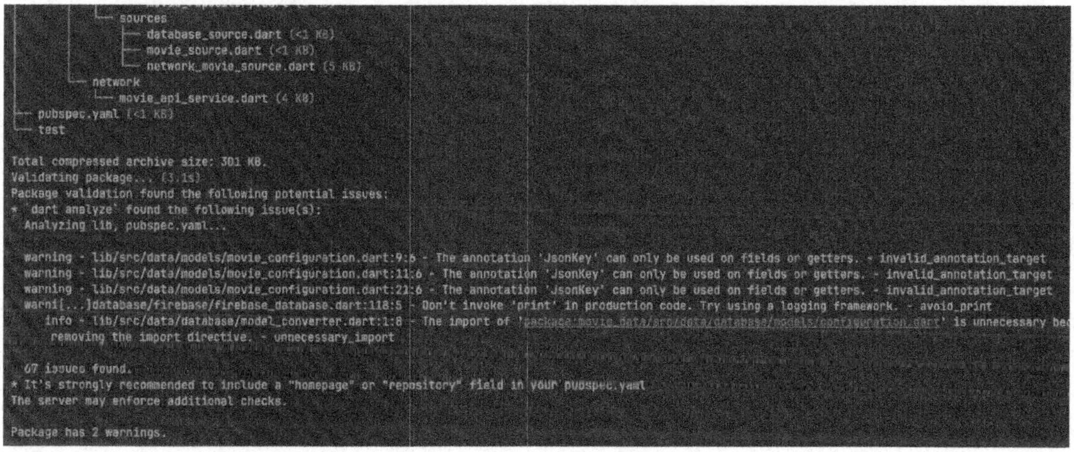

*Figure 16.5: Successful publish dry run*

# Conclusion

In this chapter, you learned all about packages and how to create a new package. You then learned how to fix any errors that come with refactoring a project with a package. Finally, you learned how to register to become a verified publisher and how to publish a package.

In the next chapter, you will learn all about platform channels and plugins. This will help you understand plugins and how you would go about creating your own package for Android and iOS and accessing native systems.

# Join our book's Discord space

Join the book's Discord Workspace for Latest updates, Offers, Tech happenings around the world, New Release and Sessions with the Authors:

https://discord.bpbonline.com

# CHAPTER 17

# Platform Channels and Plugins

## Introduction

In this chapter, you will learn about plugins and when you need to use them or build your own. There are many third-party plugins that provide the backbone for Flutter's functionality and should be what you use if you need native functionality. If that functionality does not exist, you can build your own. You will learn how plugins work and how to build your own SharedPreferences type plugin.

## Structure

The chapter covers the following topics:

- Writing a plugin
- Using third-party plugins
- Platform channels
- Building a plugin

## Objectives

By the end of this chapter, you will know when to use third-party plugins and when to build your own. You will understand how plugins work and communicate with the

Flutter app. You will also understand how to create and build a plugin that will replace the SharedPreferences plugin.

# Writing a plugin

Unlike a package, which is a library of Dart code, a plugin is a set of native code with a Dart front-end. Depending on which platforms are supported, you will have Android, iOS, macOS, Linux, and Windows. When a plugin is created, there are three main **.dart** files:

- `<plugin name>.dart`
- `<plugin name>_method_channel.dart`
- `<plugin name>_platform_interface.dart`

These files are the entry point into the plugin. The first file, **`<plugin name>.dart`**, is what the user of the plugin will see. These have all of the methods that can be called for this plugin. This class will, in turn, call the platform singleton instance, which will then call the channel class. The **platform** class implements the **PlatformInterface** class, which just has a constructor that takes a token. This class is itself abstract and is implemented by the channel class. This is a bit confusing, but it helps to separate interfaces from classes. The **channel** class is so named because it has an instance of a **MethodChannel**. This class is used to talk to native code. The way they do this is by sending and receiving messages. You would make a call as follows:

```
methodChannel.invokeMethod<Return Type>(String methodName, [arguments]);
```

You define what method names that will be available and then the user calls a method in the plugin class. Remember that the main plugin name (defined by how you created the plugin) will contain all of the methods the user of the plugin will see.

In this chapter, we will be creating a shared preferences plugin. This will duplicate the current shared preferences but will demonstrate how to create a plugin and implement it in Android and iOS. We will not be creating any other platform code, but if you would like to expand on it, you can create the Windows, macOS, or Linux versions.

# Using third-party plugins

In Android Studio, there is an External Libraries section in the Project view. If you open up the Flutter Plugins section, you will see all of the plugins we are currently using in our project:

*Figure 17.1*: Movie plugins

As you can see in *Figure 17.1*, there are a lot of them. When you need native functionality that Flutter does not provide, then it is highly recommended that you first search for an existing plugin from **pub.dev**. You can do a search and will usually find multiple plugins that do what you need. The only thing you need to do is determine which plugin is best.

Do this by viewing the plugin's ratings, documentation, and examples. Before you fully commit to a plugin, it might be wise to do a test with the plugin to make sure it handles all of your needs. For example, there are many video plugins, all with different features. Do you need a plugin that works on certain platforms? If it does not, you can eliminate that plugin. Does it have all of the features you need? If not, you can eliminate that one. What happens if you search all available plugins and nothing matches what you are looking for? If you find one that is close to what you want, you can fork that plugin and modify it yourself (assuming it has a license that allows you to do that). That will give you a head start in building a plugin. I needed a plugin that worked on iOS and Android and used Bluetooth to connect to a specific device. Since this was a very specific need, it was decided to write our own plugin. Luckily, we had native code examples we could use for this. We had older iOS and Android apps that had this implemented, so we could copy a lot of the code over.

# Platform channels

Platform channels are a way for Flutter apps to communicate with native code running on a device. They provide a bidirectional communication channel between Flutter and native code. The idea is for a Flutter app to tell a plugin to perform an action on the native side and have the plugin execute that action and return a result. Channels work by sending messages between Flutter and the native code. These messages are serialized in a format that both sides can understand. The **MethodChannel** is the most common channel and is used to invoke methods on the native side and return a result. **MethodChannels** just require a name that needs to be the same on both sides of the channel. On the native side, you would create a **MethodChannel** with a channel name and the type of messenger used to process messages. This is usually a **BinaryMessenger**. If you have your own way of sending messages, you would implement your own messenger. To create a **MethodChannel** you would use the following:

```
channel = MethodChannel(flutterPluginBinding.binaryMessenger, "<channel name>")
```

This **binaryMessenger** comes from the **onAttachedToEngine** method, which looks as follows on Android:

```
    override fun onAttachedToEngine(flutterPluginBinding: FlutterPlugin.FlutterPluginBinding) {
```

It looks like this on iOS:

```
  public static func register(with registrar: FlutterPluginRegistrar) {
```

The easiest way to start working on a Plugin is to use the **flutter create -template=plugin** command. This creates the needed starting project for you. This will consist of the following:

- Dart-based project for the plugin.

- Example project to test your plugin.

- Platform folders for each platform that is iOS, Android, etc.

Inside the Dart-based project, you will have a lib folder with three files. If the project is named **movie_plugin** then they will be:

- **movie_plugin.dart**

- **movie_plugin_method_channel.dart**

- **movie_plugin_platform_interface.dart**

The **MoviePlugin** class will define all of the methods that are available for this plugin. This file will just call methods from the **MoviePluginPlatform** class. The **MoviePluginPlatform** extends the **PlatformInterface** which has a few methods for identifying it and then dummy methods. These methods throw an **UnimplementedError**. The reason for this is that each platform has to implement this method. If they do not, then this error will be thrown. For example, if you write the Android native portion but then try to run the app on iOS, you will get this error. This will remind you that you have to implement iOS. The **MoviePluginPlatform** creates a static instance of the **MethodChannelMoviePlugin** class. As its name implies, this class creates a **MethodChannel** with the name **movie_plugin**. The **MethodChannelMoviePlugin** class then calls the **invokeMethod** function on the method channel that takes a return type, the string value of the method name, and any arguments. The argument types are dynamic, meaning they can be anything that can be serialized. The author usually uses JSON as it is easy to use on both sides of the plugin. An example would be:

```
return methodChannel.invokeMethod<String?>('getString', {'key': key });
```

This calls the native **getString** method passing in a map argument with a key value. The return value is a nullable string, meaning that the call may not find a string. Just remember that it looks like:

```
return methodChannel.invokeMethod<return value>(method name, list of
arguments);
```

One other important channel type is the **EventChannel**. This is a great way to send messages from the plugin to the user. This class takes a messenger and a channel name like the **MethodChannel**. In the native code, you need to set a stream handler. This handler must implement the **onListen** and **onCancel** methods. The **onListen** method will return an **EventSink** class that you will use to send messages. The **EventSink** interface looks like:

```
public interface EventSink {
    void success(Object var1);

    void error(String var1, String var2, Object var3);

    void endOfStream();
}
```

Sending JSON values of events to the **success** method works well. The Flutter app will then listen to the **EventChannel** and handle any events. **EventChannels** are a great way for a Flutter app to listen for events that have not been specifically requested. For example, you may get a native Bluetooth event that you want to send to your Flutter app.

# Building a plugin

For this chapter, we will be building a plugin that will replace the **shared_preferences** plugin. This plugin saves primitive values to local storage. This is a relatively easy set of methods. For the Android portion, it will use the **SharedPreferences** class, and for iOS, it will use the **UserDefaults** class.

# Creating the plugin

While you can create the plugin through your IDE, we will be creating it through the terminal so you can see the parameters needed. Since we are building this for Android and iOS, we will be specifying those platforms. To create the plugin, you will use the **flutter create** command with the plugin template. The steps are as follows:

1.  From the terminal, go to the folder above your project:

    ```
    cd ..
    ```

2.  Type:

    ```
    flutter create --org=com.bpb --template=plugin
    --platforms=android,ios movie_plugin
    ```

    This will create a plugin with a **com.bpb.movie_plugin** package with Android and iOS native code.

3.  Open the project from your IDE. For Android Studio, you can also open up the Android project that is part of this plugin. The reason is that Android Studio handles the project as an Android project when you open up that folder. So, you will have your **movies**, **movie_plugin**, and **movie_plugin/android** projects open. In the **movie_plugin** project, you will first see the **README.md** file. This has some dummy information that you will need to change if you want to publish your plugin. Open up **pubspec.yaml**. Most of this looks the same as a regular Flutter project. There are two main differences:

    *   No **publish_to** field

    *   Extra **homepage** field

There is also an **example** project inside. This project is useful for testing the plugin. We will be using this project to bring up a simple one-screen app for testing shared preferences:

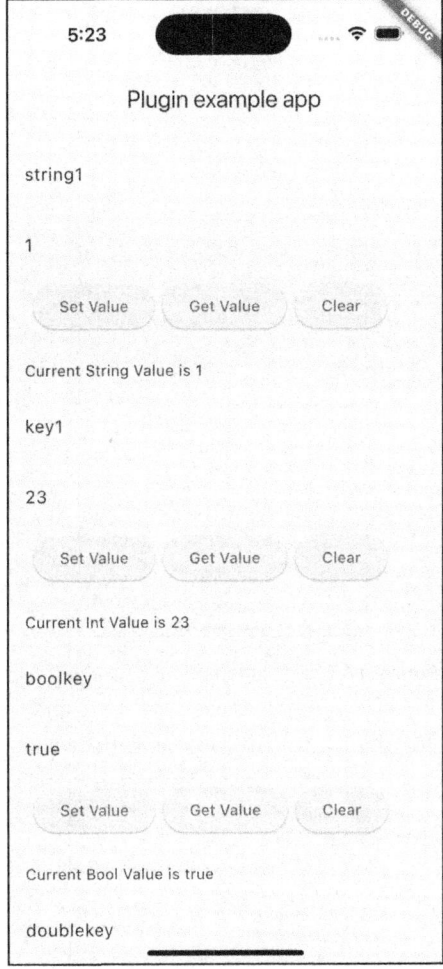

*Figure 17.2: Plugin example app*

This has four sections. The first one is for setting the key/value pair for strings, the second for ints, the third for Booleans, and the fourth for doubles. This will allow us to test setting, retrieving, and clearing values. You will want to enter a key and then a value, click the **Set Value** button and then click the **Get Value** button to see if the value shows up in the line below. Then try pressing the **Clear** button and then the **Get** button to make sure it is gone. If all of these areas work, you know your plugin is working. If they do not, you can fix that area.

# Building the plugin

In the `movie_plugin` project, you will see the three generated files. Open up `movie_plugin.dart`. This has a generated `getPlatformVersion` default method. Try running the example project. It should look like:

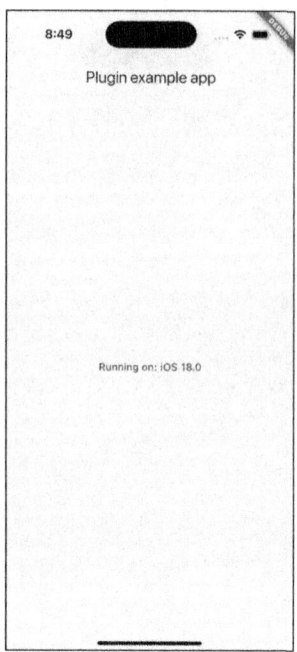

*Figure 17.3: iOS starting plugin example app*

This is running on iOS. For Android, it will look as follows:

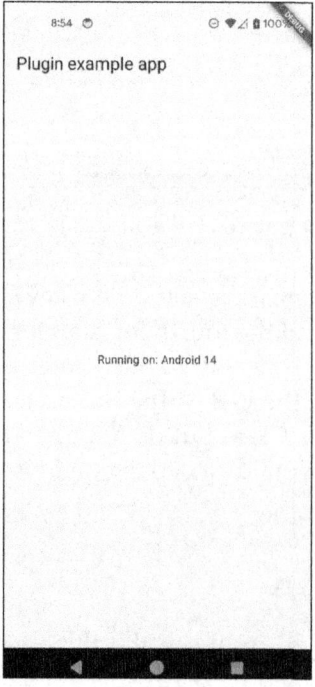

*Figure 17.4: Android plugin example app*

# Android plugin

Now, open up the Android project. This will be the Android folder inside of the **movie_plugin** folder. While this project builds from the main **movie_plugin** project, Android Studio does not know anything about the Flutter system. If you open **MoviePlugin.kt**, you will see lots of errors for files it cannot find. While you could edit these files knowing that the main **movie_plugin** project would be able to build them, it is easier to work in this project with everything compiling correctly in this sub-project. We will do some gradle magic to fix this. The steps are as follows:

1. Open up **settings.gradle**. Add the following:

```
pluginManagement {
    def flutterSdkPath = {
        def properties = new Properties()
        file("local.properties").withInputStream { properties.
load(it) }
        def flutterSdkPath = properties.getProperty("flutter.sdk")
        assert flutterSdkPath != null, "flutter.sdk not set in local.
properties"
        return flutterSdkPath
    }
    settings.ext.flutterSdkPath = flutterSdkPath()

    includeBuild("${settings.ext.flutterSdkPath}/packages/flutter_
tools/gradle/")

    repositories {
        google()
        mavenCentral()
        gradlePluginPortal()
    }
}

plugins {
    id "dev.flutter.flutter-plugin-loader" version "1.0.0"
    id "com.android.library" version "8.1.4" apply false
    id "org.jetbrains.kotlin.android" version "1.9.24" apply false
}
```

What this does is set a variable to point to **your local.properties** file which should have the location of where Flutter is installed. It will then include the Flutter gradle build file and then apply some plugins.

2. Open **build.gradle**. Add the following to the top of the file:

```
def localProperties = new Properties()
def localPropertiesFile = rootProject.file('local.properties')
if (localPropertiesFile.exists()) {
    localPropertiesFile.withReader('UTF-8') { reader ->
        localProperties.load(reader)
    }
}

def flutterRoot = localProperties.getProperty('flutter.sdk')
if (flutterRoot == null) {
    throw new GradleException("Flutter SDK not found. Define location
with flutter.sdk in the local.properties file.")
}
```

This does the same thing and gets the location of Flutter.

3.  Find the dependencies section and add this line:

```
// This allows the Plugin code to compile
compileOnly files("$flutterRoot/bin/cache/artifacts/engine/android-
arm64/flutter.jar")
```

4.  Do a Gradle sync. This can be done by either of these two buttons.

*Figure 17.5: Gradle sync*

Going back to **MoviePlugin.kt**, you will see that all of the errors are gone. You can now start work. Since we are working on replicating the **SharedPreferences** plugin we will want all of the methods that we use in the **Prefs.dart** file:

1.  Remove this import as it is not needed:

```
import androidx.annotation.NonNull
```

2.  Add an enum for all of the method calls we will support above the **MoviePlugin** class:

```
enum class MethodCalls(val value: String) {
    GetString("getString"),
    SetString("setString"),
```

```
    Clear("clear"),
    ContainsKey("containsKey"),
    GetInt("getInt"),
    SetInt("setInt"),
    GetDouble("getDouble"),
    SetDouble("setDouble"),
    GetBool("getBool"),
    SetBool("setBool"),
}
```

This just defines some enums we can use that will define in one place the strings that should be used. Note that it is important that the strings match both name and case.

3.  Before the **onAttachedToEngine** method add the following fields:

    ```
    private lateinit var context: Context
    private lateinit var sharedPreferences: SharedPreferences
    ```

    Then add the imports needed. This will let us save a **Context** and create a **SharedPreferences** instance.

4.  Add the following to the **onAttachedToEngine** method after the channel setup:

    ```
    context = flutterPluginBinding.applicationContext
    sharedPreferences = context.getSharedPreferences("movie_plugin",
    Context.MODE_PRIVATE)
    ```

    Luckily, the passed in **flutterPluginBinding** has a **Context** we can use. This is needed to get the **SharedPreferences**.

5.  In the **onMethodCall** call, replace the code with:

    ```
            Log.e("MoviePlugin", "onMethodCall: ${call.method}")
            when (call.method) {
                MethodCalls.GetString.value -> {
                    val key = call.argument<String>("key")
                    Log.e("MoviePlugin", "key: $key")
                    if (key == null) {
                        result.error("INVALID_ARGUMENT", "Key cannot be
    null", null)
                        return
                    }
                    getString(key, result)
                }
            }
    ```

Add the **Log** import. This will help us when we are testing. This is just the **getString** call. Notice that we have not written the **getString** method yet. What this does is check the string of the **call.method** and match it to our **enum** value. The **MethodCall** class also contains arguments. For the **getString** call, we are expecting a **key** argument, and it will return a nullable string. We return an error if the key argument is not found. We then pass the key and the result class to the **getString** method. For plugins, it is critical to set the result value for the caller to check the result.

6. Add the **getString** method to the bottom of the file:

```
private fun getString(key: String, result: Result) {
    val value = sharedPreferences.getString(key, null)
    Log.e("MoviePlugin", "getString: key: $key value: $value")
    result.success(value)
}
```

This method takes the key and uses the **sharedPreferences** class to get the string associated with that key. We then set the result's success method with that value. Note that this value can be null. We will be doing something similar for the other types.

7. Add the **setString** method:

```
private fun setString(key: String, value: String, result: Result) {
    val commitResult = sharedPreferences.edit().putString(key, value).commit()
    Log.e("MoviePlugin", "setString: key: $key value: $value commitResult: $commitResult")
    result.success(commitResult)
}
```

This method will save the value with the given **key**. In Android, you need to call the **edit** method, call **putXXX**, and then the **commit** method.

> **Note: There are newer ways to do this in Android, but we will just be covering the easiest way.**

Next, we need to add two methods for clearing and checking for the key:

8. Add the clear and **containsKey** methods:

```
private fun clear(result: Result) {
    val commitResult = sharedPreferences.edit().clear().commit()
    result.success(commitResult)
}
```

```
        private fun containsKey(key: String, result: Result) {
            val value = sharedPreferences.contains(key)
            result.success(value)
        }
```

Remember to always call **result.success** or **result.error**.

9. Add the int methods:

```
        private fun getInt(key: String, result: Result) {
            val value = sharedPreferences.getInt(key, 0)
            result.success(value)
        }

        private fun setInt(key: String, value: Int, result: Result) {
            val commitResult = sharedPreferences.edit().putInt(key,
    value).commit()
            result.success(commitResult)
        }
```

10. Add the Double methods:

```
        private fun getDouble(key: String, result: Result) {
            val value = sharedPreferences.getFloat(key, 0.0f).toDouble()
            result.success(value)
        }

        private fun setDouble(key: String, value: Double, result:
    Result) {
            val commitResult = sharedPreferences.edit().putFloat(key,
    value.toFloat()).commit()
            result.success(commitResult)
        }
```

11. Add the Boolean methods:

```
        private fun getBool(key: String, result: Result) {
            val value = sharedPreferences.getBoolean(key, false)
            result.success(value)
        }

        private fun setBool(key: String, value: Boolean, result: Result)
    {
            val commitResult = sharedPreferences.edit().putBoolean(key,
    value).commit()
            result.success(commitResult)
        }
```

12. Now, return to the **onMethodCall** method and add the handling of the **setString**, clear and **ContainsKey** methods:

```
MethodCalls.SetString.value -> {
    val key = call.argument<String>("key")
    val value = call.argument<String>("value")
    Log.e("MoviePlugin", "key: $key value: $value")
    if (key == null) {
        result.error("INVALID_ARGUMENT", "Key cannot be
null", null)
        return
    }
    if (value == null) {
        result.error("INVALID_ARGUMENT", "value cannot
be null", null)
        return
    }
    setString(key, value, result)
}

MethodCalls.Clear.value -> {
    clear(result)
}

MethodCalls.ContainsKey.value -> {
    val key = call.argument<String>("key")
    if (key == null) {
        result.error("INVALID_ARGUMENT", "Key cannot be
null", null)
        return
    }
    containsKey(key, result)
}
```

13. Add the int method calls:

```
MethodCalls.GetInt.value -> {
    val key = call.argument<String>("key")
    if (key == null) {
        result.error("INVALID_ARGUMENT", "Key cannot be
null", null)
        return
    }
    getInt(key, result)
}
```

```
        MethodCalls.SetInt.value -> {
            val key = call.argument<String>("key")
            val value = call.argument<Int>("value")
            if (key == null) {
                result.error("INVALID_ARGUMENT", "Key cannot be
null", null)
                return
            }
            if (value == null) {
                result.error("INVALID_ARGUMENT", "value cannot
be null", null)
                return
            }
            setInt(key, value, result)
        }
```

14. Add the Double calls:

```
        MethodCalls.GetDouble.value -> {
            val key = call.argument<String>("key")
            if (key == null) {
                result.error("INVALID_ARGUMENT", "Key cannot be
null", null)
                return
            }
            getDouble(key, result)
        }

        MethodCalls.SetDouble.value -> {
            val key = call.argument<String>("key")
            val value = call.argument<Double>("value")
            if (key == null) {
                result.error("INVALID_ARGUMENT", "Key cannot be
null", null)
                return
            }
            if (value == null) {
                result.error("INVALID_ARGUMENT", "value cannot
be null", null)
                return
            }
            setDouble(key, value, result)
        }
```

15. Add the Boolean calls:

```
            MethodCalls.GetBool.value -> {
                val key = call.argument<String>("key")
                if (key == null) {
                    result.error("INVALID_ARGUMENT", "Key cannot be
null", null)
                    return
                }
                getBool(key, result)
            }

            MethodCalls.SetBool.value -> {
                val key = call.argument<String>("key")
                val value = call.argument<Boolean>("value")
                if (key == null) {
                    result.error("INVALID_ARGUMENT", "Key cannot be
null", null)
                    return
                }
                if (value == null) {
                    result.error("INVALID_ARGUMENT", "value cannot
be null", null)
                    return
                }
                setBool(key, value, result)
            }
```

# Plugin files

So far, we have just built the Android portion of the plugin. The movie app needs an interface to talk to, and that is where the **movie_plugin.dart** file comes in. This is the entry point and main interface for the plugin. What we need is a way for the movie app to talk to this dart entry point, which then calls the appropriate native code. In our case, either Android or iOS. It does this by sending the method call on the **MethodChannel**. The running native code will be listening on that channel for the method call. Let us start with the **MoviePluginPlatform** class:

1.  Open up **movie_plugin_platform_interface.dart**.

2.  Remove the **getPlatformVersion** method.

3.  Add the following methods. These methods will not do anything but are the interface for the plugin.

    ```
    Future<String?> getString(String key) async {
      throw UnimplementedError('getString has not been implemented.');
    ```

```
  }

  Future setString(String key, String value) async {
    throw UnimplementedError('setString has not been implemented.');
  }

  Future clear() async {
    throw UnimplementedError('clear has not been implemented.');
  }

  Future<bool?> containsKey(String key) async {
    throw UnimplementedError('containsKey has not been
implemented.');
  }
  Future<int?> getInt(String key) async {
    throw UnimplementedError('getInt has not been implemented.');
  }

  Future setInt(String key, int value) async {
    throw UnimplementedError('setInt has not been implemented.');
  }

  Future<bool?> getBool(String key) async {
    throw UnimplementedError('getBool has not been implemented.');
  }

  Future setBool(String key, bool value) async {
    throw UnimplementedError('setBool has not been implemented.');
  }

  Future<double?> getDouble(String key) async {
    throw UnimplementedError('getDouble has not been implemented.');
  }

  Future setDouble(String key, double value) async {
    throw UnimplementedError('setDouble has not been implemented.');
  }
```

Notice the **UnimplementedError**. This will be thrown on any platform that has not been written or implemented yet.

4. Open up **movie_plugin_method_channel.dart**.

5. Add the same **MethodCalls enum** above the class:

```
enum MethodCalls {
  getString('getString'),
  setString('setString'),
  clear('clear'),
```

```
    containsKey('containsKey'),
    getInt('getInt'),
    setInt('setInt'),
    getBool('getBool'),
    setBool('setBool'),
    getDouble('getDouble'),
    setDouble('setDouble');

    final String value;

    const MethodCalls(this.value);
}
```

6. Now replace **getPlatformVersion** with:

```
@override
Future<String?> getString(String key) async {
  return methodChannel.invokeMethod<String?>(MethodCalls.
getString.value, {'key': key });
}

@override
Future setString(String key, String value) async {
  return methodChannel.invokeMethod<void>(MethodCalls.setString.
value, {'key': key, 'value': value });
}

@override
Future clear() async {
  return methodChannel.invokeMethod<void>(MethodCalls.clear.
value);
}

@override
Future<bool?> containsKey(String key) async {
  return methodChannel.invokeMethod<bool>(MethodCalls.containsKey.
value, {'key': key });
}
@override
Future<int?> getInt(String key) async {
  return methodChannel.invokeMethod<int?>(MethodCalls.getInt.
value, {'key': key });
}

@override
Future setInt(String key, int value) async {
```

```
      return methodChannel.invokeMethod<void>(MethodCalls.setInt.
value, {'key': key, 'value': value });
  }

  @override
  Future<bool?> getBool(String key) async {
    return methodChannel.invokeMethod<bool?>(MethodCalls.getBool.
value, {'key': key });
  }

  @override
  Future setBool(String key, bool value) async {
    return methodChannel.invokeMethod<void>(MethodCalls.setBool.
value, {'key': key, 'value': value });
  }

  @override
  Future<double?> getDouble(String key) async {
    return methodChannel.invokeMethod<double?>(MethodCalls.
getDouble.value, {'key': key });
  }

  @override
  Future setDouble(String key, double value) async {
    return methodChannel.invokeMethod<void>(MethodCalls.setDouble.
value, {'key': key, 'value': value });
  }
```

This just calls the **invokeMethod** call with the name of the method and the arguments.

7. Open **movie_plugin.dart** and replace **getPlatformVersion** with:

```
Future<String?> getString(String key) async {
  return MoviePluginPlatform.instance.getString(key);
}

Future setString(String key, String value) async {
  return MoviePluginPlatform.instance.setString(key, value);
}

Future clear() async {
  return MoviePluginPlatform.instance.clear();
}

Future<bool?> containsKey(String key) async {
  return MoviePluginPlatform.instance.containsKey(key);
```

```
    }
    Future<int?> getInt(String key) async {
      return MoviePluginPlatform.instance.getInt(key);
    }

    Future setInt(String key, int value) async {
      return MoviePluginPlatform.instance.setInt(key, value);
    }

    Future<double?> getDouble(String key) async {
      return MoviePluginPlatform.instance.getDouble(key);
    }

    Future setDouble(String key, double value) async {
      return MoviePluginPlatform.instance.setDouble(key, value);
    }

    Future<bool?> getBool(String key) async {
      return MoviePluginPlatform.instance.getBool(key);
    }

    Future setBool(String key, bool value) async {
      return MoviePluginPlatform.instance.setBool(key, value);
    }
```

This will call the **MoviePluginPlatform**'s version of each method. If you look at the files on the left you will see several files that have a red underline. This means they all have errors.

8. Delete the **movie_plugin_method_channel_test.dart** and **movie_plugin_ test.dart**. files in the **example/test** folder. We will be writing tests in the next chapter.

9. Delete the **plugin_integration_test.dart** file in the **example/integration_ test** folder.

Note that tests will be written in the next chapter that discusses writing tests.

# Example plugin app

In order to test our plugin, it helps to have an example app that we can test with. *Figure 17.1* shows what the app will look like. All of the code will be in **main.dart**.

1. Delete the **initState** and **initPlatformState** methods along with _ **platformVersion** variable.

2. Open up **main.dart** in the **example/lib** folder. We need text controllers for each field. Add the controllers and strings after the **_moviePlugin** variable:

```
    TextEditingController stringKeyTextController =
TextEditingController();

    TextEditingController stringValueTextController =
TextEditingController();

    TextEditingController intKeyTextController =
TextEditingController();

    TextEditingController intValueTextController =
TextEditingController();

    TextEditingController boolKeyTextController =
TextEditingController();

    TextEditingController boolValueTextController =
TextEditingController();

    TextEditingController doubleKeyTextController =
TextEditingController();

    TextEditingController doubleValueTextController =
TextEditingController();

    String currentStringValue = '';

    String currentIntValue = '';

    String currentBoolValue = '';

    String currentDoubleValue = '';
```

3. Replace the **build** method with:

```
    @override
    Widget build(BuildContext context) {
      return MaterialApp(
        home: Scaffold(
          appBar: AppBar(
            title: const Text('Plugin example app'),
          ),
          body: CustomScrollView(
            slivers: [
              SliverList(
                delegate: SliverChildListDelegate(
                  [
// TODO Add Fields
                  ],
                ),
              ),
            ],
          ),
```

```
      ),
    );
  }
```

4. Replace the TODO with:

```
                Padding(
                  padding: const EdgeInsets.all(16.0),
                  child: Column(
                    crossAxisAlignment: CrossAxisAlignment.start,
                    children: [
                    ],
                  ),
                ),
```

5. For the children add the first two text fields:

```
                    TextField(
                      decoration: const InputDecoration(
                        border: InputBorder.none,
                        hintText: 'String Key',
                        // hintStyle: TextStyle(color: Colors.
black),
                      ),
                      textInputAction: TextInputAction.next,
                      controller: stringKeyTextController,
                    ),
                    const SizedBox(
                      height: 16,
                    ),
                    TextField(
                      decoration: const InputDecoration(
                        border: InputBorder.none,
                        hintText: 'String Value',
                      ),
                      textInputAction: TextInputAction.done,
                      controller: stringValueTextController,
                    ),
```

6. Add the first button row and the text:

```
                    Padding(
                      padding: const EdgeInsets.all(8.0),
                      child: Row(
```

```
                              children: [
                                ElevatedButton(
                                    onPressed: () async {
                                      if (stringKeyTextController.
text.isNotEmpty &&
                                          stringValueTextController.
text.isNotEmpty) {
                                        await _moviePlugin.setString(
                                            stringKeyTextController.
text,
                                            stringValueTextController.
text);
                                      }
                                    },
                                    child: const Text('Set Value')),
                                const SizedBox(
                                  width: 8,
                                ),
                                ElevatedButton(
                                    onPressed: () async {
                                      if (stringKeyTextController.
text.isNotEmpty) {
                                        final currentString = await
_moviePlugin
.getString(stringKeyTextController.text);
                                        if (currentString != null) {
                                          setState(() {
                                            currentStringValue =
currentString;
                                          });
                                        }
                                      }
                                    },
                                    child: const Text('Get Value')),
                                const SizedBox(
                                  width: 8,
                                ),
                                ElevatedButton(
                                    onPressed: () async {
                                      final currentString =
                                          await _moviePlugin.clear();
                                      if (currentString != null) {
```

```
                              setState(() {
                                currentStringValue = '';
                              });
                            }
                        },
                        child: const Text('Clear')),
                  ],
                ),
              ),
              const SizedBox(
                height: 16,
              ),
              Text('Current String Value is
$currentStringValue'),
              const SizedBox(
                height: 16,
              ),
```

7. Add the Int fields and text:

```
              TextField(
                decoration: const InputDecoration(
                  border: InputBorder.none,
                  hintText: 'Int Key',
                  // hintStyle: TextStyle(color: Colors.
black),
                ),
                textInputAction: TextInputAction.next,
                controller: intKeyTextController,
              ),
              const SizedBox(
                height: 16,
              ),
              TextField(
                decoration: const InputDecoration(
                  border: InputBorder.none,
                  hintText: 'Int Value',
                ),
                textInputAction: TextInputAction.done,
                keyboardType: TextInputType.number,
                inputFormatters: <TextInputFormatter>[
                  FilteringTextInputFormatter.digitsOnly,
```

```
                          ],

                          controller: intValueTextController,
                        ),
                        Padding(
                          padding: const EdgeInsets.all(8.0),
                          child: Row(
                            children: [
                              ElevatedButton(
                                  onPressed: () async {
                                      if (intKeyTextController.text.
isNotEmpty &&
                                            intValueTextController.text.
isNotEmpty) {
                                          await _moviePlugin.setInt(
                                              intKeyTextController.text,
                                              int.
parse(intValueTextController.text));
                                      }
                                  },
                                  child: const Text('Set Value')),
                              const SizedBox(
                                width: 8,
                              ),
                              ElevatedButton(
                                  onPressed: () async {
                                      if (intKeyTextController.text.
isNotEmpty) {
                                          final currentValue = await _
moviePlugin

.getInt(intKeyTextController.text);
                                          if (currentValue != null) {
                                            setState(() {
                                              currentIntValue =
'$currentValue';
                                            });
                                          }
                                      }
                                  },
                                  child: const Text('Get Value')),
```

```
                              const SizedBox(
                                width: 8,
                              ),
                              ElevatedButton(
                                  onPressed: () async {
                                    final currentString =
                                    await _moviePlugin.clear();
                                    if (currentString != null) {
                                      setState(() {
                                        currentIntValue = '';
                                      });
                                    }
                                  },
                                  child: const Text('Clear')),
                            ],
                          ),
                        ),
                        const SizedBox(
                          height: 16,
                        ),
                        Text('Current Int Value is
$currentIntValue'),
                        const SizedBox(
                          height: 16,
                        ),
```

8. Add the Boolean text fields:

```
                        TextField(
                          decoration: const InputDecoration(
                            border: InputBorder.none,
                            hintText: 'Bool Key',
                            // hintStyle: TextStyle(color: Colors.
black),
                          ),
                          textInputAction: TextInputAction.next,
                          controller: boolKeyTextController,
                        ),
                        const SizedBox(
                          height: 16,
                        ),
                        TextField(
```

```
                        decoration: const InputDecoration(
                          border: InputBorder.none,
                          hintText: 'Bool Value',
                        ),
                        textInputAction: TextInputAction.done,
                        controller: boolValueTextController,
                      ),
                      Padding(
                        padding: const EdgeInsets.all(8.0),
                        child: Row(
                          children: [
                            ElevatedButton(
                                onPressed: () async {
                                  if (boolKeyTextController.text.
isNotEmpty &&
                                      boolValueTextController.
text.isNotEmpty) {
                                    await _moviePlugin.setBool(
                                        boolKeyTextController.
text,
                                        boolValueTextController.
text == 'true');
                                  }
                                },
                                child: const Text('Set Value')),
                            const SizedBox(
                              width: 8,
                            ),
                            ElevatedButton(
                                onPressed: () async {
                                  if (boolKeyTextController.text.
isNotEmpty) {
                                    final currentBool = await _
moviePlugin
.getBool(boolKeyTextController.text);
                                    if (currentBool != null) {
                                      setState(() {
                                        currentBoolValue =
'$currentBool';
                                      });
```

```
                    }
                  }
                },
                child: const Text('Get Value')),
            const SizedBox(
              width: 8,
            ),
            ElevatedButton(
                onPressed: () async {
                  final currentBool =
                  await _moviePlugin.clear();
                  if (currentBool != null) {
                    setState(() {
                      currentBoolValue = '';
                    });
                  }
                },
                child: const Text('Clear')),
          ],
        ),
      ),
      const SizedBox(
        height: 16,
      ),
      Text('Current Bool Value is
$currentBoolValue'),
      const SizedBox(
        height: 16,
      ),
```

9. Add the double fields:

```
      TextField(
        decoration: const InputDecoration(
          border: InputBorder.none,
          hintText: 'Double Key',
          // hintStyle: TextStyle(color: Colors.
black),
        ),
        textInputAction: TextInputAction.next,
        controller: doubleKeyTextController,
      ),
```

```
                    const SizedBox(
                      height: 16,
                    ),
                    TextField(
                      decoration: const InputDecoration(
                        border: InputBorder.none,
                        hintText: 'Double Value',
                      ),
                      textInputAction: TextInputAction.done,
                      keyboardType: TextInputType.number,
                      inputFormatters: <TextInputFormatter>[
                        FilteringTextInputFormatter.
allow(RegExp(r'^\d+\.?\d{0,2}')),
                      ],

                      controller: doubleValueTextController,
                    ),
                    Padding(
                      padding: const EdgeInsets.all(8.0),
                      child: Row(
                        children: [
                          ElevatedButton(
                              onPressed: () async {
                                if (doubleKeyTextController.
text.isNotEmpty &&
                                        doubleValueTextController.
text.isNotEmpty) {
                                    await _moviePlugin.setDouble(
                                        doubleKeyTextController.
text,
                                        double.
parse(doubleValueTextController.text));
                                }
                              },
                              child: const Text('Set Value')),
                          const SizedBox(
                            width: 8,
                          ),
                          ElevatedButton(
                              onPressed: () async {
                                if (doubleKeyTextController.
```

```
text.isNotEmpty) {
                                final currentValue = await _
moviePlugin

  .getDouble(doubleKeyTextController.text);
                                if (currentValue != null) {
                                  setState(() {
                                    currentDoubleValue =
'$currentValue';

                                  });
                                }
                              }
                            },
                            child: const Text('Get Value')),
                        const SizedBox(
                          width: 8,
                        ),
                        ElevatedButton(
                            onPressed: () async {
                              final currentString =
                              await _moviePlugin.clear();
                              if (currentString != null) {
                                setState(() {
                                  currentDoubleValue = '';
                                });
                              }
                            },
                            child: const Text('Clear')),
                      ],
                    ),
                  ),
                  const SizedBox(
                    height: 16,
                  ),
                  Text('Current Double Value is
$currentDoubleValue'),
```

Now, run the example app on Android. Fill in the string key and value and press the **Set Value** button. After entering **MyStringKey** for the key and **MyStringValue** for the key, pressing the **Set Value** button and then the **Get Value** button, you should see the text field show the value:

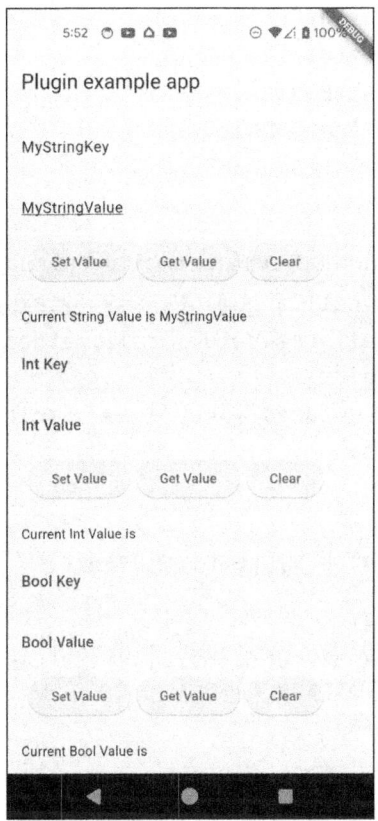

*Figure 17.6: Testing plugin*

Go ahead and test the other fields to make sure they work. If they do not, then you will need to debug or print logging statements to find out why.

# iOS plugin

Now that we know Android works, it is time to build out the iOS side. Luckily, this will entail just one file. In the plugin's **ios/Classes** folder, open up **MoviePlugin.swift**. This is the swift file for our plugin. We will be writing almost the same code as in Android's Kotlin but using Swift. The steps are as follows:

1. Add the **MethodCalls** enum above the class:

```
enum MethodCalls: String {
    case getString = "getString"
    case setString = "setString"
    case clear = "clear"
    case containsKey = "containsKey"
    case getInt = "getInt"
```

```
    case setInt = "setInt"
    case getBool = "getBool"
    case setBool = "setBool"
    case getDouble = "getDouble"
    case setDouble = "setDouble"
}
```

2.  Inside of the handle method, replace the current code with:

```
    let args = call.arguments as? [String: Any]
switch MethodCalls(rawValue: call.method) {
case .getString:
  guard let key = args?["key"] as? String else {
    result(false)
    return
  }
  getString(key: key, result: result)

case .setString:
  guard let key = args?["key"] as? String, let value =
args?["value"] as? String else {
    result(false)
    return
  }
  setString(key: key, value: value, result: result)

case .clear:
  clear()
  result(true)

case .containsKey:
  guard let key = args?["key"] as? String else {
    result(false)
    break
  }
  containsKey(key: key, result: result)

case .getInt:
  guard let key = args?["key"] as? String else {
    result(false)
    return
  }
  getInt(key: key, result: result)
```

```
    case .setInt:
      guard let key = args?["key"] as? String, let value =
args?["value"] as? Int else {
        result(false)
        return
      }
      setInt(key: key, value: value, result: result)

    case .getBool:
      guard let key = args?["key"] as? String else {
        result(false)
        return
      }
      getBool(key: key, result: result)

    case .setBool:
      guard let key = args?["key"] as? String, let value =
args?["value"] as? Bool else {
        result(false)
        return
      }
      setBool(key: key, value: value, result: result)

    case .getDouble:
      guard let key = args?["key"] as? String else {
        result(false)
        return
      }
      getDouble(key: key, result: result)

    case .setDouble:
      guard let key = args?["key"] as? String, let value =
args?["value"] as? Double else {
        result(false)
        return
      }
      setDouble(key: key, value: value, result: result)

    default:
      result(FlutterMethodNotImplemented)
    }
```

While this code looks a bit different, it is very similar to Android. The only differences are the switch statement and the **guard/let** commands that are common in Swift. The **guard/let** is a way to set a variable, and if the condition is false, return false.

3.  Add the string methods:

```swift
func getString(key: String, result: @escaping FlutterResult) {
  let defaults = UserDefaults.standard
  result(defaults.string(forKey: key))
}

func setString(key: String, value: String, result: @escaping
FlutterResult) {
  let defaults = UserDefaults.standard
  defaults.set(value, forKey: key)
  result(true)
}
```

This uses the **UserDefaults** class for iOS, which can store and retrieve simple values, just like Android's **SharedPreferences**.

4.  Add the clear and **containsKey** methods:

```swift
func clear() {
  let defaults = UserDefaults.standard
  if let appDomain = Bundle.main.bundleIdentifier,
    let prefs = defaults.persistentDomain(forName: appDomain)
  {
    for (key, _) in prefs {
      defaults.removeObject(forKey: key)
    }
  }
}

func containsKey(key: String, result: @escaping FlutterResult) {
  let defaults = UserDefaults.standard
  let value = defaults.object(forKey: key)
  result(value != nil)
}
```

5.  Add the int methods:

```swift
func getInt(key: String, result: @escaping FlutterResult) {
  let defaults = UserDefaults.standard
  result(defaults.integer(forKey: key))
}
```

```
    func setInt(key: String, value: Int, result: @escaping
FlutterResult) {
        let defaults = UserDefaults.standard
        defaults.set(value, forKey: key)
        result(true)
    }
```

6. Add the bool methods:

```
    func getBool(key: String, result: @escaping FlutterResult) {
      let defaults = UserDefaults.standard
      result(defaults.bool(forKey: key))
    } .

    func setBool(key: String, value: Bool, result: @escaping
FlutterResult) {
        let defaults = UserDefaults.standard
        defaults.set(value, forKey: key)
        result(true)
    }
```

7. Add the double methods:

```
    func getDouble(key: String, result: @escaping FlutterResult) {
      let defaults = UserDefaults.standard
      result(defaults.double(forKey: key))
    }

    func setDouble(key: String, value: Double, result: @escaping
FlutterResult) {
        let defaults = UserDefaults.standard
        defaults.set(value, forKey: key)
        result(true)
    }
```

Now, run the example app on an iPhone or iOS simulator. You should see the same screen, and the results should be the same. If you get any compile errors, check to make sure you entered the code correctly.

# Movies app

That takes care of the Android and iOS plugin package.

1. Return to the movies package and open the **pubspec.yaml** file.

2. Add the following after the **movie_data**:

```
movie_plugin:
    path: ../movie_plugin
```

This will add the **movie_plugin** plugin.

3. Do a Pub Get.

4. Open **providers.dart**. Replace the prefs entry and add one for the **movie_plugin**:

```
@Riverpod(keepAlive: true)
Prefs prefs(PrefsRef ref) {
    return Prefs(ref.read(moviePluginProvider));
}

@Riverpod(keepAlive: true)
MoviePlugin moviePlugin(MoviePluginRef ref) {
    return MoviePlugin();
}
```

This replaces **SharedPreferences** with our movie plugin.

5. In a terminal run:

**dart run build_runner build**

6. Open up the **prefs.dart** file in the **utils** directory.

7. Replace the preferences variable with:

```
final MoviePlugin preferences;
```

8. Remove the **SharedPreference** import and add the **MoviePlugin** import.

9. Change all of the methods to:

```
Future setString(String key, String value) async {
    preferences.setString(key, value);
}

Future<String?> getString(String key) async {
    return await preferences.getString(key);
}

Future setInt(String key, int value) async {
    preferences.setInt(key, value);
}

Future<int?> getInt(String key) async {
    return preferences.getInt(key);
```

```
}

Future setBool(String key, bool value) async {
  preferences.setBool(key, value);
}

Future<bool?> getBool(String key) async {
  return preferences.getBool(key);
}

Future setDouble(String key, double value) async {
  preferences.setDouble(key, value);
}

Future<double?> getDouble(String key) async {
  return preferences.getDouble(key);
}
```

The only difference is that these return a **Future** of the value. If you look at the files that have errors, the only one left is the **genre_screen.dart**. Since our version of **prefs** returns futures, we need to change the code a bit to wait for the values.

10. Open **genre_screen.dart**. Go to the **saveSelectedGenres** method. Replace the contents with:

```
final prefs = ref.read(prefsProvider);
final genreNameList = genreStates.map((state) => state.genre.name).toList();
await prefs.setString(genreStringKey, genreNameList.join(','));
```

11. Replace the first two lines of the **getSelectedGenres** method:

```
final prefs = ref.read(prefsProvider);
var genreNameList = (await prefs.getString(genreStringKey))?.split(',');
```

Try running the Movies app on both Android and iOS. Go to the Genre screen and select a few genres. If you stop and restart your app, it should remember the genres you selected.

That was a lot of work, but you created your very own plugin that is very similar to one on **pub.dev**. Now you know how to build your own, so that any time you come across any missing functionality in Flutter that is implemented on the native side, you will be able to build your own. You can also use what you learned in the last chapter to publish this plugin just like you would a package.

# Conclusion

In this chapter, you learned about plugins and how to build them. You learned that you need to write native code for each platform you support. While a lot more difficult than writing straight Flutter Dart code, it is very satisfying to create a plugin that implements native code. If your plugin is useful, publish it on **pub.dev** and share it with others. Who knows, you could become a famous plugin developer.

In the next chapter, we will implement tests for our plugin as well as tests for the movie app. This will help us be assured that our plugin and app function the way they should, and if anything breaks in your code, your tests should let you know before it is too late.

## Join our book's Discord space

Join the book's Discord Workspace for Latest updates, Offers, Tech happenings around the world, New Release and Sessions with the Authors:

**https://discord.bpbonline.com**

# CHAPTER 18
# Testing and Performance

## Introduction

Flutter is a very fast framework, and normally, you will not need to worry about performance. However, there are times when parts of your app may show performance problems. In addition, testing your app will ensure that it performs the way you expect and is as fast as you need it to. In this chapter, you will learn about the different types of testing, how to write tests for your app or plugin, how to write UI tests, and how to view performance information. With this information, you can make sure new code does not break existing functionality by monitoring tests and making sure they do not break. You will also be able to find areas in your app that are slowing down parts of your app. Flutter includes a lot of tools for writing tests and measuring your app's performance.

## Structure

The chapter covers the following topics:

- Testing
- Unit testing
- Widget testing
- Integration
- Performance

# Objectives

By the end of this chapter, you will know about the three different types of testing and how to write those tests. You will know when to write unit tests when to write widget tests, and when to write integration tests. Finally, you will understand how to use Flutter's DevTools to measure performance.

# Testing

Testing is a way to make sure your app functions properly and, more importantly, that it will catch changes in your code that break how your app works. Testing helps identify bugs in your code and can even be used in the creation of code. In **test-driven development (TDD)**, you write your tests first before you write your code. While we will not be using this in this chapter, it is a popular way to write code because you have several advantages:

- **Improved code quality**: Testing improves the code you write because it has to be testable.

- **Higher test coverage**: By writing tests first, you ensure you have more tests covering all parts of your app.

- **Higher confidence**: More tests make you more confident that your code will work the way you expect.

The way testing works is:

- **Write a failing test**: Write the test that tests what you want your class to achieve. You will have to write the bare minimum for the class, but with no functionality, it will fail.

- **Fix the failing test**: Write code that causes the test to pass.

- **Refactor**: Clean up the code.

- **Repeat**

In Flutter (and other platforms), there are three different types of tests:

- **Unit tests**: Test a single class or method. This will be for testing how a function or class works.

- **Widget tests**: Test a single Flutter widget. This test will ensure the widget performs properly in multiple states. For example, a switch shows that it is on when that state is set and off when the state has been turned off.

- **Integration tests**: Tests parts of an app and the integration of multiple screens. This could be a sign-in screen with dialogs and other screens associated with the sign-in functionality.

One nice feature of tests is that there are mocking libraries that allow you to mock functionality. For example, say you have an API for logging into a system. You may not want to have to log a user in to run a test. By using a mocking library, you can mock the API, and have it return login information or just return that the user is logged in.

# Unit testing

Unit tests are usually the easiest to write. They are usually just Dart code and not Flutter. They will test to make sure the function returns the correct value for the different input values. These are usually pretty easy to maintain, but they only test a very small part of your app and only give you confidence in that one function. Unit tests do not test UI but functionality. You could use it to test a view model or classes that perform calculations. All unit tests go in the **test** folder.

Each test file in the **test** folder will need to import the **test** package:

```
import 'package:test/test.dart';
```

Each test will have a main function. Inside that function, you will usually use the **test** method that takes the name of the test and a function. This looks like:

```
testWidgets('<name of test>', (WidgetTester tester) async {

}
```

The testing package contains functions that will test the values of your tests. This is the **expect** function. This takes the actual value, a matcher, and a reason string that will be printed if it fails. This looks like:

```
Expect(<actual result>, <what we should get>, 'optional reason why it failed')
```

This is how you make sure your test is producing the correct result. If this fails, the whole test fails. If you perform a computation and that function should always return the same value given a certain input, then if that function changes, your test will fail, and you will either have to fix your function or change the test to reflect the change.

# Movie plugin unit test

We will be writing a unit test to test the functionality of the methods of the **MoviePlugin**. While we are not running on an actual device, we need to mock the underlying storage. Mocking is a way to create *fake* classes that either do nothing or return values that we want them to. This way, we can test the actual class without worrying about the other classes it uses. For the **MoviePlugin** class, we need to mock the prefs portion of the plugin. Let us create the movie plugin test:

1. Open the **movie_plugin** project.
2. Add the test dependency. In a terminal type:

    ```
    flutter pub add dev:test
    ```

3. In the **test** folder, create a new file named **movie_plugin_test.dart**.

4. Add the following imports:
```
import 'package:test/test.dart';
import 'package:movie_plugin/movie_plugin.dart';
import 'package:movie_plugin/movie_plugin_platform_interface.dart';
import 'package:plugin_platform_interface/plugin_platform_interface.
dart';
```

5. Create the **MockMoviePluginPlatform** class:
```
class MockMoviePluginPlatform
    with MockPlatformInterfaceMixin
    implements MoviePluginPlatform {
  // Add Code Here
}
```

Note that **MockPlatformInterfaceMixin** is part of Flutter's plugin platform interface.

6. Create a map to store the preferences:
```
Map<String, dynamic> mockPrefs = <String, dynamic>{};
```

7. Start implementing the methods of the **MoviePluginPlatform**:
```
@override
Future clear() {
  mockPrefs.clear();
  return Future.value(true);
}

@override
Future<bool?> containsKey(String key) {
  return Future.value(mockPrefs.containsKey(key));
}
```

These two methods will clear the map and return the value of the **containsKey** method of the map.

8. Add the string methods:
```
@override
Future<String?> getString(String key) {
  return Future.value(mockPrefs[key]);
}

@override
Future setString(String key, String value) {
```

```
    mockPrefs[key] = value;
    return Future.value(true);
  }
```

9. Add the int methods:

```
  Future<int?> getInt(String key) async {
    return Future.value(mockPrefs[key]);
  }

  @override
  Future setInt(String key, int value) async {
    mockPrefs[key] = value;
    return Future.value(true);
  }
```

These just use the map to set and retrieve values.

10. Add the Boolean methods:

```
  @override
  Future<bool?> getBool(String key) async {
    return Future.value(mockPrefs[key]);
  }

  @override
  Future setBool(String key, bool value) async {
    mockPrefs[key] = value;
    return Future.value(true);
  }
```

11. Add the double methods:

```
  @override
  Future<double?> getDouble(String key) async {
    return Future.value(mockPrefs[key]);
  }

  @override
  Future setDouble(String key, double value) async {
    mockPrefs[key] = value;
    return Future.value(true);
  }
```

Now that we have the mock class written, let us start writing the tests.

12. Add a main function after the **MockMoviePluginPlatform** class:

```
void main() {
}
```

13. Add the first test for the **setString** method:

```
test('setString: Add One item', () async {
  MoviePlugin moviePlugin = MoviePlugin();
  MockMoviePluginPlatform fakePlatform = MockMoviePluginPlatform();
  MoviePluginPlatform.instance = fakePlatform;

  expect(await moviePlugin.setString('Test', 'Value 1'), true);
});
```

This test creates the **MoviePlugin** class and sets the **MoviePluginPlatform.instance** to our mock platform. We then call the **setString** method and make sure it returns true. This is just a very simple test to make sure we get the expected value back. You will usually want to build your tests up from simple to more complex and make sure you test all conditions that could happen. In writing tests, you will find yourself thinking about different scenarios that could happen with your code. This will help you in writing your code and you may find a test that your code does not cover.

# Groups

You can also combine your tests into groups. You would use the group just like the test method by giving it a name and then the function. That function will have multiple test functions. It would look something as follows:

```
group('Test All String methods', () {
  test('setString: Add One item', () {
    <Code here>
  });

  test('setString: Add One item and then clear', () {
    <Code here>
  });

  test('setString: Add One item and then get the string', () {
    <Code here>
  });
});
```

1. Click on the green **Run** button to run the test. You should see:

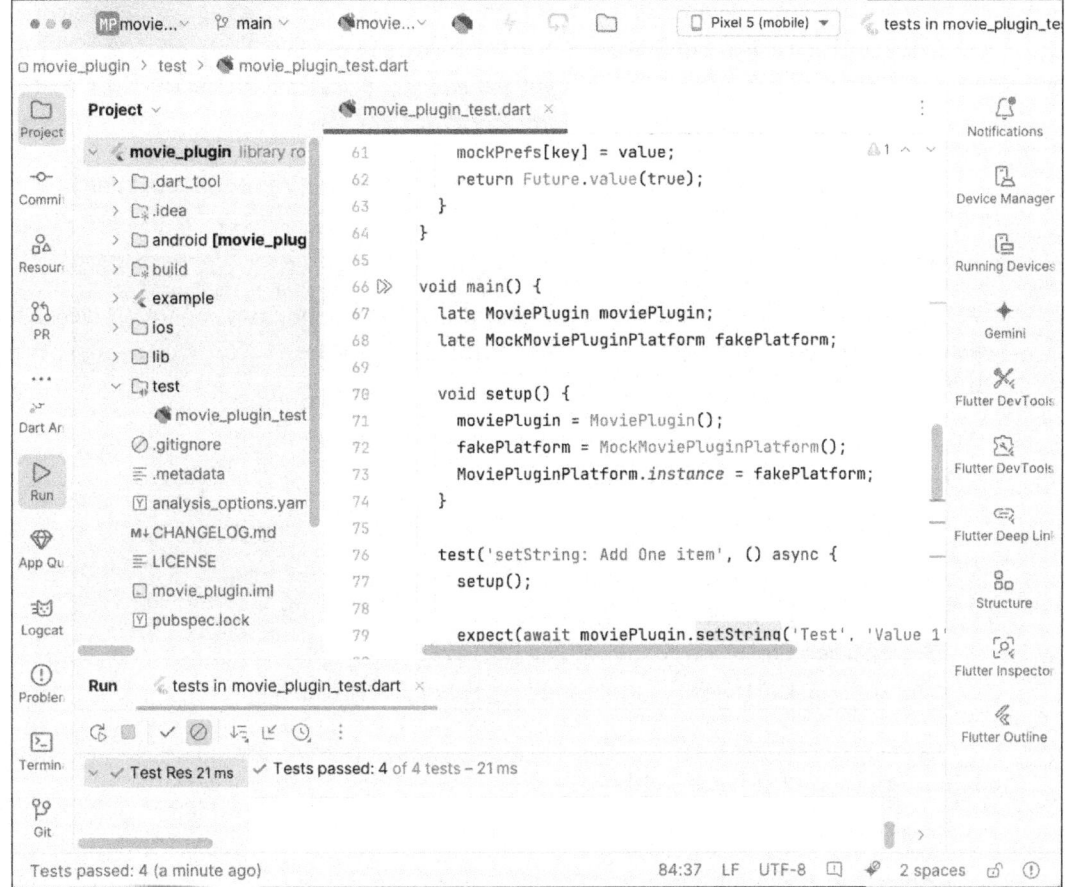

*Figure 18.1*: First test

2.  Add the next test for the clear and **containsKey** functions:

```
test('setString: Add One item and then clear', () async {
  MoviePlugin moviePlugin = MoviePlugin();
  MockMoviePluginPlatform fakePlatform = MockMoviePluginPlatform();
  MoviePluginPlatform.instance = fakePlatform;

  expect(await moviePlugin.setString('Test', 'Value 1'), true);
  expect(await moviePlugin.clear(), true);
  expect(await moviePlugin.containsKey('Test'), false);
});
```

Here, we set the string, clear it, and then make sure that it does not still exist. Try running these tests. What other tests can you think of?

3.  Next, test setting the value and verifying that the value exists:

```
test('setString: Add One item and then get the string', () async {
  MoviePlugin moviePlugin = MoviePlugin();
  MockMoviePluginPlatform fakePlatform = MockMoviePluginPlatform();
  MoviePluginPlatform.instance = fakePlatform;

  expect(await moviePlugin.setString('Test', 'Value 1'), true);
  expect(await moviePlugin.getString('Test'), 'Value 1');
});
```

We have tested some strings, but we should test the other types as well. We will test ints. We are starting to see some duplicate code here. You can create other methods for setup.

4.  Add some variables and create a new method just under main:

```
late MoviePlugin moviePlugin;
late MockMoviePluginPlatform fakePlatform;

void setup() {
  moviePlugin = MoviePlugin();
  fakePlatform = MockMoviePluginPlatform();
  MoviePluginPlatform.instance = fakePlatform;
}
```

5.  Now replace all this code with:

```
setup();
```

Your first test will look like:

```
test('setString: Add One item', () async {
  setup();

  expect(await moviePlugin.setString('Test', 'Value 1'), true);
});
```

6.  Write the int test:

```
test('Test Ints', () async {
  setup();

  expect(await moviePlugin.setInt('IntKey', 1), true);
  expect(await moviePlugin.getInt('IntKey'), 1);
  expect(await moviePlugin.containsKey('IntKey'), true);
  expect(await moviePlugin.clear(), true);
  expect(await moviePlugin.containsKey('IntKey'), false);
});
```

The other tests are left as an exercise for you.

# Widget testing

As the name implies, widget testing involves testing just one widget at a time. These tests are still in the test folder and run in memory on the development machine and not on a real device. This makes these tests very fast. Luckily, there is the **flutter_test** package provided by Flutter. This package provides the **WidgetTester** class and the **testWidgets** function, which provides a **WidgetTester** for each test. It also provides Finder classes for searching for widgets. Then, you will use **Matcher** constants to verify the widget. You will need to import the **flutter_test** package. You should already have it in **pubspec.yaml**, but it will be in the **dev_dependencies** section and look as follows:

```
dev_dependencies:
  flutter_test:
    sdk: flutter
```

With the **WidgetTester** class, there are a few important methods. For testing widgets, the **pumpWidget** method will display your widget. There is also a **pumpAndSettle** method that will wait for all animations to finish, and there are no more frames to display. Once you have your widget displayed, you need to find it and test it to make sure it is displayed the way you expect. Flutter provides the **Finder** class that has many methods for finding widgets. A few important methods:

- **text**: Find a **Text**, **EditableText**, or **RichText** widget with the given text.
- **textContaining**: Find the **Pattern** of text in the above widgets.
- **widgetWithText**: Look for descendants that are of type **Text** with the given text string.
- **image**: Find an image.
- **byKey**: Find a widget with the given key.
- **bySubtype**: Find a widget by sub-type, that is, **StatefulWidget** will find all classes that subclass it.
- **byType**: Find widgets of a certain type.
- **byIcon, widgetWithIcon**: Finds a widget containing an icon.
- **byTooltip**: finds widgets with the given tooltip text.

There are also several methods that let you search through all widgets and make a decision on each widget. One of the most important methods is the **byWidgetPredicate**. Here is a helper method you can use:

```
Finder findWidgetOfType(Type type) {
  final finder = find.byWidgetPredicate((widget) {
    if (widget.runtimeType == type) {
      return true;
    }
  }
```

```
    return false;
  });
  return finder;
}
```

The callback receives a widget, and it checks to see if the **runtimeType** is of a given type. There are many ways can create helper functions to search for widgets of your making.

Once you find the widget you are looking for, you will use the **expect** method with the following matcher types:

- **findsOneWidget**: Asserts that there is only one widget found.

- **findsNothing**: Asserts that no widget was found.

- **findsWidgets**: Asserts that at least one widget was found.

# First widget test

Since we have several widgets that we have built over time, they are great candidates for testing. To start creating a widget test, the steps are as follows:

1. Open up the **movies** project.

2. In the **test** folder, create a new file named **widget_tests.dart**.

3. Add the following imports and the **main** function:

```
import 'package:flutter/material.dart';
import 'package:flutter_test/flutter_test.dart';
import 'package:movies/ui/widgets/text_icon.dart';

void main() {
}
```

4. Add the first test for testing the **TextIcon** widget:

```
testWidgets('Test TextIcon', (WidgetTester tester) async {
  await tester.pumpWidget(TextIcon(
    text: const Text('Test'),
    icon: IconButton(
        onPressed: () {},
        icon: const Icon(
          Icons.favorite_outlined,
          size: 24,
        )),
  ));
  final textFinder = find.text('Test');
  expect(textFinder, findsOneWidget);
});
```

5. Try running the test. You should see an error. In the case of the **TextIcon** widget, the **IconButton** requires the **MaterialApp** or **WidgetsApp** to be the parent. Modify the **pumpWidget**:

```
await tester.pumpWidget(MaterialApp(home: TextIcon(
  text: const Text('Test'),
  icon: IconButton(
    onPressed: () {},
    icon: const Icon(
      Icons.favorite_outlined,
      size: 24,
    )),
  )));
```

6. Now, try running, and your test will pass.

Another simple test is to add a search for the icon.

7. After the expected, add the following:

```
final iconFinder = find.byIcon(Icons.favorite_outlined);
expect(iconFinder, findsOneWidget);
```

8. Run the test again.

The next test will be a bit more complex. We want to test the **ButtonRow** widget. To do that, we need to display the widget and tap on the favorite icon. Create a new test in the same file:

9. Add the new test:

```
testWidgets('Test ButtonRow', (WidgetTester tester) async {
  await tester.pumpWidget(MaterialApp(home:
ButtonRow(favoriteSelected: true, onFavoriteSelected: () {

  },
 });
```

This test is for the **ButtonRow** widget that we want to test by pressing the favorite button. We do not need to handle the favorite callback.

10. Next, find the Favorite button and make sure it exists:

```
final textFinder = find.text('Favorite');
expect(textFinder, findsOneWidget);
```

11. Now find the **TextIcon** by finding the **anscestor** of the **Text** widget and then the icon button by finding the **descendant** of that widget:

```
final textIconFinder = find.ancestor(of: textFinder, matching:
find.byType(TextIcon));
```

```
final iconButton = find.descendant(of: textIconFinder, matching:
find.byType(IconButton));
    expect(iconButton, findsOneWidget);
```

12. Now find the Icon under that and make sure it is white:

```
    var iconFinder = find.descendant(of: iconButton, matching: find.
byType(Icon));
    var icon = tester.widget(iconFinder);
    expect((icon as Icon).color, Colors.white);
```

The **tester.widget** method is useful for getting the actual widget. This way we can test the color of the widget.

13. Now tap the button, wait for the animation to finish, and make sure the icon is red.

```
    await tester.tap(iconButton);
    await tester.pump(const Duration(seconds: 3));
    await tester.idle();
    iconFinder = find.descendant(of: iconButton, matching: find.
byType(Icon));
    icon = tester.widget(iconFinder);
    expect(icon.color, Colors.red);
```

14. Run the test to make sure it passes.

These are two examples of testing a widget. As you may have noticed, you will not see the test on your device. To do that, we will move on to integration testing.

# Integration testing

So far, we have just tested the code and individual widgets. To test your app, you need to run integration tests. This runs your app on a device and allows you to interact with the screen as well as navigate to other screens. Usually, you will test the functionality of a specific area. For example, you could test a sign-in page. You would have a test user that you can use to sign in and verify that the user successfully signed in. You could also test entering invalid data and see how the UI responds.

> **Note: If you read articles about navigating flutter_driver, that is an older technology and should not be used.**

One area that would be good to test is movie loading and scrolling. The **MovieListing** class does some complex paging. What if we could run a test that navigates to the **MovieListing** page and scrolls several pages' worth of data? To do this, we will create an integration test that sets up the app, similar to the way it does in **main.dart,** and then run a **testWidgets** function. We will then start the **MainApp**, click on the first **More** button, go to the **MovieListing** screen, and then scroll several pages and verify that the page list contains a certain amount of items. This is a bit complex, so we will step through each part:

1.  Create a new folder at the top level named **integration_test**.

2.  Create a new file named **movie_tests.dart**.

3.  Add the following imports:
    ```
    import 'package:colorize_lumberdash/colorize_lumberdash.dart';
    import 'package:firebase_core/firebase_core.dart';
    import 'package:flutter/material.dart';
    import 'package:flutter_dotenv/flutter_dotenv.dart';
    import 'package:flutter_riverpod/flutter_riverpod.dart';
    import 'package:flutter_test/flutter_test.dart';
    import 'package:infinite_scroll_pagination/infinite_scroll_pagination.dart';
    import 'package:lumberdash/lumberdash.dart';
    import 'package:movie_data/movie_data.dart';
    import 'package:movies/firebase_options.dart';
    import 'package:movies/main.dart';
    import 'package:movies/ui/screens/home/title_row.dart';
    import 'package:movies/ui/widgets/movie_row.dart';
    import 'package:movies/utils/utils.dart';
    ```

    These will be the imports needed for the test.

4.  Add the **main** function and the initialization (this looks just like the main, except we are not using Crashlytics). Add the **main** function:
    ```
    void main() async {
      final binding = IntegrationTestWidgetsFlutterBinding.
    ensureInitialized();
      binding.framePolicy = LiveTestWidgetsFlutterBindingFramePolicy.
    fullyLive;
      WidgetsFlutterBinding.ensureInitialized();
      putLumberdashToWork(withClients: [
        ColorizeLumberdash(),
      ]);
      await Firebase.initializeApp(
        options: DefaultFirebaseOptions.currentPlatform,
      );
      if (!isWeb()) {
        await dotenv.load(fileName: '.env');
      }
    // TODO Add Test
    }
    ```

This is the same code as in the main except for the first two lines.

5. Replace the TODO with the test:

```
testWidgets('Test scrolling the Movie Listing', (tester) async {
  // Build our app and trigger a frame.
  await tester.pumpWidget(const ProviderScope(child: MainApp()));
});
```

6. After the **pumpWidget**, add code to find the more button:

```
await tester.pumpAndSettle(const Duration(seconds: 1));
final moreButtonFinder = find.byType(TitleRow);
expect(moreButtonFinder, findsAtLeast(1));
```

This waits for the app to load, finds the **TitleRow**, and asserts that at least one was found.

7. Add the code to find the first **More** button and tap on it:

```
final firstMoreButton = moreButtonFinder.first;
final textButtonFinder = find.descendant(of: firstMoreButton,
matching: find.byType(TextButton));
await tester.tap(textButtonFinder);
await tester.pumpAndSettle(const Duration(seconds: 1));
```

This finds the first More button (there are several) and then finds the **TextButton** inside of it. It then taps on that button.

8. Open **movie_listing.dart** and add a scrolling controller. This is needed for our test. After the **_pagingController**, add the following:

```
final _scrollController = ScrollController();
```

9. Below the **pagingController** in the **PagedListView**, add the following:

```
scrollController: _scrollController,
```

10. Back in **movie_tests**, find the Movie Listing (a **PagedListView**) and get the paging and scrolling controllers:

```
final movieListFinder = find.byType(PagedListView<int,
MovieResults>);
expect(movieListFinder, findsOneWidget);
final movieList = tester.widget(movieListFinder);
final pagingController = (movieList as PagedListView).
pagingController;
final controller = movieList.controller;
```

11. Next, get the first **MovieRow** and figure out its height and then what a page of **MovieRows** heights are:

```
    final renderRow = tester.renderObject(find.byType(MovieRow).first)
  as RenderBox;
    final rowHeight = renderRow.size.height;
    final pageHeight = rowHeight * 20; // 20 items/page
    var currentPosition = pageHeight;
```

12. Scroll five times, and then make sure we have 120 items. (6x20)

```
    for (var i = 0; i < 5; i++) {
      controller?.jumpTo(
        currentPosition,
      );
      currentPosition += pageHeight;
      await tester.pumpAndSettle(const Duration(milliseconds: 500));
    }
    await tester.pumpAndSettle(const Duration(seconds: 1));
    expect(pagingController.itemList?.length, 120);
```

This uses the paging controllers **itemList** to check how many items have been loaded.

13. Run the test and make sure it works.

Note: You may need to do flutter clean and flutter pub get commands to get the tests to work.

# Performance

Now that you have your app written, it is time to think about performance. How does it perform starting up? How much time does it take to transition to other pages? Are certain actions taking too long? If your app is on the market, are customers complaining about something taking too long? Flutter itself is fast, drawing at 60 frames per second, but there are a number of ways you can accidentally slow that down. Slow loading times, unresponsiveness, and increased battery consumption will cause users to abandon your app.

# Widget tree

You can slow your screen down by having overly complex widget trees (the set of widgets that make up your screen). You can also slow it down by not breaking your screen into individual widgets. In other words, instead of one long build method, breaking sections into their own widget class. This causes Flutter to optimize drawing and not redraw widgets that do not need to be drawn. If you have one long build method and you call **setState**, the whole tree will need to be redrawn. Using large images can also slow things down as well. Using stateless widgets is faster as well. Try and use them if you do not have any state. Also, do not do any background tasks in the UI. Minimize the use of clipping as that can affect rendering performance. Make sure you follow the recommended lint warnings and make as many widgets constant as possible.

# DevTools

One of the best tools for measuring performance is Flutter's DevTools. It provides the following tools:

- **Performance view**: Timing and performance information.
- **CPU profiler**: Record and profile a session.
- **Memory profiler**: Analyze memory usage.
- **Debugger**: Set breakpoints, check the console, and call stack.
- **Network**: View network calls. Shows methods and duration.
- **Logging**: Shows logging information.
- **App size**: Analyze app snapshots.

You can access these tools from the right side of Android Studio, as shown in the following figure:

*Figure 18.2*: Tools

This is a suite of developer tools as shown in the following figure:

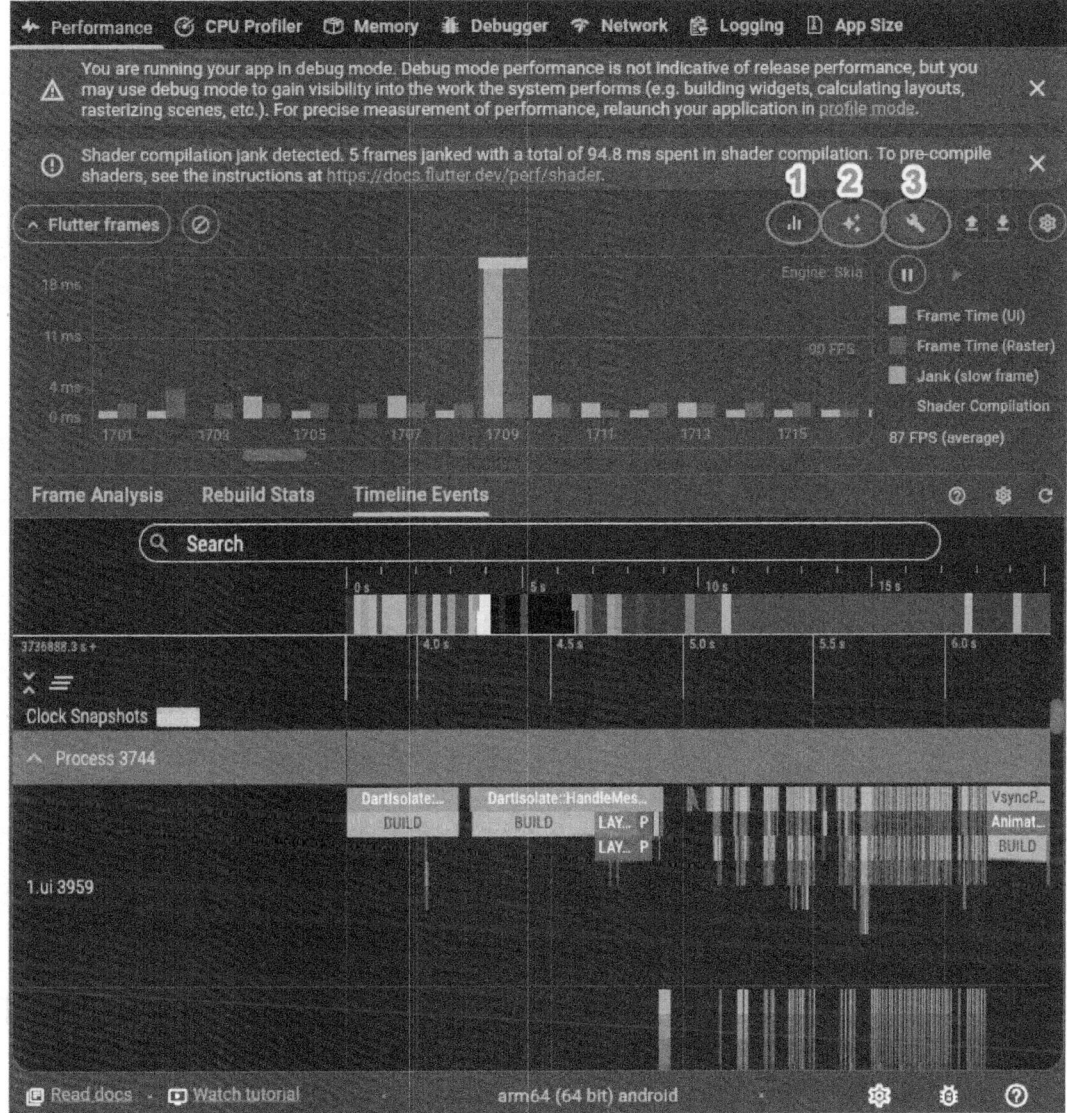

*Figure 18.3: Performance tools*

This is the **Performance** tab. There are many things you can do on this page. Pressing button number, one overlays the performance graph on the app. Pressing number two brings up another dialog for adding more options:

These options can be used to add more detail to the timeline, but be aware that **frame times may be negatively affected.**

When toggling on/off a tracing option, you will need to reproduce activity in your app to see the enhanced tracing in the timeline.

☐ **Track widget builds** · Adds an event to the timeline for every Widget built.                          More info ☑

     ○ within your code      ○ within all code

☐ **Track layouts** · Adds an event to the timeline for every RenderObject layout.                          More info ☑

☐ **Track paints** · Adds an event to the timeline for every RenderObject painted.                          More info ☑

                  Adds an event to the timeline for platform channel
☐ **Track platform channels** · messages (useful for apps with plugins). Also periodically     More info ☑
                       prints platform channel statistics to console.

*Figure 18.4: Performance options*

Pressing number three opens up options for rendering:

After toggling a rendering layer on/off, reproduce the activity in your app to see the effects. All layers are rendered by default - disabling a layer might help identify expensive operations in your app.

☑ Render Clip layers · Render all clipping effects during paint.                          More info ☑

☑ Render Opacity layers · Render all opacity effects during paint.                          More info ☑

☑ Render Physical Shape layers · Render all physical modeling effects during paint.                          More info ☑

☐ Track widget build counts · Tracks widget build counts for each Flutter frame.

*Figure 18.5: Rendering options*

The next tab is the **CPU Profiler**:

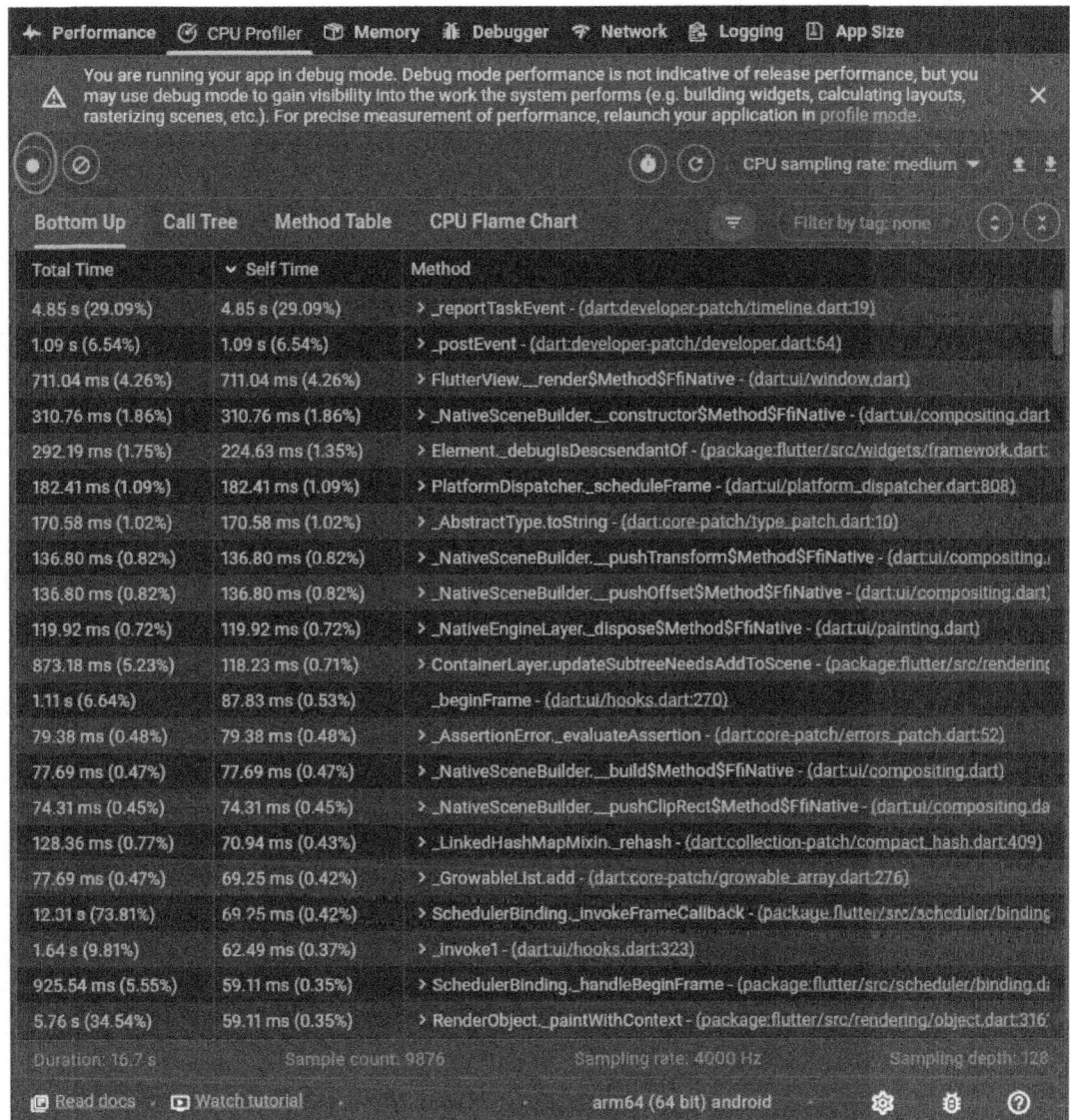

*Figure 18.6*: CPU Profiler

Pressing the circled button will start recording. Once you press the button again, it will show you details. This will show you the time and percentage each task took. Most of these will be Flutter The next tab shows the memory usage of all the classes. You can sort and filter to see how much memory your classes are taking. As you can see here, images will usually take up most of your memory. The CPU flame chart is a nice way to see:

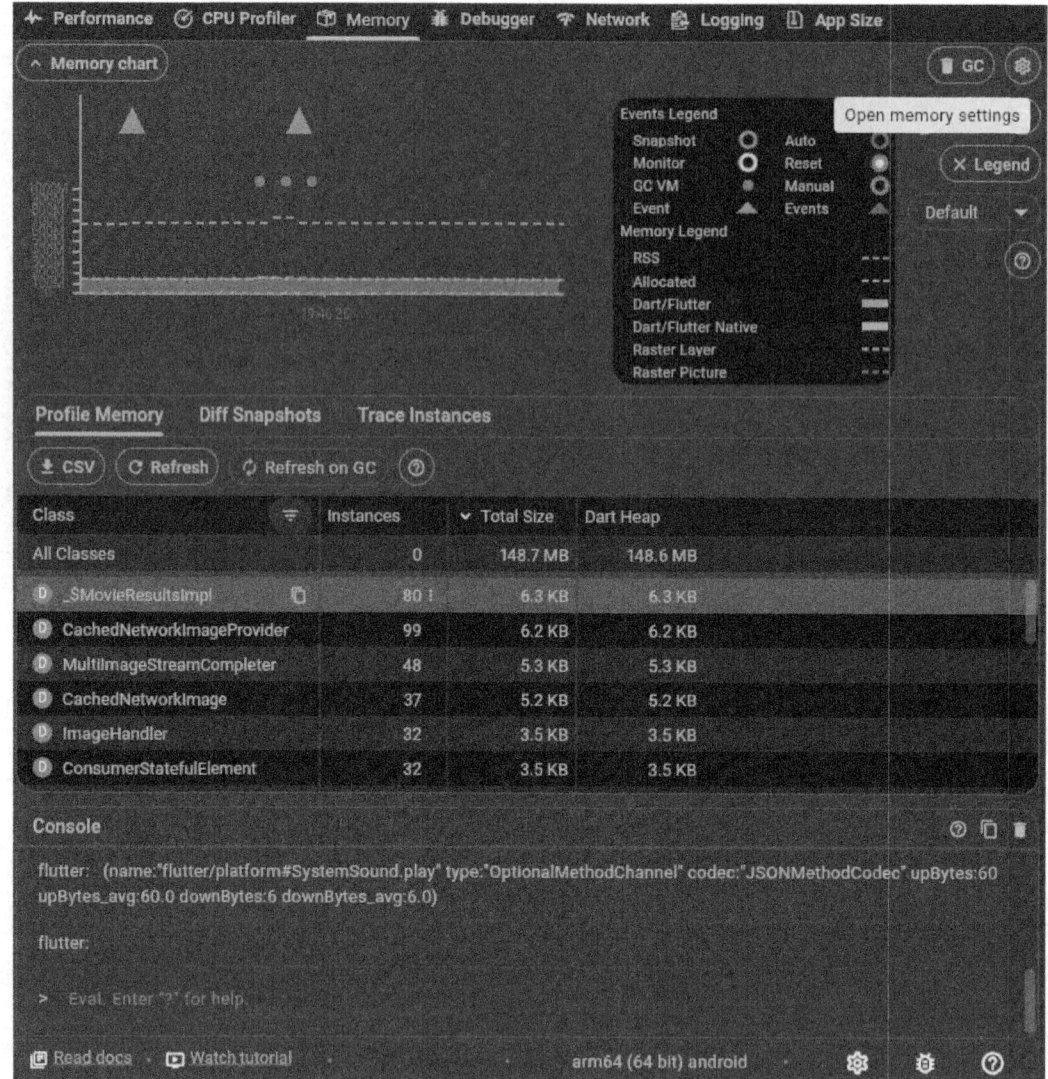

*Figure 18.7*: Memory

Skipping the **Debugger** tab, we next have the **Network** tab. This shows all of the API calls you make as well as calls to retrieve images and videos.

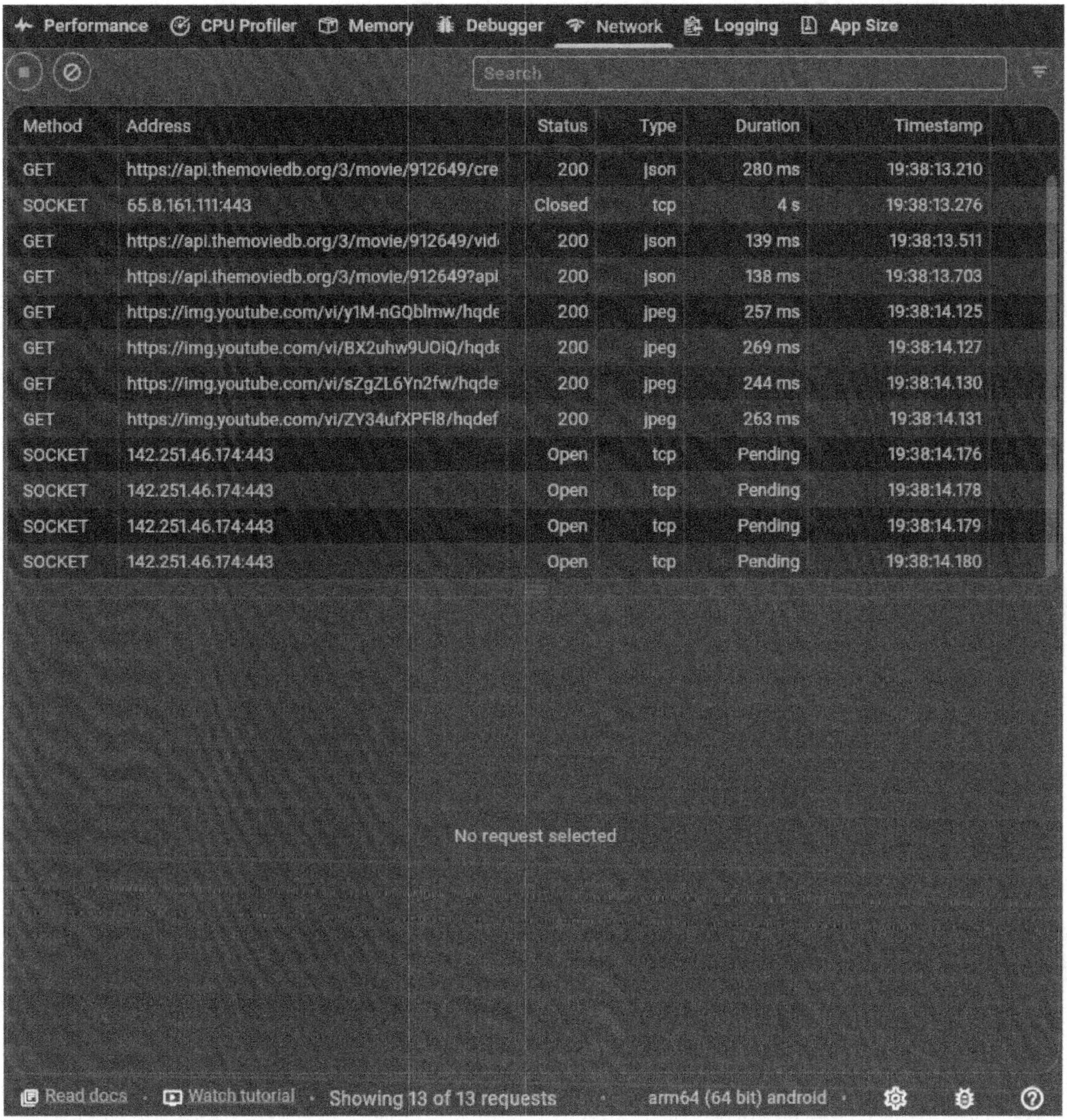
Performance
CPU Profiler
Memory
Debugger
Network
Logging
App Size
Search
Method
Address
Status
Type
Duration
Timestamp
GET https://api.themoviedb.org/3/movie/912649/cre 200 json 280 ms 19:38:13.210
SOCKET 65.8.161.111:443 Closed tcp 4 s 19:38:13.276
GET https://api.themoviedb.org/3/movie/912649/vid 200 json 139 ms 19:38:13.511
GET https://api.themoviedb.org/3/movie/912649?api 200 json 138 ms 19:38:13.703
GET https://img.youtube.com/vi/y1M-nGQblmw/hqde 200 jpeg 257 ms 19:38:14.125
GET https://img.youtube.com/vi/BX2uhw9UOiQ/hqd 200 jpeg 269 ms 19:38:14.127
GET https://img.youtube.com/vi/sZgZL6Yn2fw/hqde 200 jpeg 244 ms 19:38:14.130
GET https://img.youtube.com/vi/ZY34ufXPFl8/hqdef 200 jpeg 263 ms 19:38:14.131
SOCKET 142.251.46.174:443 Open tcp Pending 19:38:14.176
SOCKET 142.251.46.174:443 Open tcp Pending 19:38:14.178
SOCKET 142.251.46.174:443 Open tcp Pending 19:38:14.179
SOCKET 142.251.46.174:443 Open tcp Pending 19:38:14.180
No request selected
Read docs
Watch tutorial
Showing 13 of 13 requests
arm64 (64 bit) android

***Figure 18.8:** Networking*

You can see the status of the network call (200 is a success), the type, and the time it took to get the value. Here we have some images, and you can see how long it took to download. Luckily, we use the **`CachedNetworkImage`** package that will cache that image and not download it again.

Next is the **Logging** tab. The author prefers using Android Studio's console and using their own logging. This shows more system logs:

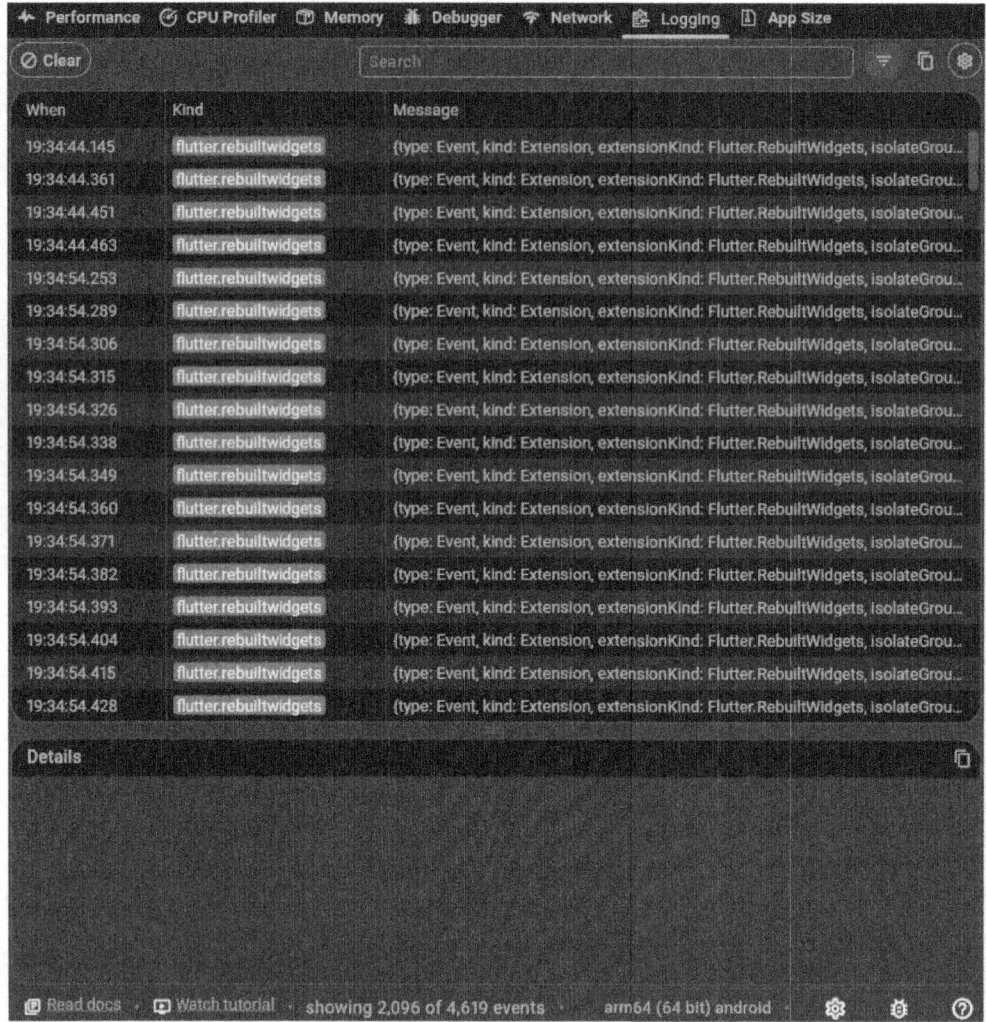

*Figure 18.9: Logging*

Take some time to get to know these tabs and see what you can learn about the app.

# Conclusion

In this chapter, you have learned how to write three different kinds of tests. Unit tests for business logic, widget tests for your individual widgets, and integration tests for your full app. This will help you make sure your app works the way it should and does not regress when you make changes. Finally, you learned how to view the performance of your app and use the tools Flutter provides to see what is happening with your app and where there are performance bottlenecks. In the next chapter, you will learn how to build and publish your app to the Google Play Store and the Apple App Store.

# CHAPTER 19

# Building and Publishing

## Introduction

In this chapter, you will learn how to build a release app for both Android and iOS that you can then publish to both the Google Play Store and the Apple App Store. This is a big step that involves learning about signing apps, creating accounts on the different stores, and finally publishing your apps. You will create developer accounts for both the Google Play Store and the Apple App Store. This will allow you to publish your apps to the respective stores. To create a polished app, you will need to create icons that the user will see in the store and on their phones. This is the final step in your journey to build mobile apps.

## Structure

The chapter covers the following topics:

- Google developer account
- Apple developer account
- Icons
- Android release
- App store
- Play Store

# Objectives

By the end of this chapter, you will have created developer accounts on each platform, created release builds for both Android and iOS, created icons to make a polished app and then finally published those apps on the Google and Apple Stores. You should understand what is needed to publish your app on both platforms.

# Google developer account

To publish a release version for Android, you will need a developer account on Google Play Store. The steps to create one are as follows:

1.  Go to **https://play.google.com/console/signup**.

2.  Sign in using your Google account.

3.  On the next page, choose a type of account: Organization or Yourself:

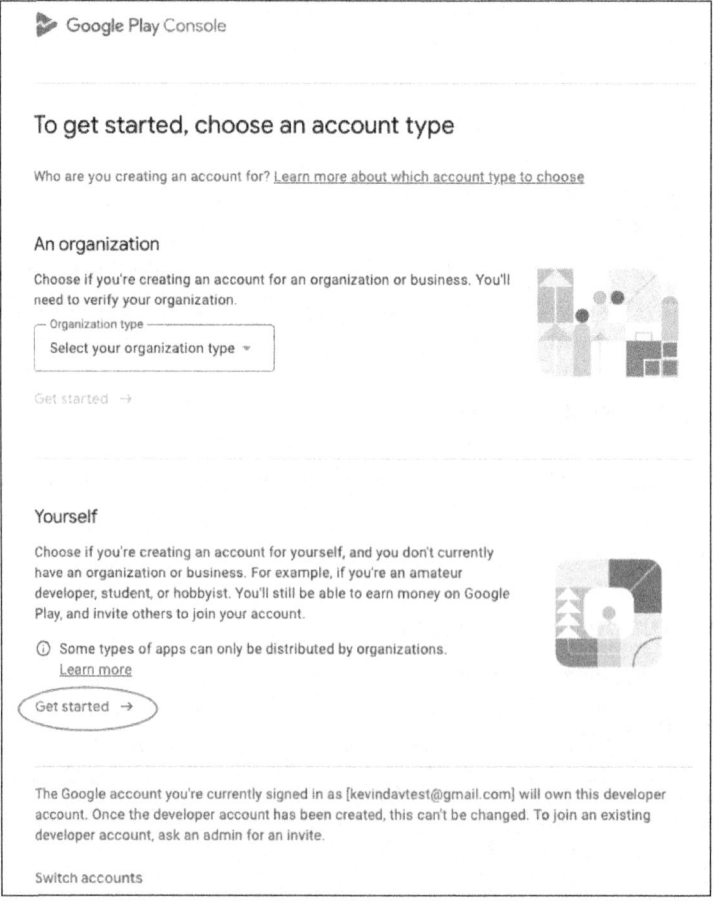

*Figure 19.1: Console signup*

4. The next page shows the info on what you will need to create an account:

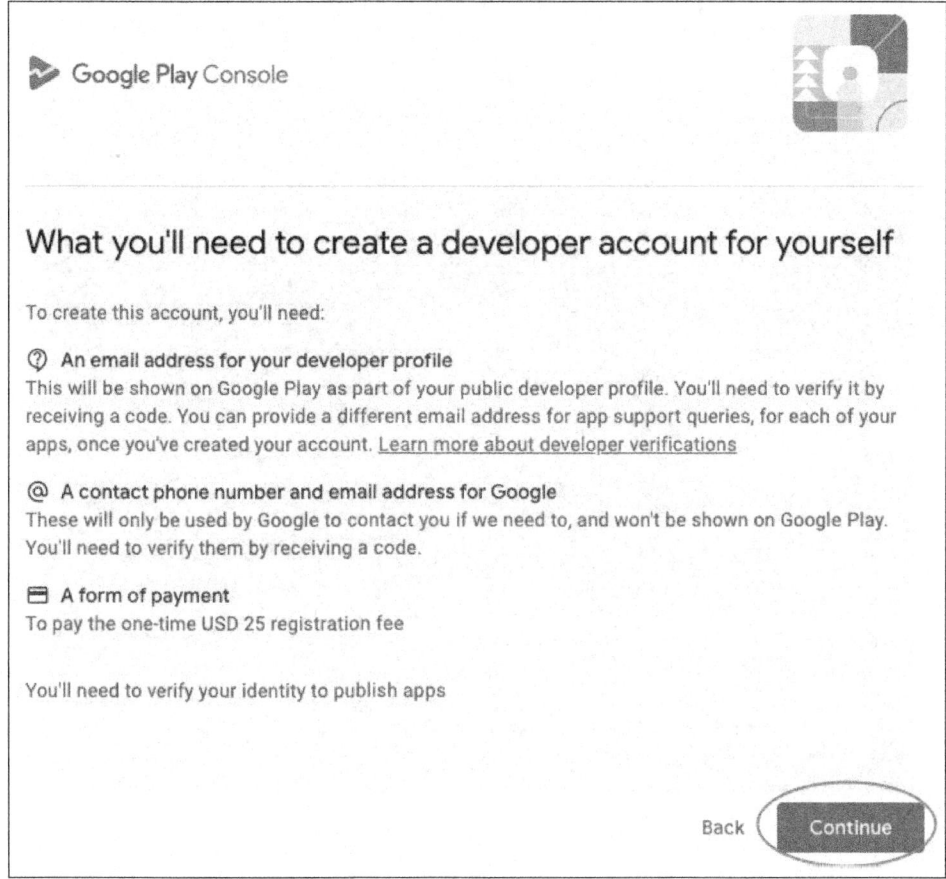

*Figure 19.2: Account creation info*

5. Press **Continue** to follow the instructions to create your account.

This will get you started. In the **Play Store** section, you will learn how to create a new app and publish your app.

# Apple developer account

To start creating an Apple account, go to **https://developer.apple.com/programs/enroll/**. Note that you will need to pay $99 / year for an account. The following is the start enrollment page:

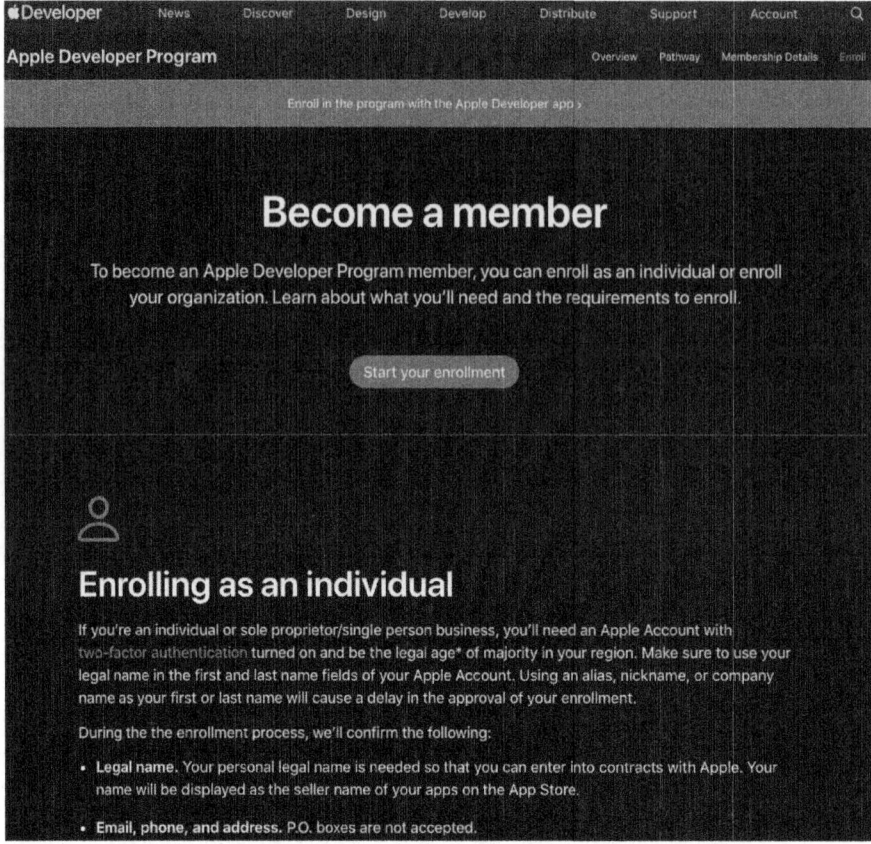

*Figure 19.3: Apple developer enrollment*

The steps to create an account are as follows:

1.  Click on **Start your enrolment**.
2.  Click on the **Create yours now** link:

*Figure 19.4: Apple sign-in*

3. Fill out the form and finish creating your account:

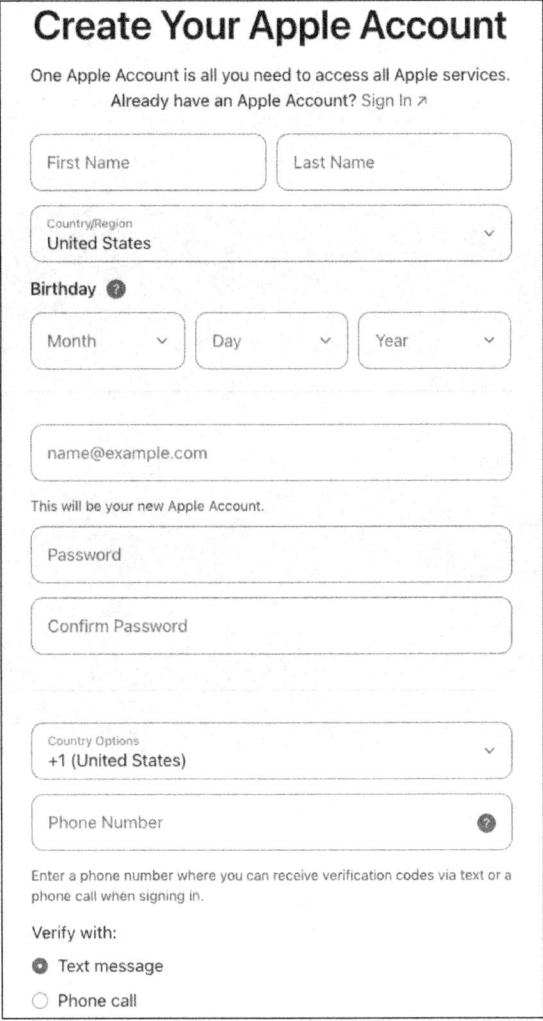

*Figure 19.5: Account creation*

4. Return to the main page and click on **Certificates**:

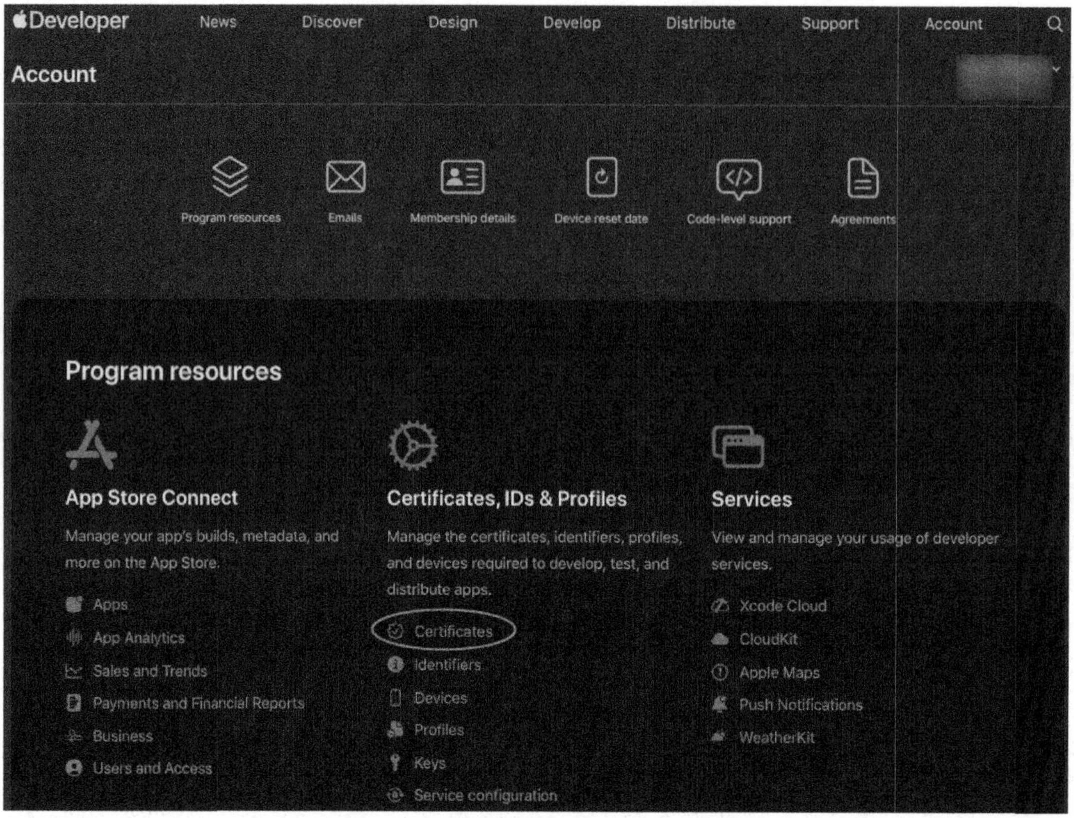

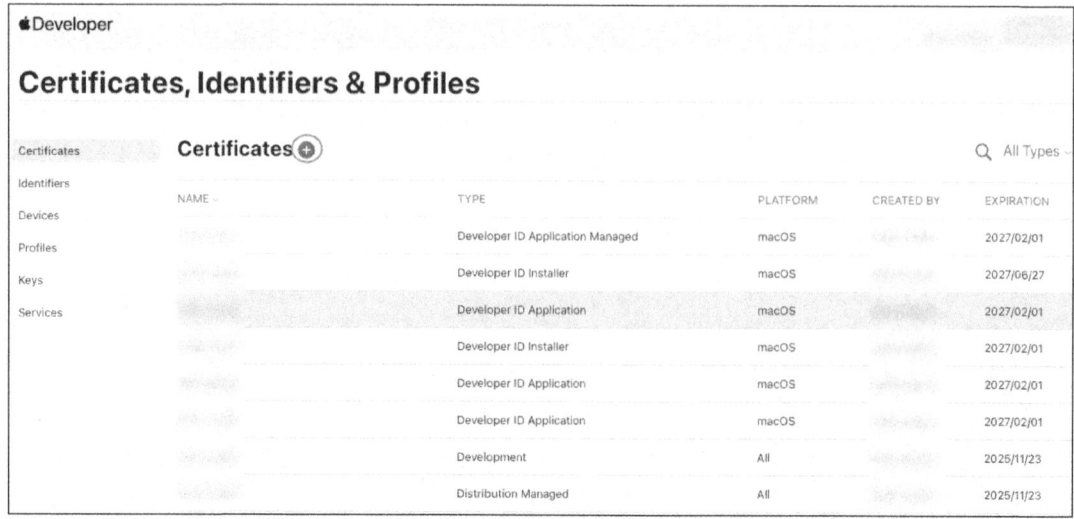

*Figure 19.6: Main page*

5.  Click on the blue plus button next to **Certificates**:

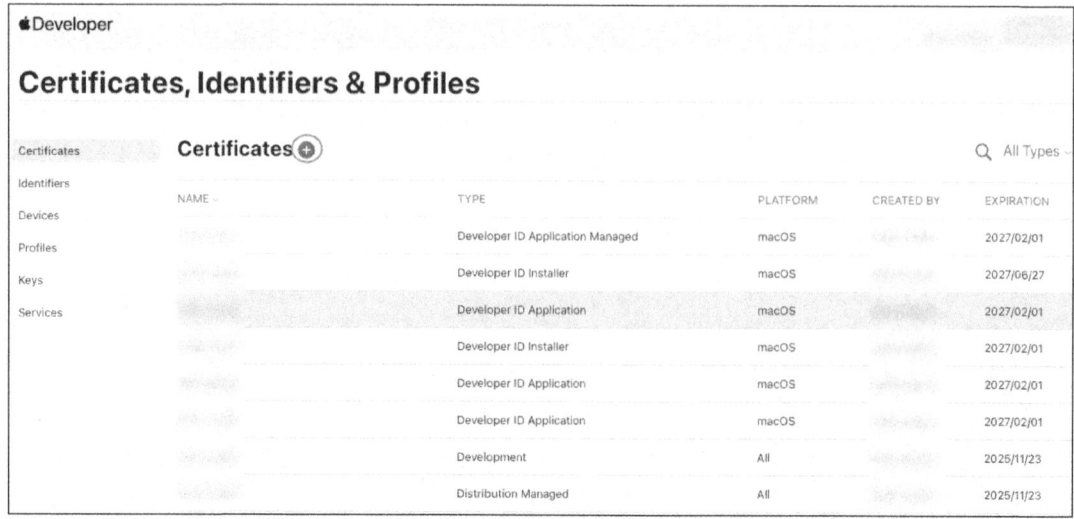

*Figure 19.7: Certificates page*

6. You will need to create both an Apple development certificate and an Apple distribution certificate. Click on **Apple Development** and then **Continue**.

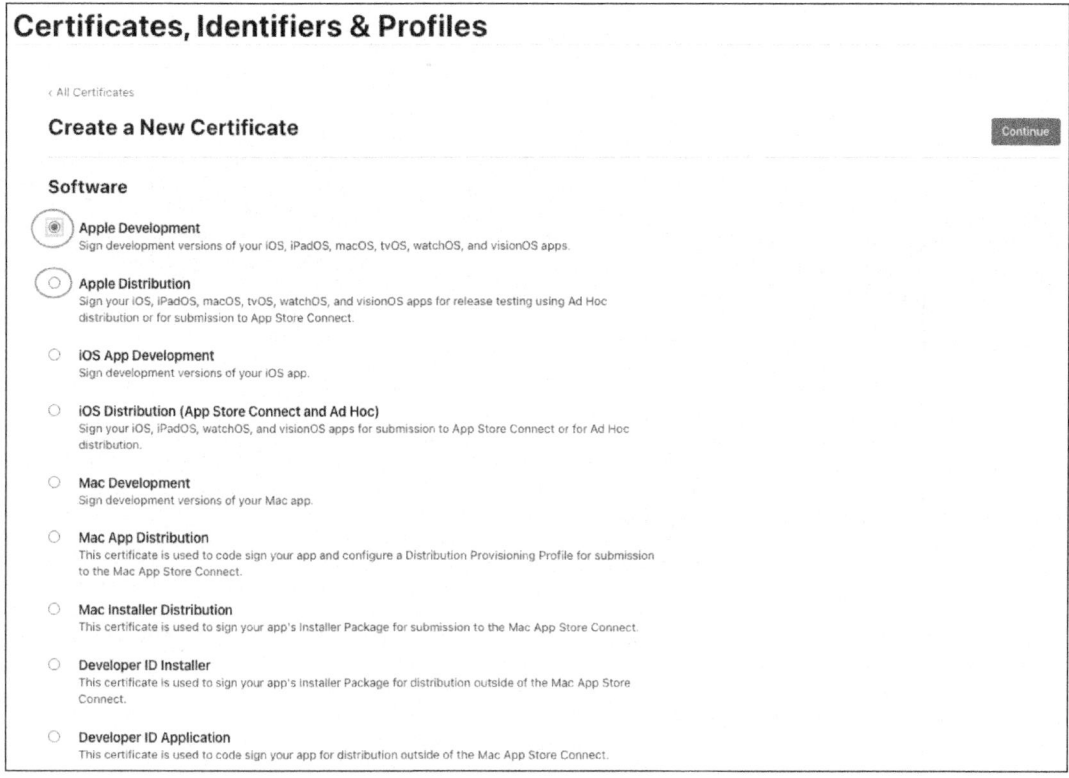

*Figure 19.8*: *New certificate*

7. Before you do that, you will need to create a Request for Certificate. You can do that by opening up the **KeyChain access** app on the Mac and using the **Certificate Assistant**. Choose **Request a Certificate From a Certificate Authority**:

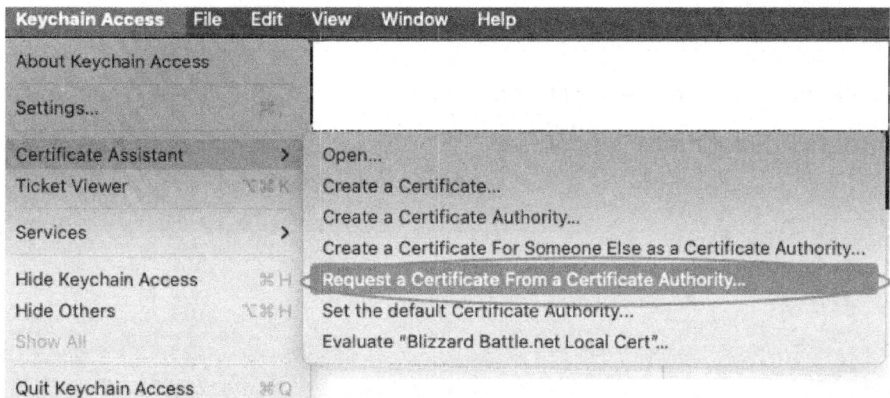

*Figure 19.9*: *Request New Certificate*

8. Enter your email and name and choose **Saved to disk**:

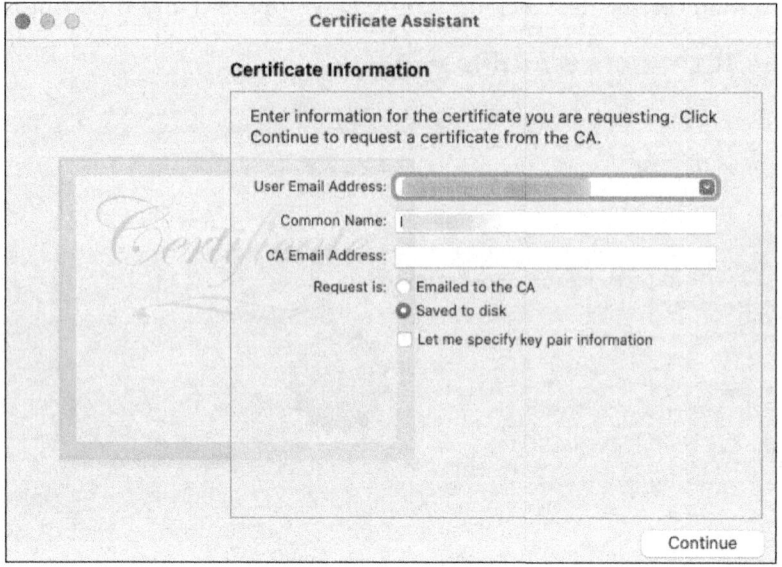

*Figure 19.10: Certificate Information*

9. Click **Continue** and save the file in a known location. Return to the developer webpage:

*Figure 19.11: Create New Certificate*

10. Click on **Choose File** and select the file you just created. Then click **Continue**:

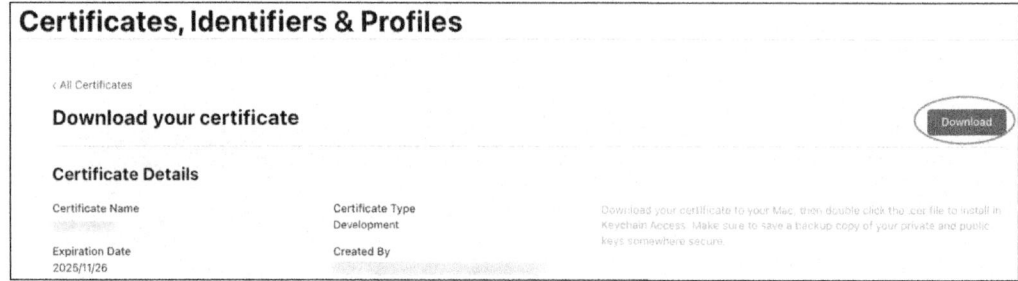

*Figure 19.12: Download certificate*

11. Download the certificate and double-click on it. The Mac should install it in your **Keychain Access** app.

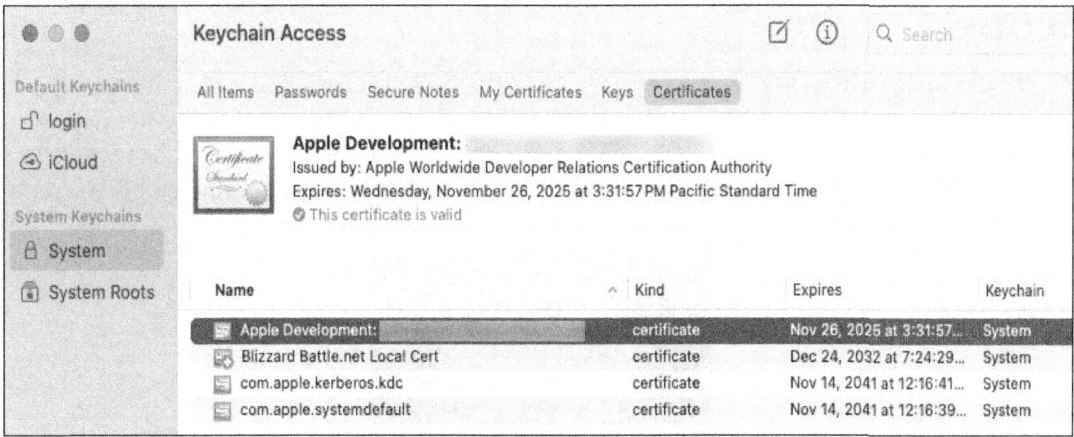

*Figure 19.13*: *Keychain access*

12. Do the same with the **Distribution Certificate**.

13. Go to your profile to view your Team ID.

14. Return to Xcode, open the **Settings** from the **Xcode** menu, and go to the **Accounts** tab.

15. Login to your Apple account. Your screen will look something as follows:

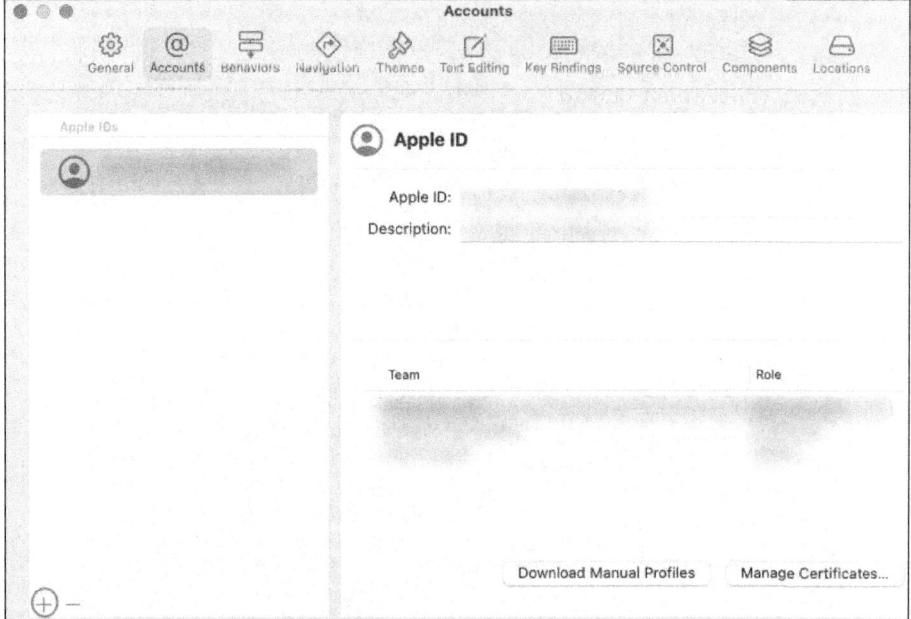

*Figure 19.14*: *Accounts*

This is where you can see your team and manage your certificates.

# Icons

When you are ready to release your app, one of the most important aspects of your app is how it looks. One of those areas is the icon from your app. This is the image the user sees when they find your app in the app store and click on it to start your app. You can have a designer create a custom icon, find a website, or use AI image generation tools to create one. You can use Google's Imagen 3 to generate one, like the one below:

*Figure 19.15*: *Icon image*

We can use this image for both sets of icons. A good tool for creating icons is **Icon Maker Pro**. You can get this on the Mac App Store. The following is Icon Maker Pro with our new image dragged onto the image area:

*Figure 19.16*: *Icon Maker Pro*

Make sure you do not use **Rounded Corner** for iOS. For the following platforms: Android, iOS and iPad platforms, press the **Generate icons** button and save the files to a directory.

# Android icons

Android icons go into the **android/app/main/res/mipmap-xxxx** folders, where *xxxx* refers to each resolution that Android uses for its icons. Icon Maker Pro creates individual files, with each file having the resolution type at the end. You need to rename and move each file to the Android mipmap folders:

1. In the Finder, rename each file to remove the resolution at the end so it is just **ic_launcher.png**.

2. For each file, move it into the proper mipmap folder with that resolution. Do this one file at a time.

3. Next, copy the higher-resolution file into the drawable folder.

4. In Android Studio, open **launch_background.xml** in the drawable folder.

5. Change the code to point to this file:

```
<?xml version="1.0" encoding="utf-8"?>
<!-- Modify this file to customize your launch splash screen -->
<layer-list xmlns:android="http://schemas.android.com/apk/res/
android">
    <item>
        <bitmap
            android:gravity="center"
            android:src="@mipmap/ic_launcher" />
    </item>
</layer-list>
```

This file is referenced in the **AndroidManifest.xml** file and is used to create the launcher icon.

6. Do the same for the **launch_background.xml** file in the **drawable-v21** folder.

# iOS icons

For iOS, the easiest way to change the icons is in Xcode. After creating the icons in Icon Maker Pro, add the icons. The steps are as follows:

1. Select the **Assets** folder in Xcode.

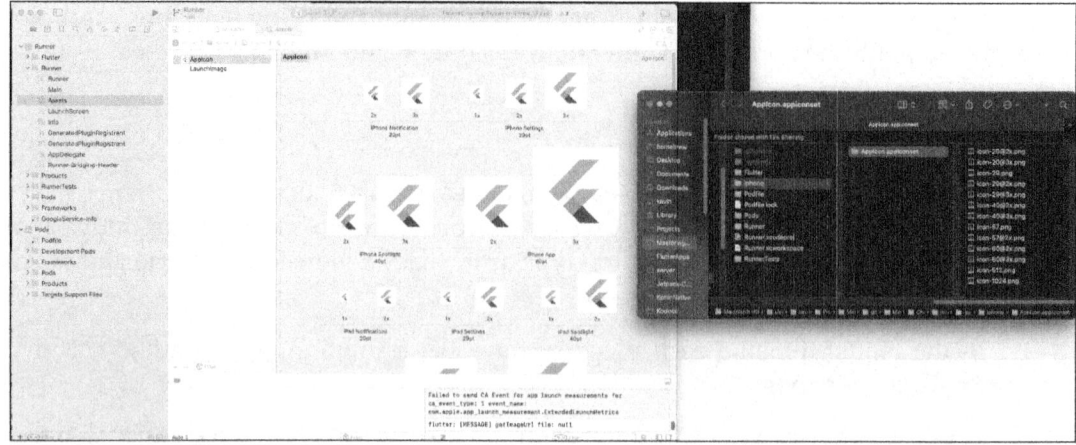

*Figure 19.17: Xcode assets*

This is the default Flutter icon.

2.   Drag each icon matching the size from the Finder. (It will tell you if you put in the wrong size). **icon-20.png** goes to the first image and so on until it looks like:

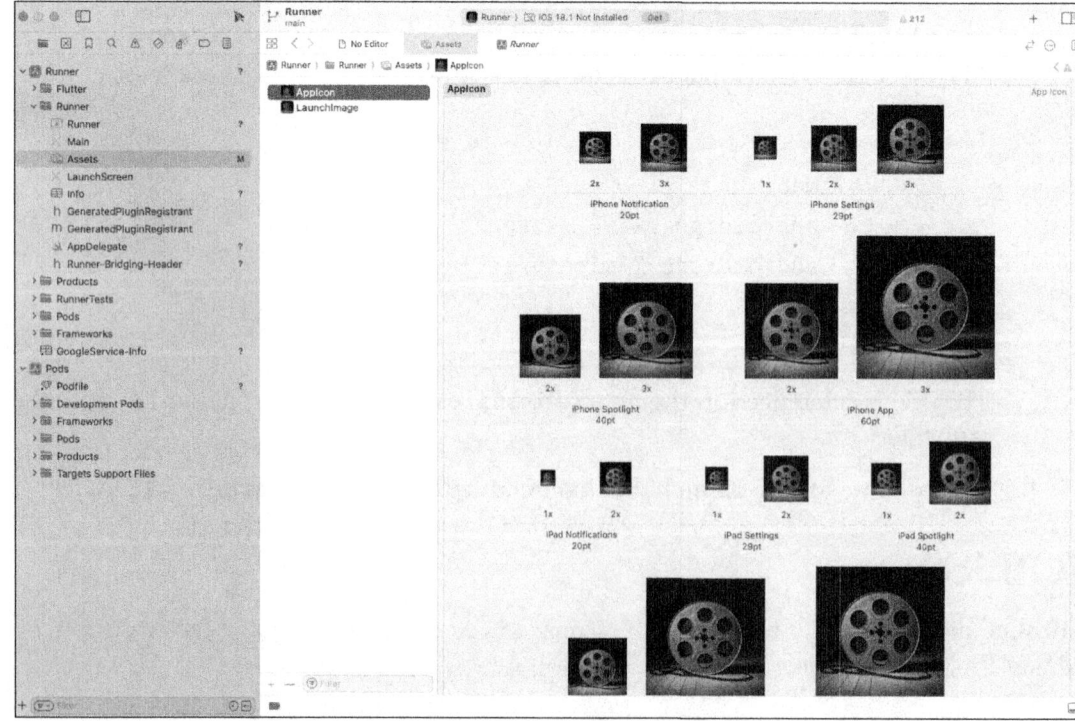

*Figure 19.18: Final icons*

Make sure you use the different iPad images created by Icon Maker Pro.

# Android release

So far, in this book, we have been creating debug builds to test. In order to submit your app to the Google Play Store and the Apple App Store, you need to create a release version of your app. This version will be smaller, as all of the debug information has been removed, and in many cases, the code has been obfuscated to hide the code. Release builds are also signed so that users can be assured that they are getting the app from the original developer. To create a release app for Android, you will need to do a few extra steps. You will need a keystore to store your cryptographic keys. This is a secure file designed to protect sensitive information. To sign your app and submit it to the Google Play Store, you will need to create this file and update the **build.gradle** file. The steps are as follows:

1. In the terminal app, go to the Android folder of your project.

2. You should have the Android tools in your path (if not, type the full path. If all else fails, Android Studio will have downloaded the Android tools, and you can find that location in the **Settings | Languages and Frameworks | Android SDK panel**). Type:

   ```
   keytool -genkey -v -keystore movies-release.keystore -alias movies
   -keyalg RSA -keysize 2048 -validity 10000
   ```

   This will prompt you to enter information and will create the keystore **movies-release.keystore** file. You need to fill in the information about yourself and your company. Remember your passwords.

3. Open up the **app/build.gradle** file in Android Studio. After the **flutterVersionName** definition add:

   ```
   // Add the keystore information from the key.properties file
   def keystoreProperties = new Properties()
   def keystorePropertiesFile = rootProject.file('key.properties')
   if (keystorePropertiesFile.exists()) {
       keystoreProperties.load(new
   FileInputStream(keystorePropertiesFile))
   }
   ```

   This looks for a file named **key.properties** to load in with passwords for the keystore. This file should be added to the **.gitignore** and not checked into Git.

4. Replace the **buildTypes** with:

   ```
   signingConfigs {
       release {
           if (keystorePropertiesFile.exists()) {
               keyAlias keystoreProperties['keyAlias']
               keyPassword keystoreProperties['keyPassword']
   ```

```
            storeFile keystoreProperties['storeFile'] ?
file(keystoreProperties['storeFile']) : null
            storePassword keystoreProperties['storePassword']
        } else {
            println('Keystore file not found')
        }
    }
}

buildTypes {
    release {
        signingConfig signingConfigs.release
        minifyEnabled true // Enable code shrinking and
obfuscation
        proguardFiles getDefaultProguardFile('proguard-android-
optimize.txt'), 'proguard-rules.pro'
    }
}
```

This uses the definition of the keystore file to load the keystore information.

5.  Create a new file in the **android** folder named **key.properties**.

6.  Add the following and add the password you used to create the keystore file:

```
storeFile=../movies-release.keystore
storePassword=<your store password>
keyAlias=movies
keyPassword=<your key password>
```

To create an Android release, there are two different types of files that can be generated: APK and a bundle file that ends with **.aab**. Google recommends using bundle files so we will be doing that.

7.  In the terminal, in the movies directory type:

**flutter build appbundle --release**

This will create a file in the **build/app/outputs/bundle/release** folder.

# App store

To publish your app to the app store, you will need your Apple Developer account and will need to go to **https://appstoreconnect.apple.com/** and log in. You will see a page with links to different areas of the site. Find the identifiers link:

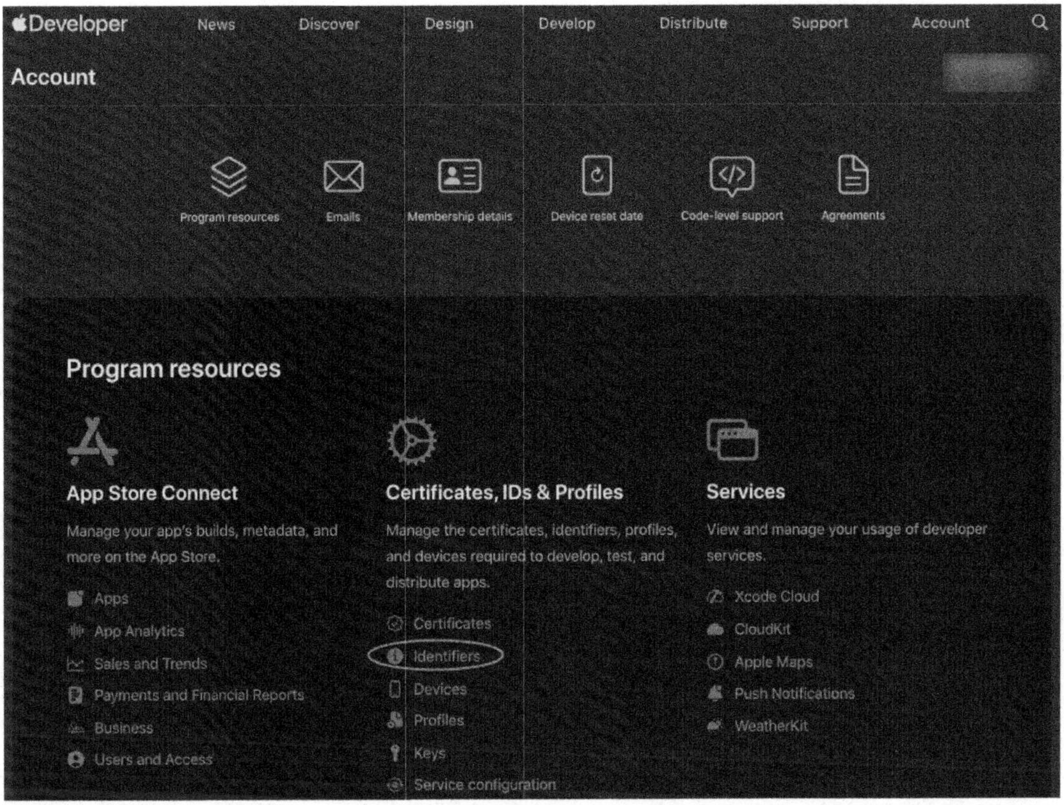

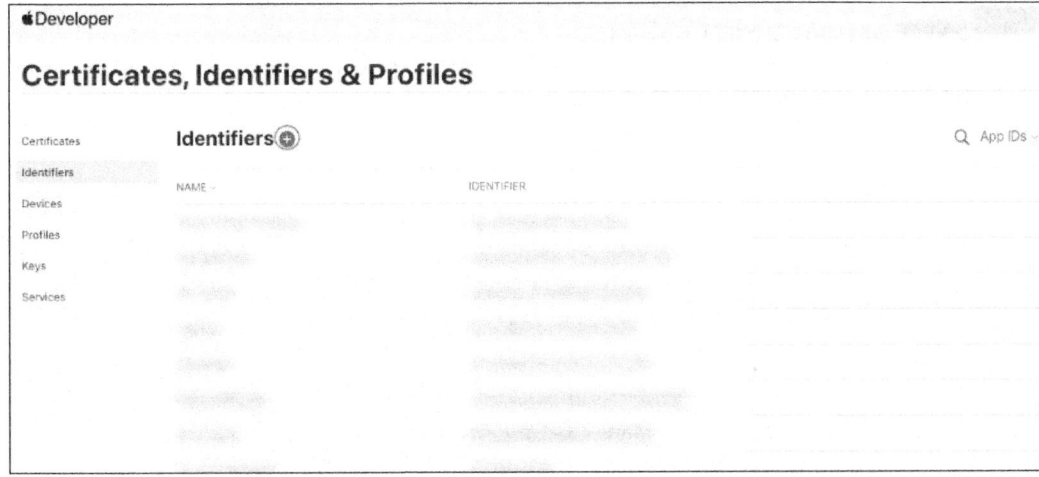

*Figure 19.19*: *App Store Connect*

You need to create an identifier for your new app. The steps are as follows:

1.  Click on the **Identifiers** link, as shown in the following figure:

*Figure 19.20*: *Identifiers*

2. Click on the blue plus image to create a new identifier:

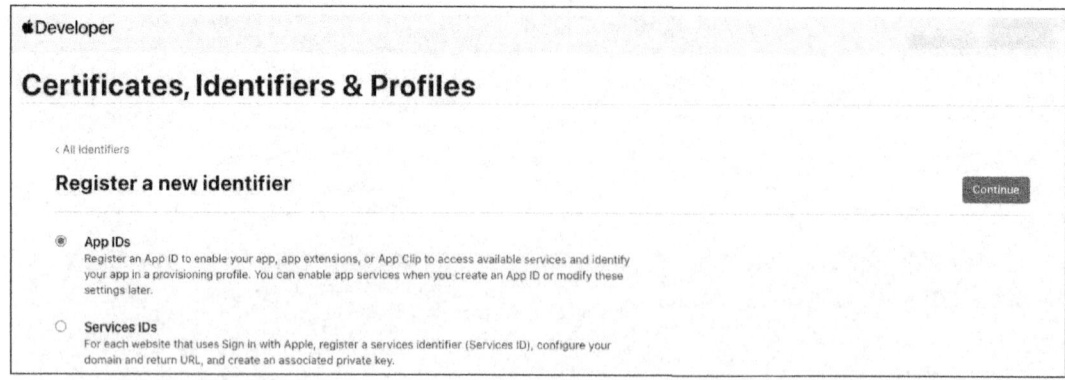

*Figure 19.21: App Id*

3. Make sure **App IDs** are selected, and press **Continue**. This will register your unique App ID:

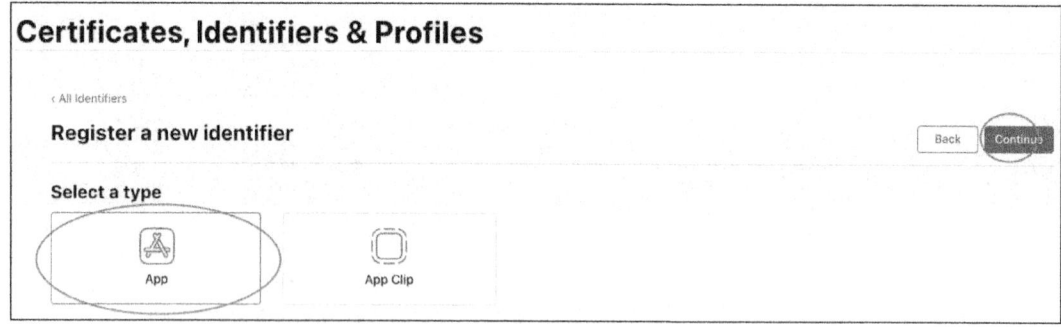

*Figure 19.22: Id type*

4. Select **App** and press **Continue**:

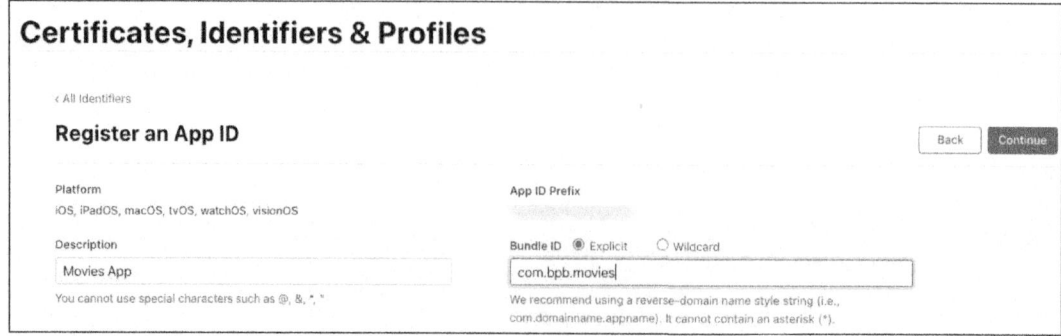

*Figure 19.23: Register Id*

5. Enter a description and bundle ID, and press **Continue**:

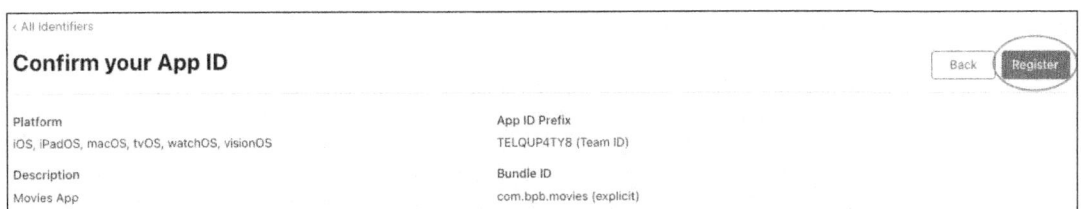

*Figure 19.24: Confirm register*

6. Click **Register**.

7. Complete any other required settings. For example, there is a requirement for the **Digital Services Act Compliance**. The dialog looks as follows:

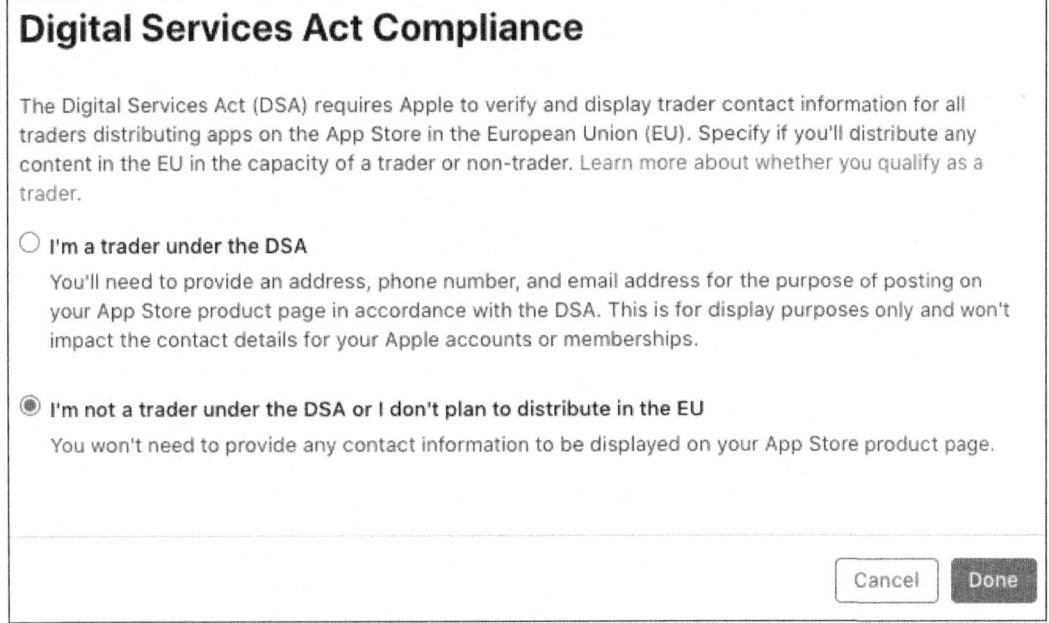

*Figure 19.25: Digital Services Act*

8. Create a new app. Find the blue plus button and press it to create a new App:

*Figure 19.26: New App*

9. Fill in the information on the app:

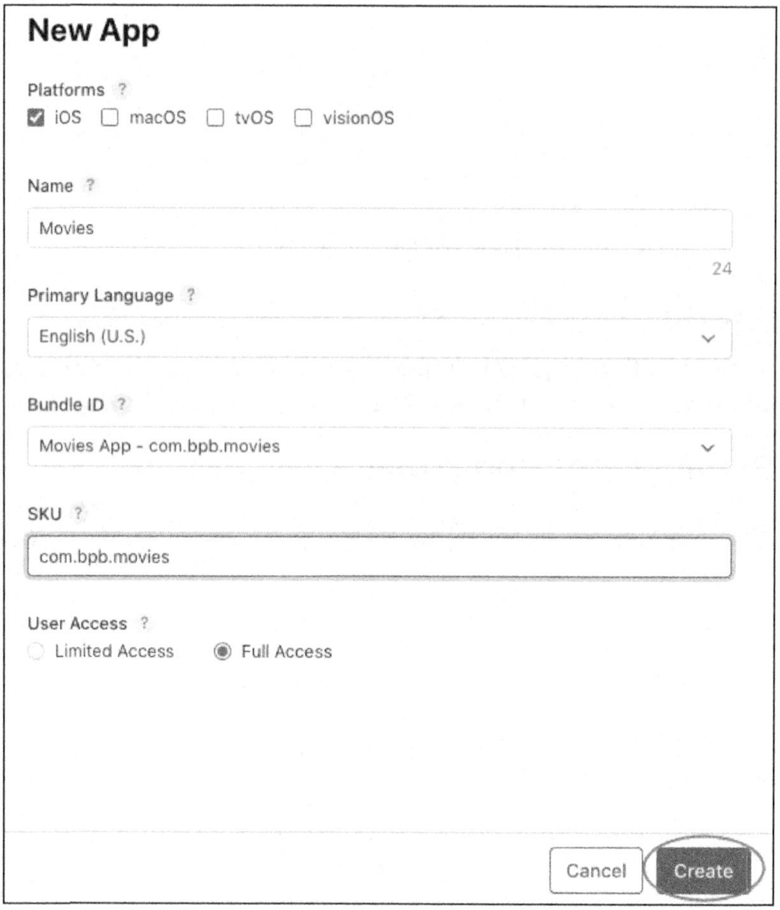

*Figure 19.27: New App information*

10. Fill in the information and press **Create**.

# iOS release build

To build an iOS release, you will need an Apple account. Like Android, you can build the release from the command line like:

```
flutter build ipa --release
```

This will create an **ipa** file in the **build/ios/ipa** folder. Here is how to build from Xcode:

1.  Open the project in Xcode.

2.  Build a release build:

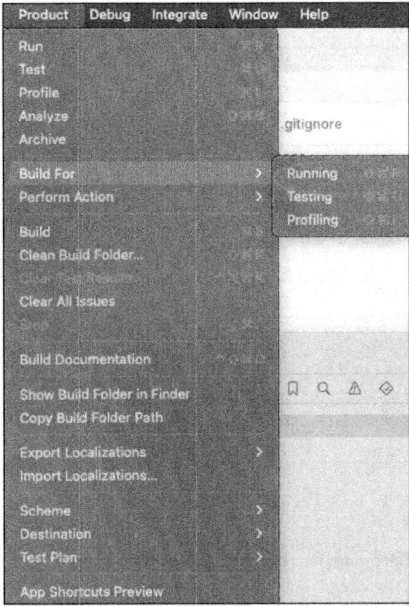

*Figure 19.28: iOS Release build*

This will take some time. Once it has finished, you will want to create an archive. This is the final file that will be published in the store.

3.   Create an archive by choosing **Product | Archive**. This will create an iOS `.ipa` file:

*Figure 19.29: Archives*

4. Press **Distribute App**:

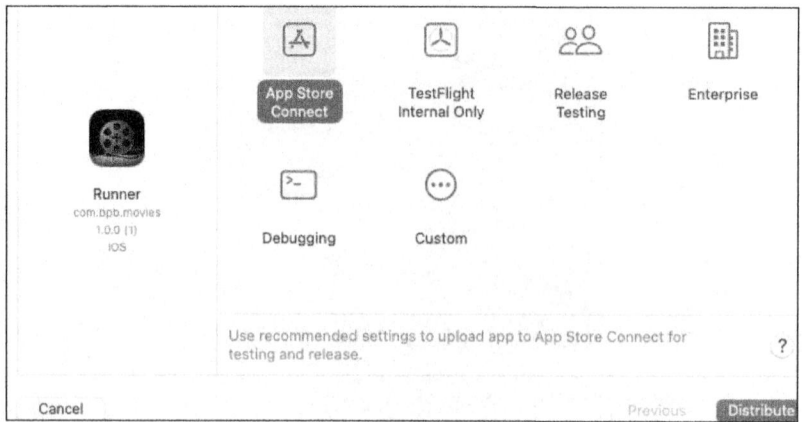

*Figure 19.30: Distribute*

5. Press **Distribute** to send the file to the App Store.

If everything works correctly, you will receive an email shortly that mentions your app is in review. You will then need to wait for Apple to approve. You will probably receive emails asking you to fix issues. This is normal.

# Play Store

At **https://play.google.com/console,** you will see something like the following (minus existing apps). To publish your app on the Play Store, you will need to create an app. The steps to do so are as follows:

1. Press the **Create app** link:

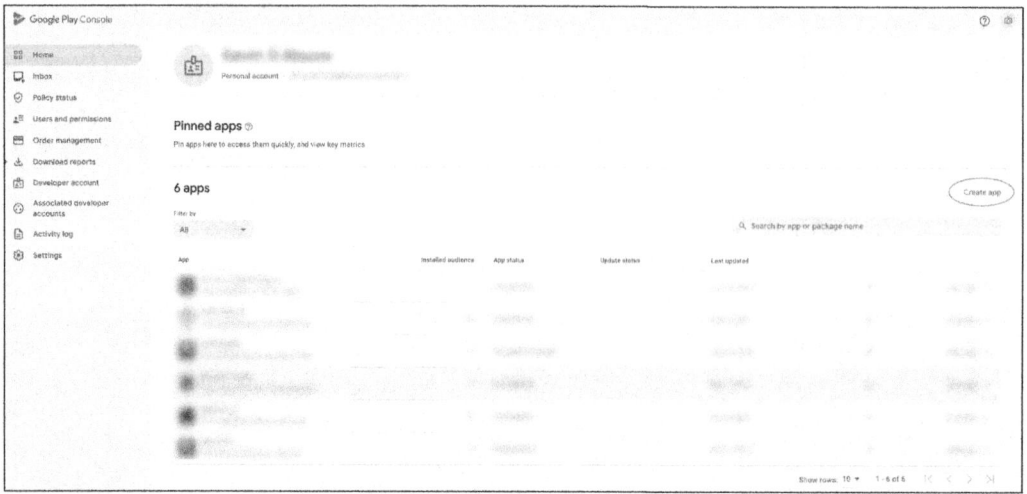

*Figure 19.31: Console Home*

2.  Fill in the **App details** and press the **Create App** button:

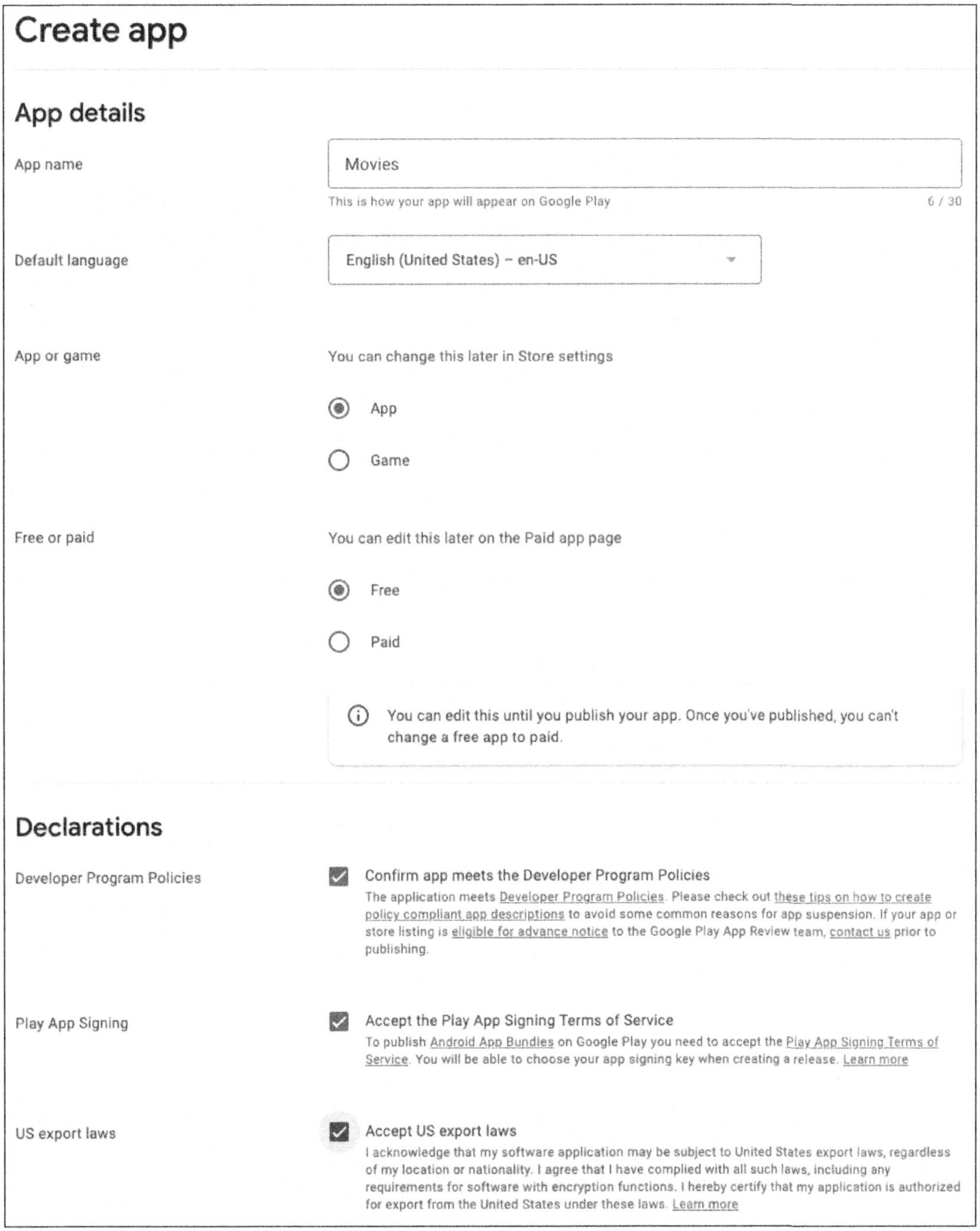

# Create app

## App details

| App name | Movies |
|---|---|

This is how your app will appear on Google Play                                    6 / 30

| Default language | English (United States) – en-US ▾ |
|---|---|

**App or game**

You can change this later in Store settings

⊙ App

○ Game

**Free or paid**

You can edit this later on the Paid app page

⊙ Free

○ Paid

ⓘ You can edit this until you publish your app. Once you've published, you can't change a free app to paid.

## Declarations

**Developer Program Policies**

☑ Confirm app meets the Developer Program Policies

The application meets Developer Program Policies. Please check out these tips on how to create policy compliant app descriptions to avoid some common reasons for app suspension. If your app or store listing is eligible for advance notice to the Google Play App Review team, contact us prior to publishing.

**Play App Signing**

☑ Accept the Play App Signing Terms of Service

To publish Android App Bundles on Google Play you need to accept the Play App Signing Terms of Service. You will be able to choose your app signing key when creating a release. Learn more

**US export laws**

☑ Accept US export laws

I acknowledge that my software application may be subject to United States export laws, regardless of my location or nationality. I agree that I have complied with all such laws, including any requirements for software with encryption functions. I hereby certify that my application is authorized for export from the United States under these laws. Learn more

*Figure 19.32: Create app*

3.  You will be taken to the **Dashboard**. Click the **View the tasks** link:

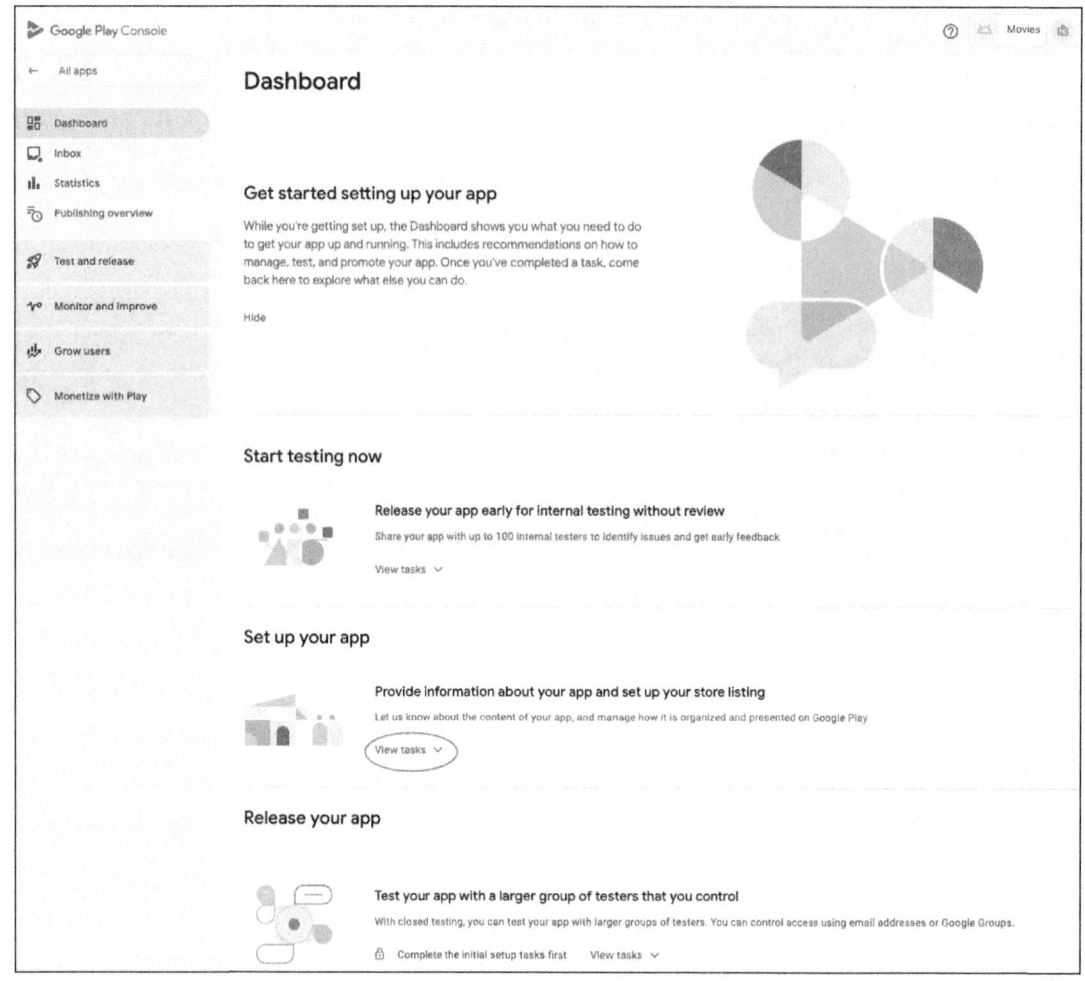

*Figure 19.33: Dashboard*

4.   You will see a long list of tasks that need to be addressed:

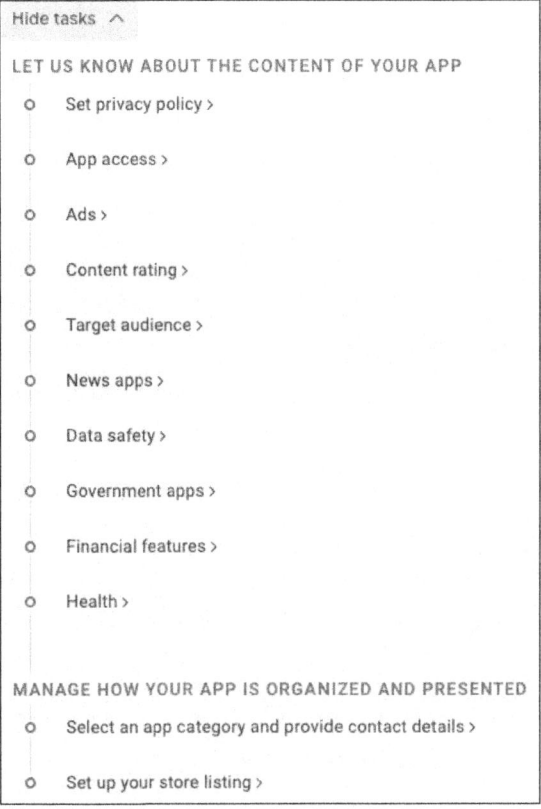

*Figure 19.34*: *Tasks*

5. Start with the privacy policy. You will need a URL to a valid privacy policy. The author used the Termly website to create a privacy policy, but you can use your own or find another website. It is then added to their website. The following is the start of the **Privacy Policy** section:

*Figure 19.35*: *Privacy Policy*

6. Continue filling out all of the pages associated with the privacy policy.

7. Next, click on the **App access** section. Choose one of the options:

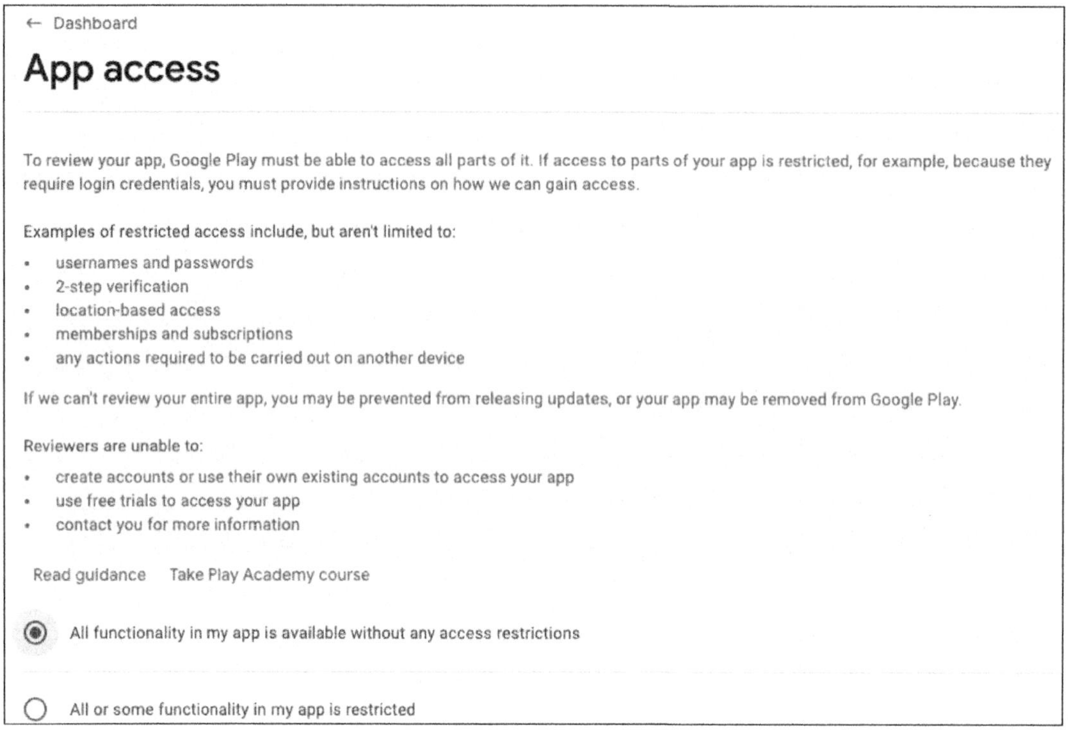

*Figure 19.36: App access*

8. Next, click on the **Ads** and answer any questions:

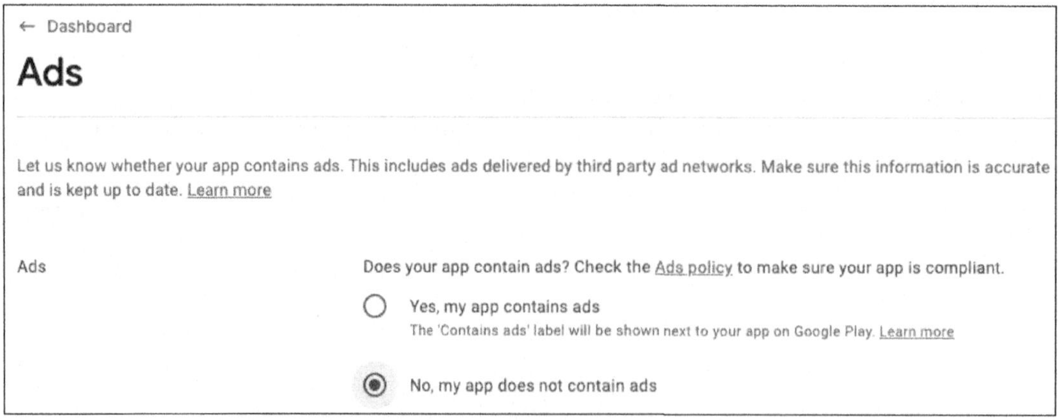

*Figure 19.37: Ads*

9. Next is **Content ratings** and filling out the questionnaire:

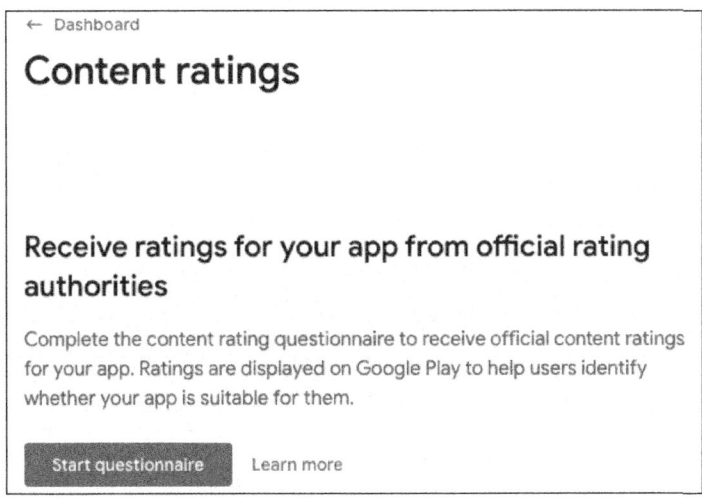

**Figure 19.38**: *Content ratings*

10. Next, fill out the **Target audience and content** section:

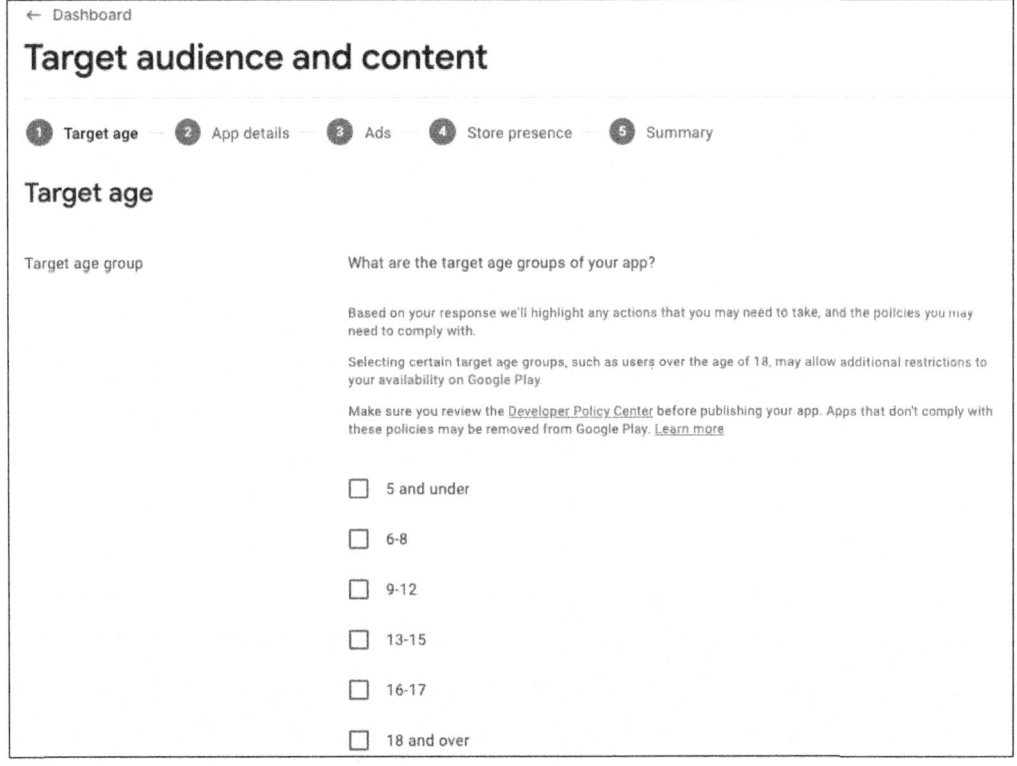

**Figure 19.39**: *Target audience*

11. Next is the simple **News apps** section:

← Dashboard
News apps
Let us know whether your app is a news app. This helps us make sure you comply with the Google Play News policy. Learn more
News apps
Is your app a news app?
No
Yes
I confirm my app complies with the Google Play News policy

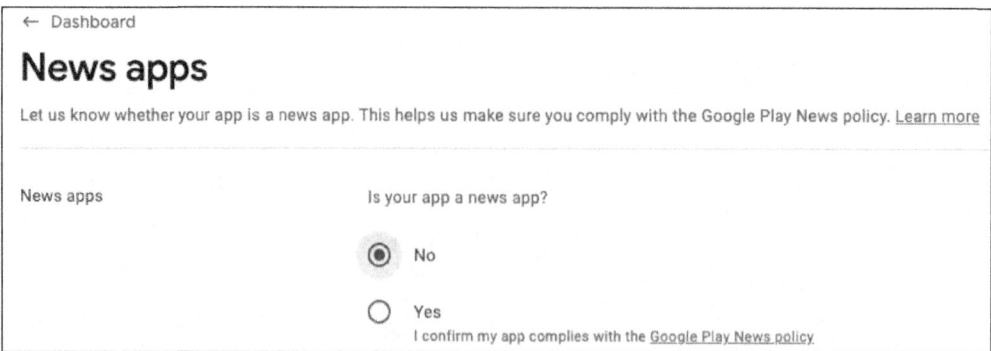

***Figure 19.40***: *News apps*

12. Then, **Data safety**:

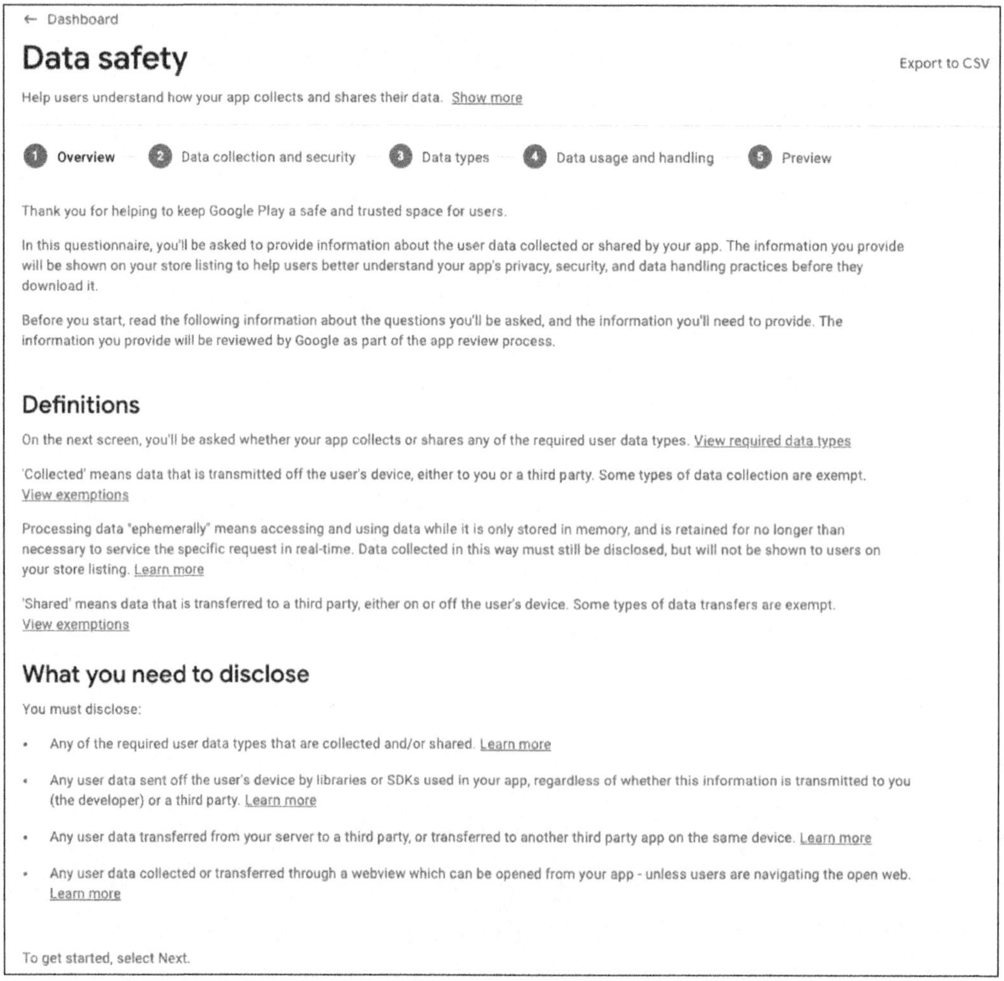

← Dashboard
Data safety
Export to CSV
Help users understand how your app collects and shares their data. Show more
1 Overview
2 Data collection and security
3 Data types
4 Data usage and handling
5 Preview
Thank you for helping to keep Google Play a safe and trusted space for users.
In this questionnaire, you'll be asked to provide information about the user data collected or shared by your app. The information you provide will be shown on your store listing to help users better understand your app's privacy, security, and data handling practices before they download it.
Before you start, read the following information about the questions you'll be asked, and the information you'll need to provide. The information you provide will be reviewed by Google as part of the app review process.
Definitions
On the next screen, you'll be asked whether your app collects or shares any of the required user data types. View required data types
'Collected' means data that is transmitted off the user's device, either to you or a third party. Some types of data collection are exempt. View exemptions
Processing data "ephemerally" means accessing and using data while it is only stored in memory, and is retained for no longer than necessary to service the specific request in real-time. Data collected in this way must still be disclosed, but will not be shown to users on your store listing. Learn more
'Shared' means data that is transferred to a third party, either on or off the user's device. Some types of data transfers are exempt. View exemptions
What you need to disclose
You must disclose:
• Any of the required user data types that are collected and/or shared. Learn more
• Any user data sent off the user's device by libraries or SDKs used in your app, regardless of whether this information is transmitted to you (the developer) or a third party. Learn more
• Any user data transferred from your server to a third party, or transferred to another third party app on the same device. Learn more
• Any user data collected or transferred through a webview which can be opened from your app - unless users are navigating the open web. Learn more
To get started, select Next.

***Figure 19.41***: *Data safety*

13. Then **Government apps**:

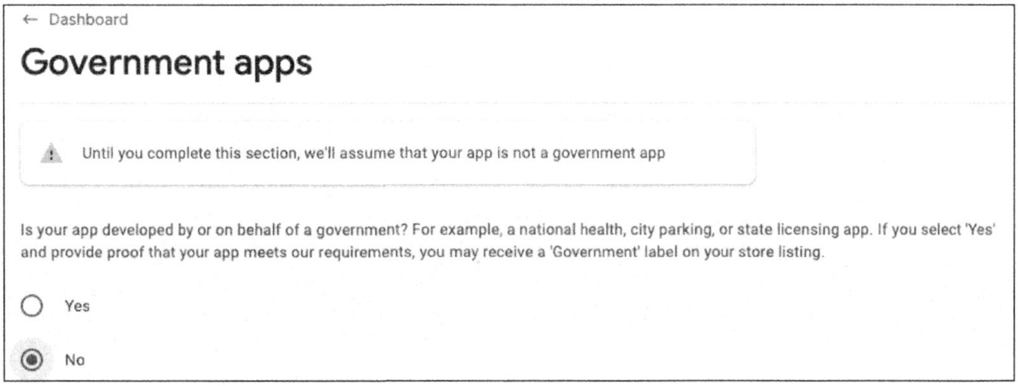

*Figure 19.42*: *Government apps*

14. **Financial features**:

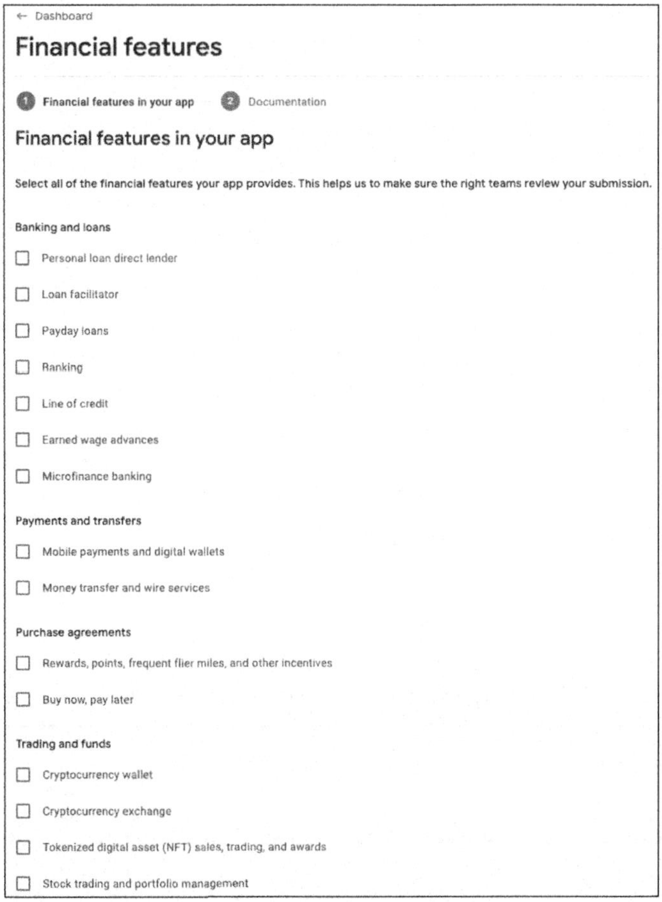

*Figure 19.43*: *Financial features*

15. Health:

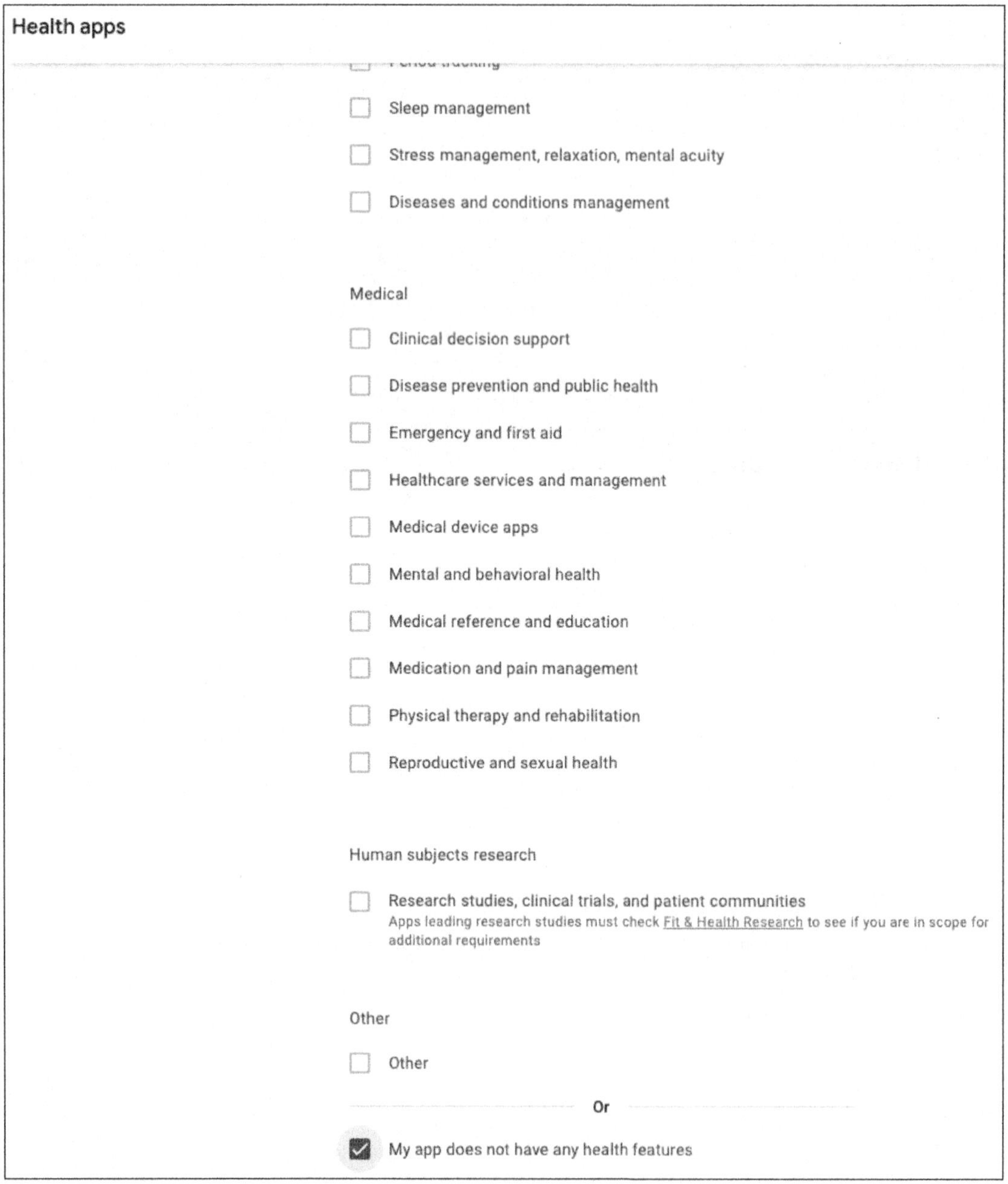

Figure 19.44: Health

16. Next, fill out the **Store settings** app category and store listing details:

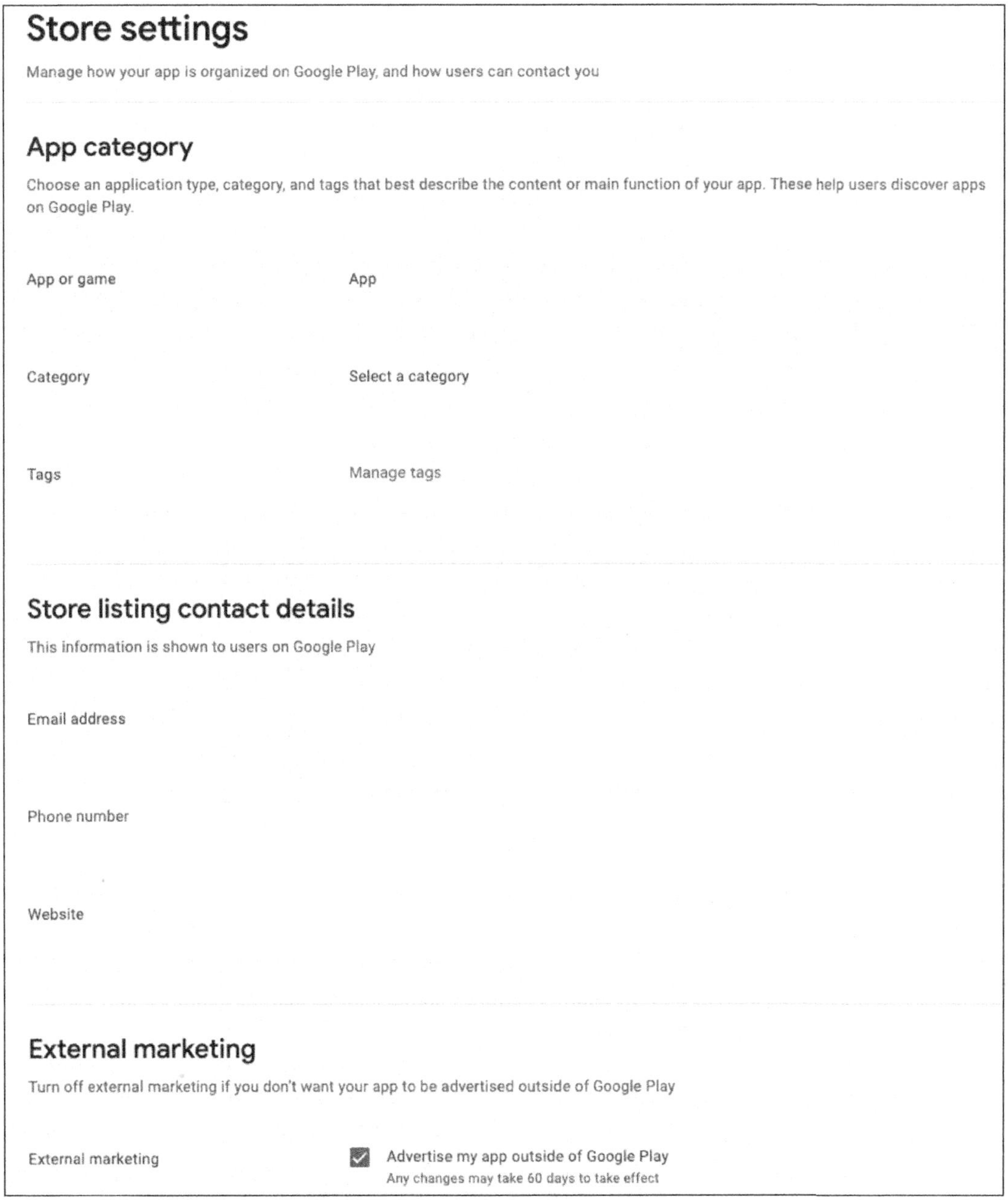

# Store settings

Manage how your app is organized on Google Play, and how users can contact you

## App category

Choose an application type, category, and tags that best describe the content or main function of your app. These help users discover apps on Google Play.

| | |
|---|---|
| App or game | App |
| Category | Select a category |
| Tags | Manage tags |

## Store listing contact details

This information is shown to users on Google Play

Email address

Phone number

Website

## External marketing

Turn off external marketing if you don't want your app to be advertised outside of Google Play

| | |
|---|---|
| External marketing | ☑ Advertise my app outside of Google Play |
| | Any changes may take 60 days to take effect |

*Figure 19.45*: *Store settings*

17. Finally, fill out the store listing:

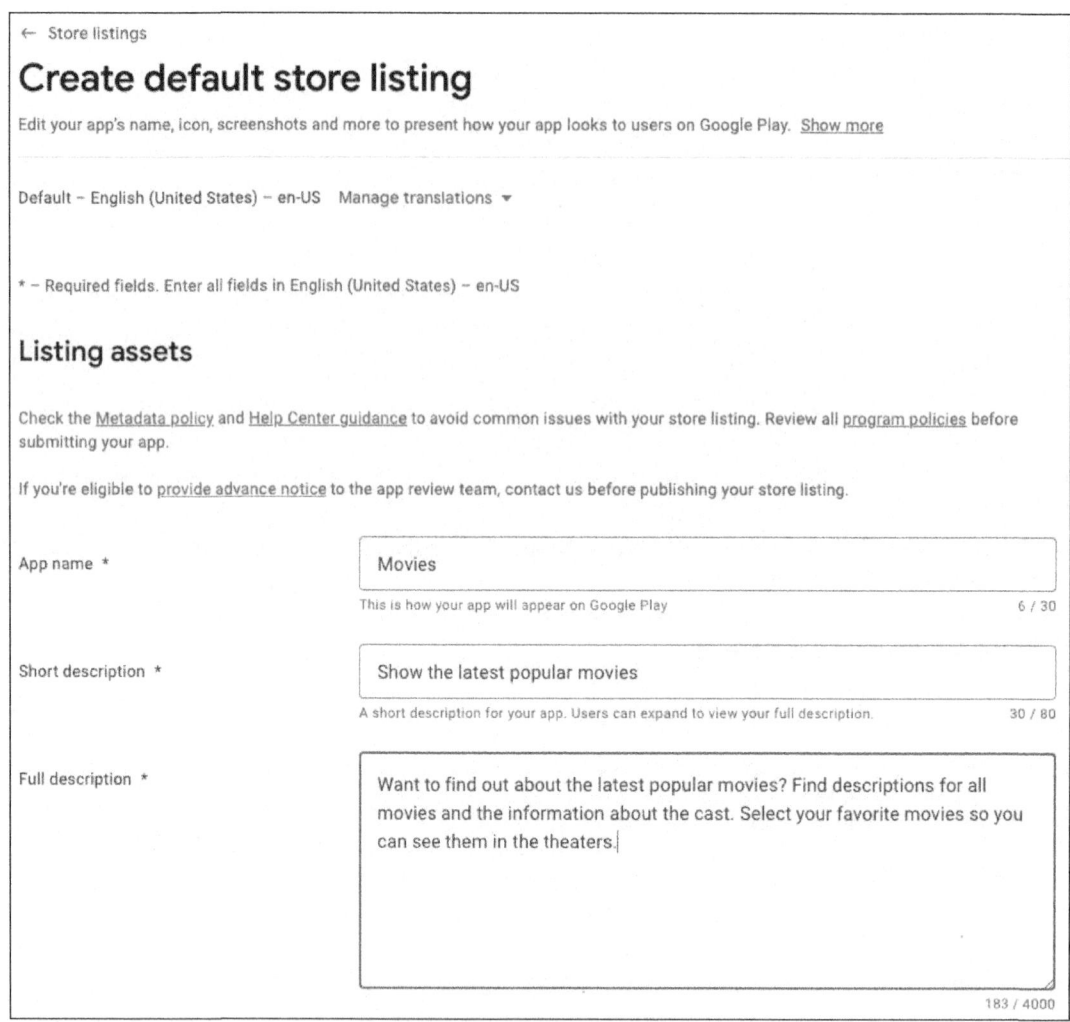

*Figure 19.46: Store listing*

18. Now, it is time to release your app. Return to the dashboard. You can either create a release for testing or go straight to release. If you have users that will test for you, it is recommended that you create a test track. To create a new release, choose **Create a new release**:

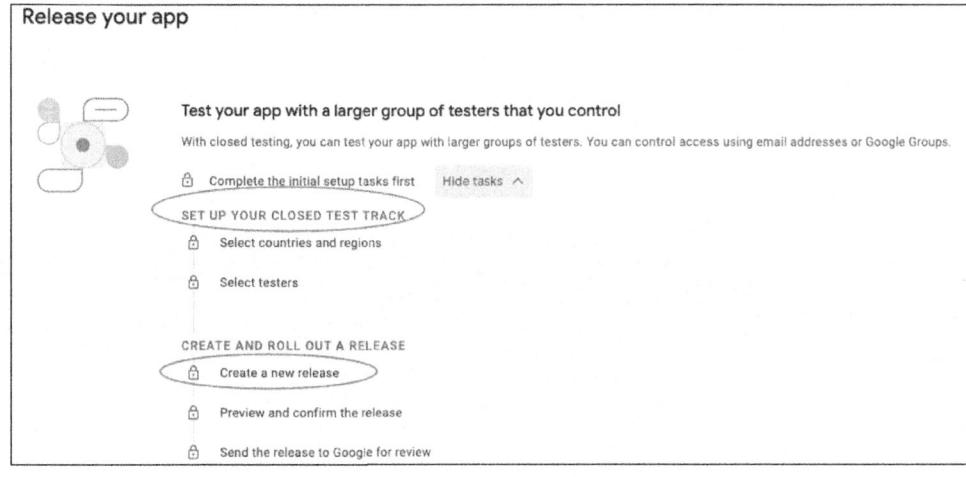

**Figure 19.47**: *Release your app*

19. Set the app type and category:

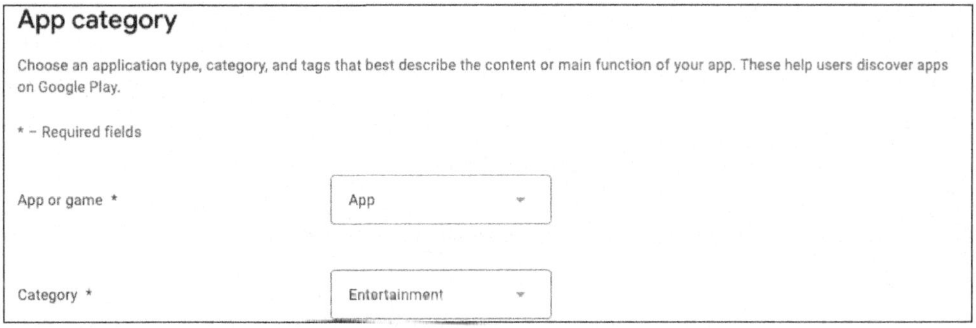

**App category**

Choose an application type, category, and tags that best describe the content or main function of your app. These help users discover apps on Google Play.

* – Required fields

App or game *            App ▾

Category *               Entertainment ▾

**Figure 19.48**: *App category*

20. Fill out the store listing contact details:

**Store listing contact details**

This information is shown to users on Google Play

* – Required fields

Email address *

Phone number

Website

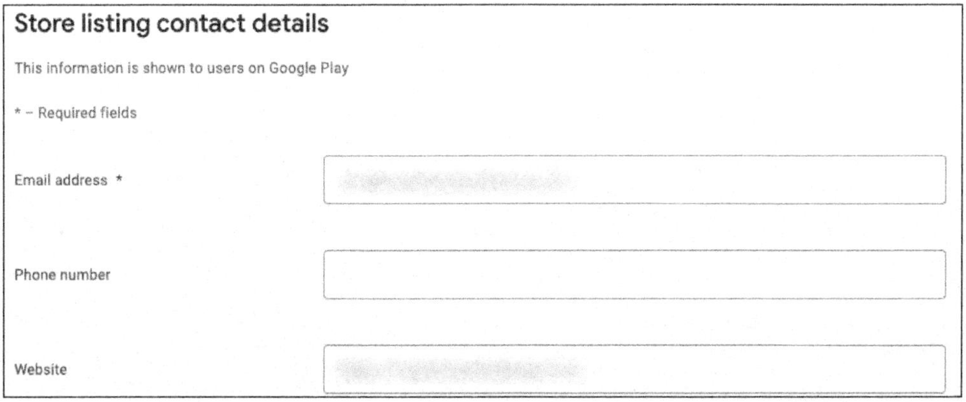

**Figure 19.49**: *store listing contact details*

21. Select the countries and regions you want to release your app to:

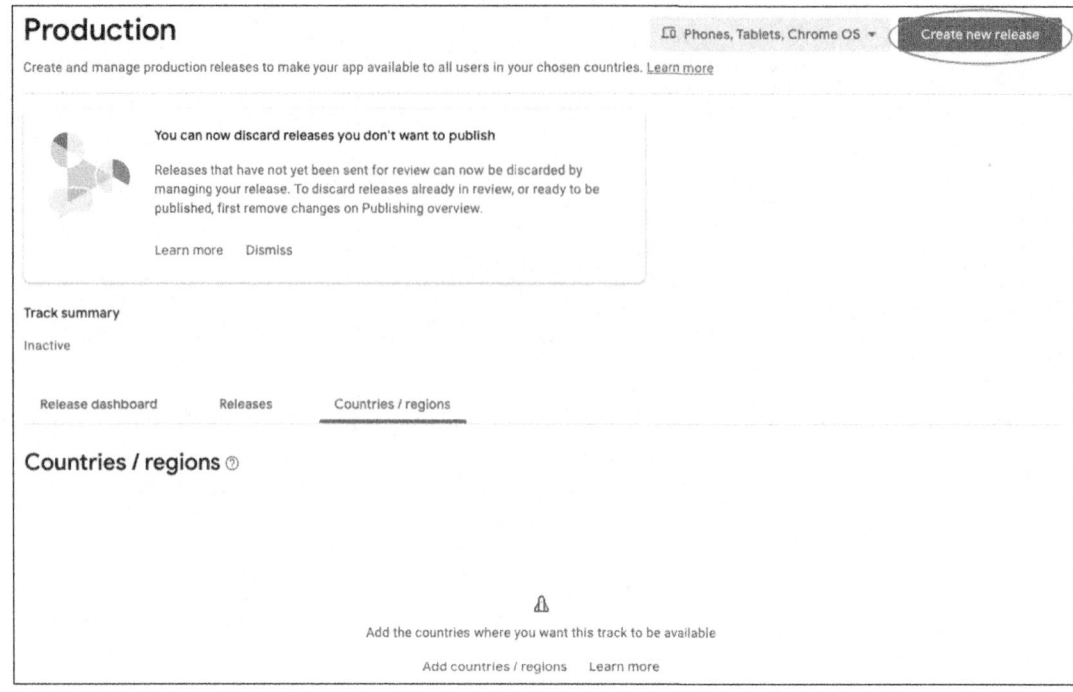

*Figure 19.50*: Countries

22. Now, to create the release. Choose **Create a new release**:

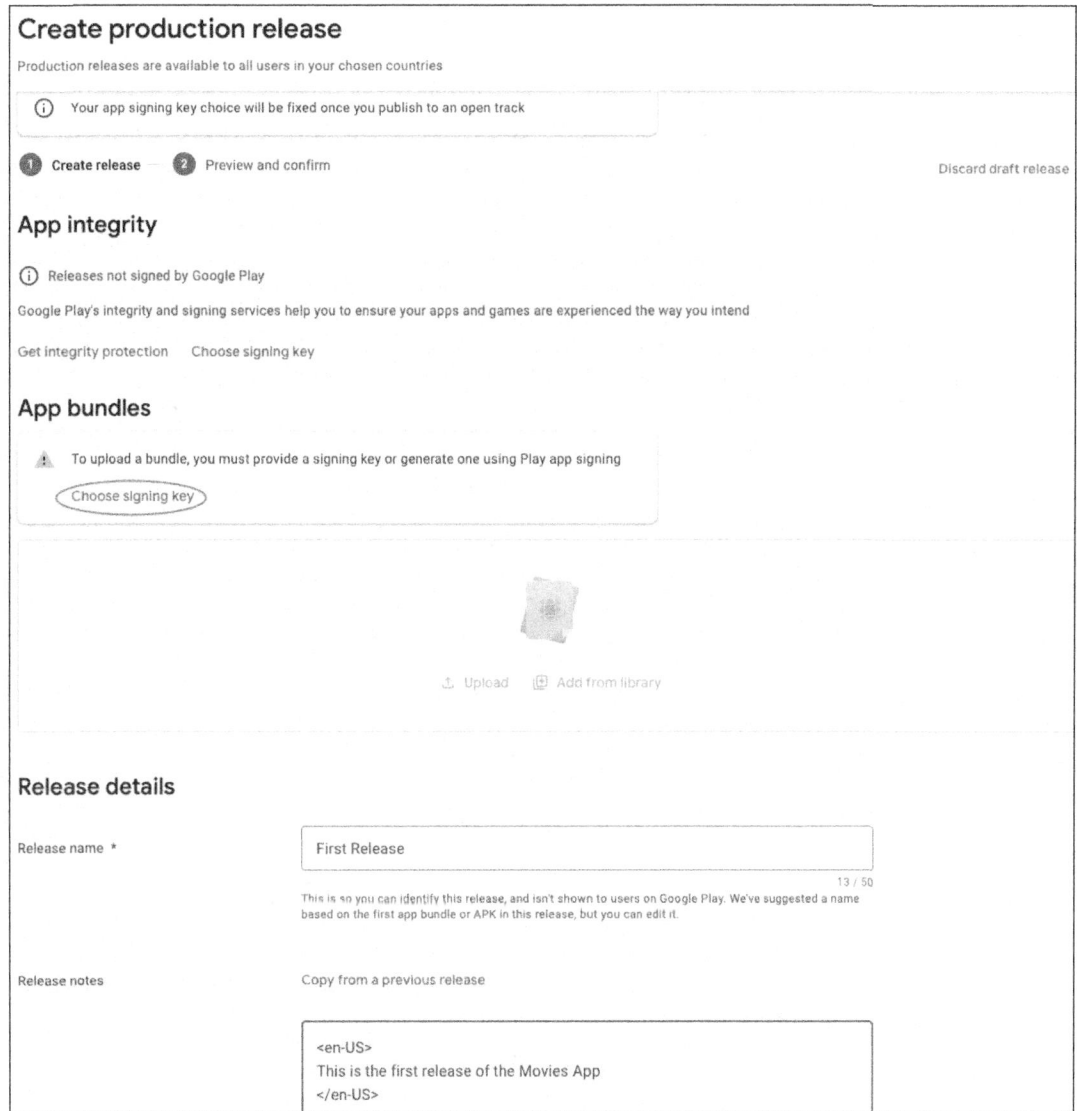

**Figure 19.51**: *Production release*

23. Choose a signing key. It is recommended to let Google manage signing. This helps so you do not have to keep track of the key yourself. Enter the release details. Add as much detail to explain why the user would want to update, as this is what the user will read on the Play Store.

24. Click the **Upload** button and upload the **.aab** file you created earlier. If everything goes well, you will have to wait for Google to review your app and approve it.

# Conclusion

In this chapter, you learned how to build a release app for both Android and iOS that you could then publish to both the Google Play Store and the Apple App Store. You now know what it takes to build and publish. This completes your journey in creating and publishing your app. Congratulations! You have learned a lot, and this should help you as you continue on in your development career.

## Join our book's Discord space

Join the book's Discord Workspace for Latest updates, Offers, Tech happenings around the world, New Release and Sessions with the Authors:

**https://discord.bpbonline.com**

# Index

Printed in Great Britain
by Amazon

60645617R10319